The Ears of Hermes

The Ears of Hermes

*Communication, Images,
and Identity in the Classical World*

Maurizio Bettini

Translated by
William Michael Short

THE OHIO STATE UNIVERSITY PRESS • COLUMBUS

Copyright © 2000 Giulio Einaudi editore S.p.A.
All rights reserved.
English translation published 2011 by The Ohio State University Press.

Library of Congress Cataloging-in-Publication Data
Bettini, Maurizio.
 [Le orecchie di Hermes. English.]
 The ears of Hermes : communication, images, and identity in the classical world / Maurizio Bettini ; translated by William Michael Short.
   p. cm.
 Includes bibliographical references and index.
 ISBN-13: 978-0-8142-1170-0 (cloth : alk. paper)
 ISBN-10: 0-8142-1170-4 (cloth : alk. paper)
 ISBN-13: 978-0-8142-9271-6 (cd-rom)
 1. Classical literature—History and criticism. 2. Literature and anthropology—Greece. 3. Literature and anthropology—Rome. 4. Hermes (Greek deity) in literature. I. Short, William Michael, 1977– II. Title.

PA3009.B4813 2011
937—dc23

2011015908

This book is available in the following editions:
Cloth (ISBN 978-0-8142-1170-0)
CD-ROM (ISBN 978-0-8142-9271-6)
Paper (ISBN: 978-0-8142-5615-2)
Cover design by AuthorSupport.com
Text design by Juliet Williams
Type set in Adobe Garamond Pro

CONTENTS

Translator's Preface   vii
Author's Preface and Acknowledgments   xi

Part 1. Mythology

Chapter 1   Hermes' Ears:
Places and Symbols of Communication in Ancient Culture   3

Chapter 2   Brutus the Fool   40

Part 2. Social Practices

Chapter 3   *Mos, Mores* and *Mos Maiorum*:
The Invention of Morality in Roman Culture   87

Chapter 4   Face to Face in Ancient Rome:
The Vocabulary of Physical Appearance in Latin   131

Part 3. Doubles and Images

Chapter 5   Sosia and His Substitute: Thinking the Double at Rome   171

Chapter 6   Ghosts of Exile:
Doubles and Nostalgia in Vergil's *Parva Troia*   200

Chapter 7   Death and Its Double:
Imagines, Ridiculum and *Honos* in the Roman Aristocratic Funeral   225

Chapter 8   Argumentum   238

Bibliography   255
Index   275

TRANSLATOR'S PREFACE

This English translation of Maurizio Bettini's *Le orecchie di Hermes* follows the publication of the original Italian edition by ten years and the appearance of *Anthropology and Roman Culture* by twenty. Yet even a decade after *Le orrechie*'s initial publication, it is difficult to overstate the significance of this work for Anglophone classicists. Conceived as a companion volume to *Anthropology and Roman Culture,* this collection of essays presents a new phase of Bettini's scholarship that both broadens and sharpens the focus of the approach he articulated there. In *Anthropology and Roman Culture,* Bettini introduced several specific lines of inquiry and theoretical perspectives that have characterized his unique brand of Roman anthropology. The essays in this volume reflect Bettini's ongoing commitment to an unambiguously "emic" level of cultural analysis, and here readers will find further evidence of how successfully Bettini continues to integrate traditional techniques of classical studies with modern anthropological theories and methods. In particular, this book demonstrates the potential of bringing aspects of Clifford Geertz's symbolic anthropology and Yuri Lotman's cultural semiotics to bear on an understanding of Roman cultural forms. The two chapters that frame the work exemplify this approach. In "Hermes' Ears" Bettini analyzes a series of myths and beliefs associated with that god in order to explore, through a kind of Geertzian "thick description," the place of vocal communication in the Roman imaginary—tracing the highly intricate "web of meanings" (to use one of Geertz's terms) that surrounds this god through ritual practice, social behavior, folk belief, and mythological representation. The analytical movement in this case runs from symbol to structure, asking how the diverse meanings of Hermes/Mercury as a cultural category manifest themselves throughout the Roman semiosphere. In "Argumentum," on the other hand, Bettini reconstructs a cultural model that underwrites Roman society's interest in and practice of the interpretation of signs—moving conversely from structure to symbol in explicating the Roman conception of inference from signs through an analysis of *argumentum*'s various senses and contexts.

By applying to the study of Roman society and culture the same anthropological "gaze" that Jean-Pierre Vernant and Marcel Detienne have dedicated so fruitfully to Greek culture, Bettini thus succeeds in offering original insights valuable to philologists, archaeologists, scholars of the literary tradition, historians, anthropologists and historians of art alike. In Part 1 (*Mythology*), for example, Bettini reconstructs a representative mythological story, demonstrating by comparison with beliefs and stories from other cultures how the legend of Brutus incorporates conventional themes and images of folklore—belying the still widespread belief that Roman culture eschewed the mythic and the fantastic. In the second part (*Social Practices*), Bettini looks at behavior and interaction in the public space, showing first how the Roman *mores* are a socially constructed category whose meaning varies according to what Maurice Halbwachs called "social frameworks," then how Roman culture's divergent metaphorical understandings of physical appearance in general and of the face in particular (*os, vultus, forma*, and so on) interact with what were perceived as the important traits of the "person" at Rome and the way in which this "person" was represented publically. Along with "Face to Face in Ancient Rome," the three chapters that comprise the third part (*Doubles and Images*) return to the central theme of Bettini's *The Portrait of the Lover* (University of California Press, 1999), namely, Roman society's obsession with doubles and images. Whereas his previous focus was on the literary motif of the lover wooing the substitute image of his or her absent beloved, now Bettini addresses this unique aspect of Roman culture as it shapes Sosia's interpretation of his encounter with his own *Doppelgänger* in Plautus' *Amphitruo;* then through a reflection on the meaning of *imagines, effigies,* and *simulacra* in Roman culture; and finally in relation to aristocratic funerary practices under the Republic.

Laura Gibbs produced early drafts of some chapters, which I then systematically revised and reworked to agree in style, tone and expression with my own translations of the remaining bulk of chapters. These were completed at various times and for various purposes, often because I found them germane to my own research. The English translation excludes some chapters of the original Italian edition which were felt not to relate directly to the book's central thematic thread, while a more recent essay by Bettini on "Death and Its Double" has been added to Part 3 as a contribution to the field's ongoing conversation about representations, and understandings, of death in antiquity. At the author's direction, all the chapters have been newly revisited and re-edited, and in some places brought up to date, in preparation for publication.

    A final word, before I let the author speak for himself (as it were). It is one of the pleasures of academic research to read Bettini's work in Italian, as he is as great a stylist as he is a scholar. I have a very distinct memory of sitting down for the first time with this book, given to me as a gift by a fellow student, and finding myself unable to put it aside. Perhaps because Bettini is also an accomplished author of narrative fiction, his academic writing often reads like a novel, the stories he weaves compelling you to turn page after page. In these pages, Bettini illuminates a world that is, as he reminds us, in many ways similar, but more often very different from our own. In my translation I have tried to capture the newness and excitement of visiting this world through his prose. My wish, therefore—perhaps a coin, and a whisper into the ears of Hermes will grant it—is that he speaks through me without any sense that I have validated that well known Italian caveat of "traduttore, traditore." If it is Bettini's own voice that you hear across these pages, I will have succeeded.

W. M. Short
San Antonio, TX

AUTHOR'S PREFACE AND ACKNOWLEDGMENTS

Is it possible for someone forced to learn Latin in four years and under threat of the rod to ever develop lasting affection for classical literature? Not normally—and Samuel Butler was no exception. Having suffered such treatment from an early age, in fact Samuel developed an enduring hatred of the classics. This was not the outcome that his father, the Reverend Thomas Butler, had hoped for when he decided to teach his son the language of Cicero and Virgil, of course. Nor did he have this end in mind when he sent young Samuel away to receive lessons from Professor Kennedy, celebrated professor of classical languages at Shrewsbury. (Describing his experience at the school, the scholar would later write: "You are surrounded on every side by lies.") Despite his father's great hopes, however, that is exactly how things turned out. Samuel learned to hate the classics—except for Homer—just as he learned to hate Tennyson, whom his grandfather, the respected Bishop Butler, had revered.

In the course of his life Samuel became a writer and thus had the opportunity to voice many sentiments that others in his position might have felt compelled to keep quiet. In his autobiographical novel *The Way of All Flesh*, the character Ernest (Samuel's counterpart) submits an important article for publication in the academic journal edited by his college. In a nutshell, the hypothesis advanced in this article was that Aristophanes, a writer as perceptive as he was outspoken, had given expression to the Athenians' true feelings for their dramaturges: disgust. According to Ernest/Samuel, the Greeks frequented the theater in the same spirit as his contemporary Englishmen went to church: they went because everyone else did, though they were bored to death by sermons. Apparently, when someone learns to hate something as a child, that hatred is true and lasting! (As for Tennyson, Samuel was pleased to discover—and recount—that the poet laureate was actually an avid collector of dirty jokes and quite foul-mouthed . . . in private, naturally).[1]

Someone who detests Greek theater and compares it to the church in which his father and grandfather had preached each Sunday morning, is surely deserving of our confidence—not because his opinions were necessarily correct, but because they were, at the very least, original. In fact, Butler had a number of idiosyncratic ideas about the classics. The reader will recall, for example, *The Authoress of the Odyssey*, a book in which Butler suggested a solution to the knotty problem of the "differences" between the *Iliad* and *Odyssey*, arguing that the *Odyssey* had been written by a woman[2]—a decidedly unusual proposition, even if Butler was not the first to make it.[3] Or, the reader will think of those pages of *Erewhon* in which Butler describes the system of education used in that strange (and remarkably postmodernist) country his lively imagination had dreamed up "over the range." Even if somewhat disguised, the classics make an appearance there as well:

> The main feature in their system is the prominence which they give to a study which I can only translate by the word "hypothetics." They argue thus—that to teach a boy merely the nature of the things which exist in the world around him, and about which he will have to be conversant during his whole life, would be giving him but a narrow and shallow conception of the universe, which it is urged might contain all manner of things which are not now to be found therein. To open his eyes to these possibilities, and so to prepare him for all sorts of emergencies, is the object of this system of hypothetics. To imagine a set of utterly strange and impossible contingencies, and require the youths to give intelligent answers to the questions that arise therefrom, is reckoned the fittest conceivable way of preparing them for the actual conduct of their affairs in after life.
>
> Thus they are taught what is called the hypothetical language for many of their best years—a language which was originally composed at a time when the country was in a very different state of civilisation to what it is at present, a state which has long since disappeared and been superseded.

---

1. On these aspects of Butler's biography, see Henderson 1967, 4ff.
2. Butler 1897.
3. Cf. Bettini 1994, 104ff.

Many valuable maxims and noble thoughts which were at one time concealed in it have become current in their modern literature, and have been translated over and over again into the language now spoken. Surely then it would seem enough that the study of the original language should be confined to the few whose instincts led them naturally to pursue it.

But the Erewhonians think differently; the store they set by this hypothetical language can hardly be believed; they will even give any one a maintenance for life if he attains a considerable proficiency in the study of it; nay, they will spend years in learning to translate some of their own good poetry into the hypothetical language—to do so with fluency being reckoned a distinguishing mark of a scholar and a gentleman.[4]

No doubt readers are meant to understand "the hypothetical language" as a reference to Latin—the language that Samuel's father, armed with a rod, began to teach him when he was just four years old. The tone is ironic and surely Butler would have preferred that the inhabitants of Erewhon had devoted the better years of their children's lives not to "the hypothetical language" but to something more concrete. It is easy to imagine what the author's judgment would be of "giving a maintenance for life" to anyone who "attains a considerable proficiency in the study of it," as was the case of Professor Kennedy of the Shrewsbury school. Sometimes hatred serves us better than affection, however, and for this reason we invite the reader to take seriously Butler's metaphorical invention—the classics as "hypothetics," a way of opening our eyes to all the possibilities that may be encountered in the universe, including those that do not belong to the here and now.

In my opinion, Butler's hatred of the classics actually led him to an appropriate way of thinking. Here we may cite the opinion of Michel de Montaigne, as well. Montaigne had learned Latin at an even earlier age than Butler, apparently even before he learned French. In contrast to Butler, however, Montaigne demonstrated throughout his entire life an extraordinary love for the classics. He wrote: "Though I be engaged to one forme, I doe not tie the world unto it, as every man doth. And *I beleeve and conceive a thousand manners of life.*"[5] Here is another example of "hypothetics"—imagining and conceiving a thousand other manners of life precisely because, as the Erewhonians would later claim, "to imagine a set of utterly strange and impossible contingencies" constitutes the best form of education. The practice of a system of "hypothetics," or the exercise of continually imagining "a thousand manners of life," as Montaigne did, helps us to not only

---

4. Butler 1975, 185f.
5. Montaigne 1970, 300.

appreciate the richness of what is possible, but also console ourselves about the anguish of the present (or what everyone believes is the present). For in fact, as the Erewhonians suggested, the universe "might contain all manner of things which are not now to be found therein."

I HAVE CHOSEN to begin this book speaking about Butler and his hatred for the classics (and of the use that the Erewhonians made of "hypothetics") not merely for the pleasure of citation. The fact is that I find myself to some degree sympathetic to his situation (including a certain hostility for teaching Latin in the way that it was taught to Butler). Yet I am even more enthusiastic about the possibility that in modern culture the classics can function precisely as "hypothetics"—in other words, as a starting point for thinking about the "thousand manners of life," as Montaigne advocated. It is this perspective that I have tried to take in putting together *The Ears of Hermes*. I am convinced, in fact, that the Greeks and Romans, though in some respects very similar to us, most often conceived things in a much different way than we do, and are able, therefore, to open our eyes to so many "possibilities" of life that otherwise we might not be able to see. The Greek and the Romans told exciting—yet different—stories. They elaborated profound—yet different—symbols. Above all, they confronted problems in many ways similar to those we find ourselves confronting today—e.g., the permanence of memory and the snare of forgetfulness, the perils of identity and the strategies necessary for constructing it, the pretensions of moral absolutes and the relativity of customs, and so on—yet with a different approach, because their worldview and the resources of their culture were different than ours. All these analogies and discrepancies constitute an extraordinary deposit of "hypothetics," a rich vein of alternate potentialities that the presence of the classics—thanks to the care devoted to them by so many generations of readers and scholars—permits us to continue mining. Why would we not choose to do so?

Certainly not because some of our contemporaries allege that the classics long ago ceased being relevant, and that, in order to be a citizen of the world, it is enough to know English and computer science. And certainly not because others are instead preoccupied with keeping the classics all to themselves, pruning them of all that would render them of interest to modern culture. Perhaps they should remember Erewhon and the fact that the universe "might contain all manner of things which are not now to be found therein."

CHAPTER 6 originally appeared in *Classical Antiquity* 16 (1997): 8–33. Chapter 7 is a revised version of an essay that originally appeared in *Hoping for Continuity: Childhood, Education and Death in Antiquity and in the Middle Ages,* edited by Kateriina Mustakallio et al., Rome: Institutum Romanum Finlandiae, 2005: 191–202. My thanks to Mark Griffith and Kateriina Mustakallio for permission to reprint.

PART 1

Mythology

ONE

Hermes' Ears

Places and Symbols of Communication in Ancient Culture

Every god has his own style. Mercury, for example has little wings on his feet. He is a Nepman and a rogue.[1]

—M. Bulgakov, The Capital in a Notebook, *1991*

Communication has its places—and these are also, or above all, symbolic. Inhabitants of the modern world inevitably tend to associate communication with the telephone, the fax machine, the computer keyboard, the television or the radio. These are undeniably technical, powerful "places"; but most of all, they are places removed from the human body and its topography. The same is true of memory and its counterpart, forgetfulness, two spheres of human experience that are intimately associated with communication. In fact, when we imagine where memory is "located," our modern experience most often suggests the image of one of the many written and electronic archives that we have amassed. Writing, in other words—along with that deceptive transformation of writing, visual or vocal "recording"—has long held us in its power: for us, even what is spoken becomes "written" once it has been recorded and our fleeting visual experiences—shows, exhibitions, the events we attend—unexpectedly take the form of an archive, a reusable store of information thus resembling a book or document.

---

1. Bulgakov 1991, 121. "NEP" stands for *Novaja Ekonomičeskaja Politika*, or the "New Economic Policy" introduced by Lenin in 1921.

Symbolically speaking, as well, our own experience of communication has been dissociated from human physicality and transformed into a kind of "bodiless" communication: ears, tongue and memory (which, along with forgetfulness, is located "somewhere" inside of us) have all ended up outside of us, living an almost autonomous existence. Entrusted to the telephone and to the Internet, communication among human beings has become more and more frequently detached from physical interaction. Even silence—when it occurs!—is no longer a palpable void that surrounds us and muffles conversation: it is the phone line going dead, the television blinking off into noiseless darkness or the computer terminal failing to connect.

But it was not always so.

The Lord of Communication

In the market-square of Pharae in Achaea stood the stone image of a bearded Hermes.[2] Before it, an altar, also of stone, was adorned with bronze lamps held in place by lead stays. This statue had prophetic powers and according to Pausanias the ritual prescribed for consulting the god was this:[3] if someone wished to ask something of Hermes, he was to come at evening, burn incense on the altar, fill the lamps with oil and light them. Leaving a coin on the altar on the right side of the statue, he was to whisper his question into the god's ears. He was then to quit the square, holding his hands over his ears. Once outside, he was to remove his hands from his ears, and whatever voice he heard in that instant he was to interpret prophetically.

The Greeks referred to the practice of divination in which words heard on the breeze were attributed predictive value by the term *klēdonismos* ("divination by means of *klēdōn*").[4] The word *klēdōn* (< *kleō*, "to tell of") in turn denotes a "sound" or "voice" that someone perceives by chance, an omen in the form of a word or rumor that circulates through the air of its own accord, revealing the will of the gods. Divination by means of oblative signs was not exclusive to Greece, however. Other Mediterranean and non-Mediterranean peoples were also familiar with this practice: it was long practiced in the folkloric traditions of Europe, for example.[5] The Romans, for their part, held vocal *omina* in great esteem, considering them equally prophetic as voices caught out of thin air—candid, involuntary phrases that contained

---

2. Cf. Vernant 1965c; Moggi and Osanna 2000, 309.
3. Paus. *Desc.* 7.22.2ff.
4. See Halliday 1967, 229. For Egypt, see Paus. *Desc.* 7.22 and Frazer 1898, 152ff.
5. On the Mesopotamian *egirrú*, see Bottéro 1974.

a profound and often crucial message for the person to whom they were addressed.[6]

In all such cases, it was simply a question of knowing how to recognize the supernatural significance of such voices—how to apprehend and then interpret these "words." Crassus, for example, failed to understand that the man on the quay of the port of Brundisium hawking Caunian figs by yelling *"Cauneas!"* was not simply advertising his goods. The fig seller was actually warning him not to take a sea voyage to his own death by shouting *cau' n(e) eas* ("do not go!"), using the apocopated pronunciation of the imperative *cave* ("beware lest . . . ") characteristic of the spoken language.[7] Crassus' mistake, to his misfortune, was that he did not expect a prophecy in this form. In the case of Hermes at Pharae, of course, it was impossible to be caught off guard: the faithful petitioner paid money to consult the oracle; he whispered a specific question in the god's ear and knew precisely at what moment the *klēdōn* would come to him.

Looking more closely at the god involved in *klēdonismos* at Pharae, it appears that Hermes was involved in divination by means of "voices" also outside of this particular context. A phallic herm from Pithanes in Aeolis, for example, bears the inscription *Hermēs Klēdonios*.[8] Hermes' function as the disseminator of fortuitous messages is not surprising. As the god of chance discovery, anything that anyone happened upon by accident could be referred to in Greek as "a gift of Hermes" (*hermaion*),[9] and Hermes also played a role in the ancient practice of casting lots, where meaningful "randomness" was of central importance.[10] It is all the more understandable, then, that the market square—the realm of Hermes—was used as a place in which to receive prophetic *klēdones:* the market was naturally filled with people speaking and shouting, and Greeks generally appear to have paid much attention to *sumbola* there.[11] The market square was in fact a place of exchange and encounter in every respect, corresponding fully to the nature of Hermes, god of the market, passages, open spaces, exchange and commerce.[12]

---

6. For the etymology of *omen,* see Benveniste 1962, 10ff. On the divinatory characteristics of the vocal *omen,* see Bouché-Leclercq 1882, IV, 77ff. and Bloch 1963, 79ff.

7. This famous case is reported by Cic. *Div.* 2.84. For the phonetics, see Hofmann 1936.

8. See Bouché-Leclerq 1882, II, 400 and Usener 1948, 267. On Hermes and divination, see also Brown 1990, 99ff. Further information is given in the note of Moggi and Osanna 2000, 309.

9. Cf., e.g., Soph. *Ant.* 397; Plat. *Phaed.* 107c; *Sym.* 176c; *Gorg.* 486e, etc. Brown 1990, 39ff. interprets this expression as a vestige of the practice of "silent trade" known elsewhere in ancient Greece—a type of exchange practiced *in absentia,* in which one of the two partners leaves an object in a certain place, the other coming to collect it later, leaving his payment in its place.

10. For Hermes and the *klēros,* cf. Arist. *Pax* 365 and the scholia ad loc.; and Brown 1990, 101.

11. Cf. the fragment of the comic poet Philemon cited by Clem. Alex. *Strom.* 7.4.25 (= Poet. Com. Graec. fr. 100 Kassel-Austin), and see Halliday 1967, 230 n. 2.

12. See the discussion of Vernant 1965c. For an original prospective on how Hermes' "space"

Hermes, in short, was the god of circulation and everything circulated around him: coins, prophetic signs, merchandise, encounters, *klēdones*. In Greek religious thought, Hermes might be said to represent what today we might define more prosaically by the term "communication": He was the herald (*kērux*) and messenger (*angelos*), functioning as a kind of channel for communication between the transmitter and addressee of a certain message.[13] Accustomed as we are to carrying telephones in our pockets, we easily forget that in antiquity such methods of long-distance communication corresponded to the figure of the *angelos,* the *kērux,* the *nuntius* and the *orator.* Hermes was the religious representation of all this.

As the god of communication, a specific and—from our point of view—significant part of the body was sacred to Hermes in antiquity: the tongue. As the philosopher Cornutus (*Comp.* p. 21) says, Hermes "is called the messenger (*diaktoros*) because . . . he leads (*diagein*) our thoughts to the souls (*psuchai*) of those near us: for this reason, they consecrate the tongue to him."[14] This unambiguously religious association of Hermes with the organ of vocal articulation places the god squarely in the camp of one of the most fundamental aspects of human interaction: linguistic communication. Plato sustains that Hermes "has to do with language (*logos*)" and that for this reason he should be called "Eiremes," from *eirein* ("to say").[15] In Hesiod, we find the story of how Hermes endowed Pandora with "lies, devious speech, a mischievous nature" and above all "a voice."[16] The Roman scholar Macrobius described Mercury as "in control of the voice and, indeed, of speech" (*vocis et sermonis potentem*).[17]

From this perspective, it is interesting to note that for Cornutus Hermes literally was "the word" (*logos*), and all his other attributes derive from this fundamental characteristic. We have already seen Hermes *diaktoros* functioning as a kind of linguistic vector. His "penetrating" and "perspicuous" nature is also emphasized, as well as his "swiftness in vocal articulation"[18]—the same features that characterize effective linguistic communication. In Cornutus' interpretation, linguistic exchange dominates all of Hermes' other roles: he is the "herald" (*kērux*) because "by means of a sonorous voice (*phōnē*) all that is signified through language reaches the ears" and the "messenger"

---

is developing in contemporary culture and society, see Guastella 1997, 1ff.

13. Hom. Hymn. in Merc. 3, "swift messenger of the immortals"; Hes. *Erg.* 80, "herald of the gods"; cf. Brown 1990, 24ff.

14. See Halliday 1967, 231 n. 2.

15. Plat. *Crat.* 407e–408b. On Hermes the "inventor of language," see Dornseiff 1922, 7, esp. n. 4.

16. Hes. *Erg.* 77ff.

17. Macr. *Sat.* 1.12.20.

18. Cornut. *Comp.* p. 21.

(*angelos*) because "we know the will of the gods from the meanings (*ennoiai*) that are brought to us through language." Even Hermes' most customary attribute—his winged shoes—refers to language, since this "accords with the fact that words are said to be 'winged' (*pteroenta*)." Hermes, then, is the religious category of "conversation" in all its forms.

Aelian also considered Hermes the father of language, but because his work concerned the nature of animals, he considered it worth mentioning what animal most directly represented (the Egyptian) Hermes in his linguistic function: the ibis. Aelian remarks that this bird, which was particularly dear to the god, "resembles the nature of language in its appearance (*eidos*): its black feathers can be compared to a kind of silent language directed inwards; its white feathers, to language that is directed outwards and heard by others, like a kind of servant and messenger of what exists inside."[19] Language, like Hermes, is a messenger: its function is to bring "inside" and "outside" into communication. However, the ibis' feathers neatly characterize language not only because they represent the human communicative faculty as the vector of some hidden "inner world." The image of its black and white plumage also captures the notion that language has a "black" and a "white" side—that silence and introversion are just as much a part of language as articulated speech.

Aelian speaks of "black" and "white" feathers, but the analogy between the ibis and language is not limited to its plumage. Aristotle mentioned a popular belief that "crows and ibises join in sexual union with the mouth, and among quadrupeds the weasel gives birth through its mouth. Anaxagoras says this, as well as some other natural philosophers, but he discusses it only very superficially and without reflection."[20] Aelian also discusses the belief that the ibis performs coitus orally, adding that this bird not only conceives but also gives birth through the mouth.[21] In this, the ibis resembles the weasel, which was traditionally believed to give birth through the mouth and to which some sources attribute the corresponding ability to conceive through the ears.[22]

In view of the analogy between the weasel and the ibis as animals that "give birth through the mouth," it is interesting to note that Plutarch also discusses the weasel as a symbol of language. Explaining why the Egyptians venerated the asp, the weasel and the scarab, he notes that "many believe that

---

19. Ael. *Nat. anim.* 10.28. These beliefs probably relate to the Egyptian god Theuth, identified with Hermes, to whom the ibis was sacred (cf. Plat. *Phaedr.* 274c). Hermes/Theuth was considered the inventor of the letters of the alphabet; see below.
20. Ael. *Gen. anim.* 6.756b (= Anaxagoras fr. A 114 Diels and Kranz). See Bettini 1998, 162ff.
21. Ael. *Nat. anim.* 10.28
22. Cf. Ant. Lib. *Met.* 29; Plut. *Is. Os.* 74.381a; Physiologus 21; Isid. *Etym.* 12.3.3, etc.

the weasel conceives through the ears and gives birth through its mouth and that this is an image of the origin of language."[23] Language has its origin in the mouth and ears: in this sense, the weasel, whose reproductive cycle goes "from mouth to ear," is an excellent representation of this human phenomenon. We do not know if the ibis belonged to the realm of speech because of its reproductive habits: Aelian only mentions the color of its feathers. The close association of this bird with language appears to be reinforced, however, by similar beliefs about the weasel.

The symbolic role that birds play in connection with Hermes as the god of language is worth exploring. As the conveyor of spoken language and guide of the flow of words from tongue to ears, Hermes was believed also to have invented the letters of the alphabet and revealed to men how to capture "flighty" vocal expressions in fixed signs.[24] In one of his mythographic *resumés,* Hyginus recounts how the idea of the alphabet occurred to the god: "Some say that it was Mercury [who invented letters], from the flight of cranes, which when they fly express the letters of the alphabet" (*alii dicunt Mercurium ex gruum volatu, quae cum volant litteras exprimunt).*[25] Dante resorted to a similar comparison in describing the wailing host of lecherous men that approached him as cranes that fly "forming long lines in the air."[26] The flight of the crane is *graphical,* then, just as the ibis' plumage is *oral.*

The ibis' oral character manifests itself in a system of simple oppositions: black/white, speech/silence. The crane's "graphicness," however, depends on a rather more complex articulation of the wings and the body, which together are capable of forming the set of graphemes necessary for writing. It is only a mythographic fantasy, of course, that the flight of birds put the idea of *litterae* into men's minds. This fantasy, moreover, was possible only when the concept of writing so pervaded the world of mental representations that even the manner in which birds fly could be imagined as "alphabetic": men looked to the sky and there too observed lines of writing.

The notion that avian flight patterns could function as a written code was probably also suggested by the divinatory practice of "reading" such patterns. If birds were capable of transmitting *signa* in their features and through the patterns they made in the sky, why could this not also function as a true and proper alphabet? This idea—that the flight of birds was able to inscribe "winged words"—represents a striking paradox: "wings," like those

---

23. Plut. *Is. Os.* 74.381a.
24. Again speaking of Hermes/Theuth of Egyptian divination: cf. Plat. *Phaedr.* 274d; Diod. Sic. 1.16.1; Cic. *Nat. deor.* 3.56; Plin. *Nat. hist.* 7.192, etc. Cf. the long note in Pease 1881, II, 1112ff. and Dornseiff 1922, 7ff.
25. Hyg. *Fab.* 277. cf. Philost. *Her.* 3.33.11.
26. Dante, *Inferno* 5.46–7.

of Hermes' sandals, both carry words away and fix them permanently in writing. But Hermes, god of language and communication, is always there.

Focusing on the ritual at Pharae again, one thing in particular strikes our attention: the consistency with which a certain symbolic value is assigned to a part of the body that functions as a kind of complement to the tongue—that is, to the ears. The petitioner poses his question by whispering directly into the god's ear, while he protects himself from receiving false or useless omens by covering his ears with his hands. He chooses the right moment for receiving the *klēdōn* by then freeing his hands from them. Hermes, god of the tongue, thus takes on another role as god of the ears. Perhaps not coincidentally, Hermes could be represented in the act of "covering his ears" with his hands:[27] Apollo besets Hermes with accusations and in response, the child-god utters two typical acoustic "omens" (*oiōnoi*): he burps loudly and sneezes.[28] "By dint of such omens," Apollo declares, he will surely find his stolen cows—and it will be Hermes to show him the way. Hermes then leaps to his feet and runs off, "covering his ears"—precisely the same sequence of gestures that the petitioner at Pharae performs when he takes his leave of the god's statue. Another aspect of the cult of Hermes refers to his ears and their communicative function: At Athens, there was a statue dedicated to Hermes *Psithuristēs*, "The Whisperer."[29] According to Pausanias,[30] Hermes received this epithet "because men who gather there hold secret discourses and whisper to each other whatever they want to say."[31] Hermes could be represented explicitly as the god of whispering—i.e., "speaking in the ear"—thus receiving in the form of an epithet what the petitioner at Pharae addressed to him in practice.

Hermes' relationship with "ears" fits his role as the god of language, since communication can only occur, as the French proverb goes, *de la bouche à l'oreille*: both organs are necessarily to the process.[32] Plutarch's symbolism of the weasel demonstrates this neatly; he also asserts that the ears of gossip-mongers "do not communicate with the soul, but with the tongue. For this

---

27. Hom. Hymn. in Merc. 305ff. The text is difficult to interpret, however: see the note in Cassola 1975, 532ff.
28. On the powers of the sneeze and other involuntary bodily sounds, cf. Deonna and Renard 1994, 117ff.
29. The evidence is collected by Usener 1948, 267, n. 52, who relates this epithet to the ritual at Pharae. On the "whisper" and Hermes "the Whisperer," see Soverini 1994, 433–60 and 1992, 811ff.
30. Paus. fr. 330 Schwabe (= Y I, p. 221 Erbse).
31. Cf. Eust. ad Hom. Od. 20.8; Usener 1948, 267 n. 5. For Brown 1990, 14ff., Hermes' "whisper" relates to the god's characteristic magical abilities (in magic, the whisper has an important role).
32. In Mesopotamian culture, the ears were considered the site of intellectual progress: cf. the "divinations with four ears" discussed by Bottéro 1982, 131.

reason, the words that most people are able to hold on to when they hear them, gossipmongers let slip away."³³ The mouth and the ears are so closely connected that the god who oversees communication necessarily deals with both.

Linguistic acts do not, however, consist solely in the emission of sound and auditory reception (As a symbol of language the weasel thus represents an ideal interpretation of communication): beyond speaking and listening, understanding and interpreting messages are also necessary components of the process of communication. These also fell within the purview of Hermes. Again according to Cornutus, the fact that Hermes' mother was named Maia was supposed to mean that "the word (*logos*) is the foundation of speculation (*theōria*) and research (*zētēsis*).³⁴ In fact, wet-nurses are called *maiai* because they bring babies into the light, just as happens in an investigation (*ereuna*)." Hermes, then, was also the god of research and investigation.

Beyond Cornutus' speculations, it is interesting that Hermes' own name was connected with words such as *hermēneus*, *hermēneia*, and *hermēneuein*, which all refer to interpretation and translation from one language to another.³⁵ As the god of interpretation and translation, Hermes established communication not only in commercial exchange, but also when translating from one language or culture to another. The same relationship between commercial and linguistic mediation is captured by the Latin term *interpres*, which properly referred to the mediator of business transactions:³⁶ an *interpres* was the person who established a "price" (*-pres*) "between" (*inter-*) two parties. The linguistic "interpreter" was thus equivalent to the mediating figure that assisted two parties in concluding commercial transactions by negotiating a price.

Hermes' function at Pharae can be reconsidered within the perspective of the relationship between translation and the world of the market, as well. Through the "voices" and "sounds" of the market, Hermes established communication between men and gods (or more exactly, between men and their destiny). Translating Fate into a *klēdōn*, he allowed men to understand the obscure will of the gods and, in doing so, achieved what was perhaps the most difficult type of communication. As Cicero says, when the gods speak

---

33. Plut. *Garr.* 1.502d. For the connection between hearing and the brain, cf. Arist. *Gen. anim.* 744a and Pettine 1992, 126.

34. Corn. *Comp.* p. 23.

35. Cf. Bosshardt 1942, 36ff. Note that in Plato (*Crat.* 407e), Hermes is explicitly defined as "interpreter" (*hermēneus*). Chantraine 1968, 373 doubts this etymological connection; cf. Krahe 1939, 175ff., esp. 181.

36. Cf., e.g., Plaut. *Curc.* 434, *quod te praesente isti egi, teque interprete;* Cic. *Fam.* 10.11.3, *utor in hac re adiutoribus interpretibusque fratre meo et Laterense et Eurnio nostro.* Cf. Ernout-Meillet 1965, 320). On the Latin terminology of translation, cf. Traina 1989, 96–99.

to us and we are not able to understand them, they are like "Carthaginians or Spaniards that come to speak to us in the Senate without an interpreter" (*Poeni aut Hispani in senatu nostro loquerentur sine interprete*).[37] They speak a foreign language, in other words—and Hermes, god of mediation, has to translate.

Hermes stands at the very center of discourse. The entire process of communication—speaking and hearing, the mouth and the ear—constellates around him. Above all, he is at the center of the most delicate part of the linguistic operation: interpretation. To use Aelian's imagery, Hermes has the ability to turn the ibis' black feathers white, to make explicit what was implicit, and to bring "out" what might otherwise have remained "in." It is perhaps surprising, then, to see Hermes implicated in a moment that seems, at least at first glance, to involve the opposite of spoken discourse: the moment, that is, when linguistic communication fails just as it has begun.

Hermes Is in the Building

The Messenger arrived unexpectedly. In the commotion of the wedding feast, he appeared like any of the others among the crowd of guests, and so the drinkers failed to notice the god's mysterious entrance. Hugging his divinity close like a drenched cloak, he blended into the throng of revelers as he passed:

> . . . Aber plötzlich sah
> mitten im Sprechen einer von den Gästen
> den jungen Hausherrn oben an dem Tische
> wie in die Höh gerissen, nicht mehr liegend,
> und überall und mit dem ganzen Wesen
> ein Fremdes spiegelnd, das ihn furchtbar ansprach.
> Und gleich darauf, als klärte sich die Mischung,
> war Stille; nur mit einem Satz am Boden
> von trübem Lärm und einem Niederschlag
> fallenden Lallens, schon verdorben riechend
> nach dumpfem umgestandenen Gelächter.
> Und da erkannten sie den schlanken Gott,
> und wie er dastand . . .

---

37. Cic. *Div.* 2.131. It is interesting that among the names (and functions) of the Mesopotamian divinity was also that of "interpreter": cf. Bottéro 1982, 114.

> But suddenly
> one of the guests, among the conversations
> saw the young master of the house at the head of the table
> as if, no longer lying there, he had risen up on high
> and all about and with all his being
> mirrored something strange and frightening that spoke to him.
> And as soon as the confusion had cleared,
> was there silence; with only the remains on the ground
> of a gloomy din and an echo
> of dying murmurs, already tainted
> that stank of deaf laughter restrained.
> And then he recognized the swift god,
> and how he stood . . .

This is the marriage feast of Admetus, and Hermes the Messenger has entered the room to announce to the young groom that he must die. When? At once. The god's entrance was discreet, but his appearance was no less frightening for that. What is most striking in Rilke's lines, in fact, is the perfect coincidence of the god's epiphany and the sudden descent of silence upon the room. The change that has come over Admetus (who already makes his way out the banquet as if enchanted by "something strange and frightening that spoke to him") is noticed by one the guests "among the conversations" that echo throughout the room. When the confusion clears, a great silence predominates ("und bald . . . war Stille"), which the echo of dying laughter and confused murmurs only makes more oppressive. Now Hermes is there and everyone knows it.

In constructing the opening of his celebrated *Alkestis,* it is hard to imagine that Rilke did not have in mind Plutarch's assertion that "when in some gathering silence suddenly descends, they say that Hermes has entered the room."[38] The modern poet has written a work of poetry that is objectively Greek and a Plutarchean proverb, dramatized in the form of a story, gives Admetus' German wedding its tragic atmosphere. There is nothing forced in any of this, though. Greeks or no Greeks, it is distressing when, for no apparent reason, conversation fails and silence descends upon a group of people who previously had been engaged in lively chatter. It is as if the unexpected break in conversation suggested the entrance of the supernatural. The total synchrony of events, perhaps, creates the suspicion that "something strange" has insinuated itself among us. Even today in France, Germany and England people commonly declare in similar situations that "an angel has

---

38. Plut. *Garr.* 2.502ff.

passed";[39] in Christian culture, the messenger of the Lord assumes the role of Hermes, the winged messenger, but the substance has not changed. The winged Christian angel conveys a silence of equal foreboding.

In ancient Rome, sudden silences at banquets were considered ominous: "It has been remarked," Pliny writes, "that the participants at a feast may suddenly fall silent, but only if the banqueters are of an even number. In such circumstances, everyone's reputation is at risk"[40] (Connected as they are with chthonic deities, even numbers are inauspicious).[41] Pliny relates this "sudden silence" to the fact that somewhere someone is "speaking badly" of the guests (*isque famae labor est*), almost as if a malevolent voice besmirching the good reputation of the guests possessed the strange power of being able to halt conversation from afar.[42]

Rilke was a master of supernatural silences. By the time dessert was served at Urnekloster's dinner, for example, the ghost of Cristina Brahe had "crossed through the room already deserted . . . through an indescribable silence, in which was only heard the tinkling of a glass" ("durch den nun freigewordenen Raum vorüberging . . . durch unbeschreibliche Stille, in der nur irgendwo ein Glas zitternd klirrte"). Here, too, a trace of sound—a tinkling like the muffled murmurs in *Alkestis*—only makes the silence more terrifying:

> "Wer ist das?" schrie mein Vater dazwischen.
> "Jemand, der wohl das Recht hat, hier zu sein. Keine Fremde. Christine Brahe."—Da entstand wieder jene merkwürdig dünne Stille, und wieder fing das Glas an zu zittern.
>
> "Who is it?" shouted my father, interrupting my grandfather.
> "Someone who has every right to be here. Not a stranger. Christine Brahe."
> Then that strange silence returned and the glass began to tremble again.

Silence is a mark of the dead. In the afterlife, no one speaks, and anyone of that realm—Hermes, an angel of the Lord, the ghost of Cristina Brahe—necessarily causes conversation to fail. In fact, death itself is absolute silence: this is why Hermes, represented as the *psuchopompos* ("escort of

---

39. On the folkloric beliefs concerning "sudden silences," see Wolters 1935, 95; Deonna and Renard 1994, 110ff. Frazer 1911, II, 299) records that in Bavaria at the moment in which conversation fails there is the custom of saying, "Someone has crossed their legs."
40. Plin. *Nat. hist.* 28.27.
41. See Deonna and Renard 1994, 120.
42. The passage is difficult to interpret. According to Wolters 1935, 93ff., sudden silence was believed to signal the arrival of hostile demons. See also Deonna and Renard 1994, 119.

souls"), radiates the silence characteristic of the world beyond. If Hermes is in the building, gloomy quiet prevails,[43] just as conversation that takes place between and with the gods is by definition silent.[44]

This consideration only partially explains Plutarch's proverb (The meaning of a proverb is always richer and fuller than the explanation some unilateral interpretation provides). The complexity of Hermes' own nature—as the god of voices, the tongue, the ears and linguistic communication in general—permits a better understanding of the meaning of the silence provoked by the god's unexpected arrival. The fact is that Hermes, the lord of all communication, controls both speech and silence: to use Aelian's metaphor, both the ibis' white and black feathers are in his power. In fact, when Macrobius described Mercury as "in control of the voice and speech," he must also have meant to refer to his power over silence—to his ability *not* to grant the voice or speech.

Speaking aloud and remaining silent are two faces of the same coin, and Hermes displays them both. This is why Hermes, as the god of thieves, makes dogs fall silent at the dark of night, truly behaving as the "Dog Strangler" (*kunanchēs*), as his epithet indicates.[45] Hermes had demonstrated this ability at the very beginning of his career, when, as a child, he stole Apollo's cows.[46] The little thief reentered his mother's cave "without the dogs barking"; nor "did he make any sound as normally happens when touching the ground."[47] Hermes "had launched upon the dogs that guarded them an attack of lethargy and *kunanchē*."[48] The *kunanchē* that Hermes inflicts upon the dogs is a kind of "sore throat"[49] that keeps them from barking, as if strangled. In other words, just as it lies in Hermes' power to grant the capacity to speak, so too he can take it away.

---

43. Deonna and Renard 1994, 120ff.

44. Cic. *Div.* 1.129 observed that "the spiritual faculties (*animi*) of the gods perceive reciprocally without eyes, ears or tongue that which each experiences (for which reason, men, even when the express a desire or a wish in silence, do not doubt that the gods here them). See Scarpi 1983, 31–50, esp. 36.

45. Hipponax fr. 2.1 Degani, with a rich apparatus of further evidence. On the dog in Greek culture, see Franco 2000.

46. Hom. Hymn. in Merc. 142ff.

47. Similar is the "silence" and "deafness" that the small thief asks of the old man who has seen him pass by Apollo's cows: "having heard me, be deaf, and say not a word" (92ff.). The text also alludes to the conspiratorial behavior of the thief: "I did not see, I know nothing, I did not hear others speak of it; I could not tell you" (263ff.).

48. Ant. Lib. *Met.* 23.2.

49. *Kunanchē* is a term used to indicate a disease of the throat characteristic of dogs (Arist. *Anim.* 604a; Ael. *Nat. animal.* 4.40) as well as angina in human beings (Corp. Hipp. 2.7.16 Littré, etc.).

Lupus in Fabula

Let us follow this thematic thread. In Latin, a specific expression was used to indicate the unexpected arrival of someone in the middle of a conversation about that very person: *lupus in fabula* ("the wolf in the tale").[50] The grammarian Pompeius explains: "You are speaking about someone and this person suddenly shows up. You say: *lupus in fabula.*"[51] This expression has many parallels in both ancient and modern languages, and these too often involve the "wolf": in Greek, there was "If you only mention the wolf . . . ," with the same meaning as *lupus in fabula,*[52] while medieval Europe knew the saying *mentio si fiet, saepe lupus veniet.*[53] An adage known in Tuscany is "chi ha il lupo in bocca, l'ha sulla groppa" ("who has the wolf in his mouth, has it on his back"), while in France it is "quand on parle du loup, on en voit la queue" and in Germany, "wenn man den Wolf nennt, so kommt er gerennt."[54]

These expressions correspond to the traditional prescription never to name malicious or dangerous beings in order to avoid their sudden appearance.[55] Similar proverbs have the devil in the role of the wolf: cf. "speak of the devil, and horns will sprout." In Spain, the wolf or devil appears to be substituted by another, equally malevolent figure in the proverbial saying, "en nombrando el ruin de Roma, luego asoma." This is similar to the Italian "persona trista, nominata e vista," while in China a figure known as General Cao Cao fulfills this function in the proverb "shuo Caocao, Caocao jiu dao" ("when you speak of Cao Cao, he comes immediately").[56] From this comparative evidence, we may infer that at Rome the expression *lupus in fabula* was employed to mean that the person who suddenly appeared had actually been summoned into the conversation simply by naming them. This was

---

50. E.g., Ter. *Ad.* 537; Cic. *Att.* 13.33.4. Cf. Plaut. *Stich.* 577, *atque eccum lupum in sermone.* See Otto 1890, 199ff.; Battaglia 1956, 292ff.); and the collection of materials in Valenti Pagnini 1981, 3ff. The entry concerning this proverb in Tosi 1991, 433, n. 927 is very useful.
51. Comm. art. Don. p. 311 Keil.
52. "Said of those who unexpectedly appear when they are named" (Corp. Paroem. Graec. [Apostolius] 6.50 = Leutsch 1851, I, 377). Cf. Corp. Paroem. Graec. [Diogenianus] 4.64 (= Leutsch 1851, I, 241) and Suda ει.67 (= Adler 1931, II, 519).
53. Walter 1964, n. 14777. With small stylistic differences, the same proverb recurs also in n. 8628, 23503, 27174 and 30312.
54. Arthaber 1989, 364ff. In modern Greek, there is also the proverb *katá phoné kaí ho gaídaros,* in which "the donkey" (*ho gaídaros*) replaces "the wolf."
55. Otto 1890, 199ff. For the prohibition against "naming" the wolf, cf. Peuckert 1987, 9, 782ff.
56. For the "ruin de Roma," see Arthaber 1989, 364ff. "Ruin" means "wretch, trickster, crafty old devil," etc. For the etymology of this expression and its most ancient evidence (also proverbial), see Corominas 1954, 4, 86ff. For the Chinese proverb, see Mathews 1972, 884: Cao Cao was a powerful general of the 2nd c. ce who, in later traditions, became the incarnation of evil itself.

most likely the origin of the proverb, though this observation merits greater amplification.

All these beliefs and proverbs presume the curious notion that simply speaking about someone actually involves them in conversation (if only partially and imperfectly). Something similar occurs in the *Iliad*, when, returning from their celebrated "Night Raid," Odysseus and Diomedes appear in the Achaean camp at the precise moment that Nestor had been speaking of them: "The conversation was not but finished, and already they had arrived."[57] The notion that speaking about someone effectively brings about the appearance of that individual is clear in the Roman belief we have already cited above from Pliny: evidently, the sudden onset of silence was attributed to the fact that, somewhere, someone was slandering those sitting at the banquet (*isque famae labor est*).

In these circumstances, the person who constitutes the topic of conversation is obviously outside the conversation. Nevertheless, he or she perceives what is happening in the distant conversation by means of the silence that occurs within the present (that is, in-progress) conversation in which he or she is currently involved. It is almost as if the "present" conversation were being interrupted by a "distant" conversation in which one of the (present) participants has become the (distant) subject of conversation. This interruption, however, is not the same as entering into another circle of communication: the person being spoken about in the "distant" conversation simply stops communicating with his or her interlocutors in the "present" conversation, without actually entering into communication with those who are speaking about him.

Pliny records another Roman belief that seems to suggest the same thing: "it is commonly held that people can perceive when they are being talked about by others by a ringing in their ears" (*quin et absentes tinnitu aurium praesentire sermones de se receptum est*).[58] This belief still circulates in some modern societies in proverbial form, although the Roman "ringing" has been substituted by "buzzing" or "humming."[59] Here, the individual who is the (distant) topic of conversation senses a kind of disturbance in their

---

57. Hom. *Il.* 10.540. This comparison was made by Erasmus (*Ad.* 2.5.50).

58. Plin. *Nat. hist.* 28.24. Cf. Stat. *Silv.* 4.4.26; Front. *Ep.* 26.15; Poet. Lat. Min. IV, 62 Baehrens. See also Wolters 1935, 47ff. and Tosi 1991, 6, n. 7.

59. Statements of the type "orecchia manca, parola franca; orecchia destra, parola mal detta" (in Zeppini Bolelli 1989, 122), implying that either the right or the left ear buzzes depending on whether the person is being spoken of "well" or "badly," are already ancient: see Wolters 1935, 49 and Browne's *Pseudodoxia Epidemica* (V, XXIII, 6) in Wilkin 1852, II, 82: "When our cheek burneth or ear tingleth, we usually say that somebody is talking of us. . . . Which is a conceit hardly to be made out without the concession of a signifying genius, or universal Mercury, conducting sounds unto their distant subjects, and teaching us to hear by touch."

own (present) communication, as if they had somehow been attracted into a conversation in which they cannot, however, fully participate. Thus they perceive only a vague sensation of that remote discourse.

In such cases, we might say that only the phatic function of communication has been activated:[60] the "ringing" or "buzzing" signals that a channel of communication with another conversation has opened, but no effective message can be transmitted along this channel. Nevertheless, speaking about someone distant seems to produce a kind of sympathy with them. In some way, this act draws them into the present conversation, as in the case of *lupus in fabula*—even if in this instance the attraction towards the conversation in progress is so strong that the person does actually appear.

Let us try, then, to disentangle the cultural web of which *lupus in fabula* is only the first strand. Behind it, there is not only the belief that, once named, a malignant creature (the wolf, the devil) suddenly appears, but also the more general conviction that speaking about someone establishes a kind of sympathetic relationship with that person, and that even if they do not appear, nevertheless they perceive their role as the topic of conversation. These cultural models form the foundation of *lupus in fabula*.

THE ORIGIN OF a proverb is one thing; its manner of signification is another. A proverb is in fact a refined semiotic mechanism, whose operation may be schematized as follows: the proverb expresses a certain ("logical" or "real") situation, which is invariable, through a set of images, which may vary infinitely;[61] for example, as Greimas notes, the situation "act before it is too late" may be expressed through the set of images that includes expressions such as "strike while the iron is hot" (Europe), "shape the chalk while it is soft" (Swahili) and "cook the gourd while the fire is hot" (ancient Hebrew).[62] In the case of *lupus in fabula*, the situation that is being expressed is "the person about whom we have been speaking has just arrived," while the set of images used to express this situation includes the arrival of the wolf, the devil, the *ruin de Roma*, the *persona trista* and so on. To begin our analysis of *lupus in fabula*, therefore, we will look at the (variable and varied) images used to express it, rather than dwelling upon the (invariable) situation expressed by the proverb. And this set of images prompts an immediate

---

60. Cf. Malinowski 1953, 296ff. and Jakobson 1966, 188ff.

61. I use the categories of Permiakov 1979, 163–79. Greimas (1974, 325) attributes a similar semiotic function to the proverb when he insisted on the "connotative" character of proverbial language, meaning by this "the transfer of meaning from one semantic place (that intended by the signifier) to another."

62. Greimas 1974, 323–29.

question: When the person about whom we have been speaking suddenly appears, why do we consider this situation so disturbing that we express it through the image of a wolf or the devil?

Another Tuscan proverb that is still in use today to mean that the person who suddenly appears was just "on the tongue" of the interlocutors, appears to employ a slightly less troubling image: "se eri un fico, eri in bocca" ("if you were a fig, you would be in my mouth"). The image should not mislead us, though; the proverb actually sets up the poor person who suddenly appears on the scene as about to be "eaten" by the speakers. Here, then, it is not the person who is being spoken about that inspires fear, but the interlocutors themselves.

The two types of proverb that we have now seen—one that assimilates the person being spoken about to a wolf or the devil, and one that likens him to a fig in the mouth of the interlocutors—appear to function symmetrically. The situation remains unchanged, but the images used to express that situation orient its meaning in opposite directions. In the first case, the speakers are threatened by the unexpected arrival of the person they have been speaking about, while in the second, the person who has been the subject of conversation finds himself at the mercy of those who have been speaking about him. But why should this specific situation be the cause of so much anxiety that it comes to be expressed proverbially through such unsettling images?

To answer this question, let us consider the connection between *lupus in fabula* and the theme of "unexpected silence." When the person being spoken about actually appears, it is clear that dialogue cannot continue as before; it must in some sense be interrupted. Commenting on a passage of Terence in which the expression *lupus in fabula* appears, the grammarian Aelius Donatus suggests an interesting linkage between this situation and sudden silences:

> LUPUS IN FABULA: silentii indictio est in hoc proverbio, et eiusmodi silentii, vel in ipso verbo ut ipsa fabula conticescat, quia lupum vidisse homines dicimus, qui repente obmutuerunt; quod fere his evenit, quos prior viderit lupus, ut cum cogitatione in qua fuerint etiam verbis et voce careant.[63]

> LUPUS IN FABULA: There is an assertion of silence in this proverb and of a silence so immediate that the discourse be interrupted even in the middle of a word. Of those who suddenly fall silent, we say in fact that they "have

---

63. Comm. ad Ter. Ad. 537. I follow the text of the manuscripts (*fabula* V, *syllaba* others). Wessner 1905 corrects this to *ut in ipso verbo vel ipsa syllaba conticescat*, depriving *conticescat* of a subject and rendering Donatus's observation rather banal.

seen the wolf." This occurs to those whom the wolf sees first, that they are left without words and without voice in the middle of a thought.

According to Donatus, *lupus in fabula* relates to a belief that the wolf, coming upon someone unexpectedly, robs them of their ability to speak.[64] The wolf, then, is capable of producing "sudden silence" in the same way Hermes' entrance into a room does. Here, however, the fearsome, disturbing creature that causes silence is not a god but an animal, and—significantly— this animal's power to bring about silences resides in its gaze. That is, if a wolf furtively casts his glance upon someone, that person will be unable to express whatever it is that they had in mind at that moment.

Again, the situation presupposed by *lupus in fabula* always remains the same—"the person we were talking about has arrived"—but the range of images used metaphorically to express this situation has increased. According to Aelius Donatus' explanation, the sudden arrival of the person being spoken of interrupts the conversation at its middle by depriving the speaker of his voice, as if he were under the spell of the wolf's bewitching gaze. Scholars have normally rejected this interpretation of the proverb in favor of one based on the prohibition of naming the wolf or the devil in order to prevent its appearance. There is no need to choose one or the other, however. As a creation of folklore, a proverb is capable of sustaining the coexistence of diverse models of belief in its imagery. Donatus' explanation expands the set of images used by the proverb and, in doing so, further clarifies its meaning. By referring to the enchanting powers of the wolf to rob someone of their voice, *lupus in fabula* is capable of expressing the belief not only that the spoken-of person appears at the sound of his name, but also that his appearance brings silence down upon the interlocutors. The full sense of the proverb encapsulates both meanings: "If you speak of the wolf, the wolf appears and takes away your voice," and this is a figurative way of saying, "we are speaking about someone, and when they appear we must be quiet." At any rate, rejecting Donatus' explanation out of hand is untenable for another reason: the ancient sources concur in their appeal to the theme of the wolf's gaze to explain the proverb's origin.[65]

Donatus' interpretation of *lupus in fabula* only reinforces the disconcerting nature of the images used to express this situation. Arriving on the

---

64. Cf., e.g., Plin. *Nat. hist.* 8.80; Hor. *Carm.* 3.27.3; Serv. ad Ecl. 9.53 On this, see Otto 1890, 200ff. and Valenti Pagnini 1981, 5. Pitrè (1889, 463) records a Sicilian expression "lu vitti lu lupu" or "lu ciarmau lu lupu" referring to "someone hoarse."

65. Cf. Isid. *Etym.* 12.2.24, (*lupus*) *de quo rustici aiunt vocem hominem predere, si eum lupus prior viderit. unde et subito tacenti dicitur: lupus in fabula. certe si se praevisum senserit, deponit feritatis audaciam* and 1.37.28; Anec. Helv. 273.11 Hagen, *sic homines malum de aliquot loquentes, ipsum, de quo loquuntur, si supervenire viderint, sermo eorum deficit.*

scene, the person being spoken of not only acts like the wolf (i.e., appearing when named), but also possesses a kind of bewitching gaze that robs the speaker of his or her voice. Relating this proverb to beliefs about the wolf's gaze, Servius makes this connection explicit: "The natural philosophers also confirm that the voice is robbed from whomever it [sc. the wolf] has seen first. From this comes the proverb *lupus in fabula,* which is used whenever the person being spoken of arrives and by his presence cuts off the ability to speak" (*etiam physici confirmat, quod vox detrahitur ei, qui primum viderit. unde etiam proverbium natum est 'lupus in fabula,' quotiens supervenit ille, de quo loquimur, et nobis sui praesentia amputat facultatem loquendi*).[66] Appearing in the middle of a conversation of which he has been the subject, the intruder—like the wolf's gaze—terminates all communication on the spot. From this we may conclude that *lupus in fabula* presupposes a situation in which the spoken-of person sees the interlocutors first, catching them in the act of speaking about him. It is almost as if he was already there; perhaps he has heard what was being said about him. Because the interlocutors cannot know how much the interloper has heard, they are in a position of weakness. This is the first reason for the disturbing character of this communicative situation.

Upon the interloper's arrival, conversation must end; otherwise embarrassment ensues. The interlocutors are compelled to be quiet and to interrupt the conversation even in mid-word, if necessary. From this perspective, the situation of *lupus in fabula* partly resembles that of aposiopesis or *reticentia*.[67] As for the concrete progression of this interruption, however, *lupus in fabula* seems to offer two possibilities:

a) Silence falls spontaneously, as if the wolf had seen the interlocutors first;
b) Silence does not fall spontaneously, and then, to revive the conversation, the proverb is recited.

Donatus identifies an interesting aspect of the proverb in this regard,

---

66. Serv. ad Ecl. 9.54.
67. Aposiopesis involves the interruption of a phrase already begun and the onset of a silence or pause. There are differences, however: while the silence introduced by aposiopesis presupposes the presence of some kind of internal block (intense emotion, fear of breaking the rules of social control, etc.), the silence of *lupus in fabula* assumes the existence of an external block (the person who appears). Moreover, aposiopesis does not strictly interrupt communication, as it may first appear: rather, it maintains and in fact intensifies communication by recourse to the instrument of silence. *Lupus in fabula,* on the other hand, is a a true (and not rhetorical) interruption of the dialogue. On the linguistic, rhetorical, and anthropological function of aposiopesis, see the excellent study of Ricottilli 1984, 13–45.

when he remarks that *lupus in fabula* contains an explicit and immediate "assertion of silence" (*indictio silentii*). The grammarian seems to mean that if silence descends upon the interlocutors at the precise moment in which the interloper appears, it is the proverb itself—pronounced by one of the interlocutors as an "assertion of silence"—that interrupts the conversation. The proverb expresses two things, then: first, what normally happens when the interloper appears and the conversation is interrupted, and second, what must occur when that person arrives. Thus, in addition to its regular descriptive function, *lupus in fabula* also has a performative function.

Not only this. Beyond encapsulating both the statement "silence has descended upon us, because the person we were speaking about has arrived" and the exhortation "be quiet, the person we were speaking about has arrived," *lupus in fabula* has a third dimension of meaning: it also indicates its place in the dialogue. At least in theory, *lupus in fabula* should always be last in a conversation, since its utterance prohibits a response: if the interlocutor responds, he violates the "assertion of silence" that the proverb represents. *Lupus in fabula*, then, necessarily marks the end of one dialogue and the beginning of another—one that involves the newly arrived individual. One further observation. Used in this way, it is obvious that the expression *lupus in fabula* cannot be addressed to the person who was the subject of conversation. If it is the last utterance that the interlocutors exchange in their present dialogue, by necessity it cannot involve the person whose arrival signals the beginning of a new conversation.

Let us now explore the other dimension of the proverb, the image of the fig in the speaker's mouth. On first consideration, it does not appear that the mere utterance of this expression produces silence, as *lupus in fabula* does. In fact, the situation it defines is quite different. While *lupus in fabula* is the closing utterance of the old dialogue, "if you were a fig, you would be in my mouth" is the opening statement of the new one. Its utterance effectively transforms the interloper into a full-fledged participant of the conversation. As we have said, these two proverbs thus work in complementary fashion: *lupus in fabula* functions as an "assertion of silence" and an effective interruption of conversation, while "if you were a fig, you would be in my mouth" functions as an explicit opening of dialogue. Unlike *lupus in fabula*, which cannot be addressed to the newly arrived individual, "if you were a fig, you would be in my mouth" *must* be.

Addressing one's self directly to the new arrival and openly declaring that not moments ago they had been the very topic of conversation naturally presumes great psychological self-assuredness on the part of the interlocutors. In effect, the proverb communicates the following information to the interloper: "We have seen you and we are so sure of our own situation that we have no difficulty in telling you that we have just been talking about you." The new arrival may justifiably worry, then: "What could these people have been saying about me? There is nothing to be done about it—whatever they say, I will never know if that is truly what they were saying. I am totally in their hands; in fact, I am in their mouths: 'if I were a fig, they would be eating me.'"

Both *lupus in fabula* and the situation typified by the proverbial expression "if you were a fig, you would be in my mouth" presuppose a rather curious game between the interlocutors and the person who has been the subject of conversation. As we have seen, this game involves the give and take of gazes, and everything depends on who spots whom first. Its true complexity, moreover, emerges from the density of animal beliefs that furnishes the proverb with its set of images. Isidore of Seville describes what happens in each case: "Concerning the wolf, peasants say that a man loses his voice, if the wolf sees him first. For this reason, when someone suddenly falls silent, we say *lupus in fabula*. On the other hand, if we realize that we have been seen, the wolf loses its bravery and ferocity."[68] In other words, while the effect of the wolf's gaze upon man is silence, that of man's gaze upon the wolf is something else entirely: the animal becomes tame, it "loses its bravery and ferocity." Projecting this image upon the situation defined by *lupus in fabula*, the interlocutors who catch sight of the interloper and address him openly ("if you were a fig, you would be in my mouth") correspond to someone who realizes that he has been seen by the wolf; the intruder is tamed—the wolf is no longer frightening and the hunter has become the prey. In such situations, the spoken-of person finds himself in a position of weakness in respect to his interlocutors.

Now that we have considered the images used to encapsulate a certain situation—two people who have been speaking about someone when that person unexpectedly arrives—in the form of a proverb, it is time to consider the situation itself. From a strictly linguistic point of view, this situation is perhaps explicable within the framework of Émile Benveniste's theory of verbal person, which he developed from the work of Arabic grammarians.[69]

According to these grammarians' interpretation of grammatical "person," the first person corresponds to "he who speaks," the second to "he to whom one addresses one's self," and the third to "he who is absent." Consistently with this formulation, Benveniste suggests that the only "true" grammatical

---

68. Isid. *Etym.* 12.2.24.
69. Benveniste 1966, 252ff. Benveniste's study has been take up again by Lazzeroni 1994, 267ff., according to whom, along with the "correlation of personality" theorized by Benveniste that opposes the first and the second person to the third, there is also a "correlation of subjectivity" that opposes the first person to the second and the third.

persons of the verb are the first and second, while the so-called "third person" is in fact a "non-person" represented without any markings of individuality. Transferring this idea to the pronouns, we might say that "I" and "you" are "real" personal pronouns with true referential values, while "he" and "she" refer to the individual about whom one is speaking only as a member of the set of "others."[70] This is why in some languages the words for "he" and "she" can function as allocutives when the speaker wishes to distance his or her interlocutor in some way, whether out of respect or disdain. By addressing "you" as "he" or "she" (as, for example, in Italian an interlocutor may be addressed as *Lei*—that is, with a third person pronoun), the interlocutor is in some sense depersonalized, distanced below or above their natural status of "person." Outside of such cases, it is impossible to address "he" or "she" as "you." We can speak of "he," "she" or "it" as the subject of conversation, but we cannot make that third person into a second person. By definition, a "he," "she" or "it" is absent.

The situation presupposed by both *lupus in fabula* and "if you were a fig, you would be in my mouth" thus corresponds to the break that occurs when the system of oppositions between "person" and "non-person," between "those present" and "those absent" falls apart. If the person about whom one is speaking exists necessarily outside of the conversation, what happens when that person unexpectedly appears, penetrating into a linguistic space that does not concern strictly concern them? Communication fails, and conversation is interrupted. In addition to this linguistic observation, our anthropological analysis of the images used for expressing this situation also allows us to describe a state of mind. The situation defined by these proverbial expressions is perceived as so "uncanny" (in Freud's sense) that it is likened to the arrival of a wolf, to the silence imposed by that animal's bewitching eye or a kind of metaphorical mastication. The entrance of "he" or "she" into a conversation that concerns "him" or "her," resulting in the transformation of that "he" or "she" into an interlocutor (a "you"), creates anxiety both in the person speaking about the "he" or "she" and in the "he" or "she" who discovers him- or herself as the subject of the others' talk. Put in different terms, according to cultural convention the individual as topic of conversation and as personal (grammatical) subject must remain distinct: they must never meet. If they do happen to meet, communication ceases to function and the situation created by this encounter takes on a rather disagreeable and disturbing quality.

The psychic and emotional disturbance caused by such situations probably relates to beliefs about slanderous talk. In these circumstances, silence

---

70. Benveniste 1966, 252.

occurs not only because some "other" is being talked about, but because that person is being disparaged. This is similar to the situation described by Freud when he notes that "cultured" men immediately refrain from vulgar speech when a woman enters the room, whereas "in country taverns" the same event prompts scurrilous joking.[71] In one ancient source for *lupus in fabula*, the silence imposed upon the original interlocutors is in fact explicitly related to their slanderous talk.[72] Moreover, when the proverb appears within "conversational" contexts (rather than metalinguistic discussions), it often appears from the communicative situation that the interloper is being spoken of in categorically negative terms. In one case, the conversation turns on the greedy character of the parasite Gelasimus, who then suddenly shows up;[73] in another, Syrus explains how he means to wheedle something skillfully out of the *senex* Demea, who then unexpectedly appears.[74] Must we conclude, therefore, that the uneasiness provoked by this kind of situation corresponds only to breakdown of the rules of discretion and decency—that something is being said about someone that could not be said to them directly, and that this inconsistency is perceived as unpleasant and embarrassing for everyone?[75]

Such an explanation would be only partial, since slanderous talk is only sporadically associated with the use of *lupus in fabula*. Frequently, the proverb is used in contexts that contain no suggestion whatsoever of maliciousness towards the conversational interloper.[76] In fact, only one of the many numerous ancient explanations of this proverb mentions that the spoken-of person was the object of slander; normally, authors do not even mention this possibility.[77] Our own linguistic and cultural competence suggests, moreover, that the use of such expressions is independent of libelous intent: the unexpected appearance of the spoken-of person is enough to motivate our use of these conversational formulae.

Disparaging talk therefore appears to occupy an extreme position within the situation defined by *lupus in fabula*, although this position is not always substantially different from that occupied by the simple and neutral fact of "speaking about" another person. Indeed, experience teaches us that we

---

71. Freud 1972a, 89.

72. *Anec. Helv.* 273.11 Hagen. For an analogous relationship of triangulation occurring in acts of insulting, cf. Luc. *Calum.* 6ff.

73. Plaut. *Stich.* 574ff.

74. Ter. *Ad.* 533ff.

75. In this sense, the situation of *lupus in fabula* is very similar to that presupposed by aposiopesis (see above, 20n67), when speech is interrupted precisely out of fear of violating some rule of social behavior.

76. Cf., e.g., Cic. *Att.* 13.33.4, *de Varrone loquebamur, lupus in fabula: venit enim ad me.*

77. Cf. Otto 1890, 199ff.

often speak of others primarily because we wish to criticize them: often, then, the extreme situation is what effectively occurs—or at any rate what the "interloper" fears is occurring. This does not imply, however, that the reason for the uneasiness, embarrassment or disturbing character of situation resides only in that it may be defamatory. The phenomenon is in fact much more general.

We have already remarked that cultural convention pretends, quite paradoxically, that people are not (and ought not to be) spoken of by others—or at any rate that people are distinct and different entities when they are being spoken about and when they themselves are participating in dialogue. But this is obviously just a matter of convention; we know things do not really work like that. This is why the belief persists that when someone is the subject of some remote conversation, they can perceive what is happening there through a ringing in the ears or because of the failure of their own conversation. This belief underscores the fact that it is difficult, if not impossible, to make two distinct entities out of a person as subject of the conversation and as the "real" individual. A conversation *about* someone imperceptibly tends to become a conversation *with* that person—even if this phenomenon is limited to ringing in the ears. When cultural convention is blatantly contradicted and the individual *qua* interlocutor comes to coincide with the person *qua* topic of conversation because that individual has in fact appeared, a sensation of rupture and uneasiness arises. But what kind of anthropological situation is created in such circumstances?

Situations of this sort negatively affect the identity of the "interloper." If we discover that someone has transformed "us" into the subject of a conversation ("if you were a fig, you would be in my mouth"), it is like encountering a "double" of ourselves that has been circulating unimpeded in others' conversations. This is what happens to Sosia in Plautus' *Amphitruo*, when he finds himself standing before another 'Sosia'; or to Euripides' Helen, when she learns that it was only her *eidōlon* ("image") that was seduced by Paris, first causing the Trojan War and now roaming the seas with her husband Menelaus. Conversely, when the participants in a conversation discover that the person about whom they have been speaking is there before them in flesh and blood (*lupus in fabula*), it is like seeing the ghost of a dead man: the absent person has suddenly and disconcertingly become present.

Perhaps, then, the Arabic grammarians' definition of the third person— "he who is absent"—has a much more profound anthropological meaning than its use as a linguistic label suggests: by definition, "he who is absent" lives in another world, absent just as the dead and supernatural beings are absent. This is why the spoken-of person—like Hermes *psuchopompos* or Cristina Brahe—brings silence in tow. In short, the situation of *lupus in fabula* and "if you were a fig, you would be in my mouth" is perceived as anxiety producing precisely because it involves the fracture of someone's identity and a crisis of "presence." When this cultural convention falls apart, it reveals a sort of divided "I," exposing the interloper to the existence of his Double, or revealing the presence of the "original" of the verbal substitute ("he" or "she") that had been constructed by the participants of a conversation. And when this occurs, everyone is stunned into silence.

Death and Oblivion

Death is silence and it cannot be any other way.[78] Of their very nature, we cannot speak with the dead. They are absent, existing only in our memories or in conversations of which they are the subject. The dead are not "subjects" with whom we can sit down and have a conversation. For this reason, a dead man who returns and speaks inspires great fear. There is another condition, however, that relates to silence and that similarly distinguishes death from life: forgetfulness. When silence reigns, it is notoriously also impossible to remember: for example, when Odysseus goes to speak with the Dead in Homer's *Odyssey*, he discovers that only "the mind of Teiresias is solid. Only to him do the gods grant a mind full of sense, even in death, while all the others flit about like shades."[79] The dead do not have minds, sense or memories: Anticlea, Odysseus' own mother, recognizes her son only after drinking the blood of the slaughtered victims. They do not remember anything of mortal life; that is why Seneca defines them as "forgetful of themselves" (*oblitos sui*).[80]

Because the kingdoms of the living and the dead must remain distinct, Hades extends oblivion over all that came before. Above all, these two worlds must not communicate: In Vergil, souls destined for reincarnation drink from the fountain of Lethe in order to forget the experiences that they have already lived and to be able to confront the new life that awaits them.[81] Something similar happens at the oracle of Lebedea, where in the cave of Trophonius those wishing to consult the oracle act out a kind of mock descent into Hades. The petitioner must drink the water of two fountains before descending—*lēthē*, "in order to reach a state of oblivion concerning

---

78. In Hippocratic medicine, the onset of "silence" is always bound to disease or to "death" (just as the "voice" is connected to health and "life"): see Ciani 1983, 159–72.

79. Hom. *Od.* 10.493ff. For the intellectual deficiencies of the dead (and the "cruelty" of the Greeks' description of them), see Vermeule 1979, 23ff.

80. Sen. *Herc. fur.* 292.

81. Verg. *Aen.* 6.713ff.; cf. Hom. *Od.* 11.152ff. The case of Pythagoras, who recalls everything about his preceding lives, is exceptional: cf. Diog. Laert. 8.4.

all that they had thought up to that moment" and *mnēmosunē*, "in order to remember everything that they had seen in their descent."[82] As Vernant puts it, "he drank from the first and immediately forgot everything to do with his human life, and, like a dead man, he entered into the realm of Night."[83]

The association of forgetfulness and death is found in other mythological tales. When Orpheus, leaving the underworld, violates the injunctions of Persephone by turning to look back at Eurydice, he is overcome by a fit of forgetfulness.[84] At that moment, Lake Avernus resounds three times and Eurydice is swallowed up again by the infernal regions. Orpheus' failure of memory thus brings about the death of his beloved, as if in the act of forgetting he had again brought on that condition of perennial oblivion in which Eurydice had remained before her unexpected liberation. The denouement of Ariadne's story explores the same symbolic connection. Overwhelmed by her misfortune, the girl asks the Eumenides that the young hero Theseus bring ruin upon himself and his family with the same "state of mind" (*mens*) he had when he left her on the deserted island. These are the sinister threats of a woman scorned and near the end; but the "state of mind" (*mens*) in which Theseus had abandoned her was the casual forgetfulness of a faithless lover.[85] And again, it is a failure of memory that brings about the death of Aegeus, the hero's father, who had asked his son to hoist a white flag on his return as a sign of his success and safety. Theseus, who up to that moment had remembered everything "with sure memory" (*constanti mente*), now has his *mens* "wrapped in blind darkness;" "forgetful in spirit" (*oblito . . . pectore*), he brings about his father's death, when the old man throws himself from the rocks.[86]

Life and death must never communicate and so silence stands between them. When death enters among the living, conversation fails. In the same way, death must not preserve any memory of life. Thus, silence and forgetfulness are two complementary aspects of the noncommunication that regulates the interaction of this world and the next. Even if communication between the living and the dead were possible, such a conversation would be between those who remember (the living) and those who live in total oblivion of themselves (the dead). What, then, of those moments when the failure of conversation and the failure of memory appear to intersect, as if in

---

82. Paus. *Desc.* 9.39.8. For other, less complete descriptions of the oracle of Trophonius, see the sources collected by Frazer 1898, 2000ff.

83. Vernant 1965a. On the relationship between death and forgetfulness in the Greco-Roman tradition, see now Brusatin 2000, 3ff.

84. Cf. Verg. *Georg.* 4.488, *immemor*. Cf. Verg. *Georg.* 248, *qualem Minoidi lucum / obtulerat mente immemori*.

85. Cat. 64.200ff.

86. Cat. 64.208ff.

short circuit—when conversation is interrupted because a speaker suddenly realizes that he has forgotten what he wanted to say?

In one of his letters, Seneca describes a peculiar figure of his times, Calvisius Sabinus:

> He was exceedingly wealthy and had the nature and patrimony of a freedman. I have never seen a man more indecorously blessed. He had such a bad memory that sometimes he forgot Odysseus' name, sometimes Achilles', sometimes Priam's, whom he knew about as well as we know our teachers. No old slave *nomenclator*, who cannot recall for his master the exact names but invents them, ever saluted the citizens as poorly as he did the Achaeans and the Trojans. Nevertheless, he wanted to appear learned, and for this reason, he came up with the following expedient: he bought some slaves at a rather high price, one of whom knew Homer by heart, another Hesiod, and then assigned each of the others one of the nine lyric poets. You must not be surprised at the fact that he had paid so dear for them, given that he had not found them already instructed but had had them prepared for this purpose. When he had finally procured this troupe of slaves, he really began to annoy his guests. He would keep them all at the ready at the foot of the couch, to ask them from time to time some verse that he wished to cite—but he would also interrupt them in the middle of their speech. Satellius Quadratus, an exploiter of stupid rich people . . . once suggested to him to hire some grammarians to pick up the leftovers after dinner. And when Sabinus said to him that each of those slaves cost him one hundred thousand sesterces, the other retorted, "You could have bought as many bookcases full of books for less." But Sabinus had convinced himself that he knew everything that those slaves did, just because they belonged to him.[87]

Calvisius Sabinus cuts a rather pathetic figure. If his learned slaves somewhat resemble the Greek Carmadas—who according to Pliny "recited by memory, on request, the volumes of an entire library, as if he were reading them" (*quae quis exegerat volumina in bibliotheca legentis modo repraesentavit*)[88]—their master is more like the grammarian Orbilius Pupillus Beneventanus, who earned himself the surname *Oblivio Litterarum* because he had forgotten everything he once knew by the time he was one hundred years old.[89] Unlike the poor Orbilius, however, Calvisius Sabinus possessed

---

87. Sen. *Ep. mor.* 27.5ff.
88. Plin. *Nat. hist.* 7.89.
89. Suet. *Gramm. rhet.* 9. The epithetic was given to him in an epigram of Furius Bibaculus (fr. 3 Courtney).

sufficient economic resources to remedy this terrible inconvenience; he simply bought others' memories, convinced that he himself would somehow possess their intellectual capabilities thereby. Perhaps Sabinus took literally the principle of Roman law that "we acquire not only through ourselves, but also through those whom we have in our *potestas, manus* or *mancipium*."[90] As the owner of a troupe of slaves who "possessed" good culture and (more importantly) excellent memories, Sabinus considered himself to possess those spiritual endowments in turn, believing that "he knew everything that those slaves did, just because they belonged to him." Notwithstanding the best efforts of the slaves that he kept at the ready at the foot of his couch like some vocal library or an online archive, still he stumbled in pronouncing the words they had recalled for him not a moment before. Conversations in Calvisius Sabinus' house must have failed often—and not because Hermes had entered the room or because an interloper had appeared unannounced. The obstacle to communication was Sabinus' terrible memory, and it was no help trying to revive it by purchasing those extraordinary slaves. Perhaps what happened to Calvisius Sabinus was the same thing that had happened to Messala Corvinus, of which Trimalchio also complains: "I have such a good memory, that often I forget what my own name is."[91]

The truth, as Pliny says, is that "in man, there is nothing so precarious [as memory]":

> morborum et casus iniurias atque etiam metus sentit, alias particulatim, alias universa. ictus lapide oblitus est litteras tantum; ex praealto tecto lapsus matris et adfinium propinquorumque cepit oblivionem, alius aegrotus servorum, etiam sui vero nominis Messala Corvinus orator. itaque saepe deficere temptat ac meditatur vel quieto corpore et valido.[92]

> It suffers the injuries of sickness or of a fall, and even of fright: sometimes partially, sometimes totally. A man struck by a rock forgot the letters of the alphabet; another, falling from a very high roof, forgot his mother, his relatives and his friends; yet another, overtaken by sickness, did not recognize his slaves, while the orator Messalla Corvinus could not even remember his own name. The memory attempts and conspires to flee from us even when our body is safe and unharmed.

---

90. Gai. *Instit.* 2.86ff., 3.164 and 221. Cf. De Zulueta 1963, II, 80, "The basic principles are that a *paterfamilias* inevitably acquires what his dependants acquire."
91. Petr. *Satyr.* 66, *tam bonae memoriae sum, ut frequenter nomen meum obliviscar.* This is a proverbial expression: cf. Otto 1890, 244. On Messalla Corvinus, see Plin. *Nat. hist.* 7.90.
92. Plin. *Nat. hist.* 7.90.

The memory is in constant danger and forgetfulness waits patiently in ambush—even when we are in good health (or believe that we are). This is why some suspected that failures of memory—especially when sudden—were caused by magical arts. Cicero, for example, recounts that during the defense of Titinia, Curio spoke after him but "suddenly forgot the case in its entirety and he said that this occurred because of Titinia's potions and enchantments" (*subito totam causam oblitus est idque veneficiis et cantionibus Titiniae factum est*).[93]

It would be easy to make Calvisius Sabinus the archetype of the many learned and cultured people who believe it is their right to usurp and exploit others' intelligence to their own ends, convinced that they know everything others do for the simple reason that they belong to their *familia*. But Sabinus' fragile and deficient memory inevitably brings us from the comedy of knowledge to the darkness of tragedy: Sabinus, overcome by oblivion, forgetful of the words that his learned assistants have just whispered to him, resembles a soul of the Homeric *Nekuia*. The *phrenes* ("spiritual faculties") of the dead in the *Odyssey* are equally unstable (*empedoi*);[94] their heads are "worn out" (*amenēna karēna*),[95] and their minds are "senseless" (*aphrades*).[96] Sabinus also seems like one of those "shadows of the weary" (*eidōla kamontōn*).[97] Indeed, instead of a slave who knew Homer by heart and could provide him with citations from the *Odyssey*, Sabinus should have had someone actually perform it—pouring him a little sacrificial blood to drink, as Odysseus did for Teiresias, to make him remember.

Living Archives

Above, Seneca produces an interesting comparison in describing Calvisius Sabinus' *défaillances* by employing the technical term for a slave employed for the specific purpose of reminding a forgetful or distracted master of the names of those he encountered in the course of his business (*nomenclator*). The image of this *comparandum* is fitting: a bad *nomenclator* who mistakes the names of those his master must greet represents very well the gaffes of someone who mistakes one Homeric hero for another. In the Senecan account, however, this reference to the *nomenclator* anticipates the appearance of those learned slaves whose duty was to remind their master of the

---

93. Cic. *Brut.* 217.
94. Hom. *Od.* 10.493,
95. Hom. *Od.* 10.521 and 536, 11.29 and 49,
96. Hom. *Od.* 11.476,
97. Hom. *Il.* 3.278, 23.72; *Od.* 11.476, 24.10,

texts he had forgotten, and who function in a manner very similar to the *nomenclatores*. Here, we enter the fascinating realm of "memory aids"—but not in the sense of mnemonic devices, mental maps, techniques of memorization, notes or memoranda that take advantage of writing (or in more modern times, of printing).[98] Instead, we are about to encounter a kind of living instrument of memory, a figure whose duty and function was to combat forgetfulness—to remember and to make others remember.

There were various such figures at Rome. *Nomenclatores* were employed to remind their masters of the names of *clientes;* or, during elections, to allow the candidates to create a false sense of familiarity with their constituents.[99] (Otherwise, a Roman citizen might be compelled to use the generic appellative *dominus*, roughly translatable as "Sir").[100] There were also *monitores*, whose job was to stand next to the orator in the forum and remind him of what he should say or do.[101] The same word also denoted what we might call a theatrical "prompter" as well as *libri commentarii*.[102]

When memory fails, help is needed—and in a culture where writing had not yet supplanted orality in the task of conserving and archiving information, "memory aids" might be not only lists of "talking points" or agendas, but also the living memories of human beings. (From this perspective, it is interesting that *libri commentarii* as well as "prompters" in a theater could be defined as *monitores:* begging pardon for the pun, it is almost as if the designation of those *written* instruments still preserved some memory of their *oral* predecessors.) Consider, for example, the words of Euryalus to Odysseus when the hero presents himself in disguise. The arrogant suitor says that Odysseus does not seem to him "a man expert in contests, but rather one who sails upon the sea in a ship of many oars, who commands merchant sailors and cares for the cargo, goods and alluring gain."[103] In the Homeric text, the expression *phortou . . . mnēmōn* means literally "mindful of the cargo." On the significance of this term, the ancient Homeric exegetes make some observations that are worth considering.[104]

According to a scholiast's comment on *Odyssey* 8.163, it was a *mnēmōn* who "remembered what the value of each piece was."[105] Homer's use of this

---

98. See the fascinating discussion of Bolzoni 1995.
99. Cf. Cic. *Att.* 4.1.5; *Mur.* 77. The name *nomenclator* was also given to the slave who reminded his master of the names of those who came to salute him in the morning at home. Sen. *Ben.* 1.3.10; see also *Ep. mor.* 19.11; *Brev. vit.* 14.5.
100. Cf. Sen. *Ep.* 1.3.1, *obvios, si nomen non succurrit, 'dominos' salutamus;* Mart. 1.112 and 5.57.
101. Cic. *Verr.* 1.52; *Orat.* 2.24.99; Quint. *Inst. orat.* 6.4.9, etc.
102. Fest. *Sign. verb.* p. 122 Lindsay; Paul. Fest. p. 123 Lindsay.
103. Hom. *Od.* 8.159ff.
104. Cf. Bischoff 1932; Gernet 1968, 153ff.; and Vernant 1965a.
105. Cf. Dindorf 1855, 366ff.

expression, moreover, indicated to some—again according to the scholiast—that the heroic age did not know the use of the alphabet: "they say that they kept the cargo in memory because they did not have knowledge of letters." The scholiast goes on to say that it was for this reason—i.e., the maintenance of cargo lists—that the Phoenician traders invented the alphabet. In ancient usage, however, the word *mnēmōn* was applied to both the "secretary" (*grammateus*) and the "provisioner" (*epimelētēs*).

The *mnēmōn*, then, appears to have been a kind of on-board commissary and, at the same time, a cargo manifest—someone who both took care of those on board and also registered the value of each piece of merchandise in memory. In the absence of writing, the inventory of goods corresponded not to a written document, but to a person—the *mnēmōn*—who functioned as an archivist, paradoxically also constituting the archive itself. The Phoenicians invented the alphabet to free the *mnēmōn* from this difficult task, wishing to delegate to the more trustworthy expedient of writing the data that previously had burdened the memory.

In this sense, the polarity between the two Greek expressions—the more recent *grammateus* and the more ancient *mnēmōn*—takes on almost emblematic value. The word *grammateus* derives from *gramma* ("letter of the alphabet") and therefore provides us with a "written" equivalent of the ancient mnemonic functionary. Plato amuses himself in an elegant metaphorical construction by reversing the two terms of the question, defining "memory" (*mnēmē*) as "our *grammateus*" and describing it while he registered the impressions that he received in written form (*graphein*).[106] In other words, "graphic" reasoning had already so pervaded the world of information and communication that, for Plato, "memory" itself could become a scribe. In Latin, too, terms such as *obliviscor, oblivio* and (even more transparently) *oblittero* take their meaning from the act of erasing a surface on which letters have been traced:[107] that is, "forgetfulness" has assumed the form of an erasure—the cancellation of what has been written.

RETURNING TO THE *mnēmōn*. Although little evidence remains, it is apparent that this figure played an important role in myth and heroic tales:[108]

---

106. Plat. *Phil.* 39a. The dialectic between oral and written memory, or oral and written communication, was obviously maintained for a long time in Greece—in, e.g., the case of the *grammateús*, the city's "public reader" who "gave voice" to the letter written by Nikias (Thuc. *Hist.* 7.8–10). Nikias decided to entrust his message to writing because he feared the "obscuring" it would have undergone "through a messenger" (*en tōi angelōi*): see the analysis of Guastella 1997, 15ff.

107. Cf. Ernout-Meillet 1965, 455.

108. Cf. Tümpel 1894, II, 2, 3075ff.

for example, in the story of Achilles and Tenes,[109] Thetis prohibits her son from killing Tenes because he has been honored by Apollo—and Achilles was destined to die if ever he killed someone of Apollo's line.[110] Thetis therefore assigns a slave to stay beside Achilles to remind him of this prohibition. Unknowingly, however, Achilles kills Tenes and, when he realizes what he has done, also kills the slave who had failed in his duty. In Lycophron the slave is actually named "Mnemon," revealing his function through his name. Lycophron also mentions the interesting detail that the slave failed in his task because he had been "conquered by forgetfulness" (*lēthargōi sphaleis*).[111]

Eustathius provides ample evidence of other *mnēmones* of heroic legend,[112] beginning with an account of the story of Chalcon Kyparisseus who, according to Asclepiades of Mirlea,[113] was assigned as "*mnēmōn* and squire" to Nestor's son Antilochus. Nestor had received an oracle that his son "should keep away from the Ethiopian," and therefore assigned Chalcon to his son to remind him of this. Chalcon, however, fell in love with Penthesilea and ran to help her and thus was killed by Achilles. Antilochus was in turn killed by Memnon (the "Ethiopian") and Chalcon's body was impaled by the Greeks. Eustathius remarks that "*mnēmones* were given also to other heroes," as in the case of Achilles already mentioned. According to Timolaus of Macedonia,[114] even Patroclus had his own *mnēmōn* named Eudoros, who was assigned to Patroclus "so he would not drive too far forward" during the battle. But Eudoros was killed by Pyraichmos, who was then killed by Patroclus—and Patroclus, as we know, was himself killed by Hector. According to Antipatros of Acanthus, Hector, too, had a *mnēmōn*[115] named Daretes Phrygius whose task it was to remind him "not to kill anyone dear to Achilles." After deserting his post, however, Daretes was killed by Odysseus—and Hector's

---

109. Plut. *Quaest. Graec.* 28; Lyc. *Alex.* 241ff. and Tzetzes's scholion ad loc.; Apoll. *Ep.* 3.26. On the anthropological meaning of "forgetting" in this myth, see Lévi-Strauss 1983a, 253–61.

110. See the scholion of Tzetzes ad Lyc. *Alex.* 241ff.

111. Lyc. *Alex.* 241–2.

112. Comm. ad Hom. Il. 11.521. Cf. Halliday 1928, 133ff., who does not, however, comment on this other than to note its late, literary character. It is useful to note that the account of Eustathius is echoed by the *resumé* of Ptolomaeus Chennus's *Nova Historia* given by Photius (*Bib.* 147a). On Ptolomaeus Chennus, see "Ptolemaios Chennos" in *RE* XXIII, 2, 1959, col. 1862.

113. A grammarian of the 1st c. BCE: see "Asklepiades von Myrlea" in *RE* II, 2, 1896, coll. 1628ff.; Jacoby 1957, III C, 548–51; and Müller 1851, III, 298ff. The fragment is not reported in either of these works; but see Jacoby 1957, I A, 296ff.

114. A grammarian of the 3rd c. BCE: see "Timolaos ék Makedonías" in *RE* II, VI A:1, 1936, col. 1275ff. and cf. Müller 1851, IV, 521.

115. Perhaps an author invented by Ptolomaeus Chennus: see "Antipatros von Akanthos" in *RE* I, 2, 1894, col. 2517. Jacoby 1957, I A, 296–97 has a section dedicated to Antipater of Acanthus, in which he cites the text of Eustathius and that of Ptolomaeus Chennus from Photius. No entry either in the commentary or in the *Nachträge* corresponds to the text, however.

fate is well known. According to Eresius,[116] Protesilaus also had a *mnēmōn* named Dardanus of Thessaly. Protesilaus' father had assigned Dardanus to his son after receiving an oracle that "he would die if he was the first to disembark." Protesilaus was later killed by a "Trojan man" (*Dardanos anēr*) because of Dardanus' inattentiveness to his task.[117] Photius catalogues other *mnēmones*:[118] Odysseus' father is supposed to have given to his son a Cephallenian *mnēmōn* by the name of Muiscos, while Achilles is supposed to have had a Carthaginian *mnēmōn* named Noemon. As may be seen, Achilles always has *mnēmones* with very significant names: Mnemon's name derives from "memory" itself (*mnēmē*), whereas Noemon's comes from "intelligence" (*nous*).

The figure of the *mnēmōn* seems to be inserted into well-known episodes of Homeric myth—the heroic deaths of Achilles, Patroclus, Antilochus, Hector, Protesilaus and so on—almost as a touch of tragic irony. These are all heroes who receive explicit condemnations of fate and for this reason are given *mnēmones* with the specific task of keeping them from their own destinies. Consequently, the figure of the *mnēmōn* is entrusted with the part of the story or event that we know from the most traditional variants of the myth to have been the cause of the hero's death. Thus, Achilles' *mnēmōn* had the task of reminding him "not to kill a descendant of Apollo," Hector's the task of reminding him "not to kill someone dear to Achilles," Protesilaus' that of reminding him "not to disembark first" and so on. No *mnēmōn*, however, can stand in the way of destiny. According to the logic of myth, the *mnēmōn* must always fail in the task he has been assigned; the story demands that the *mnēmōn* play the paradoxical role of he who remembers (and makes others remember) and he who forgets.

There are various reasons for the *mnēmōn*'s failure: it may be a matter of explicit—but otherwise unexplained—forgetfulness (Mnemon); of love (Chalcon), desertion (Daretes) or simple absentmindedness (Dardanus of Thessaly). In this last case, the story is particularly clever. At the end, we learn that a *mnēmōn* named "Dardanus" was probably the least suitable of all to play the role of bodyguard for Protesilaus, given the homonymy he shared with the man destined to kill the hero. Here, the *mnēmōn* has the paradoxi-

---

116. An author known only to Eustathius: cf. "Eresios" in *RE* VI, 1, 1907, col. 420. In Ptolomaeus Chennus, the story is attributed to Antipater of Acanthus. In the *apparatus criticus*, Jacoby 1957, I A, 297 notes that before "Eresios" the name of the author has been lost.

117. The killing of Protesilaus by a "Dardanian man" (*Dardanos anēr*) is told by Hom. *Il.* 2.701 and therefore the story represents a somewhat fantastic re-elaboration of the Homeric line. Cf. Thraemer, 1901. This obscure Homeric mention had been explained in various ways already in antiquity, attributing to the mysterious "Dardanian" the identity of Aeneas, Hector, Euphorbus and so forth. Cf. Leaf 1900, I, 103 ad loc.

118. Phot. *Bibl.* 147a.

cal task of defending the hero from "himself": he was supposed to be the faithful "double" of his charge but turned out to be that of his assassin.

In this type of story, the *mnēmōn* acts as a kind of *alter ego* for the hero. Like an image reflected in a mirror, he is supposed to warn and remind the hero of something—even if in the event he deliberately does not do so or does not succeed in doing so. The *mnēmōn* thus functions as a kind of external memory bank for the hero—a walking *monumentum*, as it were. This figure thus closely resembles the Roman *monitor* entrusted with the task of reminding his master of a single event. (In other cases, the same effect is obtained by modifying a significant part of the body: for example, letting one's hair grow—or shaving it—until a certain goal had been achieved, somewhat as we do when we change the position of a ring or tie a knot in a handkerchief.)[119]

Modern culture is highly sensitive to the theme of information storage. It is therefore worth considering the role of the *mnēmōn, monitor* and *nomenclator* from the perspective of modern theory of "distributed cognition," which explores the ways in which human beings entrust a part of our cognition and memory to some aspect (or indeed many aspects) of our external environment. This process permits us to "unload" our minds of excess data that would otherwise be difficult to utilize.[120] In this light, *mnēmones, monitores* and *nomenclatores* were clearly more powerful than the classic knot in a handkerchief, the agenda, the card file and most modern data storage systems. These individuals not only contained information, but also were capable of producing it whenever needed. In roughly technological terms, we might say that these ancient figures were themselves "databases" that provided a kind of interactive "software" program for accessing all the information contained on the "disk." The limited development of written culture as well as the easy availability of "human instruments" in Roman society guaranteed that even memory aids and information support systems were realized through a form of human interaction.

Finally, there are those cases in which the *mnēmōn* served a public and specifically juridical function. We know of certain *mnēmones* whose duty was to "remember the religious calendar" (*hieromnēmonein*), for example.[121] As Gernet notes in his famous study, the *mnēmōn* "prefigures in Greece char-

---

119. Her. *Hist.* 1.82.7–8 recounts that after losing Tirea, the Argives forbade anyone to allow their hair to grow and prohibited the women from wearing gold jewelry until they had regained it. The Spartans decreed the opposite: although they had never worn their long hair up to that moment, they decide that from then on they would let it grow.
120. See the well-known work of Norman 1995, 139–54, as well as Vigotsky 1987, 81ff.
121. Ar. *Nub.* 624.

acteristic institutions of modern law, such as the archive and recording."[122] The title of *mnēmones* later passed to the magistrates charged with preserving written documents; but having no knowledge of writing, the so-called Law Code of Gortyn was entrusted to a group of *mnēmones* who functioned as assistants to the magistrates, as true and proper "living records." The *mnēmōn* had not only the capacity to remember and to make others remember the past; above all, he possessed the authority of memory. He enjoyed the dignity of an archive and was as reliable as only written documents are for us.

"Stuffed Ears" and the Location of Memory

Let us return to Rome. A gloss informs us that the *nomenclatores* who reminded candidates of the names of their constituents had a peculiar nickname: *fartores* (literally, "stuffers" or "fillers"). Paulus Festus explains: "*nomenclatores* are called *fartores* because without anyone realizing it they 'stuff' all the names of the people whom the candidate must greet into his ear" (*fartores nomenclatores, qui clam velut infercirent nomina salutatorum in aurem candidati*).[123] The metaphor is almost ridiculous; actually, it is probably comic,[124] since it corresponds to certain images found in Plautus: for instance, charged with carrying a message to Toxilus, the slave-girl Sophoclidisca remarks, "I will approach Toxilus; I will load his ears with the things I have been charged with telling him" (*conveniam hunc Toxilum; eius auris quae mandata sunt onerabo*).[125] Jokes in Roman political life were apparently inspired by the comic poets and grammarians, diligent collectors of words, noted down these creations of the vernacular language in their scholarly lexicons, making them objects of erudition.

The metaphor is telling, however: the *nomenclator* who whispers the name of some unfamiliar individual into the candidate's ear behaves as a *fartor*—a professional "stuffer" of animals (especially birds) or sausage maker.[126] The candidate's ears are like an empty skin into which the slave stuffs the names of those the candidate should (but does not) recognize. That is, the ears function as a place where the memory "keeps" words.

---

122. Gernet 1968, 285; Vernant 1965a.
123. Paul. Fest. p. 78 Lindsay. Cf. also Acro's scholion on Hor. *Serm.* 3.3.229.
124. Cf. Müller 1975, I, 88), *comica, ut videtur, horum hominum appellatio*.
125. Plaut. *Pers.* 182, conveniam hunc Toxilum; eius auris quae mandata sunt onerabo Cf. Sen. *Ep. mor.* 1.3.4, *in quaslibet aures quidquid illos urit exonerant*.
126. Cf. *TLL* VI, 287, 8ff. For *fartor* in the sense of *saginator*: Plaut. *Truc.* 105; Ter. *Eun.* 257 (and Eugraphius's commentary); Hor. *Serm.* 2.3.229; and, above all, Col. *Re rust.* 8.7.1, "it is the task of the *fartor* to fatten the chickens, not the peasant's"; for *fartor* in the sense of "sausage-maker," cf. Donatus ad Ter. Eun. 257, *fartores qui insicia et farcimina faciunt*.

Within this metaphorical field, we may once more consider the weasel. Besides being thought to conceive through the ears and give birth through the mouth—as we have seen—the weasel was also apparently believed to conceive through the mouth and give birth through the ears. This belief also relates to language:

> The Law (*Leviticus* 11:29) says: Do not eat the weasel or anything like it. The Physiologus said of the weasel that it has this nature: its mouth receives from the male and, having conceived, it gives birth from the ears. There are some who eat the sacred bread in church, *but as soon as they have left, they reject the word from their ears,* like the impure weasel. And they become like the deaf asp that seals its own ears.[127]

To express that someone needs to be reminded of something, why does Roman culture say "to stuff the ears"? By the same token, why can forgetting what one has heard be likened to having one's ears "emptied"? Because in the process of oral communication, information must of course pass through the ears. But I suspect memory is also directly involved in the "stuffed ears" of he who must not forget and in the "empty ears" of he who rejects the words that he has heard. Let us see.

Horace, desperately beset by that infamous babbling *garrulus* who has decided to torture him at all costs, is rescued only by the unexpected arrival of someone embroiled in a court case with the annoying man.[128] Wishing to drag the importunate man off to court, Horace's savior asks the poet, *licet antestari* ("Are you disposed to bear me witness?") and he responds, *ego vero oppono auriculam* ("Obviously, I offer my earlobe"). Blabbermouths are a curse;[129] but what of Horace's earlobe? Porphyrio explains its significance: "The adversary of the annoying man asks Horace if he would be disposed to bear him witness, so as to allow him to drag the man before the praetor.... When someone called another to witness, he touched him on the earlobe and said to him 'Are you disposed to bear me witness?'" (*adversarius molesti illius Horatium consulit an permittat se antestari, iniecta manu extracturus ad praetorem quod vadimonio non paruerit . . . porro autem qui antestabatur, auriculam ei tangbat atque dicebat, 'licet te antestari?'*).[130]

The act of touching someone on the earlobe has symbolic value and serves precisely to remind someone of something. We know this from other

---

127. Physiologus 21.
128. Hor. *Serm.* 1.9.75ff.
129. Cf. Plut. *Garr.* 2.503a.
130. Comm. in Hor. Serm. p. 165.

evidence as well:[131] Vergil recounts that when Apollo addressed him, the god "pulled my ear and admonished me" (*aurem / vellit et admonuit*).[132] The poet had abandoned his duty; rather than writing pastoral poetry, herding flocks and singing a *carmen deductum*, he had turned to celebrating kings and battles. By pulling one of his ears, the god meant to remind him of this. Likewise, Seneca wishes that there were "some guardian that could pull my ear (*aurem subinde pervellat*) at the right moment, distance us from gossiping and protest against the praises of the masses."[133] In other words, touching and pulling the ear was a gestural translation of the verb *admonere*. For this reason, touching someone's earlobe was a customary invitation for him or her to appear before a magistrate on one's behalf.[134]

But why, for the Romans, did the act of touching the earlobe function in this way? Pliny explains the meaning of the gesture as follows: "The memory is situated in the earlobe and by touching it, we call someone as a witness. Likewise, the place behind the right ear is dedicated to Nemesis, where we pass our ring finger after having touched it with the lips, as if to replace there the pardon that we ask of the gods for our words" (*est in aure ima memoriae locus, quem tangentes antestamur; est post aurem aeque dexteram Nemeseos . . . quo referimus tactum ore proximum a minimo digitum, veniam sermonis a diis ibi recondentes*).[135] As part of a "symbolic anatomy" associating the faculties or sentiments of the soul with certain parts of the body—Pliny informs us that according to popular belief the site of *vitalitas*, for example, was the knees—the earlobe functioned as the seat of memory.[136] Since memory was "located" in the earlobe, touching or pulling that part of the body served as a way to jog the memory—just as touching someone's knees initiated an act of supplication, an appeal to their most intimate *vitalitas*.

A final observation on the mnemonic powers of the ears. Plutarch asserts that the hearing duct connected directly to the *psuchē* ("soul"):[137] in other words, that between the ear and the individual's spiritual faculties a direct channel of communication existed. In this regard, what Pliny has said about

---

131. See Otto 1890, 48.
132. Verg. *Ecl.* 6.3.
133. Plin. *Ep.* 94.59.
134. This symbolic gesture lives on today in certain cultures, although the modern act seems to have assumed an almost exclusively punitive or prohibitive meaning: it is used to warn someone (usually a child) not to repeat a certain action: cf. Morris 1983, 256ff. Nevertheless, a good tug on the ear—even if it is only metaphorical—preserves some connection with the sphere of memory and still has the value of an admonition. It is possible, moreover, that something of this ancient custom's meaning remains in the modern habit of pulling someone's ears on their birthday as a solemn reminder of how far they have come in life.
135. Plin. *Nat. hist.* 11.251.
136. Plin. *Nat. hist.* 11.250.
137. Plut. *Garr.* 1.502d.

the "place of Nemesis" merits further comment.[138] According to Pliny, when someone wishes to ask pardon of the gods for some imprudent word they have uttered (thus potentially inviting the arrival of Nemesis), it is customary to pass the ring finger across the lips and then to "put it back" behind the lobe of the right ear. Was this to signify that in the future one would be mindful not to commit the same mistake again? This gesture is almost equivalent to tugging one's own ear to remind one's self not to repeat such an anger-provoking blunder, and thus to screen one's self from the vengeance of the gods. In fact, even in some modern cultures—for example, in Turkey and southern Italy—touching the ear has apotropaic value.[139]

We also learn from Pliny that "some placate anxiety by passing a bit of saliva behind the ear with their finger" (*alius saliva post aurem digito relata sollicitudinem animi propitiat*).[140] As often in the case of gestures, they are difficult to define and interpret unambiguously—but it is possible that in the act of passing the ring finger behind the right ear after touching it to the lips as well in passing saliva behind the ear with the finger, the "meanings" of self-admonition, saliva's apotropaic power,[141] and even unrelated, nervous movement caused by situational anxiety all coexist. In such cases, by touching meaningful parts of our body we communicate directly with ourselves, using a language whose deepest meanings we have only partially forgotten.

We could continue this journey through the symbolic places of memory and oblivion, language and silence at some length, to prove just how much the cultures of antiquity differ from our own—at least with regard to communication and its symbology. But we will stop here, since we seem to have come full circle to the ears—the ears of Hermes, god and symbol of communication.

---

138. Cf. also Plin. *Nat. Hist.* 28.22. For the goddess Nemesis, see Wolters 1935, 31ff.
139. Morris 1983, 259–64 explains this gesture as the equivalent of "touching a metal," with reference to an earring that is no longer worn. Pliny demonstrates that this explanation is incorrect.
140. Plin. *Nat. hist.* 28.25.
141. Cf. also Plin. *Nat. hist.* 28.36, *veniam quoque a deis spei alicuius audacioris petimus in sinum spuendo*. Cf. also Petr. *Sat.* 74. On the powers of saliva, see Elworthy 1895, 414ff.

TWO

Brutus the Fool

Morio dictus erat: viginti milibus emi.
redde mihi nummos, Gargiliane: sapit.

—Martial, Epigrams 8.13

Non v'ha dubbio che quel che si narra in specie di Bruto presenta per la maggior parte
le caratteristiche della leggenda e della poesia popolare.

—G. De Sanctis, Storia dei Romani, 1926

Aut fatuum aut regem nasci oportet—"It is well to be born either a King or a Fool," or so the saying goes:[1] in both cases, paradoxically, the advantages are the same. Traditional wisdom holds that the Fool and the King—the bottom and the top of the pyramid, the two extreme points of the spectrum—are actually more alike than their differences might lead us to believe. Brutus, unable to be King, was clever enough to follow the wisdom of the proverb: becoming a Fool, he shielded himself from the treacheries of his deceitful cousin Tarquin. Only he, with his superior intelligence, understood that the Fool is closest to the King and that by taking just a short step he could slip into the place of the King. And by then it was too late for his enemies; for the truth is, no one expected it.

In following this paradoxical strategy, Brutus has well-known and noble fellows: not only Hamlet,[2] that other "false fool" who sought vengeance for

---

   1. Sen. *Apoc.* 1.1. Cf. Otto 1890, 299, who believes the proverb was "re-adapted" by Seneca, but gives no reason for this assumption.

   2. In the course of this essay, I will refer exclusively to the story narrated by Saxo Grammaticus in *Gesta Danorum*, with some Nordic variants as collected by Gollancz 1926 and others, rather than to the (perhaps better known) versions of François de Belleforest and William Shakespeare. Further information is taken from Hansen 1983.

his father's death from a murderous and incestuous uncle and then became lord of the land, but also Khusràw, son of Siyavish. As Firdawsi recounts in the *Book of Kings*,[3] Khusràw's uncle, Afrasyab, had had his brother, the king, murdered. Khusràw feigned madness at his uncle's court in order to allay any fear that he might retaliate, finally succeeding in his efforts to retake his father's throne. In the company of such false madmen we may also number David, at the court of King Achis;[4] Odysseus, who feigned madness to avoid going to Troy until he was betrayed by the hateful Palamedes;[5] and Solon, who, when war broke out between Athens and Salamis, resorted to a similar expedient in order to express certain disagreeable opinions without risk of danger.[6]

The closest analogies run among the stories of Brutus, Hamlet and Khusràw. With only slight variation, the same web of familial relationships presents a young man who avenges the murder of his father (Tarquin killed Brutus' older brother as well as his father)[7] and reclaims his rightful position on the throne from a murderous maternal uncle (Brutus), paternal uncle (Hamlet) or maternal grandfather (Khusràw) by the same stratagem: feigning insanity. Given that the same "plot" appears to have existed in Rome, Denmark and Persia,[8] it is certainly understandable why De Santillana and Von Dechend would take such striking correspondences between these stories as the basis for hypothesizing a single mythic "architecture":[9] a man who speaks of the heavens and of Time in a forgotten language. As attractive as this theory is, it is also improbable and flawed, above all in sacrificing the story itself to its presumed "meanings," as if the tale did not

---

3. Firdousi 1876, II, 339ff.
4. 1 Samuel 21:11–13.
5. Hyg. *Fab.* 95; cf. Apoll. *Ep.* 3.7.
6. Plut. *Sol.* 8.1ff.; Just. 2.7. On this episode, see Lanza 1997, 41ff. Tac. *Ann.* 6.24 recounts that when Drusus was dying, he feigned *dementia* in order to curse Tiberius.
7. Dion. Hal. *Ant. Rom.* 4.68.2; Liv. *AUC.* 1.56.7. etc. Dionysius tells us that Tarquin killed also the Brutus's father, Marcus Junius. Sources for the story of Brutus: Liv. *AUC.* 1.56; Dion. Hal. *Ant. Rom.* 4.68ff; Diod. Sic. 10.22; Cic. *Brut.* 53; Ov. *Fast.* 2.717ff.; Val. Max. 7.3.2; Anon. *De vir. illustr.* 10.2; etc. A complete account in Münzer 1931; Ogilvie 19565, 216ff.
8. These stories have been the subject of numerous "genetic" and comparative studies, in which Brutus has been compared to heroes of the Irish, Indian and Finnish traditions (Jiriczek, Lessmann, Zenker and Setälä: cf. Jones 1986, 126 and 145). As a "type," this legend was also of great interest to Freudian psychoanalysis, because of the relationship between Oedipus and Hamlet (recognized already by Freud 1966, 246): cf. Rank 1987, 86ff.; Jones 1986, 126ff.; and, more recently, Bloom 1996, 331ff., on Hamlet and Freud. On the relationship between the stories of Brutus and Hamlet, see above all Powell 1894, 28ff.; Davidson 1980, II, 59f. n. 64. There are also some scant mentions in Frazer 1911, 291 n. and 505f. A detailed comparison between the tales (and other Nordic variants of the Hamlet story) goes beyond our interests here: Hansen 1983, 25ff., interpreting these stories as related "genetically." Wiseman 2003 identifies different "layers" of the Brutus legend to show how variations in the narrative reflect changes in sociopolitical context.
9. De Santillana and von Dechend 1983, 35ff.

merit interest of its own, as if to make it attractive the scholar's task were to find other (and in particular "metaphysical") references within it. But the story itself is worth listening to, for it is the tale of a Fool who poses riddles to his "wise" and "intelligent" enemies—in other words, the tale of a "truth" that conceals and camouflages itself in "error" in order to remain true, and with such an insinuating force that it bends the powerful to the Fool's will. This is certainly a worthwhile theme, even if behind the Fool's riddling it is impossible to discover some *raison raisonnante* that, once the veil of Time has been removed, resurfaces with archaic solemnity to address the universe's greatest questions. Patience if Hamlet remains Hamlet and Brutus remains Brutus; after all, is that so little? Nothing is gained—and probably much is lost—by swapping Hamlet for some astral philosophy. Perhaps it is only that we have lost the habit of *reading* stories, then, and our inability to pay attention to them makes us wish to change them into something they are not. Worse still, perhaps we have lost the habit of *listening* to stories. And our sources recount the story of Brutus so fragmentarily and so weakly that it has become almost incomprehensible; certainly, some patience will be required.

The Hero Speaks and Acts Nonsense

Dionysius of Halicarnassus recounts that Tarquin, believing Brutus to be truly dim-witted, dispossessed him of all his paternal inheritance but what was strictly essential. Thereafter, Tarquin permitted him to live with his sons—not out of any consideration for the bond of kinship that united them (Tarquin was Brutus' *avunculus*, "maternal uncle"), but "to make the boys laugh by speaking nonsense and doing what only the truly stupid do."[10] At this point, we should probably imagine the narrator enumerating a series of examples demonstrating the hero's stupidity—the nonsensical things said and done by Brutus that would eventually earn him that nickname, meaning "dull, stupid."[11] But what exactly did Brutus say or do that was so foolish?

---

10. Dion. *Ant. Rom.* 4.69.1.
11. Dion. *Ant. Rom.* 4.68.2. Cf. Liv. *AUC.* 1.66.8. Niebhur's (1873, I, 423ff.) thesis that the legend of "feigned stupidity" was created to provide an aetiological explanation for this *cognomen* is well known (and was taken up by Accame 1949, 251 as well as by Alföldi 1965, 83, with slight modifications). Pais (1926, II, 170ff.), on the other hand, transformed Brutus into a divinity (against De Sanctis 1956, 394ff.). Cook (1905, 300ff.) reached the same conclusion independently of Alföldi, and also divinized Lucretius Tricipitinus and others (against Piganiol 1917, 256). On the problem of the historicity of this figure, see Mommsen 1864, 111ff.; Cook 1905; Groh 1928, 290ff., particularly in relation to the sources; Gjerstad 1962, 48 n. 1; Alföldi 1965, 83; Bloch 1965, 77 and above all Momigliano 1975, 293ff. Vague remarks in Gagé 1976, 57ff.

Chapter 2. Brutus the Fool   43

We know nothing concretely, because Dionysius limits himself to a few generic hints and other sources are completely silent on this score; apparently, this was part of the story that was not deemed worthy of transmission. We can suppose, however, that this part of the story did in fact exist, because structurally it is necessary to the plot. So we know only that we could have known and that we have been unlucky, which can only increase our displeasure.

Two long fragments of a *tragoedia praetexta* by Accius bearing the title *Brutus* have survived.[12] The first contains the account of one of Tarquin the Proud's dreams, and the second the explanation that was given of this dream by certain dream interpreters. In brief, Tarquin's dream and its interpretation go something like this: the "most beautiful" of a pair of rams is sacrificed by a king, understood metaphorically as Tarquin's murder of Brutus' older brother; the second ram, however, attacks the king, making him fall to the ground, understood metaphorically as Brutus overturning the king's power.[13] The seers' interpretation naturally emphasizes the link between the ram (*aries*) in Tarquin's dream and the man Tarquin considered "to be as stupid as an animal" (*esse . . . hebetem aeque ac pecus*). We do not know at what point in the action of the Accian *praetexta* this dream occurred—indeed, we know nothing whatsoever of the plot. However, judging from the dream's outline of a character thought to be "dull" (*brutus*), but who is in reality quite astute, it is reasonable to assume that the subject of the play was Brutus and his adventures as (false) *stolidus,* employing on stage all the resources of the bewildered and bedeviled Fool who conceals beneath his ambiguous phrases a burning desire for revenge. If that is the case, what we have is a "Hamlet" produced over 1700 years before Shakespeare's masterpiece—or better, what we would have had, had the nameless divinity in charge of conserving classical texts not demonstrated her avarice once again, thereby favoring the primacy of the pale Danish prince.

But to continue. Suetonius recounts that the emperor Claudius, who seems to have been truly stupid, once attempted to rehabilitate his reputation by claiming that he was only feigning stupidity:

> ac ne stultitiam quidem suam reticuit simulatamque a se ex industria sub Gaio, quod aliter evasurus perventurusque ad susceptam stationem non fuerit, quibusdam oratiunculis testatus est: nec tamen persuasit, cum intra breve tempus liber editus sit, cui index erat moron epanastasis, argumentum autem stultitiam neminem fingere.[14]

---

12. Fr. 19ff. Ribbeck³.
13. Cf. fr. 12ff. Ribbeck³.
14. Suet. *Claud.* 38.3. Last and Ogilvie's (1958, 476ff.) interpretation is somewhat too

And not even his own stupidity did he conceal, claiming in some speeches that he had feigned it on purpose under Gaius [i.e., Caligula], because otherwise he would have been destined to succumb and would not have reached the position that he had. But he did not succeed in convincing anyone, because sometime afterward a book was circulated that was entitled *The Refutation of the Idiots,* the argument of which was that no one can fake stupidity.

Writing those *oratiunculae* in his own defense, Claudius must have invoked the legendary paradigm of Brutus in demonstration of the shrewdness of his own *stultitia* (or, if nothing else, to indulge his natural tendency for historical scholarship). Moreover, in sustaining the thesis that stupidity cannot be feigned, his detractors must have made reference to the story of someone who had in fact been successful at this. Unfortunately, nothing remains of these texts—although admittedly much worse losses have occurred.

How, then, are we to imagine Brutus in his disgraceful role of *ludibrium* at the king's court?[15] When Tarquin sends his sons to Delphi, he sends Brutus as their companion for the sole purpose that they may mock and insult their cousin:[16] Brutus, in other words, is chosen specifically for derision and abuse. This is the normal fate of the Fool, however. Before reaching the throne, Claudius had been considered precisely "one of the *ludibria* of the court."[17] Thus Suetonius:

> quotiens post cibum obdormisceret . . . olearum aut palmularum ossibus incessabatur, interdum ferula flagrove velut per ludum excitabatur a copreis. solebant et manibus stertentis socci induci, ut repente expergefactus faciem sibimet confricaret.[18]

> Whenever he would fall asleep after a meal, he would be attacked with olive or date pits. At times, the entertainers would keep him awake by hitting him with sticks or rods, as if in jest. They also had the habit of putting women's slippers on his hands, while he snored, so that he would rub himself on the face when he woke up.

---

reductive: according to their understand, the source of Claudius' pretext was "evidently the myth of Brutus in Livy." But why only Livy? On this passage of Suetonius, see also Guastella's (1999, 209) remarks, with sources and bibliography on the truth or falsity of Claudius's stupidity.

15. Cf. Dion. *Ant. Rom.* 4.68.2; Liv. *AUC.* 1.56.9.
16. Dion. *Ant. Rom.* 4.69.2.
17. Suet. *Cal.* 23.3; *Nero* 6.2; cf. Cass. Dio. 60.3.7.
18. Suet. *Claud.* 8. See also Guastella's (1999, 149) note, with other useful references.

Besides suffering the indignations required by the script, the false Fool must also have done everything in his power to confirm the impression of his own stupidity—"talking nonsense and doing what only the truly stupid do," as Dionysius says. Khusràw's grandfather Afrasyab asks him: "Wouldn't you like to learn how to write? Don't you want to take revenge upon your enemies?" and the boy responds: "There is no more cream in the milk: I'd like to chase all the shepherds from the desert."[19] After his father and two older brothers are murdered, a similar question is posed to Brjám, the "Hamlet" of modern Icelandic folklore, and his little brothers:[20] "Where do you feel the pain most?" Brjám's younger brothers beat their chests and so are killed, while Brjám slaps his rear and sneers—and so is spared, deemed too stupid to be dangerous. Brjám leads directly to Saxo Grammaticus' Amelethus (Amleth)[21] who, upon returning from his tryst with the future Shakespearian Ophelia, is mockingly interrogated about their love making. "On what couch?" his enemies ask, to which he answers: "On a mare's hoof, a cock's crest and the roof beams."[22]

The "false Fool" must not only speak but also act nonsense. Before the eyes of Menelaus and Agamemnon, Odysseus yokes an ox and a horse and goes about Ithaka with a dunce's cap (*pileus*) on his head.[23] It is a shame that the celebrated painting by Euphranor of Corinth no longer stands in the sanctuary of Artemis at Ephesus; as Pliny describes it, it depicted "Ulysses, feigning madness, as he yokes an ox with a horse, men wearing the *pallium* as they think, and a leader as he sheathes his sword" (*Ulixes simulata insania bovem cum equo iungens et palliati cogitantes, dux gladium condens*).[24] Here, the conspicuous stupidities of the (false) fool arouse the doubt and concern of those "thinking" men (*cogitantes*) who observe him. Solon, too, went about in public "completely unkempt in the manner of the insane" (*deformis habitu more vecordium*), with the dunce's cap on his head,[25] and David, disguising his appearance at the court of Achis, stumbled upon the shutters of the door and let himself fall, drool running down his beard.[26] Finally, at the court of Feng, Amleth lay on the floor covered in ash, trying to harden some curved rods in the fire;[27] later, he mounted a horse backwards (leading

---

19. Firdousi 1876, II, 342.
20. See Powell 1894, 405; Gollancz 1926, 73 and Hansen 1983, 13ff.
21. See below, 68ff.
22. Sax. Gramm. 3.6.11.
23. Hyg. *Fab.* 95. For the *pileus,* see Schöne 1872, 125ff., but with caution; Samter 1894, 535ff.; and Lanza 1997, 41ff., on the "cap" worn by Solon.
24. Plin. *Nat. hist.* 35.129.
25. Justinus 2.7; Plut. *Sol.* 8.1f.
26. 1 Samuel 21:11–13.
27. Sax. Gramm. 3.6.6.

it by its tail instead of its reins);[28] and when his companions pointed out an abandoned ship's rudder on the shore and told him it is a huge knife, he responded that it was perfect for cutting a huge side of ham.[29] And so forth.

The folkloristic typology related to "The Fool" (feigned or not) is too vast—but also too predictable—to require further examples. Psychoanalysts, who have created a clinical profile of the (false) Fool's behavior, note that this personality displays markedly "infantile" characteristics, such as a love for riddles, a predilection for dirty or obscene substances, general ineptitude and so on.[30] Possibly. What is certain is that the Fool's behavior consistently demonstrates a tendency to subvert the behavioral norms that others accept, creating a kind of "world of opposites.[31] In the stories about *true* Fools ("simpletons") collected by Thompson,[32] we find characters who confuse a gourd with an ass's egg,[33] who sow boiled seeds,[34] who cover rocks lest they catch cold,[35] and so forth. Structurally speaking, the Fool tends to put into contact cultural artifacts that, in typical behavior, have no relation to one another. And he does so by taking advantage of "contiguities" that are completely unforeseeable—metaphorical, analogical, purely linguistic and so on. The result is a world that is methodologically unexceptionable but manifestly absurd. The Fool explores the residues of cultural codes and how to short circuit them. He hits the right keys at the wrong moment and stands there waiting to see what happens.

An Eater of Bitter Figs

Perhaps I was being overly pessimistic in stating our complete ignorance of Brutus' foolish deeds. Though it is scant and vague, there is in fact some evidence of what he did and said at Tarquin's court. Moreover, as we shall see, it is evidence of a sort of serene, subtle madness, and I do not believe that Brutus acquired his fame (let alone his *cognomen*) exclusively on the basis of such behavior. But it is all that remains.

Macrobius illustrates through various examples what the Romans referred

---

28. Sax. Gramm. 3.6.8. On this motif, see Davidson 1980, 60 n. 65: it is a popular form of *ludibrium* common to many northern cultures.
29. Sax. Gramm. 3.6.10. Cf. Davidson 1980, 60 n. 67.
30. Jones 1986, 140ff.
31. In the sense of Cocchiara 1963, who does not, however, deal specifically with the theme of "The Fool" and his actions.
32. Thompson 1966², See also Thompson 1967, 269ff.
33. Thompson 1966², J 1772.1.
34. Thompson 1966², J 1932.
35. Thompson 1966², J 1873.2.

to as *grossi* ("immature figs").³⁶ Among the texts he cites is a fragment of the historian Postumius Albinus regarding Brutus:

> et Postumius Albinus annali primo de Bruto: ea causa sese stultum brutumque faciebat, grossulos ex melle edebat.³⁷

> Postumius Albinus writes about Brutus in the first book of his *Annales*; from this he showed that he was stupid and slow: he used to eat bitter figs in honey.

Brutus, pretending to be a fool, used to eat *grossuli ex melle*. Albinus' text suggests a link between the two, and this impression is enhanced by the peculiarity of the act itself: why ever would Brutus have had to eat *grossuli ex melle*? In other words, perhaps this is one of the deeds of the false Fool, miraculously transmitted thanks to Macrobius' pedantic erudition.

The absence of any context makes interpreting the fragment difficult, of course. Nevertheless, something can be said about it. According to Macrobius, "figs which are not yet mature are called *grossuli*" (*grossuli appellantur ficus quae non maturescunt*). These are the same figs that Columella advises shaking from their branches if one wishes the tree to produce again and yield ripe, edible figs.³⁸ Apparently, then, *grossuli* are what Pagani called *bottoncelli*—the hard and gristly "budlets" that represent the first stage of the fig's growth,³⁹ and which no one would ever willingly eat. Furthermore, the expression *ex melle* indicates that Brutus' *grossuli* were "in honey" or "dipped in honey."⁴⁰ Assuming that this unique choice of snack relates to the practice of conserving certain types of fruit in honey as *delikatessen*, it is still odd that Brutus would be in the habit of eating not ripe, good figs in this way, but hard and tasteless green ones.⁴¹ Although Apicius and others tell us that

---

36. Macr. *Sat.* 3.20.5ff. On *grossi*, cf. Col. *De re rust.* 5.10.10; *De arb.* 21.1; Hil. *In Evan. Matt.* 21; ecc. *TLL* VI, 2, 2336, 40ff.; Olck 1909, coll. 2100ff., 2106 and 2109.

37. Post. Alb. fr. 2 Peter. We do not know who translated the fragment into Latin. Macrobius himself (praef. 13–14) informs us that Postumius had written his *Annales* in Greek, so the Latin translation seems rather curious. See Peter 1870, cxiii; it has also been suggested that fr. 2 and 3 Peter do not belong to the Greek *Annales*, but the *poiēma* mentioned by Polybius (39.12.2): see Münzer 1953, coll. 902 ff.

38. Col. *De re rust.* 5.10.10; *De arb.* 21.1.

39. Pagani 1846, 332 and 1566.

40. Cf., e.g., Plaut. *Merc.* 139, *resinam ex melle Aegyptiam vorato;* Ter. *Eun.* 930, *ex iure hesterno panem atrum vorent;* Plin. *Nat. hist.* 23.129, *arboris ipsius cinis ex melle;* Cels. 2.30.2, *recens . . . caseus . . . ex melle* and 4.14.3, *nuclei pinei ex melle.*

41. Cf. Apic. 1.12.3 and 4; Plin. *Nat. hist.* 15.6 and 65; 19.91; Col. *De re rust.* 12.47.2–5; etc. See also Plin. *Nat hist.* 22.108; cf. Olck 1897, coll. 431ff.; *RE* XV.1, coll. 364ff., esp. 377; André 1961, 87ff. On "figs in honey": Apic. 1.12.4; Pallad. 4.10.33; *Geoponica* 10.56.5.

various fruits—and above all figs—were dipped in honey (or sugar) when not yet fully ripe, and that even sour fruits like quince[42] and bitter roots like *inula* were eaten so, it is unlikely that worthless, tough "buds" such as *grossuli* would form any part of the Roman diet. Instead, in this strange alimentary act there seems to be some hint of the hero's "foolishness," as in fact Albinus himself explicitly affirms (*"from this* he showed that he was stupid and slow: [namely the fact that] he used to eat bitter figs in honey"). Brutus the Fool eagerly devours as a delicacy something disgusting; while others eat good fruit in honey, he eats the hard, gristly buds of green figs. This must have been a cause of great amusement at Tarquin's court.

In the long series of stories that regard him, the Fool frequently eats things that others would never think of consuming. This act is consistent with what has been defined as the basic principle of the Fool's behavior: "false identification of an object."[43] In other words, someone is "a fool" when he does not correctly identify things, confusing one thing for another and confounding their attributes and functions. The "theory" of this principle is essentially articulated by Firdawsi's tale of Khusràw: there, Piran advises the young man on how to go about pretending to be a fool. "Chase reason from your mind," he suggests. "If he [Afrasyab, from whom Khusràw must defend himself] says 'war,' respond 'marriage.'" When the dreaded interview with his grandfather finally happens, the boy passes the test, and Afrasyab is truly convinced that the boy is harmless: "He's mad. I say 'head' and he responds 'foot.'"[44]

The principle of "false identification of an object" functions particularly well in the alimentary code, when the structure of cultural models distinguishing what is edible from what is not—a structure capable of signifying the opposition between "human" and "non-human," "nature" and "culture"—is confounded by the Fool's behavior. Cacasennus devours a bowlful of glue, mistaking it for gruel,[45] while Marcolfa obstinately refuses to eat the bread offered to him by the king, instead preferring his own "bread concoction."[46] There are frequent scenes of this type in the cycles of the North American Trickster, as well:[47] he boils water thinking that he is cook-

---

42. On quince, see Plin. *Nat. hist.* 16.50 and 65; Col. *De re. rust.* 12.47.2; Apic. 1.12.3; etc. On *inula,* see Plin. *Nat. hist.* 19.21.
43. Thompson 1966², J 1750–1809.
44. Firdousi 1976, II, 34.
45. Croce 1943, 177.
46. Croce 1943, 166.
47. Of course, the complex figure of the "Trickster" (buffoon and demiurge, god and scoundrel) cannot be reduced to the typological linearity of the "Fool": but the Trickster's "stupidity" nevertheless appears to have a primary role in the stories about him, as part of the intricate bundle of his distinctive characteristics. See the interesting considerations of Miceli 1984.

ing a fish (that has in fact escaped), and declares the soup to be delicious;[48] he eats certain seeds, and develops a terrible rash;[49] he abuses some medicine, and suffers the effect of laxatives.[50] Most inept by far, however, is Bertoldinus, to whom a doctor prescribes an assortment of pills to ingest and a "cure" to take "below." But the latter is covered in honey, which causes the fool to swallow the "cure" and to use the pills "below." He justifies this by saying, "Leave it to one who knows. Do you think I'm mad? It is you who have misunderstood the doctor's orders: do you really wish me to put this thing below, when it is covered in honey? I would really be an idiot then. It must be taken orally, while these little pellets must be used below. I have a brain, too, you know!"[51] Naturally, the honeyed cure "sticks in his throat and will not go up or down," and poor Bertoldinus almost suffocates.

We do not know whether Brutus, eating his *grossuli ex melle*, committed an error of alimentary identification as grave as Bertoldinus', but it is curious to note that in Roman medicine *grossi* played an important role.[52] Whatever the case may be, it is clear that the hero—like a Fool—consumed the wrong food and "from this he showed that he was stupid and slow: he used to eat bitter figs in honey," as Postumius says. Certainly, someone like that does not arouse suspicion that he is merely biding his time until he can avenge his parents.

It is perhaps disconcerting to imagine the same Brutus who swore on the blood of Lucretia, who chased out the tyrant Tarquin and who killed his traitorous sons without regret foolishly devouring disgusting green figs in honey. But it is interesting to compare the picture of the hero intent on his "foolish" meal with his depiction on a coin minted by M. Brutus around the year 59 B.C.E.[53] On one side, the coin represents a man with a round head covered by abundant hair and a thick beard. His face is gaunt, his nose noble and pointed, his brow marked by a deep furrow, his eyes set off by a conspicuous crease, almost a bag. Such iconography, which may go back to the portrait (*imago*) of Brutus carefully preserved by his descendants, is profoundly suggestive:[54] this is the severe and decisive Brutus, the first

---

48. Radin, Jung and Kerény 1965, 44.
49. Thompson 1966², J 2134.1; cf. Thompson 1967, 448.
50. Thompson 1966², J 2134.2; cf. Thompson 1967, 650.
51. Croce 1943, 131.
52. Cf. Cels. *De med.* 5.12 (*grossi in aqua cocti* have an epispastic function); Plin. *Nat. hist.* 23.125 (raw *grossi* aid the removal of warts); 23.128 (they are helpful against flatulence and, when cooked in water, help the mumps; in wine, they protect against scorpion bites, etc.); see also Marc. Empir. 10.82.
53. Rome, Museo Nazionale Romana (a reproduction in *Enciclopedia dell'arte antica*, s.v. "Bruto"). On the relationship between M. Brutus and his ancestor, cf. Flower 1996, 88ff.
54. Cic. *Phil.* 2.26 (a statue of Brutus, with sword drawn, stood instead on the Capitoline: Plut. *Brut.* 1; Dio Cass. 43.45; Plin. *Nat. hist.* 37.4; Suet. *Iul.* 80; cf. also Bettini 1988b, 190ff.). As

consul of Rome. Imagining him off somewhere in Tarquin's palace slurping up *grossuli ex melle* while the members of the court laugh at him as someone who "does not even know how to eat," increases the mystique surrounding his character.

The Hero Is Like an Animal

Through deeds of this type, Lucius Junius acquired the *cognomen* "Brutus." What does this adjective mean? In the archaic language, the meaning of this term appears to have been that of *gravis*—i.e., "weighty, heavy."[55] Later, used in reference to someone's mental faculties, the originally physical sense of "heaviness" came to signify "stupidity." Similar lexical developments—where a word denoting something physical is transferred to the intellect to indicate a lack of intellectual vivacity—can be cited: *hebes* ("smoothed, rounded; blunted")[56] and *tardus* ("slow") both also come to mean "stupid." (In Greek medicine, on the other hand, "stupidity" presupposes the prevalence of the element of water over the element of fire; in some sense, then, the fool is imagined as "watery").[57] The intellect is something intangible, and so to represent its force or weakness Roman culture relied upon kinesthetic metaphors.[58]

Brutus is a "foolish" hero (or at any rate one who pretends to be a Fool), whose name directly signifies his stupidity. In this regard, it is interesting to note that Hamlet, the philosopher-prince of Denmark, owes his name to a comparable linguistic mechanism. Powell and Gollancz have shown that the name of the hero of this ancient saga—Amloði—was used in medieval Icelandic, Norwegian and Danish (and indeed is still used) as a substantive meaning "dunce" or "simpleton."[59] A middle English reworking of the *Historia de prelis*, moreover, twice contains the word *Amlaʒe* or *Amlaugh* used as a term of derision together with words like "monkey" and "ass."[60] Although it is impossible to determine whether the word's meaning in the sense of "stupid" precedes its use as a proper name (cf. *brutus* > *Brutus*) or whether

for this iconography, it appears again almost identically on an *aureus* of 44–42 BCE, coined by L. Pedanius Costa in Macedonia. West (1933, I, 47) took this as proof of a common model, a portrait "of reconstruction"; cf. *Enciclopedia dell'arte antica*, s.v. "Bruto."

55. Fest. *De sign. verb.* 31 Lindsay, *brutum antiqui gravem dicebant*; cf. Lucr. *De re. nat.* 6.105; Hor. *Carm.* 1.34.9; *TLL* II, 2216). On *Brutus* as a *cognomen* (and on *cognomina* derived in general from deficiencies in mental capacity), see Kajanto 1965, 264ff. and Alföldi 1966, 713ff.
56. Cf. Ernout-Meillet 1965, *s.v.*
57. See Lanza 1997, 19ff.
58. Bandler and Grinder 1981, 195ff.
59. Powell 1894, 408. Gollancz 1926, 31f. and 58f.
60. Gollancz 1926, 58ff.

the hero's name began to function as a generic term because of the fame of his saga,[61] the fact remains that Hamlet's name also suggests, in some way, the theme of the hero's stupidity.

Tarquin's Dream and Ovine Stupidity

Returning to Brutus and the meaning of *brutus* in Latin: Insofar as they are endowed with a "heavy" intellect, animals also belong to the category of *bruti*[62] and, for this reason, may be used directly as models of stupidity. In Accius' *Brutus*, Tarquin tells of his dream:

> visus est in somnis pastor ad me appellere
> pecus lanigerum eximia pulcritudine;
> duos consanguineous arietes inde eligi
> praeclarioremque alterum immolare me;
> deinde eius germanum cornibus conitier,
> in me arietare, eoque ictu me ad casum dari . . .[63]

> I dreamed that a shepherd drove his wool-bearing flock of extraordinary beauty toward me. From it two rams were chosen of the same stock, and I was sacrificing the more outstanding of the two. Then its brother pointed its horns at me, and drove at me, and from the blow I fell to the earth.

And the *interpretatio* given by the seers:

> proin vide ne quem tu esse hebetem deputes aeque ac pecus
> is sapientia munitum pectus egregie gerat
> teque regno expellat . . . [64]

> Therefore take care that he whom you deem stupid as a beast does not rather have a mind extraordinarily rich in genius, and drives you from your throne.

The interpreter's explanation does not use the adjective *brutus* (substituted here by *hebes*), evidently not to give away the joke too soon by mentioning

---

61. Gollancz 1926, 31ff. On the possibility of a Nordic "translation" of *Brutus*, see Powell's (1894, 403) refutation. On the problem of Hamlet's name, Davidson's (1980, 59 n. 63) remarks are full and informative; see also Hansen 1983, 6f.
62. Plin. *Nat. hist.* 9.87; 11.183; cf. *TLL* II, 2215.
63. Fr. 19ff. Ribbeck³.
64. Fr. 33ff. Ribbeck³.

the hero by name. Furthermore, of the two rams, the one that is chosen for sacrifice by the king is defined as *praeclarior* ("more outstanding"), which corresponds to the fact that Tarquin had deemed the elder of the two Junii superior (and therefore dangerous) and had killed him for that reason. This is effectively what Dionysius says of Brutus' brother, too: "He showed his noble genius."[65] The dream, then, begins to lay bare Tarquin's mistake in choosing (and killing) the better of the two brothers *in appearance*. But this is not what interests us here. Even more important is that in the symbolism of the dream, Brutus—the Fool—is transformed into an animal, specifically a ram: that is, he who is deemed to be "just like an animal" (*aeque ac pecus*) because of his intellect actually becomes a *pecus* in the dream. Even working with Freud's *The Interpretation of Dreams* in hand, there would be nothing objectionable in this. The linguistic metaphor—*brutus* referring both to "animal" and to "fool"—is simply transformed into a dream image, Brutus coming to be represented in the form of an animal. But as always with symbols, the figure is complex and merits more detailed analysis.[66]

In Roman culture and Roman folklore (and elsewhere too) the sheep and the goat exemplify stupidity, as demonstrated not only by the imagery of proverbial and conventional language, but also by the creative imaginings of poets. The last scene of Plautus' *Bacchides*, for example, turns on a long identification between two old men and sheep (*oves*)[67] that the two shrewd sisters would have been very happy to "sheer" and that they find "stupid" (*stultae*).[68] The sheep (*ovis*) as an embodiment of stupidity in Roman culture suggests another interesting parallel with the story of Brutus: Quintus Fabius Maximus, the future Cunctator, once merited the nickname *Ovicula* ("Sheepish"), a name that Plutarch tells us was given him "for the tame and slow character that he had shown in infancy."[69] After describing Fabius' tranquil nature, his

---

65. Dion. *Ant. Rom.* 4.68.2.

66. The scene has inspired numerous interpretations. Mastrocinque (1983, 457ff.) considered it a derivation of Eur. *Elect.* 699 (the prodigious lamb of the Atreidi); see also Mastrocinque 1988, 13ff., suggesting Accius' *praetexta* as the basis for Livy's account, through Calpurnius Piso. Fauth (1976, 469ff.), on the other hand, detected in this *praetexta* a residue of ancient Etruscan symbologies. On Accius' *Brutus*: a reconstruction in Ribbeck 1875, 568ff., who suggests that the material was derived from Ennius's *Annales*, while a kind of "Verschmelzung" between Ennius and Accius provided the basis for Livy's account; Soltau (1909, 39ff. and 93ff.) typically sets Accius' and Ennius' poetic creation atop the historiographical texts, against Lenchantin De Gubernatis 1912, 444ff. and 457; Wright (1910) hypothesizes the existence of trilogy of plays entitled *Tullia, Servius,* and *Brutus;* Hermann (1948, 141ff.) suggests that Accius himself invented the theme of Brutus's "stupidity"; Michels (1951) attributes much of the story (including what is given by the historians) not to Accius but to an unknown author, perhaps Pollio; Gabba (1969, 377ff.) rightly invites us not to overburden the Accian text with political or ideological meanings; see also Gjerstad 1962, 48, n. 1.

67. Plaut. *Bacch.* 1120ff.

68. Plaut. *Bacch.* 1139.

69. Plut. *Fab. Max.* 1.3. Cf. Anon. *De vir. illustr.* 43.1; *RE* VI.2, coll. 1814ff.; Kajanto 1965, 328.

indulgence of his companions and so forth, the historian also records the fact that he "learned his lessons slowly and with great difficulty." Moreover, among those who did not know him well he had nourished "the suspicion that he was stupid and lazy." In other words, the future Fabius Maximus had gotten off to an anything but promising start! Furthermore, if one excludes the trait of tameness, Fabius' adolescence seems to resemble closely that of Titus Manlius, the future Torquatus. As a young man, Torquatus too appeared "slow," although he demonstrated a certain roughness of character as well (above all in the episode of the tribune Marcus Pomponius).[70] But he, like Fabius, also played a role of the highest order in Roman affairs, at least after his famous encounter with the giant Gallic warrior. More specifically, however, we are told by Seneca that Titus Manlius had had "a brutish and obtuse childhood" (*adulescentiam brutam atque hebetem*)[71] and by Livy that he was considered by everyone to be "of sluggish and obtuse intellect" (*hebetis atque obtusi cordis*).[72] For this reason, his father had decided to send him to the country; and in fact, Livy emphasizes, it seemed quite fitting that he would then be living "among the animals" (*inter pecudes*).[73]

A (false) Fool who as a boy carries the name of Brutus is represented as an *aries;* one who is "slow" who, again as a boy, was nicknamed Ovicula; and one who is *hebes* who is deemed by his father fit only for confinement out in the countryside *inter pecudes:* similar stories about heroes who spend their youth in folly (falsely in the case of Brutus; truly in that of Fabius and Manlius) only to mature to greatness and heroism. Lévi-Strauss' traditional opposition of nature and culture—no doubt a fundamental opposition, but one which tends to be abused because of its generality—can be easily (and quite fittingly) applied here. The dunce—that is, the marginalized, the outcast—acquires a "natural" or animalesque name or symbol, while standing against him is the culture of men who deride and reject him as an animal, only to discover later that he is truly great. One dunce that is clever and decisive; another that is tame and reflexive; and another that is rough and brutal: it is curious that at Rome the greatness of heroes—even those who are most significant to the city's history—is tied to such paradigms.

There is more to say about Fabius Maximus' *cognomen*, Ovicula. Specifically, Plutarch's report that "he learned his lessons slowly and with great difficulty" reminds us of a passage of Plautus that gives the impression of being proverbial.[74] In *Persa*, the slave woman Sophoclidisca laments the fact that her mistress feels the need constantly to repeat her orders. Reasoning that

---

70. Liv. *AUC.* 7.4ff. On the story of Torquatus and his father, see Bettini 1988b, 18ff.
71. Sen. *De ben.* 3.37.4.
72. Liv. *AUC.* 7.4.
73. Liv. *AUC.* 7.4.
74. Cf. Otto 1890, 260.

such repetition would be appropriate for someone *indocta* ("uneducated"), *immemor* ("forgetful") or *insipiens* ("stupid"), she concludes that her mistress must consider her *barda* ("stupid, slow") and *rustica* ("a bumpkin")—and yet, it has been five years since she joined her mistress's service, "when, meanwhile, if a sheep had come to school, I believe it would have learned to read and write already."[75] Evidently, the "sheep at school" that learns to read and to write is a paradigm of comic absurdity. This suggests a possibly proverbial and folkloric context for the attribution of the name Ovicula ("Sheepish") to a person who has difficulty learning in Roman culture, just as in certain folkloric traditions of Asian and northern Europe there exist stories centered around the strange and absurd consequences of a country bumpkin sending an ox to school.[76] Such stories may explain Sophoclidisca's utterance; likewise, figurative and proverbial expressions like Sophoclidisca's may frequently be transformed into ironic and silly stories.[77]

Returning to our inventory of the various animalesque representations of stupidity in Roman culture, it is worth noting the fate of *hircus* ("he-goat"). In Plautus,[78] the rude country slave Grumio receives from the slick city slave Tranio the nickname *rusticus hircus* ("rustic he-goat").[79] Earlier, Tranio had defined him also as *frutex*,[80] an expression meaning literally "piece of wood," but frequently also used in the sense of "stupid." He who is like a he-goat is also stupid. Clearer still is the proverb that Petronius puts in the mouth of the freedman Trimalchio when he grows angry with Ascyltus: *quid nunc stupes tamquam hircus in ervilia* ("Why are you standing there stupidly like a he-goat in the vetch?").[81] This sense of *hircus* seems to corroborate the interpretation of those two lines of Catullus' famous poem on the *salax taberna:*

> solis licere, quidquid est puellarum,
> confutuere et putare ceteros hircos?[82]

> That only you are allowed to fuck all the girls in the world, and to consider all others he-goats?

---

75. Plaut. *Pers.* 168ff.
76. Thompson 1966², J 1882.2; Thompson 1967, 271.
77. This is one of the ways in which novellas and stories frequently arise: cf. Šklovskij 1968, 205ff., regarding *calembour* such as "The Devil and Hell," which is transformed narratively into the novella of Boccaccio by the same name.
78. Plaut. *Most.* 38.
79. Cf. Chiarini 1972, 277ff.
80. Plaut. *Most.* 13.
81. Petr. *Sat.* 57.11.
82. Cat. *Carm.* 37.4–5.

Chapter 2. Brutus the Fool 55

I do not believe that Catullus is alluding here to the legendary "stench of the he-goat" (*hirci odor*) (or worse, to the he-goat's sexual potency—just the opposite of what the sense demands). He is simply stating that the *contubernales* should not think of everyone else as stupid "goats" whose girlfriends can be snatched from under their noses: in effect, Catullus is warning them that "we will not remain here like some *hirci in ervilia*."

The term *vervex* ("wether") has a similar sense. The aforementioned freedman of Trimalchio had earlier apostrophized Ascyltus, asking *quid rides, vervex* ("what are you laughing at, you wether?").[83] Similarly, Juvenal tells us of men who are born "in the country of the castrated bulls and under an opaque sky" (*vervecum patria crassoque sub aere*).[84] Consider, moreover, the formation of *balatro* ("babbler; jester, buffoon"), which is obviously connected with *balare* ("to bleat"), denoting the sound made by the sheep.[85] It is interesting to note that in the *scholia* to Horace's poems *balatrones* are defined as *rustici homines inepti et triviales* ("rustic fellows, inept and buffoonish").[86] The *rustici* and *inepti*—who have no idea of the ways of this world—are assimilated to sheep via *balare*, just as the awkward Grumio, the rough and stupid (*frutex*) country slave, was defined as *hircus rusticus*.

The use of the sheep and the he-goat as paradigms of "stupidity" in Roman culture should now be clear. Of course, Aristotle had already claimed that sheep and goats are "foolish" animals[87] and modern parallels can also be cited.[88] Perhaps it is most interesting, however, to note the function that this paradigm plays in the iconographic tradition. In his monumental exegesis of symbols written in 1556 and entitled *Hieroglyphica*, Pierio Valeriano, for example, addresses the representation of "stupidity" in art. The beautiful woodcut that opens the paragraph regarding this theme depicts a kneeling king, wearing a royal mantle and crown and touching the earth with his hands; next to him stands a sheep. The author remarks:

> in primis autem significatum illud super ovem comperi, ut ex eius simulacro stultitia significaretur: nam usurpatione vulgi, ovis cognomento insipientes appelantur.[89]

---

83. Petr. *Sat.* 57.2.
84. Juv. *Sat.* 10.50. Cf. Plaut. *Merc.* 567; Sen. *De const. sap.* 17.
85. Ernout-Meillet 1965, s.v. Cf. Acr. Porphy. Comm. in Horatii Sat. 1.2.2, *balatrones a balatu ovium*.
86. Hor. *Sat.* 2.3.166; cf. Jerome, *Ep.* 95.4. It is nevertheless difficult to provide a precise description of the meaning of *balatro*: cf. Ernout-Meillet 1965, s.v.
87. Lanza 1997, 24ff.
88. I mean expressions, in Italian, such as "castroneria" ("stupidity" < *castrone*, "wether") and "pecorone" ("muttonhead"); cf. also August. *Ep.* 26, *quidam tantae sunt fatuitatis, ut non multum a pecoribus differant: quos moriones vulgo appellant* ("some are so stupid that they do not differ much from sheep; popularly, they are called '*moriones*'").
89. Pierio Valeriano 1556, 74ff.

First of all, I discovered this meaning concerning the sheep, that stupidity is represented by its depiction: for in vulgar usage, stupid men are called by the nickname "sheep."

Fifty years later, Cesare Ripa, in his 1776 treatise *Iconologia*, likewise noted the importance of the sheep in representations of "stupidity." According to Ripa, "Foolishness" should be represented as "a nude woman smiling and laying obscenely upon the ground with a sheep next to her,"[90] while "Stupidity" should instead be pictured as "a woman who rests her hand upon the head of a goat"[91] and "Ineptitude" as "a woman seated with her head bowed, and next to her a sheep."[92]

Returning, finally, to Tarquin's dream. It is clear that Brutus' transformation into an *aries* ("ram") depends upon a model of ovine stupidity that was widespread in Roman cultural representation, underlying various proverbial sayings, *cognomina*, poetic images, linguistic metaphors and so on. As a symbol, however, the ram is capable of expressing a further meaning, equally operating in the story as the hero's "stupidity." An *aries* is not simply an *ovis:* instead, it is a strong, horn-bearing animal that is above all prone to the act of *arietare*—that is, "butting with the horns," as rams do. Brutus' animalesque representation is therefore capable of signifying not only his stupidity but also the force with which he is destined to overthrow the power of the king. To use a Freudian expression, Brutus' representation as a ram operates in the dream as a true and proper symbolic "condensation": the *aries* represents his "stupidity" (he is *hebes aeque ac pecus,* as the seer says) as well as the hidden and dangerous force that will allow him to drive Tarquin from the throne. At the same time, it is impossible to deny the connotations of "kingliness" and "nobility" that are expressed by the image of the ram and that fully enter into the complex bundle of symbolism, enriching its efficacy and explaining Accius' choice of symbol (if it was he who first elaborated the episode of the dream).[93] This symbolic condensation leads directly to the next part of the story, to the singular gift that Brutus offers at Delphi. Before considering that, however, another detail of the legend warrants our attention.

---

90. Ripa 1766, V, 233ff.
91. Ripa 1766, V, 247ff.
92. Ripa 1766, II, 216.
93. Cf. the observations of Fauth 1976, adding also the evidence of Artem. 2.12, where the connection between "ram" and "king" is clear.

A Talking Dog

As Ogilvie notes, Zonaras recounts a unique element of the Brutus story.[94] Tarquin had in fact been terrified by a series of disquieting dreams: in a garden, some vultures attack a gathering of young eagles; a serpent appears while the king is feasting with his companions, causing them to flee. Livy includes the dream of the serpent,[95] while Dionysius adds a story about a pestilence.[96] In all cases, the result is the same: Tarquin's two sons, Titus and Arruns, are sent to consult the oracle at Delphi.[97] The god responds: "Tarquin will be dethroned on that day, when a dog will speak with a human voice." Pliny appears to preserve a trace of this version, saying that among his notes were omens "that a dog spoke . . . and a serpent barked, when Tarquin was expelled from the kingdom" (*canem locutum . . . et serpentem latrasse, cum pulsus est Tarquinius ex regno*).[98] Besides the manifestation of omens recurring in Roman tradition such as an animal speaking with a human voice, it is hard to imagine that the god's enigmatic response does not allude in some way to the action of Brutus, since in fact it is he who will bring about Tarquin's fall from power. It is possible, then, that the oracular response alludes also to the hero's feigned *brutalitas,* to his animal nature that, in the end, resolves itself unexpectedly (and ruinously for the king) into the most human of capacities: speaking. Indeed, lacking a human voice (*aphasia*) appears to be one of the specific characteristics that define what is *brutus* in Roman culture. A fragment of Aphranius reads: *non possum verbum facere: obbrutui* ("I cannot speak a word: I have become *brutus*").[99] Furthermore, one of the characteristics of Titus Manlius, the future Torquatus—the *tardus* who was considered *inter pecudes*—was precisely that he was *infacundiore lingua impromptior* ("rather slow with a rather ineloquent tongue"), and Claudius was well known for his confused and difficult speech.[100] As for the image of the "dog," it is likely brought into play in order to a designate a person neglected, mistreated and despised by all. When Plautus' Amphitryon finally reaches his palace, he ends with a grand and noble salutation to his

---

94. Zon. *Hist.* 7.11. The difference in the versions is noted by Ogilvie 1965, 318.
95. Liv. *AUC.* 1.57.
96. Dion. *Ant. Rom.* 4.69.
97. In Zonaras, Brutus is not named. He is named, however, a few lines below when the story of the embassy is told from the beginning (including the gift of the "stick," the god's response, etc.). Probably Zonaras simply concatenated two different versions of the story, without mentioning this expressly.
98. Plin. *Nat. hist.* 8.153. Cf. Iul. Obseq. 103.
99. Fr. 418 Ribbeck³.
100. On Torquatus, see Liv. *AUC.* 7.4; on Claudius, see Suet. *Claud.* 4.6 and 30; Dion. *Ant. Rom.* 60.2.2; and esp. Sen. *Apo.* 5.2.

wife; but Alcmena is not so enthused, believing not only that she has already seen him, but that she has just left his company. Sosia remarks, "Although he is long awaited, she greets him hardly more than anyone would greet a dog" (*exspectatum eum salutat magis haud quisquam quam canem*).[101] Brutus, kept at the palace as a *ludibrium* for the entertainment of the members of the court, is treated no better. It is likely, therefore, that the god's enigmatic pronouncement figures the moment at which Brutus will be revealed through the image of a "dog that begins to speak like a man." Zonaras goes on to say that Tarquin was relieved by the oracle's words because "he thought that the prophecy would never come true." What he did not imagine was that the "dog" was already in the palace, and that it was already preparing to speak with a human voice.

If this hypothesis is correct, Brutus' stupidity appears to have been realized (at least in the version of the story given by Zonaras) not so much in his "speaking and acting nonsense" as in his vague and dull muteness (a kind of generic *infacundia* like Titus Manlius'). Brutus went about the palace in these conditions, despised and mocked by the powerful—"like a dog."

The Hero Poses One Riddle and Solves Another

Dionysius recounts that a pestilence descended upon Rome, afflicting young boys and girls and, in particular, pregnant women, who suffered the plague's worst affects when giving birth.[102] Tarquin therefore dispatched his sons Arruns and Titus to consult the oracle at Delphi and with them he sent Brutus—but only as an amusement for his two sons ("so they could mock and insult him," according to Dionysius; "more as an amusement than as a companion," according to Livy).[103] Having reached Delphi, the two Tarquins dutifully offered magnificent gifts to the god at the temple, whereas Brutus offered only a piece of wood. Naturally, this provoked the ridicule of his cousins (*katagelasantes*):[104] they failed to realize, however, that Brutus had in fact hollowed out the piece of wood and hidden inside it a bar of gold—an offering that Livy describes as "an enigmatic image (*per ambages*) of his own genius."[105] Thus, the hero goes to the oracle not only to interrogate the god, but also to pose riddles. Moreover, when Titus and Arruns receive a response from the god to the question they had been sent to ask,

---

101. Plaut. *Am.* 680.
102. Dion. *Ant. Rom.* 4.69.2.
103. Dion. *Ant. Rom.* 4.69.3; Liv. *AUC.* 1.56. Cf. Zon. *Hist.* 7.11. On Rome and Delphi, see Altheim 1938, 263ff. and Parke and Wormell 1956, I, 267ff.
104. Dion. *Ant. Rom.* 4.69.3.
105. Liv. *AUC.* 1.56.

they ask another question, wishing to know which of them would take the throne after their father's death. To this further enquiry, the divine voice of the oracle responds that the kingship will fall to whoever "first . . . gives his mother a kiss" (*primus . . . osculum matri tulerit*). Titus and Arruns conspire to keep their brother Sextus, who had remained at Rome, in the dark and agree to give their mother a kiss both at the same time so as to divide the kingdom between themselves. What they did not understand was that the god's response was a riddle and that to gain the throne they would first have to solve that riddle. Brutus would eventually "solve" the god's cryptic response by kissing the earth, reasoning that the earth itself is the mother of all men. But before doing so, he posed a riddle of his own—the riddle of the gold inside the piece of wood. What was the meaning of this enigmatic act? To understand its significance, it is necessary to examine some of the other details of the story: in particular, the theme of pestilence.

An Oedipal Plague

In Propp's terms,[106] pestilence functions in narrative as the "initial lack" or loss that a hero must somehow remedy. Immediately following the onset of plague, in fact, the hero is sent to the place where he will have to confront and surmount his main task. The pestilence afflicting Tarquin's Rome is akin to other plagues of what we might call an "Oedipal" type, targeting young boys and girls and especially pregnant women. This plague occurs, moreover, in a city whose king is a criminal—an assassin known to have conspired with a sister-in-law as perverse as he. Tarquin had murdered his father-in-law, Servius Tullius, the former king, and in the act's grim denouement mutilated the king's corpse under the wheels of a cart. Not content with this, Tarquin also murdered his brother and his own wife, his brother-in-law (Brutus' father) and his son (Brutus' brother and Tarquin's uterine nephew). Furthermore, Tarquin had engaged in sexual acts with his accomplice, his own sister-in-law. Besides killing his own father and his close relatives, that is, Tarquin had also committed incest. It is difficult to imagine there is not some link, then, between the pestilence and the king's criminality. Frequently in the ancient world (but also in many non-Western cultures), the interpretation of natural calamities and in particular of "*fléaux*" is articulated in terms of guilt and impurity: homicide, sexual transgression and similar crimes are thought to provoke the anger of divinity, bringing pestilence or famine.[107]

---

106. Propp 1966, 37ff.
107. Delcourt 1938, 32ff.; Parker 1983, 27ff.; Bettini 1985. On Dionysius' account of the pestilence, see Gagé 1955, 62 n. 1 and 67ff.

It is possible, then, that the pestilence unleashed upon Rome at that time functioned as a clear signal of the king's fast approaching hour of reckoning. In Livy's account, a serpent in Tarquin's palace replaces the pestilence as motivation for sending the embassy to Delphi;[108] grim omens presage the coming ruin of the king and, on the narrative level, motivate sending Brutus and the two Tarquins to the oracle.[109] Prompting the expedition to Delphi, the pestilence, the serpent in the palace (and it is no less a serpent that "barks," as Pliny says) and the flock of young eagles attacked by vultures in Zonaras all represent equivalent elements in the story from the point of view of narrative function.[110] Yet, we must emphasize again how fragmentary and disconnected the narrative is in our sources.[111] We are not told explicitly what questions the Tarquins ask of the oracle regarding the omens or the pestilence, nor the answer that the god offers in response. What should Tarquin do? What is the meaning of all the terrible portents? Our sources do not contain any hint of such questions; at best, the version by Zonaras offers a fragment of the response in the image of the dog speaking with the human voice. But it is clear that these are the scattered remains of a shipwrecked story.[112]

Two Intelligent Brothers and the Third, A Fool

Returning to the narrative function of the pestilence or omens—an element in which the "folk-tale" structure of the Brutus legend is most readily

---

108. Liv. *AUC.* 1.56. Livy's narrative is analyzed from a stylistic perspective by Burck 1934, 170ff.

109. Plin. *Nat hist.* 8.153.

110. Zon. Hist. 7.11. According to Schachermeyr 1932, the theme of "omens" is taken from Accius or Ennius, again attributing to a poet the connection between the embassy to Delphi and these prodigious events (or pestilence).

111. This is noted also by Parke and Wormell 1956, I, 267.

112. A section of Paulus Festus' *Epitome* on the institution of the *ludi tauri* (fr. 479 Lindsay) may also be cited in connection with the pestilence as recounted by Dionysius; cf. also Paul. Fest. *De sign. verb.* fr. 479 (Lindsay), *regnante superbo Tarquinio, cum magna incidisset pestilentia in mulieres gravidas*. Moreover, Serv. in Aen. 2.140 notes that Tarquin was ordered to establish the *ludi taurei* "from the book of the fates" (*e libris fatalibus*), on account of the fact that "every birth of the women turned out badly" (*omnis partus mulierum male cedebat*). Others suggest that these games were instituted by the Sabines *propter pestilentiam . . . ut lues publica in has hostias verteretur*; cf. Liv. *AUC.* 39.22; Wissowa 1912, 388 and 488; Gagé 1955, 62 n. 1 and 67ff. Servius also associates their name with the sacrifice of sterile heifers (*quae [vacca] sterilis est, taurea vocatur: unde ludi taurei dicti*). This agrees with a statement in Paul the Deacon's *Epitome* of Festus (fr. 479 Lindsay) that the *ludi tauri* were held in honor of the *dei inferi*, to whom sterile heifers were sacrificed (Bettini 1988b, 232).

apparent, as many scholars have noted.[113] As we have seen, the "hero" of the tale—Brutus—is accompanied by two companions, Arruns and Titus, his cousins, in accordance with the typical folkloric figure of triplication.[114] Through this mechanism, a foolish hero, sent only as a *ludibrium* for his companions (but who will overcome the test), is set in contradistinction to two intelligent companions (who actually are destined for defeat). The paradigm is regular here; in fact it is identical in terms of its narrative content to the structure of numerous other fables. The paradigm typically involves three brothers—two who are intelligent and one who is considered a fool—setting off together or individually to accomplish a specific task. In carrying out this task, or when the Fool asks permission to undertake it along with his "good" brothers, they mock him, misunderstanding his behavior and mistaking his naïve (but actually decisive) actions.

In the Norwegian fables told by Asbjørnsen and Moe, for example, "Cinder Boy" is the third of three brothers. He is described as a boy "without salt in the gourd," someone who "was not good at anything, who didn't do a darned thing; he just kept himself planted next to the hearth like a cat, digging around in the ash and whittling sticks of pine to light in the fire."[115] When he learns what his task will be—to be called a liar by the princess,[116] to make the princess laugh,[117] to cut down an oak tree that provides shade for the palace[118] and so forth—Cinder Boy asks his father's permission to accompany his brothers, but they only laugh at him when he reveals his wish to attempt the task.[119] More specifically, they insult him when he seems to treat certain apparently worthless things as absolutely crucial. For example, when he wishes to go and see who is cutting wood on the mountain (and in doing so discovers the "giver" who grants him the magical means of fulfilling the "initial lack"), his brothers tell him: "You're just like a child! You ought to learn how things go in the world."[120] Similarly, in a Russian fable entitled *The Fool and the Birch*,[121] three brothers—two who are intelligent, one who is a fool—go to market to sell their inheritance.[122] The Fool claims to have sold his part to a birch tree and is mocked by his two brothers—"oh, what a

---

113. De Sanctis 1956, 394; Parke and Wormell 1956, 267ff.; Ogilvie 1965, 218: but this recognition has never inspired any study of the nature and function of this structure.
114. Discussion and bibliography in Bettini 1988b, 150 and n. 29, and 242.
115. Asbjørnsen and Moe 1962, 114.
116. Asbjørnsen and Moe 1962, 110.
117. Asbjørnsen and Moe 1962, 112.
118. Asbjørnsen and Moe 1962, 619.
119. Cf., e.g., Asbjørnsen and Moe 1962, 342.
120. Asbjørnsen and Moe 1962, 620.
121. Afanasjev 1953, 541ff.
122. Cf. below, 69–70.

fool!"—but through this ridiculous barter he has in fact obtained a hoard of treasure.[123] In another Russian fable, *The Princess Who Solves Riddles*,[124] Ivan the Fool is the third of three brothers and is mocked by his father when he wishes to go propose a riddle to the princess:[125] "Where do you think you're going, fool? She has beheaded many men, all much better than you."[126] Of course, the Fool succeeds, shrewdly suggesting to the princess the only riddle she is incapable of solving.

Brutus the Fool and Ivan the Fool share certain curious similarities. On one hand, there is the Roman Fool, the third of three cousins, who poses riddles at Delphi, offering the god a piece of wood (actually filled with gold) and solving riddles himself. On the other hand, there is the Russian Fool, the third of three brothers, who poses riddles that are impossible to solve and like Brutus acquires the kingship (by winning the hand of the princess). Yet the most interesting analogies run between Brutus and Khusràw, especially in his enigmatic speech to his grandfather, and between Brutus and the prince of riddlers, Hamlet. Even Saxo Grammaticus' Amleth employs a brand of "clever" speech that probably has roots in the Nordic riddling tradition.[127] (In certain cases, the author himself seems not to understand the full meaning of what Amleth says!)[128] In any case, there is little doubt that the hero, speaking like a Fool, actually poses *kenningar* (riddles) in perfect skaldic style. For example, when Amleth and his companions traverse a beach and come upon a ship's rudder, they tell him that it is a huge knife, to which Amleth responds, "With this, you can cut a huge side of ham" (meaning the sea). When they ask him to look at the sand and call it flour, Amleth responds, "The storms of the spraying sea have ground it."[129] Amleth, in other words, understands tricky speech. He also poses riddles that others find incomprehensible. When he returns home after making love to a young girl (the future Shakespearian Ophelia), he is mockingly asked, "On what couch have you made love?" and responds, "On a mare's hoof, on a cock's crest and on roof beams." Making his way to the rendezvous, Amleth had in fact collected pieces of all of those

---

123. Afanasjev 1953, 541.
124. Afanasjev 1953, 62ff.
125. The tale corresponds to a frequent type: see Thompson 1966², 224ff., type 851.
126. Afanasjev 1953, 62.
127. Powell 1984, 411; Gollancz 1926, 26.
128. The historian of the Danes, himself far from the world he was describing, appears in these cases to be more a faithful "reporter" than a creative artist, which seems to speak in favor of his reliability: Powell 1984, 400.
129. Sax. Gramm. 3.6.10. The second of these riddles is cited by the skald Snaebiörn (Koch and Cipolla 1993, 152 n. 41).

things; by placing them on the ground where he and his lover would lie down together, he would not have to lie.[130] His enemies, naturally, did not see the truth hidden beneath his absurd words and responded only with laughter.[131]

Capable of understanding enigmatic speech, Amleth not only poses riddles, but also solves them, like Brutus. Consider the episode of Amleth's tryst with the future Ophelia. The hero's enemies devise this encounter in order to reveal, finally, whether or not Amleth is feigning stupidity. For this purpose, they even send a group of spies into the forest to report on his behavior. And Amleth would have been discovered, if one of his brothers had not remained loyal to him and come to his aid. The young man catches a fly, to which he fastens a piece of straw as a tail, leaving it to fly about in a spot through which Amleth must pass on his way to meet the girl. The prince notices this insect with a strange tail, stops out of curiosity, and recognizes "the silent warning to watch out for a trick" (*tacitum cavendae fraudis monitum*).[132] As a result, Amleth brings the girl to a place where no one will be able to spy on them. Naturally, the enigmatic formulation of a warning does not pose a problem for the (false) fool: he who continuously poses riddles also knows how to solve them. On the other hand, the absolute incapacity of those around the hero to comprehend what he is doing and saying remains consistent.

This brings us back to Ivan the Fool, a character who, like Brutus and Amleth, evinces a privileged connection between riddling and stupidity in culture and in creative narrative. The (false) Fool's way of speaking is enigmatic in its very structure: accordingly, he is also capable of solving the unsolvable. The riddle, like a dream or an oracle, speaks a language that is simultaneously both above and below culture: to understand and to formulate riddles, one must have a mind that is capable of encapsulating these two contradictory characteristics. This, then, is the nature of the (false) Fool: he is too clever, too intelligent to be understood and is thus mistaken for one

---

130. Sax. Gramm. 3.6.11.

131. The interpretation given of Amleth's obscure allusions is that the names of the objects listed also denote the varieties of grass that formed the lovers' "bed" (Koch and Cipolla 1993, 152 n. 43): but the text speaks of *horum omnium . . . particulae* ("fragments of all these"), an expression not particularly apt to describe vegetation. On Koch and Cipolla's interpretation, taken from Davidson 1980, 61 n. 71, who in turn took it from Dollerup 1975, see below, n. 193. Amleth has now assumed the characteristic language of the Fool: Segre 1990, 89ff.

132. Sax. Gramm. 3.6.10. For various attempts at explaining this, see Davidson 1980, 60, n. 69, with bibliography. None of the interpretations seems convincing, and the *oestrum* fitted with a blade of straw remains enigmatic: see Hansen 1983, 132f. Purely as a suggestion, I mention the possibility that the Italian proverb "aver la coda di paglia" ("to have a guilty conscience," but literally "to have a straw tail") may rest upon folkloric stories of this type (or vice versa).

"lacking sense." He is like a riddle—a discourse so profound that it unites that which cannot be together and is thus close to "senselessness."[133]

The Gold in the Sticks: "Stupid" Wood, Ill-Omened Wood

The unique offering made by Brutus to the god at Delphi is an enigma in itself; but how did the hero "pose" this riddle? Dionysius tells us that Brutus hollowed out the center of a log and placed a golden ingot inside it, and that this constituted his offering to the god.[134] He does not bother explaining the meaning of Brutus' strange behavior. Livy, however, does so in the following way: "He is said to have brought as a gift for Apollo a golden rod encased within a log of cornel hollowed out for this purpose, an enigmatic image of his own nature" (*aureum baculum inclusum corneo cavato ad id baculo tulisse donum Apollini dicitur, per ambages effigiem ingenii sui*).[135] In this way, the offering functions as a riddle symbolically figuring the hero's own feigned stupidity. The "false Fool" is represented as a "container" of worthless material that conceals a heart of gold. In some sense, then, the story reproduces its own basic narrative isotopy in the form of a riddle. Brutus' hollowed-out log reiterates the concealed, deceptive nature of his "stupidity." This symbolism functions in the case also of rings; ancient dream theory states that "solid rings are better in every case; hollow rings . . . indicate tricks or betrayals, because they hide something inside them."[136] In other words, what is hollow or hollowed out signifies deceit. But what of the material composition of Brutus' peculiar offering? The meaning of "gold" is clear: what is *aureus* is by nature also *eximius* ("valuable").[137] It is not accidental that "stupidity" is often defined in Latin as *plumbeus*;[138] in an opposition articulated according to metallurgic categories—worthless/precious, dull/splendid—he who is truly stupid is "leaden," whereas he who conceals his superior intelligence is *aureus*.

What, moreover, is the meaning of the "log" concealing or enveloping

---

133. On the connection between riddles and incest, see Bettini 1983, 137ff.; 1988, 145ff.; and 1998, 35 n. 18.
134. Dion. *Ant. Rom.* 4.69.3. Cf. Dio Cassius 2.12; Zon. *Hist.* 7.11
135. Liv. *AUC.* 1.56.
136. Artem. 2.5.
137. Cf., e.g., Lucr. *De re. nat.* 3.23; Cic. *Rosc. Amer.* 124.
138. Ter. *Heaut.* 74ff.; Cic. *Tusc. disp.* 1.28.71; Suet. *Nero* 2; etc. The metaphor could be enriched in an astronomical sense: It is well known that Saturn had among his other divine provinces also that of being in charge of "iron" (corresponding to the slowness of the planet's revolution; his connection with melancholy, etc.): Klibansky, Panofsky and Saxl 1983, 134f.

Chapter 2. Brutus the Fool 65

the gold?[139] The sources speak of a "wooden log":[140] in one case, the type of wood is specified as elder (*sabucus*),[141] in another as cornel (*cornus*).[142] The symbolism becomes clearer when we recall that in Latin the system of terms denoting (pieces of) wood—*codex* ("bark"),[143] *frutex* ("bush"),[144] *truncus* ("trunk"),[145] *stipes* ("trunk")[146]—are used as insults referring precisely to "stupidity." (In the iconological tradition, furthermore, someone stupid could be represented with a reed or wooden cane in his hand.)[147]

It appears, then, that Brutus, in dedicating a piece of wood to the god, intended to signify—through the language of folklore—his own "stupidity" as a *frutex* or *stipes*. Is there any further meaning to the choice of *sabucus* ("elder") and *cornus* ("cornel")? According to Lucilius,[148] *sabucus* was considered the worst variety of wood—*ardum, miserinum, atque infelix lignum sabucum vocat* ("He calls the *sabucus* a kind of wood that is dry, pitiful and unlucky").[149] Besides being "unlucky" (*infelix*),[150] the elder was also considered "dry" and—as far as can be told from a corrupted text—worthless. What impression would Brutus' offering have made, then, in comparison to the no doubt sumptuous gifts presented to the god by the young Tarquins?[151] To offer such a worthless piece of wood, Brutus must really have been a fool—a metaphorical *frutex*.[152] Furthermore, it is interesting to observe how figurative language seems to have preserved, even after so many centuries, the markedly negative characterization of the *sabucus,* precisely in relation to

---

139. The question does not seem to have troubled scholars, and the few interpretations that have been given are not convincing. Pais (1926, 170 n. 1) makes a reference to the cult of Apollo *kráneios* (cf. Frazer 1898, 333), treating this as a sort of "Delphic" symbol. Gagé 1955, "sans doute (?) . . . affabulation d'un symbole delphique" (or even a transposition of an ancient symbol of the *gens Iunia* unknown to scholarship). Fauth (1976, 501) hesitatingly refers to this as an allusion to the "Hirtenstab" detectable also in the scepter of the Tantalids. Mastrocinque (1988, 19 n. 10) suggests that "the primary meaning of this anecdote was that of a consecration of the regal scepter to Apollo," but the context does not point in that direction. On the Delphic episode, see more recently Feldherr 1997, 144ff., who reveals how "the concealed or hidden meaning" was characteristic of Tarquin's mode of communication, since he speaks to his sons in *ambages* just as Brutus speaks in riddles.
140. Dion. *Ant. Rom.* 4.69.3; Dio Cass. 2.11; Zon. *Hist.* 7.11.
141. Anon. *De vir. illustr.* 10.2.
142. Liv. *AUC.* 1.56.
143. Cf., e.g., Ter. *Heaut.* 877; Petr. *Sat.* 74.
144. Cf., e.g., Plaut. *Most.* 13; Apul. *Apol.* 66.
145. Cf., e.g., Cic. *De nat. deor.* 1.84; *Pis.* 19.
146. Cf., e.g., Ter. *Heaut.* 877; Cic. *Pis.* 19; *De har. resp.* 5; Petr. *Sat.* 43.3; Claud. *Eutr.* 1.126.
147. Ripa 1766, IV, 347 (design of C. Mariotti incised by C. Grandi) and 349.
148. Fr. 733 Marx.
149. The text is corrupt (unlikely an iambic correption *miserīnum:* cf. Lindsay 1894, 7ff.): *TLL* VIII, 1130 for other possible cases of *miserīnum.* Cf. Bettini 1988a, 89ff.
150. André 1964, 85.
151. Cic. *De re pub.* 2.24.6 (Tarquin), *dona magnifica Apollinem misit* (apparently referring to the preceding embassy: Altheim 1938, 263ff.; Parke and Wormell 1956, 267ff.).
152. The *sabucus* is called *frutex* by Plin. *Nat. hist.* 16.179.

"stupidity." In Giulio Cesare Croce's *Bertoldino,* Marcolfa says of his stupid son, "He is so awkward and stupid, I don't know if he is made of stucco or of elder-wood (*sambuco*)."[153] Elder is a worthless kind of wood: hollow, pithy and unfit for kindling even when it is dry. It is hollow, just as a stupid person is "hollow." Little wonder, then, that this term comes to designate the worthless and foolish man.

In Livy, the type of wood chosen by Brutus for his offering is instead "cornel" (*cornus*). For Latin speakers, this plant came in two varieties: *mas* and *femina. Cornus mas* corresponds to our "cornel," a plant of reddish and very hard wood. This variety of cornel was in fact so valued by the Romans for its hardness and rigidity that they fashioned their *hastae* ("spears") from it.[154] *Cornus femina,* on the other hand, is our "dogwood"—what Pliny calls *sanguineae frutices*[155]—a shrub with soft wood and large reddish leaves. It is hard to imagine that Brutus used *cornus mas* for his purposes; as Pliny describes it, this variety of wood is "one of the strongest and hardest."[156] Elsewhere we learn that it does not have pith (*medulla*)[157] and that it is *tota ossea* ("all bone").[158] Hollowing out a log of cornel wood would have been a real feat! Furthermore, the mention of *sabucus*—a soft and malleable type of wood—invites us to believe that we are dealing with *cornus femina,* which Pliny defines as *ligno . . . fungosa et inutilis* ("with spongy wood and useless").[159] And elder is, again according to Pliny, *fungosi generis.*[160] In other words, *sabucus* and *cornus femina* are two varieties of wood that one could conceivably hollow out, and which might serve ideally for concealing an ingot or "rod" of gold. Therefore, if, as appears most likely, Livy is referring to the *cornus femina* (*corneo cavato ad id baculo*), we should conclude that in this case as well Brutus is represented as choosing a particularly useless and worthless type of wood to make his ridiculous offering.

Brutus' choice of offering connotes the traits of uselessness, worthlessness and "stupidity," but also something worse. The elder tree is defined in Roman culture as *arbor infelix,* a characterization related to the fact that it produces *bacam nigram* ("a black berry");[161] moreover, it was associated with the so-called *furcae sabuceae* ("The Forks of Elder"), which featured centrally

---

153. Croce 1943, 104.
154. Plin. *Nat. hist.* 105.228. On the differences between the two species, the different critical meaning, etc., see Bayet 1971, 9ff.; André 1964.
155. Plin. *Nat. hist.* 16.75 and 176; cf. 19.180 and 24.73.
156. Plin. *Nat. hist.* 16.105.
157. Plin. *Nat. hist.* 16.183.
158. Plin. *Nat. hist.* 16.186.
159. Plin. *Nat. hist.* 16.105.
160. Plin. *Nat. hist.* 16.179.
161. Tarquitius Priscus in Macr. 3.20.25.

in the *supplicia annua* of the dog.[162] But dogwood, *sanguineae frutices*—the other type of wood indicated by the sources as Brutus' choice for his "stupid" offering—is also *arbor infelix*.[163] This particular detail—that these two varieties of plant are *infelix*—is likely also relevant to the story. In evaluating any story of folklore, the ethnographic context (considered as a complex of the beliefs about the particular facts and particular elements that the story puts in play) is surely significant.[164] We must pay a great deal of attention, therefore, to the specific meanings that the story's "objects" have for the culture in which it operates. The two types of wood that Brutus uses in the different variants of the story are both "ill-omened," "unlucky": *infelices*. According to Tarquitius Priscus, the *arbores infelices* as a class fall under the protection of the infernal gods,[165] and Pliny defines these same plants as "trees . . . condemned by superstition" (*arbores . . . damnatae religione*).[166] In short, they would not be considered at all appropriate for use as an offering to a god. Besides being "stupid," such an offering would perhaps be deemed unsuitable also from a religious or ritual point of view. As Livy explains, Brutus intended to represent himself—his own "outside" and his own "inside"—in his offering. As regarded his "outside," Brutus must have wished to suggest the image not only of stupidity but also, in some way, of what was "negative" or "ill-omened."

The Tenacity of Folklore: The Dunce, the Gold and the Wood

Brutus offers the god an image of his true self and of his own true intelligence, concealed beneath a façade of "stupidity." Like Plato's Silenus—the worn wooden box that conceals a statue of the god[167]—Brutus' "log" also manifests two contrasting characteristics. In this sense, the object that Brutus offers to the god appears to function as an *oxumōron*, a figure of speech that unites in a single syntagm two words or elements of opposite meaning, like Horace's *concordia discors* or Milton's "darkness visible." The most noble and

---

162. Plin. *Nat. hist.* 29.57. Cf. Aelian. *Nat. anim.* 12.35. On sacrificing dogs in Greece, see Mainoldi 1984, 37ff.
163. Tarquitius Priscus in Macr. 3.20.2f. Patricides were also punished by means of *virgae sanguineae:* Modest. *Dig.* 48.9.9.1. The specifically *infelix* and negative (and also markedly Roman) character of the *cornus femina* makes it unlikely that Brutus' offering is an allusion to the cult of Apollo *Kraneios*, as Pais thought.
164. Lévi-Strauss 1966.
165. Macr. 3.20.3.
166. Plin. *Nat. hist.* 16.108.
167. Pl. *Symp.* 215b, 221dff.; Lanza 1997, 32f.

desirable material—gold—is placed inside the most worthless and maligned material—a piece of useless and "unlucky" wood. The object is thus "oxymoronic" in the same way that the "false Fool" himself is oxymoronic, with his *sapiens insipientia*. Better yet, the false Fool is himself the oxymoron *par excellence*, since the meaning of that Greek rhetorical term is "clever fool." To designate the simultaneous coincidence of two opposites, and the linguistic effect produced by this, Greek culture hit upon the metaphor of "clever stupidity." Perhaps we had not realized that Brutus, Amleth and the other "false Fools" of folklore are in fact rhetorical figures—in a very literal sense.

Amleth's Unci: *Wooden Hooks and Clever Tricks*

When we first encounter Hamlet, or Amleth, in Saxo Grammaticus,[168] we find him wallowing in the dirt next to the hearth. In this, he is practically identical to the Norwegian "Cinder Boy" mentioned above.[169] Cinder Boy, moreover, in the opening tableau of his story,[170] was intent on tempering by flame certain sticks of pine that had been brought to light the fire. Amleth dedicates himself to a similar task: he tries to harden certain wooden *unci* ("curved stakes") in the fire. Whenever someone asks what he is doing, he responds that he is making "sharp darts for avenging my father" (*acuta ... in ultionem patris specula*), provoking the laughter, or surprise, of his interlocutors: no one has ever heard of a *curved* arrow before. But others are suspicious: is the Fool hiding something? Why care so much for fashioning these useless—senseless—objects? They are not useless and senseless objects, of course. As Saxo notes, "this thing would later aid his design" (*ea res proposito eius postmodum opitulata fuerit*). Indeed, in making those *unci*, Amleth too "was representing the hidden genius of the master through the practice of a modest art" (*exiguae artis industria arcanum opificis ingenium figurabat*), just as Brutus intended his "log of gold" as a cryptic symbol of himself and of his intellect.[171] Yet what was the (false) Fool's dark design, and how did it involve those wooden "hooks"? The story continues: Upon his return from Britain, where he had cleverly uncovered the treacherous intentions of his companions, Amleth takes advantage of the drunken stupor into which the entire Nordic kingdom has fallen to set a trap for his enemies—quite literally, since he contrives to bring down upon their heads a heavy curtain that

---

168. Sax. Gramm. 3.6.6.
169. Cf. above, 61. On the medieval *fool*'s typical trait of having a dirty face, cf. Avalle 1989, 92–111.
170. In Propp's (1966, 31f.) sense.
171. Sax. Gramm. 3.6.7.

hangs suspended from the palace ceiling, staking it to the ground with the very same wooden hooks (*unci*) for which he had been mocked (the curtain is also symbolic in the fact that it had been woven by his mother).[172] He then sets the palace on fire, killing all inside. Unlike Brutus's "log," Amleth's hooks conceal no golden rod inside: they are, as Amleth himself affirms, "sharp darts for avenging my father" (*acuta spicula in ultionem patris*). But the unusual, enigmatic, even incomprehensible shape of Amleth's *unci*, correlating to the false Fool's hidden purpose, also represent both his own "empty" stupidity and his superior intelligence: "the hidden genius of the master," as Saxo says. So in this case too it is an object—and specifically a piece of wood—that operates as a symbol of the nature of the false Fool, reproduced in the form of a material "riddle."

The narrative function played by the *unci* in Amleth's tale may be confirmed by the traditional interpretation of this episode enshrined in an Old Icelandic play on words: in that language, the word *krókr* means both "hook" and "clever trick."[173] While Saxo's account does not explicitly point to this interpretation, it is also possible that he himself did not comprehend the fullness of meaning with which the episode was endowed in his Nordic source, and was therefore limited to transmitting only the letter of the story, so to speak (which he nevertheless succeeded in doing, even without that additional meaning). If this hypothesis is correct, Amleth's "wooden hooks" are a verbal guise for what are simultaneously "clever tricks"—again reproducing, on the linguistic level, what the narrative structure already makes clear: that the Fool's "sticks" symbolize at once his stupidity and his superior ability.

A Dry Birch Full of Gold

Returning to the gold in the sticks: The Russian fable known as *The Fool and the Birch* represents a distinct and widespread type in folklore: the same basic narrative underlies, for example, the story of Vardiello in Basil's *Pentameron*,[174] part of Giufà's Sicilian cycle, and certain Georgian tales.[175] In the Russian version of this story, three brothers—two of whom are intelligent, while the third is stupid—receive an inheritance from their father. When the brothers go to the market in the city to sell their individual parts, the third brother—

---

172. Sax. Gramm. 3.6.24. The technique used for the murder recalls that of fishing for salmon (where a net is fixed precisely with stakes): Davidson 1980, II, 62 n. 81. Davidson's (1980, II, 62 n. 81) observation that Amelethus here takes on the behavior of the "trickster" is astute.
173. Evidence in Hansen 1983, 125.
174. Basile 1925, I, 4.
175. Pitré 1875, 190; Wardrop 1894, 165ff.

the Fool—passes by a forest where he notices the branches of a birch tree rustling in the wind. From this, he somehow gathers that the birch wishes to make an exchange: the birch wishes to buy the lamb that the Fool has received from his father. From the movement of the branches, the Fool also divines the exact price he will receive in return for the animal. Accepting the birch's terms, the Fool declares that he will pass by again the next day to collect his payment. When he does so, he finds no money at all—only the bones of the unfortunate animal that he had left tied to the trunk of the tree the day before and that wolves had devoured during the night. The Fool returns home empty-handed, resolving to pass by again the next day. This pattern repeats itself for a number of days, until the Fool grows so angry that he brings an axe to forest and begins striking the dry trunk of the birch tree—in a hollow of which, to his surprise, he finds a small treasure hidden there by a group of bandits.

The fable of the Fool and the birch tree, then, deals again with a stupid man, (a piece of) dry wood (or some other worthless material: in Giufà, the tree is replaced by a statue made of chalk), and a hidden trove of gold. Here, too, the Fool demonstrates (this time accidentally) that he is far more shrewd than his "intelligent" brothers, given his success in bartering a lamb for a true fortune. From this point of view, the fable belongs to the type that Thompson defined as "the good deal."[176] Of course, the narrative use to which the single "components" of the generic type are put is different here than in the tale of Brutus. But also in the case of Brutus the fable concludes with a "good deal" for the Fool. And we must not forget that folklore, as Jakobson and Bogatyrëv explain, operates precisely according to a principle of economicity:[177] folk narration is above all a restricted and regular way of telling stories, inclined to using and reusing a circumscribed number of linguistic and compositional elements to produce tales that are both a little bit the same and a little bit different.[178] In other words, it is likely that in the composition of this fable the same symbolic "material" was used to create episodes similar to that of Brutus' "gold in the sticks": the "dry wood," expressing the greatest "stupidity" and greatest "worthlessness," and a "heart of gold" signifying the polar opposite—the Fool's hidden intelligence (or economic fortune). In short, once again we see in operation the well-known principle of folktales that Fools and foolish deeds often triumph over those who believe themselves to be wise.

---

176. Thompson 1966², 244ff., type 1642.
177. Cf. also Propp 1975, 141ff.
178. At a greater level of complexity (and also "sophistication"), this phenomenon characterizes also the plots of Plautine comedy: Bettini 1991b.

Hamlet's Sticks

Saxo Grammaticus relates that when Amleth travels to Britain in the company of two faithless companions whose real purpose is to murder him en route, he shrewdly hits upon a means of escape: he devises a stratagem whereby the very king who is supposed to kill Amleth (according to Feng's perfidious plan) will instead end up killing the prince's would-be assassins.[179] The false Fool's profound genius defeats even the king of Britain, who, apprised of the situation by certain revelations he receives from Amleth, has Amleth's companions hanged. Amleth ingeniously feigns grief over their deaths, as if the favor done to him by the king were an offense: he thus also receives from the British sovereign some recompense for the loss of his men.[180] This recompense is given to Hamlet in the form of gold bars, naturally, which the prince then "took care to liquefy and infuse secretly into hollowed out sticks" (*liquatum . . . clam cavatis baculis infundendum curavit*). Amleth returns home with these sticks filled with gold, and immediately goes to the palace, still ragged and unsightly from his journey. Again feigning madness, he finds king Feng and the members of his court celebrating his funeral (they believe that Feng's plan has worked and that Amleth is already dead);[181] his arrival obviously causes some bewilderment, but the surprise soon turns again to *ludibrium* as the guests begin to blame Amleth for being alive. He is asked, finally, where his companions are, but "showing the sticks that he was carrying, he said, 'Here they are—the one and the other'—and you could not know whether he meant this more in jest or more in truth" (*ostensis quos gestabat baculis 'hic' inquit 'et unus et alius est.' quod utrum verius an iocosius protulerit, nescias*).

The episode is telling and merits discussion—not in order to deal with a part of the story that extends beyond the horizon of our interest (and which Hansen has in any case already discussed in some detail),[182] but because the question has general and rather interesting methodological implications. At least upon first consideration, it seems likely that Saxo drew the theme of the "hollowed out sticks" directly from the Brutus story. It even seems possible to identify his source: Valerius Maximus. Indeed, Stephanius notes (ad loc.) an explicit linguistic analogy between Valerius' tale of Brutus and Saxo's tale of Amleth in the expression *obtunsi . . . cordis* used by both authors in the

---

179. Sax. Gramm. 3.6.16ff. On this motif, see Davidson 1980, II, 62 n. 76.
180. An example of "wergild": on this custom, see Davidson 1980, II, 62 n. 79.
181. The theme occurs elsewhere in myth and folktale: he who is "the farthest" (because deceased) turns out, paradoxically, to be the "closest": cf. Hyg. *Fab.* 92; Bettini and Borghini 1980, 121ff. and 138ff.
182. Hansen 1983, 25ff. and esp. 33.

same context.[183] Further, and more convincing, linguistic evidence can also be cited:[184] the expression that Saxo uses to indicate the stratagem of the "gold in the log" (*aurum . . . liquatum . . . clam cavatis baculis infundendum curavit*)[185] is modeled directly after Valerius' text (*aurum . . . clam cavato baculo inclusum tulit*).[186] Here, Amleth functions as a true calque of Brutus, and François de Belleforest was correct when, in his reworking of Saxo's Amleth, he transformed the Danish hero into an accomplished student of Latin who had adopted the behavior of the "false Fool" precisely in imitation of Brutus.[187] In certain cases, literary invention goes hand in hand with philology—and sometimes even precedes it.

Saxo adapted the episode that he had found in Valerius Maximus to the structural demands of his own tale, doubling the number of logs (to bring them into alignment with the "plurality" of Amleth's companions) and giving them a new symbolic value and a narrative function. Brutus' "gold in the sticks" concealed the hero's feigned stupidity; Amleth's "gold in the sticks" permits the hero to make an affirmation that is simultaneously both true and false: encased in those sticks is the "value" of his lost companions in gold, though it would be absurd to claim that "they" are really there.[188] Nevertheless, Saxo's reelaboration correlates to a constant feature of Amleth's story: as Powell suggests, Amleth is "punctilious of verbal truthfulness."[189] Amleth's "fastidiousness" of speech was noted independently by Jones, who interpreted this from a Freudian perspective as part of Amleth's markedly "infantile" character.[190] Amleth's scrupulousness for expressing the "truth" in the false statements by which he tricks

---

183. Val. Max. 7.3.2 = Sax. Gramm. 3.6.7.

184. Powell 1894, 407; Gollancz 1926, 28 n.1; and Davidson 1980, II, 62 n. 80, limit themselves to the osbservations of Stephanius. On the other hand, the apparatus in Olrik and Raeder (1931) contains a rich list of references to Valerius Maximus. On Saxo's Latin culture in general, cf. Hansen 1983, 33ff.

185. Sax. Gramm. 6.9.11 actually uses the word *vaframentum* ("stupidity") to indicate the wisdom of the *oestrum* with straw tail. This is a rare word, used only by Valerius Maximus; in fact, the word appears three times in the passage in which the story of Brutus is recounted. This section also bears the title *De vafre dictis aut factis*.

186. Val. Max. 7.3.2 = Sax. Gramm. 3.6.21.

187. Jones 1986, 139f. Curious that Jones insists on calling our hero "Brutus the Young"; given that the younger Brutus killed his own "father" (that is, Caesar), and given that Jones's study turns on the theme of Oedipus, I would imagine this is a kind of "Freudian" slip.

188. It must be stated, then, that Valerius' text lends itself particularly well to be reworked, since its version of Brutus' offering is not so markedly polarized as the other versions we have examined. For Valerius, Brutus made this unique offering to the god not in order to allude secretly to his own condition as "false Fool," but only because "he feared that it would not be safe for him to venerate a heavenly power with an obvious gift" (7.3.2, *timebat ne sibi caeleste numen aperta liberalitate venerari tutum non esset*).

189. Powell 1894, 106.

190. Jones 1986, 141.

his enemies is in fact detectable in all of the riddles the hero poses to his enemies.[191] As Saxo says, "Desiring to be considered averse to falsity, he so mixed deceit with truth-telling that truth was never lacking in his words, but neither was the true measure of his cunning betrayed by the hint of truth"[192] (*falsitati enim alienus haberi cupiens, ita astutiam veriloquio miscuit ut nec dictis veracitas deesset, nec acuminis modus verorum indicio pateretur*).[193]

From what we have seen so far, it seems possible to draw the following conclusion: the episode of Amleth's "sticks" is modeled off a classical source—Valerius Maximus—but reworked according to the generic "isotope" of the narration into which the episode is inserted. There would seem to be no problem with this interpretation—if we were not in the fortunate position of being able to place our own reconstruction in doubt.

Conon of Lampsacus, a Greek mythographer straddling the first centuries B.C.E. and C.E., recounts a story known as *The Milesian and the Trove of Money*, as follows:[194] A certain inhabitant of Miletus, seeing his city threatened by the Persian Harpages, travels to Taormina in Sicily to deposit his money with a banker friend and then returns home. Once the danger has passed, he returns to Taormina to claim his money; his banker friend, however, though admitting to have accepted the man's deposit, refuses to give it back. After long argument, the Milesian finally summons the banker before a magistrate. The banker, therefore, contrives a stratagem: "he hollowed out a stick as if it were a flute, and hid the money that the Milesian had given him inside it, after liquefying it." He then appears in court supporting himself on this stick, feigning some malady of the feet. Finally, at the established moment, he offers the stick to the Milesian, swearing that he is returning his deposit. The Milesian becomes enraged, grabs the stick and throws it to the ground, shattering it to pieces—and thus the trick is discovered.

This story, similarly recounted by Stobaeus,[195] has many points of contact

---

191. Similarly for the rudder/*cultrum* for cutting the ham/sea (Sax. Gram. 3.6.10); for the *pulvinum*/cock's crest; and so forth (3.6.11: Amelethus actually carried pieces of these objects in his pocket).

192. Sax. Gramm. 3.6.9.

193. This narrative isotope, fundamental to the story, seems to have escaped the notice of Davidson 1980, II, 61 n. 71, who, following Dollerup, interprets as "names of plants" with a sexual connotation the "mare's hoof," "cock's crest" and "roof beam" in Sax. Gramm. 3.6.11. Yet Saxo says explicitly that Amelethus carried with him pieces of these objects *vitandi mendacii gratia;* moreover, it is for this very reason that Amelethus' statement appears absolutely absurd.

194. In Phot. *Bibl.* 186.38; Jacoby 1957, I A n. 26, 1, 38, 204ff. cf. also Men. fr. 503 Körte-Thierfelder.

195. Stob. *Ecl.* 12.85.3. Hansen (1983, 33) has demonstrated that the motif in question recurs elsewhere in other folktales (without giving the two Greek examples, however). He has noted, more-

with Saxo's story—perhaps more even than the story of Brutus has with tale of Amleth. In particular, the narrative function of the gold in the stick is identical:[196] the gold in the stick permits the hero to evade the "principle of truth," since his affirmation is simultaneously both true (the deposit really is there) and false (to all appearances, it is just a stick). What should we conclude from this similarity between the two stories? It is doubtful that Saxo Grammaticus knew Photius' version, let alone Stobaeus'—although there have been scholars who have claimed, for other reasons, that Saxo knew certain Greek epitomes of Roman history.[197] Two possibilities remain, then. First, Saxo, or his source, may have reused a folkloric motif already well known in Greece, at least in the first years of the Christian era. At the very least, the fact that such tales were circulated orally suggests this possibility. Second, Saxo, in reworking Valerius, may have independently given the motif of "gold in the stick" the same symbolic value (i.e., of concealed intellectual superiority) that this motif had once had in the past. Combining these two interpretations yields a third possibility, however: that Saxo reworked the letter of Valerius' story—his exemplary Latinity as well as his authoritative narrative *exemplum*—shaping it to the outline of a folkloric theme known to him by other means.[198]

Whatever hypothesis one chooses (and I admit I am somewhat partial to the third), one thing remains certain: folkloric creation again demonstrates the characteristics of regularity and economicity. Paradigms, motifs, structures tend to be used and reused in distant (and independent) contexts with a truly surprising degree of consistency. Only in the telling of folktales does narrative appear subject to a kind of rigid grammaticality: traits and motifs constantly repeat, elaborated in similar ways and responding to similar narrative demands. In this regard, Propp made a truly paradoxical assertion: "The phenomenon of universal resemblance [between fables] does not represent a problem for us. For us, the *absence* of such resemblances would be inexplicable" (my emphasis).[199]

---

over, that this makes a borrowing from Valerius Maximus improbable, considering instead various "derivationist" proposals advanced by preceding scholars.

196. From this point of view, the motif of Amleth's "gold in the stick" in Saxo and Conon is similar to that of Prometheus who hides fire in the *narthēx;* or of Hannibal who, in order to escape unnoticed from Crete, hides his gold *in statuis, quas secum portabat* (Justin 32.4).

197. Gollancz 1926, 28.

198. For other adaptations of Nordic themes to classical models in Saxo, see in particular Davidson 1980, 7.

199. Propp 1966, 148. Cf. also Thompson 1967, 7, "[fables] have as definite form and substance in human culture as the pot, the hoe, or the bow and arrow, and several of these narrative forms are quite as generally employed."

The Hero Falls To Earth

As we have seen, Brutus immediately comprehends what is hidden in the enigmatic—because superficially unambiguous—words of the Delphic oracle's response. When Titus and Arruns go on to ask the god which of them will inherit their father's crown, the divine voice responds that the kingdom will pass to whomever "first . . . gives his mother a kiss" (*primus . . . osculum matri tulerit*). Titus and Arruns therefore contrive to keep this secret from their brother Sextus, and to kiss their mother at the same time, so as to divide the kingdom equally between themselves. Brutus, however, realizes immediately that the god of Delphi is speaking in figures and "solves" the riddle by kissing the earth, reasoning that the earth is the "mother" of all men. Yet in Livy's account, Brutus does not simply kneel to kiss the earth, but "slipping as if he had fallen, he touched the ground with a kiss, obviously because (as he thought) the earth is the common mother of all mortals" (*velutsi prolapsus cecidisset, terram osculo contigit, scilicet quod ea communis mater omnium mortalium esset*).[200] Pretending to fall to the ground, Brutus kisses his "true" mother and thus gains power. Dionysius' account is somewhat different on this score. He sets the scene of this episode not before the temple of Delphi, but at the moment of Brutus' disembarkation in Italy.[201] In this way, "mother earth" (*terra mater*) takes on the additional aspect of "fatherland" (*terra patria*). Dionysius gives no hint of the theme of the feigned fall, moreover: Brutus simply kneels to kiss the earth, performing an ancient ritual gesture commonly practiced by those returning home after a long journey.[202] It is hard to imagine these two transformations of the story are not in some way related. Setting the episode in the context of Brutus' return home, there is no need to "motivate" the kiss:[203] disembarking, Brutus simply kneels and kisses the earth, an act to which no one would give a second thought. Ovid, on the other hand, retains the theme of "pretending": "Lying prone he gave kisses to mother earth, believed to have stumbled" (*ille iacens pronus matri dedit oscula terrae / creditus offenso procubuisse pede*).[204] Here Brutus trips, rather than slips, but this constitutes a "fall" nonetheless—and a feigned one at that.

---

200. Liv. *AUC.* 1.56.
201. Dion. *Ant. Rom.* 4.69.3.
202. Fraenkel 1962, II, 256 n. to v. 503; Ogilvie 1965, 228; on the kiss given to the earth, see in particular Lot 1949, 435ff.
203. In Propp's (1966, 80) sense of the term. See also Tomaševskij 1968, 326ff.
204. Ov. *Fast.* 2.720. Cf. Val. Max. 7.3.2, *perinde atue casu prolapsus, de industria se abiecit*. For the theme of "kissing the earth," see Thompson 1966², J 1652 and A 401.

Stupidity Drags You Down

The richest version of the Brutus story—there is little sense in speaking about the "true" version of a story of this type—is that which contains the feigned fall to earth. This act in fact corresponds to the story's fundamental narrative isotope, known already from the *aries* of Tarquin's dream (the "stupid" ram that, in reality, is strong) and above all the *baculum cavatum*. Brutus "conceals" in his fall an act that will turn out to be decisive for his future, just as in the worthless material of the "stick" he conceals gold and just as, in general, in all of his "foolish" behavior he conceals his true genius. Enveloped within the clumsy, negative act of falling, he conceals another act that presupposes his superior intelligence and that will be crucial for the final resolution of the story. Let us look more closely, then, at this new manifestation of Brutus' cleverness.

Instability of the legs and a kind of "attraction" towards the ground—a tendency, that is, to exchange the naturally and normally erect posture of a human being for a prostrate position on the ground—appears to be characteristic of the Fool (or of he who pretends to be a Fool). Claudius' hesitating gait—*dexterum pedem trahere*—is frequently mentioned.[205] In this way, the Fool's "slowness" of intellect (cf. *tardus*) has a physical complement in his plodding step. Similarly, David, pretending to be mad at the court of Achis, "let himself fall in their hands, stumbling on the door shutters."[206] David—like Brutus at Delphi—stumbles and falls; similarly, Amleth was first introduced to us "lying abject on the ground" (*abiectus humi*).[207] In a later variant of the story of Hamlet known as the *Ambales saga,* told by Arni Magnusson at the end of the seventeenth century C.E.,[208] Ambales is called Amloði (literally, "stupid") because "he continually lies in the hearth room before the ashes."[209] So too "Cinder Boy" habitually wallows in the ashes of the hearth;[210] wishing to go out in the world to perform a hero's deeds, he is told: "But remain among the ashes, stay lying in the ashes!"[211] In the iconological tradition, moreover, "stupidity" is represented as "a nude, smiling woman, lying on the ground lasciviously"[212] and "foolishness" is represented as "a woman poorly dressed, with a piece of iron on her head . . . because like iron she is heavy, and she naturally stands low, just like the fool, who

---

205. Sen. *Apoc.* 5.1; Suet. *Claud.* 2, 21, 30.
206. 1 Samuel 21:11–13.
207. Sax. Gramm. 3.6.6.
208. Gollancz 1926, 66ff. and 87ff.
209. Powell 1984, 404; Gollancz 1926, 87ff.
210. Asbjørnsen and Moe 1962, 342.
211. Asbjørnsen and Moe 1962, 342.
212. Ripa 1766, V, 80ff.

never raises his intellect."²¹³ I have already remarked that in Latin "stupidity" is often characterized as "like iron" (*plumbeus*): for example, at the end of Terence's *Heautontimoroumenos,* Menedemus says of himself, "Anything said of the stupid is appropriate in my case as well: 'blockhead,' 'trunk,' 'ass,' 'piece of iron'" (*in me quidvis harum rerum convenit / quae sunt dicta in stulto: caudex stipes asinus plumbeus*).²¹⁴

Cesare Ripa, thoroughly familiar with symbolic language, probably captured the most abstract and general connection between "stupidity" and "the earth" when he explained that the stupid man "never raises his genius" and is therefore like iron, "which by nature falls down." Doubtless, in cultural representation the opposition of "high" and "low" also functions as an indication of the distance that separates, on one hand, spirituality and intelligence, and, on the other, brutality and violence.²¹⁵ The mind is "high" and all that is spiritual, all that makes Man what he is, tends also to be "high": after all, Man is a creature whose face is turned "upward."²¹⁶ Conversely, "stupidity" naturally tends "down" to earth, and, with its uncertain gait, its stumbling, its falling, its Hamletic position "lying abject on the ground" (*humi abiectus*), reconfirms its own animal nature, its own brutishness, its own "*brutus*-ness." Those who are stupid are like animals, which "nature made prone," as Sallust says.²¹⁷

As mentioned above, the adjective *brutus* originally had the meaning of "heavy": he who is *brutus* is, by nature, "low." To make a paretymological joke like those dear to the ancient poets,²¹⁸ in falling to the earth, Brutus becomes, in effect, *brutus*. His cousins Titus and Arruns, standing in the temple of the Delphic oracle, would probably not have given this another thought; they would have found it normal for one so stupid, so *brutus*. Perhaps Brutus' fall even caused them to laugh. But understanding what impression it would have given—in other words, its cultural meaning— requires some further observations.

Mala Omina

By nature, symbols tend to disappear along with the cultures that produce

---

213. Ripa 1766, V, 320ff.
214. Ter. *Heaut.* 876–77.
215. On the opposition high/low in Roman culture, see Bettini 1988b, 176ff. and 196ff.
216. The philosophical *topos* of man's uniqueness as an animal that stands erect and looks "upward" is well known: cf., e.g., Cic. *De nat. deor.* 2.65; Hor. *Sat.* 2.2.79; Ov. *Met.* 1.85ff.; Pers. *Sat.* 2.61; Vitr. 2.1.34; Aug. *De civ. Dei.* 22.24.21.
217. Sall. *Cat.* 1, *natura . . . prona finxit.*
218. See Risch 1947, 72ff., and Bettini 1972, 261ff.

them. Often, a symbol's meaning—that is, the sense-relation that it has with the historical-anthropological context—changes until it becomes incomprehensible. In our society and culture, the act of falling probably has no more meaning than that it is an embarrassing nuisance ("I fell like an idiot!"—the topical phrase is indicative) or the harbinger of an ugly bruise. If one has a sufficiently Bergsonian "anesthésie du coeur," one may brush off one's own stumbling with a laugh or show compassion for another's by rushing to lend a helping hand. Certainly, one does not feel any sense of "disturbance," nor fear anything "hidden" in the event of a fall. But things were different in the ancient world.

In the Roman world, any act of "falling" or "stumbling"—*procumbere, prolabi, pedem offendere, impingere* and so forth—provoked an immediate sense that something was wrong. Such an occurrence in fact constituted a *malum omen* ("ill omen"), presaging only misfortune.[219] When Myrrha, accompanied by her nurse, makes her midnight journey to an incestuous meeting with her father, an owl warns her three times with its "gloomy song" (*funereum carmen*) and three times the girl stumbles (*pedis offensi*), called back by this *signum* of coming misfortune.[220] Myrrha is about to commit the terrible act of incest and her stumbling signals the imminent monstrosity she is about to undertake. Ovid also recounts that Protesilaos, setting out for the Trojan War, stumbled on the threshold:[221] *pes tuus offenso limine signa dedit* ("your foot, stumbling on the threshold, gave omens"). Protesilaus should not have gone to Troy: he was destined to die there and his stumbling indicated he was committing a grave mistake. Arriving in Africa, Caesar "fell to the earth as he disembarked" (*prolapsus . . . in egressu navis*), an event that aroused great dismay among his soldiers.[222] How could they undertake an act of war with a commander who "fell to earth" just as he was entering the theater of operations? Surely some terrible disgrace awaited them. Falling, in short, "gives an omen" (*dat signum*), as Ovid says: it is a signal that whatever is about to happen or whatever is being done is bound

---

219. The model is well known and has been frequently studied: cf. Ogle 1911, 252ff., in particular on the house-door, and therefore also on stumbling on the threshold; McCartney 1920, 217ff., who rightly analyzes the phenomenon of "stumbling" in general, rather than focusing solely on the threshold of the home; Riess 1893, coll. 29ff. and 1939, coll. 350 ff.; Frazer 1931, 136ff.; Pease 1920, 486; Bömer 1980, 155. There are numerous examples: Liv. *AUC.* 5.21.16 (cf. Val. Max. 1.5.2), Camillus falling after the capture of Veii, presaging his banishment and the fall of Rome at the hands of the Gauls; [Caesar], *Bell. Hisp.* 23, etc. The relevant passages are collected by Ogle 1911 and Bömer 1980.

220. Ov. *Met.* 10.452ff.

221. Ov. *Her.* 13.87ff.

222. Suet. *Iul.* 59; Dio Cass. 45.58.3; Frontin. *Strat.* 1.12.2.

to have woeful consequences. In other words, the "meaning" of stumbling or falling is guilt, error, and imminent disgrace.

Stories of Stumbles and Falls

Negligible superstitions? Naïve folk beliefs? Long ago we stopped treating as such any cultural model that is simply different from our own. With its cultural semantics, language demonstrates that fear of falling—signaling guilt, error or disgrace—is not an insignificant *Aberglaube*, but a window on very different way of conceiving one's relationship with destiny. In fact, even a simple survey of the terms that Latin uses to denote guilt, blame and disgrace reveals that most are taken precisely from the domain of "stumbling" or "falling." *Peccare*, the most common term designating both the act of "making a mistake" and the act of "transgressing," is derived from *pedica* ("trap for the feet; fetter").[223] A man who "makes a mistake" (*peccat*) is one who "falls into a trap," one who has his feet bound by fetters.[224] The same is true of *labi*, signifying both the act of "slipping" and the act of "failing" or "making a mistake." He who "fails" (*prolabitur*) is one who "slips." Moreover, *offendere* ("to stumble") also denotes "failure" and "ruin."[225] Even *scelus*[226]—one of the key terms in the vocabulary of guilt and transgression—probably belongs to the same semantic matrix, if indeed this word is related to the Sanskrit *skhalati* ("make a false step") and Armenian *sxalim* ("make a false step, commit an error"). *Scelus* denotes both "disgrace" and, with the additional sense of personal responsibility, "guilt," or the act of transgression.[227] Here, too, a "false step" is imagined as disgraceful and transgressive. As with *peccare*, the "false step" or "pitfall" is related on the one hand with mistakes, and on the other with moral guilt or fault. The language of the Gospel reveals the same metaphor in its use of the verb *skandalizomai:* this term is normally translated (already in the *Vetus Latina*) in the sense of "to be scandalized" or "to feel scandal," but *skandalon* again refers to a "trap" in which the foot is caught.[228] So, for example, in the King James Version of the "Parable of the

---

223. Cf. Ernout-Meillet 1965, s.v.
224. Augustine (*Conf.* 10.53) perhaps did not imagine that he was reusing an ancient metaphor, when, in regard to his tormented inclination toward the beautiful, he affirmed: *ego autem haec loquens atque discernens etiam istis pulchris gressum innecto*. Augustine fell into the "trap" of the beautiful: in short, "he misstepped" (*peccabat*).
225. Cic. *Pro Clu.* 23.63 and 36.98; *Verr.* 7.131; Sen. *Ep.* 96; etc.
226. Cf. Ernout-Meillet 1965, s.v.
227. Cf. e.g., Plaut. *Most.* 563; Liv. *AUC.* 22.10.15.
228. Chantraine 1968, II, s.v.

Sower," when we read that "And these are they likewise which are sown on stony ground . . . when affliction or persecution ariseth for the word's sake, immediately they are offended (*skandalizontai*),"[229] we should imagine that they "stumble" into affliction and that for this reason they fail. In symbolic language, "stumbling" or "falling" reveals not only that an action is wrong, but also that this action is, in some way, presaging some disgrace or a negative, blameworthy event.

Culturally speaking, the fear of falling—a belief that falling represents, in its various forms, a negative *signum*—thus appears capable of motivating an entire series of linguistic metaphors. At any rate, the analogy between the two cultural spheres—that of folk beliefs in *mala omina* and that of linguistic metaphor—seems too close for their relationship to be purely coincidental. We ought instead to think of the gap between the "literal" and "metaphorical" uses of terms such as *labi, offendere* and *peccare* as actually quite narrow, since between these two poles of the figure rests Roman culture's living knowledge that a fall or stumble directly indicates that something or someone is ill-fated, that such an event is written into the hidden mechanism regulating the meaning of human action, and brutally reveals its awful inflections. When Ovid encourages us to avoid grandiosity and to "slacken the sails," he explains: "For you are worthy of crossing the space of life without stumbling and of enjoying a splendid fate" (*nam pede inoffenso spatium decurrere vitae / dignus es et fato candidiore frui*).[230] Having a favorable destiny, in other words, is the same as "not stumbling" in the journey of life.[231]

The notion that "stumbling" and "falling" is related to error and failure can be expressed in other ways than in cultural beliefs (i.e., considering it a *signum*) or by means of linguistic metaphor. A certain type of fable frequent in European and Indian folklore involves an individual who comes to know a certain special name or magical formula, who then stumbles—and, in stumbling, instantly forgets what he has learned.[232] In this way, the belief (or the metaphor) assumes the form of a narrative; the belief in "stumbling" as a foreboding *signum* becomes a story about a person who knows something important, but then stumbles . . . bringing about the failure of his or her endeavors. The underlying link is always the same. The act of falling or stumbling betokens—or indeed produces—some negative turn of events. In

---

229. Mark 4:17.

230. Ov. *Trist.* 3.4.33–34.

231. The metaphor is the same as underlies the Greek adjective *aptaistos* ("not-stumbling"): cf. Luck 1977, II, 188. On the "journey" of life and time, cf. Bettini 1988b, 144ff.

232. Thompson 1966², D 2004.5. Cf. also J 2671, J 2671.1 and 2. On the link between stumbling and forgetfulness, see Lévi-Strauss 1983a, 259.

fact, the association between "falling" and "forgetting" specifically is quite powerful in itself. Speaking about the fragility of memory, Pliny remarks, "[the memory] feels the damage caused by disease, falling and even fear" (*morborum et casus iniurias atque etiam metus sentit*).[233] Pliny goes on to tell the story of one man who forgets the alphabet after being struck by a rock; and of another who forgets his own mother, relatives and friends after falling from a high roof.

Falls and Stumbles in the Unconscious

When I said that our own culture no longer perceives the act of stumbling as a negative "sign," nor associates this occurrence with someone's error or fault, perhaps I was being too hasty. If we believe at all in the existence of the unconscious mind—that mysterious reservoir in which our personal and collective past are preserved—we easily discover there the ancient symbolism of "falling" in all its gloomy splendor. Even if one does not believe in the unconscious, nevertheless it is interesting to find that the act of falling plays a significant role in the symbolic and iconological "dictionary" that Freud so tirelessly constructed through his research. Freud's interpretation of "falling" fits very well, moreover, with what we have already seen. In *The Psychopathology of Everyday Life*,[234] Freud explains the carelessness of the woman who stumbles over a heap of stones as she is out buying a new painting for her children's room as self-punishment for an abortion that she had had some short time ago. Freud (or more accurately, the woman) relates her fall to a "sin," an error that she perceives herself to have committed. The same symbolic value of "falling" plays an important role in the case of young Hans:[235] his phobia about "falling off a horse" is related to his unconscious desire to see his father fall—that is, die.[236] Hans himself describes the desire he has for his father "to smash against a rock, nude [that is, "barefoot"]."[237] This desire is bound up with the fact that Hans has seen his friend Gmunden,[238] with whom he was similarly engaged in sexual rivalry, actually "stumble against a rock" and "fall." As may be seen, in this kind of interpretation the fatal fall, the fall viewed as a defeat and stumbling are all entwined in dynamic symbolic production. Freud analyzes one of his

---

233. Plin. *Nat. hist.* 7.90.
234. Freud 1970, 215ff.
235. Freud 1972b, 514ff.
236. Freud 1972b, 515.
237. Freud 1972b, 514.
238. Freud 1972b, 521 and 523ff.

own dreams in a similar way, in *Dream and Telepathy*:[239] his son has gone to war and in a dream he sees his son standing on a wharf, wearing not his military uniform but a ski suit, the same he had been wearing when he had had a skiing accident. The young man stands, moreover, on a footstool—an object that Freud closely associates with falling from his own memories of infancy. Freud interprets this dream as signifying that his son had been killed in war. In Freudian dream interpretation, the theme of "falling" thus reclaims all its ominous meaning.

Brutus and Caesar

But let us return, finally, to Brutus. Falling to earth, or stumbling, the hero makes manifest—in the outward "envelope" of that action—precisely the opposite of what is about to happen. At that moment, by kissing the earth, he gains supreme power, yet gives the impression that this event is inauspicious. The moment is a crucial one—it concerns who will be the king of Rome—and Brutus falls. And yet his superior intelligence permits him to transform a moment of disgrace and error—*prolabi, peccare, scelus*—into one of great fortune. Earlier, through his offering to the Delphic god, Brutus had symbolized himself as a "container" of wood that was not only "stupid" but also "ill-omened" (*infelix*). The symbolic structure of the two actions is identical.

As mentioned above, Caesar slips and falls to earth when he disembarks in Africa—a *malum omen* at a crucial moment that creates panic among his soldiers. Caesar cleverly recovers the situation, however: "turning the omen to good, he said: 'I hold you, Africa'" (*verso ad melius omine 'teneo te' inquit 'Africa'*).[240] In Frontinus' version of the story,[241] Caesar says not "Africa" but "mother earth" (*terra mater*), while in Dio Cassius he actually seizes hold of and kisses the earth, shouting: "I have you, Africa!"[242] The situation should be familiar to us—at a crucial moment, someone "stumbling" and then suddenly "holding" the earth (not to mention the references to "mother earth" and a "kiss" given to her). To neutralize the *malum omen* signified by his stumble, Caesar adopts the behavior of Brutus, applying the paradigm of someone who, in the act of falling (and therefore producing an evil omen),

---

239. Freud 1977b, 384.
240. Suet. *Iul.* 59, Cf. Gugel 1970, 5ff., who compares Caesar's behavior with his famous contempt for omens. Perhaps it would be better to explore the link between Caesar and the "earth," which appears also in his incestuous dream (Suet. *Iul.* 7): cf. Ogilvie 1965, 218.
241. Frontin. *Strat.* 1.21.2.
242. Dio Cass. 42.58.3.

in fact establishes for himself a privileged relationship with the earth, the "mother of all men."[243]

Caesar's act provides a concrete example of how a paradigm offered by myth may function in "real" life in the form of a repetition. It is not important whether the mythic paradigm influenced Caesar's actual behavior in ingeniously (and quickly) adapting a traditional schema to the moment of his unfortunate stumbling, or the writer in recounting or readapting the story. The fact remains that this episode from Brutus' story had an important place within Roman culture, also from the perspective of its fortune: because it was constructed with good, authentic materials, this episode persisted in not only Caesar's, but also Roman society's imagination.

The Narrator's Nostalgia

We have reached the end of our discussion—not, however, without a certain feeling of nostalgia and even some regret for having spoken so long about a story we know so little about. Not only because of the trouble that the writer—and the reader—has taken, but perhaps above all because this is most immediate and incontrovertible proof of the magnitude of our loss. Looking back at this point, we see that we have lost a uniquely *Roman* way of telling stories—one similar in ways to that evoked so often above in our attempt to render its likeness from European folklore, from Saxo Grammaticus and so forth. They are simple stories, certainly. But they are also stories full of meaning, stories in which we see coalesce a set of patterns that, though basic and similar to so many others, is still capable of natural and profound symbolic expression. These plots, motifs and symbols are in fact the product of an ancient process, all that remains of the countless occasions of storytelling consumed in the arc of time and distance—at least until a certain motif, a particular symbol triumphs because of its richness and its efficacy, giving rise to new stories. But we have lost this Roman "telling."

Recollecting the conclusions of the so-called "Indianist" theory of the origin and diffusion of the fable, Joseph Bédier once observed that classical antiquity appears not to have known most of the fables that were so widely circulated in the Middle Ages.[244] The observation is as interesting as it is disconcerting. Did the ancient world not have fables? The answer must certainly be "no." Roman society had its folktales, as we have seen; it is only that this mode of narration was not deemed worthy of transmission, of being

---

243. It is very likely that this is a typical schema. Cf. Frontin. *Strat.* 1.21.1, where a similar anecdote is attributed to Scipio.
244. Bedier 1893, 253ff.

enshrined into literature. For this reason, Roman folk-telling vanished with the words and with the "*ouïdire*" of those who practiced it. We have other Roman ways of telling stories—love literature, historiography, epic and so forth. These are inarguably beautiful. But we no longer possess the popular tradition of storytelling—and that is why we have been compelled to seek it out (not without some difficulty!) embedded in the so-called "best" texts (the only ones that have been transmitted to us), like small fossil shells, far from the sea.

PART 2

Social Practices

THREE

Mos, Mores and *Mos Maiorum*
The Invention of Morality in Roman Culture

> *To reconcile ourselves to usages and customs so very opposite to our own, is a task too difficult for the generality of mankind.*
>
> —R. Wood, An Essay on the Original Genius of Homer. *1769*

One of the problems that our society has most struggled with, particularly in recent decades, is that of tolerance—the willingness to recognize that the manners and morals of "others" should not be automatically labeled as wrong, irrational or (worse still) unnatural, for the simple reason that they are different than "ours." Others may live their lives in a manner quite unlike our own—eating different foods, with different sexual habits, professing a different religion (or even none at all) and so on. But this does not imply that "we" are right and "they" are wrong (nor, of course, that they are right and we are wrong). One of the most typical manifestations of intolerance is what has long gone by the name of "ethnocentrism" or the conviction that the traditions of the society to which one belongs are inherently better than those practiced by other communities.[1] If we were to catalog here all the disasters and injustices that prejudiced intolerance of the Other has ever produced (and still continues to produce), the list would be very long indeed. Of course, intolerance and ethnocentrism do not occur exclusively in the form of violence and as part of the great historic conflicts that we all know. Bigotry is in fact a very devious kind of evil that can affect even those

---

1. On ethnocentrism, see the sensible definitions given by Taguieff 1999, 113–14.

who are otherwise quite open-minded, creeping up on them when they least expect it. For example, it is a form of intolerance to brand the habit of drinking herbal tea, very widespread among Californians, as "stupid" simply because any number of outstanding kinds of coffee may be found in the world. We may find bizarre what others prefer as an after-dinner drink, but why define such a custom as "stupid" when compared with that of drinking coffee?

Michel de Montaigne's "Thousand Manners of Life"

Intolerance and ethnocentrism are based on the pathological conviction that one's own customs—"our" customs, those of the group with which one identifies—are always better than those observed by "others." We might put it like this: Intolerance and ethnocentrism are the products of an excess of cultural identity, of the overvaluation of the traditions that define "us" (or better, what we say or believe define "us"). An excess of cultural identity is obviously a kind of illness, an illness that many factors may precipitate simultaneously: cultural narrow-mindedness, naiveté, fear, egotism, inadequate education and so forth. Obviously, I am not proposing to investigate here all the things that can lead to the overvaluation of one's own customs.[2] But we can say that one of the most effective cures for this illness is a kind of "reversal therapy"—the dedicated practice of systematically upsetting one's own point of view by taking on that of the Other and of observing one's self through another's eyes. One of the most successful practitioners of this method actually happens to have been one of the greatest thinkers of whom sixteenth-century Europe could boast: Michel de Montaigne.

In an essay very significantly entitled *De la coustume* ("On Custom"), Montaigne wrote: "Barbarians are no more a wonder to us, than we are to them."[3] Montaigne took a very ancient category of thought that opposes the "barbarians"—i.e., those who are different from us, "others"—to the group to which the subject belongs, only to immediately turn it on its head. Montaigne looks at himself ("us") through the eyes of the so-called

---

2. The distinction between excess of group-identity on one hand and necessary group-identification on the other is quite difficult: probably it is a distinction that can be more easily employed in each instance on the plan of concrete behaviors. Lévi-Strauss (1983b, 21–48) has insisted on the necessity of diversity between cultures as a method of conservation and differentiation. For a discussion of this "differentialist" position, cf. Taguieff 1999, 43–47 and 103. See also the considerations of Remotti 1996, 96ff.

3. The translations given here are those of Charles Cotton's edition of 1685 (Montaigne 1952, 44). All subsequent quotations from Cotton's translation will be cited by page number in the text, unless otherwised noted.

barbarians, and the result is this: If the barbarians appear strange to us, then we must also appear strange to the barbarians. It appears that "skeptical Montaigne," as Rousseau called him, is precisely the person to consult when we risk becoming too convinced of our own cultural identity and of the "correctness" of our own traditions. Let us read on then, but this time from Montaigne's essay "Of Cannibals":

> [E]very one gives the title of barbarism to everything that is not in use in his own country, as, indeed, we have no other level of truth and reason than the example and idea of the opinions and customs of the place wherein we live (93).

The force of *coustume*—"custom"—is tremendous.

> The principal effect of its power is, so to seize and ensnare us, that it is hardly in us to disengage ourselves from its gripe . . . from whence it comes to pass, that whatever is off the hinges of custom, is believed to be also off the hinges of reason (46).

Montaigne nevertheless succeeds in freeing himself from its grip.

> A French gentleman was always wont to blow his nose with his fingers (a thing very much against our fashion), and he justifying himself for so doing . . . asked me, what privilege this filthy excrement had, that we must carry about us a fine handkerchief to receive it, and, which was more, afterwards to lap it carefully up, and carry it all day about in our pockets, which, he said, could not but be much more nauseous and offensive, than to see it thrown away (44).

Montaigne did not, however, flee in disgust from the presence of that bizarre gentleman: quite the opposite.

> I found that what he said was not altogether without reason, and by being frequently in his company, that slovenly action of his was at last grown familiar to me; which nevertheless we make a face at, when we hear it reported of another country (44).

Montaigne was truly open-minded. When he traveled, he did so always "very much sated with our own fashions; I do not look for Gascons in Sicily; I have left enough of them at home; I rather seek for Greeks and Persians" (478). He was broadminded enough to declare that a certain love poem current among the natives of New Antarctica—what today we call Brazil—not only did not seem "barbaric" to him (and this in itself is very praiseworthy) but was in fact "perfectly Anacreontic" (97). This is perhaps going too far—but still we have to admire Montaigne for the explicit declaration that he made in the introduction to his essay "Of Cato the Younger":

> Though I be engaged to one forme, I do not tie the world unto it, as every man doth. And I beleeve and conceive a thousand manners of life.[4]

When one begins to talk about Montaigne, there is always the risk of not being able to stop.

> And, also, in the subject of which I treat, our manners and motions, testimonies and instances; how fabulous soever, provided they are possible, serve as well as the true; whether they have really happened or no, at Rome or Paris, to John or Peter, 'tis still within the verge of human capacity, which serves me to good use.... There are authors whose only end and design it is to give an account of things that have happened; mine, if I could arrive unto it, should be to deliver of what may happen (41).

A man capable of imagining and of conceiving "a thousand manners of life," an author interested more in speaking of "what may happen" than in giving "an account of things that have happened," Montaigne is probably the first *anthropologist* of the Western tradition.[5] Because of this he had such interest in understanding customs, his own and those of others.

Herodotus: Comparing *Nomoi*

Before continuing on to the second part of our study, along the path that eventually leads to these extraordinary words of Montaigne, we ought to stop and linger on at least two ancient texts. The first is that well-known episode of Herodotus' *Histories* in which the theme of "reflecting on customs" has its founding moment, as it were:

> If one made a proposal to all the men in the world, inviting them to choose what were the best customs (*nomoi*) of all, after considering the question for

---

4. The translation here is that of Florio's 1603 edition of Montaigne's essays.
5. On the oscillations internal to Montaigne's thought between cultural relativism and faith in the existence of a common basis for "reason," see above all Todorov 1989, 51–64; Remotti 1990, 56–78.

a minute each one would choose his own: everyone one is that convinced of the superiority of his own customs (*nomoi*) over all the rest. . . . And that all men are of this same opinion as far as concerns customs (*nomoi*) may be deduced from many facts, and in particular from this. During his long reign, Darius summoned the Greeks who were at his court and asked them for what price they would have agreed to eat their own dead relatives. They declared that they would do such a thing for no price whatsoever. Darius then summoned to his palace those Indians who are known as the Callatiae, who eat their parents. And with the Greeks present, who followed the proceedings by means of an interpreter, he asked the Callatiae for what price they would have agreed to cremate their dead parents. And these begged him with great shouts not to utter such impieties. Such is the force of tradition in these cases, and it seems to me that Pindar very rightly wrote "custom is the queen of all things" (*nomos pantōn basileus*).[6]

In both instances, Darius' questioning provokes a horrified refusal: for no price would the Greeks ever be disposed to do what the Callatiae do, and for no price would the Callatiae ever be disposed to do what the Greeks do. According to Herodotus, Darius' experiment confirmed his theory that all men consider their own customs (*nomoi*)—even those that seem the most bizarre—the best among all possible or imaginable traditions. At least at first glance, then, this text presents us with evidence not of the tolerance for others' customs, but, on the contrary, of the overvaluation of one's own. The Greeks show themselves to be extremely ethnocentric in this case and the Callatiae likewise. In fact, each of the participants in the experiment maintains the conviction that his customs are better than those of the other, and in one case they are actually called "impious." What seems to emerge from Herodotus' reflections is, in the first place, the impossibility of divesting one's self of one's own customs.[7] However, this is true only if one alternately takes on the point of view of the participants in Darius' experiment: first, that of the Greek, and second, that of the Callatiae. But what happens if a third point of view on the situation is assumed, that of an observer who is neither Greek nor Indian? A story is written to be read by someone, of course: what counts, then, are not so much the feelings or the opinions expressed by the actors within a narrative, as those reactions that the narrative is supposed to provoke in the external reader or addressee. We are particularly fortunate, then, since the narrative itself already offers an internal

---

6. Her. *Hist.* 3.38.3–4; the text of Herodotus is cited briefly by Montaigne in his essay *On Custom*. On the importance of this Herodotean text for the theme of reflections on customs, see the excellent discussion of Remotti 1990, 52–55.

7. Her. *Hist.* 3.38.3–4

"addressee": Darius, the Persian observer who organizes this confrontation of opinions, with whom the external reader can easily identify for the purpose of achieving a point of view external to the text.

Let us try to imagine what Darius (and along with him the reader of Herodotus) might have thought after hearing the opinions of the two interviewees. Darius could conclude not only that each community considers its own customs better than those of others, as Herodotus declares, but at the same time that these customs (*nomoi*) are also quite relative, since each rejected those of the other out of hand with exactly the same feeling of revulsion. If the Greeks reject the customs of the Callatiae and the Callatiae reject those of the Greeks, could it not be true that neither the Callatiae nor the Greeks are "right" absolutely? If Darius had wanted to go further in his thinking, he could have reached the (perhaps melancholy) conclusion that even his own customs—those that he himself shared—were equally relative. At the heart of Darius' experiment, then, there is also a good bit of skepticism: but it is this attitude that permits him to undertake such an evenhanded comparison.

We have before us, therefore, the paradox of a text that, when it emphasizes the absolute force of traditions, simultaneously opens the door to a relativistic consideration of those same traditions. Herodotus' thought is quite complex,[8] as indeed generally happens when the problem of cultural identity is at issue.[9] In laying bare the almost tyrannical sway that traditions hold over the members of a community, Darius' experiment reveals that they are relative in nature: they can be placed on the same level. Understood in this way, the Herodotean text prefigures the attitude that, more than two thousand years later, Melville Herskovits would officially term "cultural relativism"[10]—a commitment to judge others' customs not on the basis of

---

8. It is seen also in the way that the text of Pindar (*nomos pantōn basileus*, "custom is the queen of all things," fr. 169 Snell-Mähler) is recontextualized. Pindar in fact uses this maxim to justify the use of violence for asserting the Hellenic *nomos* over the barbarisms of others, as Hercules had done to the damage of Gerion and the Thracian Diomedes. Herodotus, however, does not present the Hellenic *nomos* at all as an absolute value, but—at least in terms of the "force" exercised on the individual community—recognizes the parity of the Hellenic *nomos* with that of the Indians. Cf. the discussion of Moggi 1988, 51–76, esp. 55–56 and nn. 16 and 19.

9. Taguieff (1999, 108) discusses the "dilemma" of anti-racism: is it a duty to safeguard "differences" at all costs, to preserve diversity between human cultures, or is it a duty of racial mixing to realize the unity of the human race?

10. Herskovits 1948. As is known, the theory of cultural relativism was developed by Herskovits on the basis of the critique of ethnocentrism undertaken by his teacher Franz Boas, as well as of Ruth Benedict's studies on "visions of the world" (or "patterns of culture"). It needs to be said, however, that culture relativism is a position that, though presenting itself as indisputably noble, nevertheless risks posing problems of no less importance than those it called upon to solve. In 1947, the United Nations nominated a Commission on Human Rights with the task of elaborating an international code capable of preventing future crimes like those committed by Nazism. Herskovits addressed

the observer's own parameters, but of those defined by the community under consideration. In Darius' experiment, cultural relativism and respect for differences go hand in hand: If his skepticism permits him to treat customs relativistically—depriving them of any pretension of being absolute for all men—the "tyranny" that traditions exercise over a community guarantees the respect necessary for safeguarding such differences.[11]

Cornelius Nepos: Traditionalist Relativism

Long before Herskovits, an explicit declaration of this "relativistic" principle in judging customs and cultures could be found in a Roman author who generally does not get much credit, unless it is for his easy Latin style appropriate for beginning students: Cornelius Nepos. In the preface to his work on famous foreign generals, he too follows the path of comparison, writing:

> I know very well, Atticus, that I will have numerous critics who judge the style of my writing history light and inadequate for great men, given that you can read here, for example, who was Epaminondas' music teacher or that among his many fine qualities was also skill in dancing and his mastery of flute-playing. But they will probably be people who, ignorant of Greek culture, will believe that they should only approve what conforms to their own customs (*mores*). When they learn, however, that the criterion for judging what is good and decent or reprehensible (*honesta atque turpia*) is not the same for everyone and that each thing has to be judged according to the traditions of its own ancestors (*omnia maiorum institutis iudicari*),[12] they will not be surprised that in treating the virtue of the Greeks I conformed with their customs (*mores*). It was not a shameful thing for Cimon, one of the greatest Athenians, to take his maternal cousin for a wife, because

---

this Commission to ask that the principles of cultural relativism be inserted into the list of such rights, but his proposal was refused, on the argument that cultural relativism risked rendering vain the very proposals of the commission, since, at least theoretically, it would be possible to affirm that even the crimes perpetrated by a certain community on another community could be judged not on the basis of absolute parameters, but on the basis of parameters internal to the culture of that community. In other words, cultural relativism is a form of tolerance that at every moment risks having to accept the precise opposite, i.e., intolerance (cf. Tullio Altan 1983, 70ff.).

11. From a certain point of view, Herodotus seems to anticipate the position of the "right to difference," the rejection of ethnocentrism that is based not on an idea of the universalism of the human race, but, on the contrary, on respect for the plurality of communities and identities; cf. Taguieff 1999, 104–7.

12. Nep. *De excell. duc.*, pr. 1ff. Similar considerations, even if in a slightly more scholastic mode, can be found in the anonymous Sophistic essay entitled *Dissoi Logoi*, in Diels and Kranz 1969, II, 408f., 90, 29ff.

his own fellow citizens followed that same custom, while according to our laws that would be cause for scandal. On Crete it was a sign of distinction for young men to be the lovers of many men. In Sparta, there is no widow too noble to dedicate herself to prostitution for financial gain. And again, in all of Greece it is a mark of great honor to be proclaimed victor in the Olympic Games. To set foot on stage or to act in popular spectacles was not considered dishonorable for anyone: all things that, for us, are in part defamatory, part humiliating, and part contrary to decent behavior. Instead, many things deemed quite reasonable by our customs are not so for them. What Roman would ever hesitate to take his wife to a banquet? Or what matron would abstain from showing herself in the atrium of her home or from participating in society? In Greece, however, things are different. A woman is not permitted to see visitors, unless they are her relatives and she keeps herself locked up in the most inner part of the house, called the *gynaceum*, where none but a close relative is permitted to enter.

Here, Nepos unambiguously declares that in judging cultures there is no place for the conviction that one's own customs are "right," to the exclusion of all others. Rather than hastening to the conclusion that Cimon entered into an incestuous marriage, the proper thing to do is to discover if such a marriage was considered acceptable and legitimate according to the *instituta maiorum* of the Athenians themselves. Others' customs should be evaluated only on the basis of parameters *internal* to the culture—that is, on the basis of the *instituta maiorum* that serve as the norm for the behavior of the "others" and not on the basis of what "we" consider right. This is nothing other than an unequivocal rejection of ethnocentrism and a declaration of cultural relativism.

To show that customs are relative, Nepos hits upon a very clever strategy: he catalogs a series of behaviors that Roman citizens could not but reject—passive homosexuality practiced by free youths, participation in sports activities, acting on stage and so forth—declaring that among the Greeks, all these behaviors are not only permissible, but in fact in certain cases actually honorable. But he does not stop there. Nepos has the courage to carry his relativistic rationale to its conclusion and to overturn his own point of view entirely, just as many centuries later Montaigne would invite his readers to do. In fact, Nepos explicitly suggests looking at the Roman *mores* that he himself shares through others' (that is, Greek) eyes:

> Many things deemed quite reasonable by our customs are not so for them. What Roman would ever hesitate to take his wife to a banquet? . . . In Greece, however, things are different.

Chapter 3. Mos, Mores *and* Mos Maiorum

Here, even Roman *mores* are treated relativistically, like those of the Greeks: "our" customs may appear to "them" just as unseemly as "theirs" appear to "us"—so much so indeed that the Greeks would by no means approve of "our" women and the way in which "we" permit them to behave. If Montaigne said, "the barbarians are no more a wonder to us, than we are to them; nor with any more reason," Nepos could have said, "the Greeks are no more a wonder to us, than we Romans are to them; nor with any more reason."

There is something we need to stress here, however. The example of possible Roman impropriety cited by Nepos—the behavior of "our" women—is only one, while those that he cites of the Greeks are many, as we have seen. And in the end the example that he chooses is not even all that terribly unbecoming. "Certainly," a Roman reader could have objected, "perhaps we do give our women a little too much liberty; but do you really mean to compare us with them, when they practice passive homosexuality, when they let their widows prostitute themselves, when they wrestle nude and recite on the stage . . . ?" In other words, even in a moment of the greatest intellectual honesty, when trying to relativize things to the point that the absolute rightness of one's own customs is cast into doubt, there is always the risk of giving in to the prejudice that "we" are better than "others." Ethnocentrism can creep in even by simply reducing the number of "our" behaviors that "others" may find unseemly or by choosing as an example one of "our" behaviors that, as uncouth as it may seem in the eyes of others, can never be as improper as those of the "others" in our eyes. The fact is that viewing one's own customs in a relativistic way is extraordinarily difficult. As Montaigne wrote, the force of custom is so powerful that it is capable "so to seize and ensnare us, that it is hardly in us to disengage ourselves from its gripe."

Nepos' text prompts a further consideration, which will help us make the transition to the next section of this chapter. The process that brings Nepos to his rejection of ethnocentrism and his declaration of cultural relativism—that every culture should be judged according to its own internal parameters and not according to external *mores*—involves a resolute affirmation of the central position of *instituta maiorum* in any society. The *turpia atque honesta,* says Nepos—i.e., what is good and what is bad—*omnia maiorum institutis iudicari.* In other words, Nepos' cultural relativism and his idea of tolerance derive as a logical and final consequence of the concept of tradition. For Nepos, the "traditions of the ancestors" are so important and so worthy of respect that even those of others must be treated with great deference. He therefore begins from a typically Roman cultural model: the importance of the *mos maiorum* (or the *mores atque instituta maiorum*) in defining collective behavior. We will have to speak of this at greater length below.[13] Nepos is so respectful of this cultural model, however, that he considers sacred not only Roman *instituta maiorum,* but also those of other groups. Nepos, in short, comes to reject ethnocentrism and to avow a universal right to be different, by making an appeal to what is actually extremely "traditional." No doubt, this conclusion is rather surprising—even if it is pleasantly surprising—since an overvaluation of the customs of the ancestors and of the particular group identity that derives from them is usually found in the company of attitudes that can be defined as ethnocentric rather than relativistic (and that are anything but tolerant, at any rate). It is enough to think of the notorious Umbricius of Juvenal's third satire,[14] or of any number of modern "local" movements that, in reclaiming traditional customs (dialects, food, festivals, proverbs and so on) also demonstrate a marked intolerance for the customs of other communities. Nepos provides evidence of the fact that, at least at the intellectual level, an overvaluation of the concept of "tradition"—i.e., of the *mores atque instituta maiorum*—as a model for behavior is not necessarily a symptom of ethnocentrism or of intolerance.

However, such an attitude has implications that we cannot leave unmentioned. When Nepos bases his entire relativistic theory on the centrality of the *instituta maiorum,* he shelters "other" cultures from ethnocentrism, certainly; but at the same time, he effectively protects "his own" *instituta maiorum* (i.e., those of the Romans). If the *instituta maiorum* are such an authoritative model of behavior as to guarantee respect even for some other culture's *mores* that the Romans would never accept, how could one ever dare to bring under discussion "our" *instituta maiorum,* upon which Roman identity is founded? Nepos' cultural relativism thus becomes a formidable instrument for curtailing internal attempts to introduce *mores* incompatible with "our" traditional ones. Let the Greeks do what they like, since they do it in respect of their own *instituta maiorum;* by the same token, let no Roman ever think of introducing into "our" society any *mores novi,*[15] customs that do not respect the *instituta* of our ancestors. Nepos' brand of cultural relativism holds for others' societies (and this is already a lot, of course): but for the same reason it does not and cannot ever hold for his own.

---

13. Cf. below, 97–104.
14. Juv. *Sat.* 3.58ff.
15. Cf., e.g., expressions like that of Cic. *Manil.* 9.60.2, *at enim ne quid novi fiat contra exempla atque instituta maiorum.*

Mores at Rome

In our analysis of Nepos' text, one of the words we have come across most frequently is *mos*. It is the *mores* that Nepos treats relativistically in order to reject ethnocentrism. Let us see, then, what is understood by *mos* and by *mores* in the culture to which Nepos belongs: Roman culture, of course.[16]

The Varronian Phenomenology of Mos

We may begin with ancient definitions of *mos*. As Festus tells us, *mos est institutum patrium, id est memoria veterum pertinens maxime ad religiones caerimoniasque antiquorum* ("*Mos* is an institution that we receive from our forefathers, i.e., the memory of tradition that above all regards the religion and the cult practices of the ancients").[17] Later, Isidore would say more or less the same thing: *mos est vetustate probata consuetudo, sive lex non scripta . . . mos autem longa consuetudo est de moribus tracta tantundem* ("*Mos* is a habit proved by its longevity, or an unwritten law . . . *mos* is a long habit, equally taken from the *mores*").[18] As we can see, both definitions orient *mos* squarely in the direction of "antiquity" (*memoria veterum, vetustate probata consuetudo*) and of "habit" (*mos autem longa consuetudo est*).

The most interesting considerations of *mos* belong to Varro, however. He gives us not only a definition of what this meant for him, but also a description of the way in which *mores* are formed and established—and this gives us a very interesting glimpse at the way in which Roman culture internally interpreted the anthropological value of *mores*. According to Servius, Varro defined *mos* as follows: *Varro vult morem esse communem consensum omnium simul habitantium, qui inveteratus consuetudinem facit* ("Varro wants *mos* to be the consensus of all those who live together: once this is established in time, it creates a habit").[19] Ulpian no doubt was thinking of Varro when he asserted that *mores sunt tacitus consensus populi longa consuetudine inveteratus* ("The *mores* are the tacit consent of the populace, which has been consolidated with time through long habit").[20] For a *mos* to be defined in this way, it needs to satisfy two prerequisites: first, that it be shared by a community

---

16. On *mos* and *mores*, see also the well-known article Dumézil 1954, 139ff. (not particularly useful, however, in the perspective that interests us here). On the etymology of the word, see Flobert 1973, 567ff. (adopting that of Curtius, i.e., from **me-*, "to measure").
17. Fest. *De verb. sign.* 146.3 Lindsay.
18. Isid. *Etym.* 5.3.2.
19. Serv. in *Aen.* 7.601.
20. Ulp. *Reg.* 1.4.

of people who "agree" on this *mos*, and second, that it be consolidated in time. The characteristic of "antiquity" seen in the preceding definition is now joined by that of "popular consensus." *Consensus* is a cultural model to which frequent recourse is had in Latin texts to reinforce the foundation or the legitimacy of a judgment, attitude, behavior, and so on. It is needless to cite examples.[21] But from Macrobius we learn some further information about Varro's thinking on *mos*, perhaps even more interesting than what we have already seen. Macrobius tells us that in his *Logistoricus de Moribus*, Varro states that *morem esse in iudicio animi, quem sequi debeat consuetudo* ("*mos* consists in a judgment of the spirit, and habit must follow it").[22] In this case, too, the importance of *consuetudo* is reaffirmed, as is the slow consolidation of *mos* along the temporal axis. But in this definition there is something more: *mos* is specifically defined here as something that consists in *iudicium animi*—i.e., in an interior disposition that is consolidated as a true and proper *mos* only when it is acknowledged as a *consuetudo* and affirmed as such. Here is Macrobius' paraphrase of the Varronian formulation: *mos ergo praecessit et cultus moris secutus est, quod est consuetudo* ("so *mos* came first and the observance of the *mos* followed, which corresponds to habit").[23] On its own, a *mos* is a disposition that depends on a *iudicium animi*, and so is not yet sufficient: to truly become a collective practice, there needs also to be *cultus moris*, the practice and the social acceptance of the *mos* that transforms it into a *consuetudo*.

This Varronian phenomenology of *mos* is extremely interesting. In fact, we could advance the hypothesis that Varro was able to formulate it so clearly because, besides being an author, philosopher, and antiquarian, he was also a linguist—and so he saw the possibility of transferring to the sphere of "customs"—the social creation *par excellence*—the experience that he had had considering another type of social creation: *sermo*. In fact, in the theoretical framework of his treatise *De Lingua Latina*, Varro attributes great importance to the notion of *consuetudo*.[24] In particular,[25] he creates an explicit distinction between the *consuetudo* of an individual and that of the

---

21. Cf. expressions like Liv. *AUC.* 8.35.1, *stupentes tribunos . . . liberavit onere consensus populi Romani;* Plin. *Nat. hist.* 14.72, *nec negaverim et alia [vina] digna esse fama, sed de quibus consensus aevi iudicaverit haec sunt;* Cic. *Tusc. disp.* 1.35 claims even that the *consensus* of all men corresponds to 'naturalness': *quodsi omnium consensus naturae vox est, omnesque qui ubique sunt consentiunt esse aliquid . . . nobis quoque idem existimandum est.* It is worth recalling, too, that the merits of Scipio Barbatus' son, consul in 259 B.C.E., were also defined through the model of the generalized *consensus* in the funeral oration dedicated to him (*CIL* I, 2 2.9): *honc oino ploirume consentiunt R[omane] / duonoro optumo fuisse viro / Luciom Scipione.*
22. Macr. *Sat.* 3.8.9ff. = Var. *Log.* fr. 74 Bolisani.
23. Macr. *Sat.* 3.8.12.
24. Cf., e.g., Collart 1954, 153ff.
25. Var. *Ling. Lat.* 9.2ff.

Chapter 3. Mos, Mores *and* Mos Maiorum

collective (*alia enim consuetudo populi universi, alia singulorum* ["one thing is the way of behaving of an entire populace, another entirely is that of individuals"]), establishing a hierarchy in determining linguistic usage (*in loquendo, in dicendo*): *populus enim in sua potestate, singuli illius* ("[in speaking] the populace is in its own power, but individuals are in the power of the people"); and later, *ego populi consuetudinis non sum ut dominus, at ille meae est* ("I am not, so to speak, the master of the people's habit, but the general population is of mine"). As in the case of *mos*, so in the case of language Varro distinguishes the individual dimension from the collective dimension, giving the latter predominance over the former. It is interesting that the notion of *consensus communis*, which we have seen used in the sphere of *mos*, is employed by Varro also in his capacity as a linguist, again in juxtaposition to the sphere of individual decision making. Speaking of the declension of substantives, he distinguishes two aspects of the problem: one individual, and one collective.[26] On one hand, there exists the possibility of forming substantives on the basis of individual choice, as happens with the naming of slaves, for example. If three different people have each bought a slave in *Ephesus* in *Ionia* from a merchant named *Artemidorus*, each can decide to call his own slave *Artemas* or *Ion* or *Ephesius*. On the other hand, there is the obligation to decline those names according to a scheme that does not depend on the individual's choice, but on a collective choice: in the genitive case, each one of the slave buyers is constrained to decline *huius Artemidori, huius Ionis, huius Ephesi* and so on in all cases, regardless of his own wishes. In this regard, Varro comments that *declinationem naturalem dico quae non a singulorum oritur voluntate, sed a communi consensus* ("I define 'natural declination' as that which arises not from individual will, but from common consensus"). In the determination of linguistic forms, too, then, Varro contrasts the dimension of individual will to that of the *consensus*, the agreement of the community in establishing a certain linguistic usage. *Mos* and speech appear to be social products regulated by analogous paradigms: on one hand, the *voluntas* or *consuetudo* of the individual, and on the other, the *consuetudo populi* and the *consensus communis* that impose themselves on the former. Quintilian, reflecting on the importance of *consuetudo* as the *certissima loquendi magistra* ("the surest guide by far in speaking"), says also that *consuetudinem sermonis vocabo consensum eruditorum, sicut vivendi consensum bonorum* ("I will define custom in speech as the consensus of educated men, just as custom in living [or, in *mores*] I define as the consensus of good men").[27] A practitioner of the science of language knows that "in

---

26. Var. *Ling. Lat.* 8.21ff.
27. Quint. *Inst. orat.* 1.5.3; 45.

living" the community follows paradigms similar to those that it follows in communicating: *consuetudo, consensus. Mos* and speech have no other foundation than social *consensus,* and the *consuetudo* derived from this *consensus* imposes itself on both the linguistic and moral behavior of individuals.

We can now return to the phenomenology of *mos*. The distinction that Varro makes between *mos* understood as an individual's interior disposition and its reception in the form of a *consuetudo* by means of a collective *consensus,* is actually an extremely important development. Alone, *mos* is purely an individual choice. In this light, it is interesting to note that the Varronian definition of *mos* as something consisting *in iudicio animi* echoes Terence's famous saying, *quot homines tot sententiae, suos cuique mos* ("there are as many opinions as there are men: each has his own *mos*").[28] The explicit equivalence that Terence establishes between *mos* on one side and *sententia* on the other confirms the vision of *mos* as something residing *in iudicio animi*. Actually, the fact that Terence's expression is clearly "proverbial" indicates that this vision of *mos* is something that belongs to the cultural at large.[29] In the same vein as *mos* referring simply to an individual's attitude, we may also list the numerous expressions like *meo more, tuo more, suo more, alieno more* and so on,[30] that are used to indicate the multiplicity of personal "opinions" and behaviors that may appear in the field of *mores*. These are individual choices that, precisely for this reason, are not considered shared by the collective. For this to occur, one must be accepted by the public *consensus* and then consolidated in time. In some cases, in fact, we are fortunate to be able to see this transition from personal to collective behavior—i.e., the creation of a new custom via the acceptance of a personal choice by the public *consensus*—described explicitly. Pliny, for example, recounts:

> Caesarem dictatorem post unum ancipitem vehiculi casum ferunt semper, ut primum consedisset, id quod plerosque nunc facere scimus, carmine ter repetito securitatem itinerum aucupari solitum.[31]

> The dictator Caesar, after a particularly serious fall from a chariot, was accustomed to repeat a magical formula three times before getting onto a chariot, in order to guarantee that the trip would be favorable: something that now, we know, a great part of the population also does.

---

28. Ter. *Phor.* 454.
29. Cf. Otto 1890, 166.
30. *TLL* VIII, 1526, 30ff.
31. Plin. *Nat. hist.* 28.21.

Caesar's example set a fashion,—or to say it as a Roman might, Caesar was the *auctor* of a new *mos,* and the prestige and authority that emanated from his person encouraged its adoption by others.[32] What had originally been an individual choice motivated by a personal misfortune had become a widespread behavior by Pliny's own time. Thinking back to the Varronian definition, we might say that the personal *iudicium animi* of Caesar, who was accustomed to touch wood when he mounted a chariot, gave rise to a widespread *consuetudo,* transforming his individual behavior into a collective *mos.*

The term *mos* can cover not one, but two very different cultural dimensions, then: one personal and the other collective. In the first case, *mos* derives from a simple *iudicium animi* or is an individual *sententia;* in the second case, *mos* appears instead in the form of a *consuetudo,* a *mos* shared by a certain community on the basis of a *consensus* that has become *inveteratus* with time. Needless to say, the collective dimension of *mos*—that which represents and identifies a certain "group"—is what interests us here, rather than the individual dimension of *mos.* Therefore, we will occupy ourselves essentially with this, using the Varronian definition as a point of departure for a wider phenomenology of *mos* and of *mores* in Roman culture.

Mos *and* Fas

A collective *mos* is a decision taken by a group that reaches a *consensus* on a certain behavior. This same group, then, has the capacity to consolidate this behavior in time, transforming it into a *mos* or into *mores.* This means that this process is not perceived as something absolute that imposes itself by its very nature. Quite the contrary. *Mores* are the result of collective agreement over something depending initially on a *iudicium animi,* and this agreement must then pass the test of time. In this sense, *mos* appears profoundly different from that which the Romans define as *fas* ("[divine] speech"),[33] such as that expressed in *fatum* ("destiny")—an impersonal kind of speech that by its very nature expresses the will of the gods in the form of a "divine law" that is *nefas* to violate.[34] In Roman cultural representation, *fas* is something that imposes itself independently of the individual *iudicium* of a person.

---

32. *Auctor* is the technical expression used to designate a *moris institutor;* cf. *TLL* I, 1205, 31ff., with many examples. On the meaning of *auctor,* see also Bettini 2000.
33. Cf. Cipriano 1978.
34. Benveniste 1974, 384–9. For the different between *fas* and *ius,* cf. Serv. in *Georg.* 1.269: . . . *ad religionem fas, ad homines iura pertinent.*

Fas is written directly in nature. It is a rule that prohibits the commission of certain particularly heinous and unquestionably horrible acts. For *fas* to function as a behavioral norm there is no need of a group that has reached a *consensus* on it nor of a *consuetudo* that has been consolidated in time. The difference between *mos* and *fas* is immediately evident from expressions like Tibullus' *nullus erat custos, nulla exclusura dolentes / ianua: si fas est, mos precor ille redi* ("then there was no guard; there were no doors that closed out sad lovers. How I wish that *mos*, provided it is *fas*, might return!")[35] The poet wishes that a *mos* making the life of the lover easier might return—provided, of course, that the return of such a *mos* does not violate the inscrutable rules of *fas*. *Mos* and *fas* are two different things and they may not coincide. Interesting, too, is the way in which Tacitus reports a question the legate Blaesus is supposed to have addressed to some soldiers threatening revolt: *cur contra morem obsequii, contra fas disciplinae vim meditentur?* ("Why do they contemplate violence against the *mos* of obedience and the *fas* of discipline?")[36] The text neatly distinguishes the two types of transgression: the refusal of *obsequium* is an act *contra morem*, but to disrespect military *disciplina*—a model that, at Rome, enjoyed great cultural significance[37]—is absolutely unacceptable, absurd, *contra fas*.

Majority and *Minority* Mores

Let us return to *mos*. We have seen that in the social definition of a *mos*—in its passage from a simple individual disposition to a recognized custom—everything plays on the presence of a certain group that reaches a *consensus* on it. At this point, the question must be the following: who makes up the group that through its *consensus* defines the *mores?* This is a question without a simple answer. To make our job easier, then, we will try to restrict our field of inquiry and to designate two different scenarios in which *mores* may be defined: the first involves a kind of "majority" *mores* regarding the community in its entirety, whereas the second involves a kind of "minority" *mores* regarding some subgroup of the main community. On to the first scenario, then.

---

35. *Corpus Tibullianum* 2.3.4.
36. Tac. *Ann.* 1.19.3.
37. See, e.g., Liv. *AUC.* 5.6.17, where the lack of respect (expressed by the verb *vereor*) for the *disciplina* appears at the end of a list of behaviors destructive for the city of Rome: *non senatum, non magistratus, non leges, non mores maiorum, non instituta patrum, non disciplinam vereri militiae.*

Majority *Mores*

We can begin with an example. When Sosia describes the battle against the Teleboeans in Plautus' *Amphitruo,* he says that *nos nostras more nostro et modo instruximus | legiones, item hostes contra legiones suas instruont* ("we arranged our legions according to our *mos* and our manner, while the enemy stationed their legions opposite us in their manner").[38] In Sosia's words, the Roman tactical tradition (appearing here in the guise of Amphitryon's "Theban" army) is characterized by its own particular *mos,* contrasted with that of the enemies in the same action of positioning their army. Using Varro's definition of *mos,* we might say that the group composed of Romans has reached a certain *consensus* on the rules of a military art, and that this *consensus* has become a *consuetudo:* the Romans *always* position their legions in a certain manner, according to this *mos.* In cases of this kind, the group that defines the collective *mores* corresponds to the entire community, i.e., to "the Romans." We should try to define this group more precisely, however—and in doing so, we will confront one of the most important, and also one of the most characteristic, anthropological models of Roman society.

Mos Maiorum

In the Roman representation of their collective *mores,* the group that wields decision-making power has a specific name and appearance: the *maiores.* The collective spirit of the group assumes the *persona* of the ancestors, who, because of their antiquity, grant a *mos* the necessary authority to become a *consuetudo.* Let us try to revisit *mos maiorum* in light of Varro's definition of *mos.* We will remember that, according to Varro, *mos* was "the consensus of all those who live together: once this is established in time (*inveteratus*), it creates a habit." One might say, then, that the *consensus . . . inveteratus* mentioned by Varro—the consolidation of customs along the axis of time—finds its concrete manifestation at Rome in the figure of the *maiores.* Customs that come from the *maiores* are authoritative because they are old, because they have been consolidated in time.

It is interesting to note that at Rome the *mos maiorum* may be invoked in the most disparate circumstances. There are countless examples we could cite. At times, the context can be extremely official and solemn, as when Cicero records that *quattuor omnino genera sunt . . . in quibus per senatum more maiorum statuatur aliquid de legibus* ("there are four ways in which,

---

38. Plaut. *Am.* 221ff.

according to the custom of the ancestors, a decision can be made in regard to the laws by the senate").[39] At other times, the circumstances are more common and familiar, as when at the end of Plautus' *Cistellaria* the actor turns to address the audience saying *more maiorum date plausum postrema in comoedia,* ("according to the custom of the ancestors, applaud at the end of the comedy").[40] Speaking always of theatrical practices, it is worth noting that at Rome even the choice of actors' professional undergarments was governed by a traditional "custom" (*mos*): *scaenicorum quidem mos tantam habet vetere disciplina verecundiam, ut in scaenam sine subligaculo prodeat nemo* ("actors of the theater have such respect for discretion that, according to an ancient custom, not one of them will set foot on stage without undergarments").[41] Examples could be added *ad infinitum.*

In the above discussion of Cornelius Nepos, we have already stressed how important *mos maiorum* was in Roman culture, and there is no need to dwell on the influence that this cultural model exerted on law ("the greater part of *ius* depends on *mores*, not on *leges*," remarks Quintilian),[42] religion, military discipline, the education of children, public and private behavior and so forth.[43] The range of functions covered by *mos maiorum* is extremely broad—so broad, in fact, that addressing this subject in a few pages would be practically impossible.[44] We will limit ourselves, then, to highlighting some specific, perhaps less familiar traits of *mos maiorum*—or at any rate, those more in tune with the perspective that we have taken in this study.

THE NORMATIVE FUNCTION OF *MOS MAIORUM* AND THE PRAGMATICS OF COMMUNICATION

First, the normative function exercised by *mos maiorum*. In Roman culture, *mos maiorum* is a set of rules to follow, a paradigm of behavior to which the *minores* must conform.[45] Sometimes the paradigmatic value of the *mos maiorum* is declared explicitly—in the form of a specific program

---

39. Cic. *Corn.* I fr. 24 Crawford.
40. Plaut. *Cist.* 787.
41. Cic. *Off.* 1.129.
42. Quint. *Inst. orat.* 5.10.13.
43. Cf. Rech 1936, a work conducted obviously from a point of view different from that which interests us, but nevertheless still very useful; for the function fulfilled by *mos* as a customary right (*Gewonheitsrecht*), see Peppe 1984, 88–98.
44. The bibliography on *mos maiorum*, except for a few specific works, is both endless and difficult to define (see the attempt of Bianco 1984, III, 601–6).
45. On the normative function of the ancestors in Roman culture, see also Bettini 1991a, esp. 191ff.

Chapter 3. Mos, Mores *and* Mos Maiorum

for "modeling" or "remodeling" society, for instance. According to Livy, Cato the Elder used his office of *censor* to *castigare nova flagitia et priscos revocare mores* ("suppress the disgraceful behavior of his contemporaries and reestablish ancient customs").[46] But even when no magistrate's will stands behind *mos maiorum* to enforce its observance, nevertheless the traditions of the ancients exercise an unquestionably paradigmatic function. At Rome, *mos maiorum* functioned almost as a kind of *exagium*, the instrument used to calibrate weights—a kind of *basanos* or touchstone. Sometimes the behavior of "moderns" is measured against *mos maiorum*:[47] if they conform, this serves as their justification (*dico . . . me more atque instituto maiorum fecisse* ["I declare to have acted according to the institutions and customs of the ancestors"]).[48] If they do not, there is room for censure (*nihil de me actum esse . . . more maiorum* ["nothing was done in my respect according to the customs of the ancestors"]).[49] In fact, it is worth noting that the expression *more maiorum* (and *maiorum more*), with *mos* in the ablative case, is a fixed, codified formula that is very rarely varied.[50] The grammatical rigidity of this formula corresponds well to the permanency of its function within Roman culture: when someone wants to approve or disapprove of a certain behavior, the *mos* of the ancestors is the "attendant circumstance" *par excellence*.

The normative value of *mos maiorum* ensures that this formula occurs more often than not in linguistic contexts of a strongly pragmatic nature. This second aspect of *mos* is worth investigating. If *mos maiorum*, as a cultural model, fulfills a paradigmatic function in society, this likely has some effect also on the "discourse" in which it occurs. In certain cases, the pragmatic character of the linguistic context is made explicit in the form of the phrase, as when Plautus' Stasimus exclaims, *utinam veteres hominum mores, veteres parsimoniae / potius in maiore honore hic essent quam mores mali* ("would that the ancient customs of men, the old frugalities, were more honored here than bad customs!")[51] Stasimus, bemoaning the loss of the customs of the ancestors according to *mos maiorum*,[52] makes the express wish that his fellow citizens would return to the good customs of their ancestors and abandon the *mali mores* that have displaced them. In this case, the pragmatic valence

---

46. Liv. *AUC.* 39.41.4.
47. I do not mean in this way to valorize the etymology of *mos* from **me-* ("to measure") proposed by Flobert 1973 (cf. above, n. 22), which remains quite unclear.
48. Liv. *AUC.* 34.31.16.
49. Cic. *Sest.* 73.3.
50. Cf. Rech 1936, 15ff.
51. Plaut. *Trin.* 1028ff.
52. Cf. the comment of Carmides (Plaut. *Trin.* 1030ff.), *di immortales, basilica hic quidem facinora inceptat loqui / veteran quaerit, veteran amare hunc more maiorum scias.*

of the discourse is obvious: it is expressed in the form of a wish.[53] But even when the exhortation to follow *mos maiorum* is not syntactically transparent, simply mentioning the customs of the ancestors is enough to render the discourse pragmatic. Let us take another look at an example we have just cited. If applauding at the end of a comedy is an ancestral *mos*, this means that you, too—the audience—would do well to applaud. Again, the mention of *mos maiorum* has the value of an exhortation or of an invitation. In the terminology of speech act theory, the mention of *mos maiorum* activates a kind of perlocutionary force in the discourse.[54] Any utterance regarding *mos maiorum*, in fact, is not limited to producing a certain complex of sounds or a certain linguistic meaning; more or less explicitly, it always aims at producing an effect on the interlocutor, exhorting him to justify, praise or practice certain behaviors, or to censure others.

The Athenians' Question and the Poor Definition of *Mos Maiorum*

There is another aspect of *mos maiorum* to explore. It is perhaps the most interesting, and may be introduced in the form of a question: How can the boundaries of *mos maiorum* be delineated or defined? This question has no answer, however. In fact, variability and resistance to easy definition are an integral part of the social nature of *mos maiorum*. Since we have been talking about *mos maiorum* as a cultural configuration endowed with a strongly paradigmatic value (which we expect to be rigidly codified, therefore), this appears intriguingly paradoxical. But the fluidity inscribed in the very nature of *mos maiorum* is evident from the way in which Cicero, for example, reports an anecdote about an Athenian consultation of the Delphic oracle. When the Athenians ask the god what sacred rites (*religiones*) they should practice above all, the oracle responds: *eas quae essent in more maiorum* ("those conforming to the customs of the ancestors").[55] After reflecting upon this answer, however, the Athenians return to the oracle:

---

53. Cf. also cases such as Cic. *De senec.* 2.3. *mos maiorum postulat* . . . ; *Sest.* 16, *more maiorum adligatum* . . . ; etc.

54. The reference is to the theory of Austin 1987. If we considered the situation from the perspective of the speaker—a prospective that does not interest us here—we would speak rather of the "illocutionary force."

55. Cic. *Leg.* 2.16.40. The same anecdote is told by Xen. *Mem.* 4.3.15, but much more succinctly, and without the Athenians' second question. In Xenophon, the expression that corresponds to Cicero's *mos maiorum* is *nomos poleos*.

quo cum iterum venissent maiorumque morem dixissent saepe esse mutatum quaesissentque, quem morem potissimum sequerentur e variis, respondit 'optumum.'

> They returned a second time and, affirming that the customs of the ancestors had changed many times, asked what custom specifically they should attend to among the many different ones. The oracle responded, "The best one."

The tautology of the oracle's response reveals its profound wisdom. It was the question that was naïve. How can one ask what is the "true" *mos maiorum?* Such a thing cannot be defined unequivocally. In this sense, an explicit question inevitably brings to light the fact that there is not one and only one *mos maiorum;* rather, there are many different ones, and these are often inconsistent with each other. This is why the oracle, in its response, necessarily appeals to the questioner's own faculties of judgment: relying upon his own good sense, he must understand which among the *mores maiorum* is the "best" and keep to that. We realize, then, that even *mos maiorum*—the cultural configuration to which Roman society always turns in a rigid and normative fashion—is in fact manifold and not unambiguous. At this level, customs appear more like Montaigne's "thousand manners of life" than an instruction manual for living.

The Temporal Dimension: "Old" and "New" *Mos Maiorum*

The anecdote reported above reveals that the poor definition of *mos maiorum* is due principally to the effect of time. The Athenians must have realized that "the customs of the ancients had changed many times." This presents us with a further paradox inherent to *mores:* as regards customs, time plays a double role. On one hand, it is precisely the passing of time that permits customs to become "ancient" and, as such, worthy of being observed. On the other hand, it is time that brings about their transformation or eventual abandonment. We must not forget that any process of *consuetudo* will be complemented by one of *desuetudo,* and that both these sociological forces—not merely the former—exert their influence on *mores.* If customs can be adopted, obviously they may also be abandoned—otherwise, Latin texts would not abound as they do in mournful appeals to respect *mos maiorum.* Examples are unnecessary; one need only think of Pliny's complaints of the disuse into which the ancient aristocratic custom of keeping the *imagines maiorum* in the atrium had fallen in his times (only to be replaced by pictures of athletes and busts of Epicurus).[56] It simply happened that this custom, at one time so dear to the *nobilitas,* was observed no longer and had been replaced by another.

Let us continue with this theme of the relationship between time and customs, since it is not only *desuetudo* but also *consuetudo* itself that appears to be responsible for changing *mores.* This too is an interesting paradox. As we know, the process of creating *mores* entails their consolidation through time as a *consuetudo,* giving them a necessary "antiquity." But this also means that, in the long run, customs will end up being *varii*—"many and different among themselves," as the Athenians objected to the oracle. In fact, a *consuetudo* is not defined once and only once, but continuously and without interruption, consolidating itself in customs different from those that came before. Consequently, the same force that brings about the stability of the *mores*—i.e., the progression of time and consolidation of the *consuetudo*— inevitably brings about their variety and multiplicity, as well. In the realm of *mores,* permanence and change, stability and variation are two sides of the same coin.[57] This characteristic stands in contrast to the cultural representation of *mos maiorum*—to the way in which society would like the customs of the ancients to be, an unambiguous model independent of any temporal consideration. Society almost pretends that in the realm of the *mos maiorum* time ceases to exist, substituting for it a generic reference to the *maiores,* without any other internal designation or gradation. Yet in practice things do not work like that at all: in fact, even within *mos maiorum,* it is possible to speak of customs going back to "more ancient" ancestors and of others coming from "more recent" ancestors.

Let us look at another illustrative example from the same field of religious *mores* highlighted by the Athenians' question. Lauding the importance given to the respect of cults nearly everywhere, Cicero affirms that *omnes . . . deos patrios, quos a maioribus acceperunt, colendos sibi diligenter et retinendos esse arbitrantur* ("all men . . . consider it necessary to venerate with zeal and to conserve their native gods, those that they received from their ancestors").[58] Communities venerate with particular zeal the gods handed down by their ancestors, perceiving them as "our" gods. Elsewhere again Cicero says: *iam ritus familiae patrumque servare id est, quoniam antiquitas proxime accedit ad eos, a dis quasi traditam religionem tueri* ("since antiquity comes closest to

---

56. Plin. *Nat. hist.* 35.5ff.

57. It is worth noting that already Varro, in his reflections on language, had accurately noted that the action of *consuetudo* produces, indifferently, either that which is analogous and regular or what is anomalous and irregular (Var. *Ling. Lat.* 9.1.3).

58. Cic. *Verr.* 6.132.

the gods, maintaining the rites of our fathers and of our families is practically equivalent to conserving a religion that the gods themselves have given us").[59] It is easy to imagine that on the side, standing in opposition to the *dei patrii*, are all those cults which come "from outside"—i.e., divinities that were introduced into the community at a certain point in its development, over and above the *dei patrii*. When Festus defines the *sacra peregrina* ("foreign cults"), he says that *peregrina sacra . . . coluntur eorum more, a quibus sunt accepta* ("foreign cults . . . are celebrated according to the *mos* of those from whom they were received")[60] The *sacra* that come to Rome from outside presuppose the existence of a *mos* that is not "of the ancestors," but of the people from whom these cults come. The distinction seems to be clear, then: on one hand, there are the *dei patrii*, who are venerated on the basis of the ancestral *mos*; on the other hand, there are the "new" rites, which are perceived as referring to a foreign *mos*.

But things are never so simple. This is especially true in the case of Rome's polytheistic religion, which did not prejudicially reject any divinity that it found different from the one and "true" God, as monotheistic religions tend to do. Instead, it recognized that in the course of time, new cults would inevitably enter into the religious practice of the community.[61] The episode of Jupiter's reconciliation of the Trojans and the Latins at the end of the *Aeneid* is an instructive example. Juno, who favors the Latins, fears for the integrity of their national identity, threatened as it is by the mixed marriages with the Trojans that will be the inevitable consequence of peace. Juno actually requests that the future inhabitants of Latium remain "Latin" in all respects, notwithstanding their fusion with the Trojans. She does not want the descendants of these mixed marriages to change the name of the populace—i.e., to end up being Trojans rather than Latins. She does not want them to change their language or their way of dressing. Above all, she wishes the future *propago* of this intermarriage—the Romans—to be able to found their supremacy on typical Italian *virtus*.[62] In short, Juno asks that the Latins be able to preserve intact the whole set of cultural models that constitutes the foundation of their identity—their name, their language, their manner of dress, their moral qualities. All of these fall easily under the heading of traditional *mores*. The answer that Jupiter gives to Juno's request is this:

---

59. Cf., e.g., Cic. *Leg.* 2.27.
60. Fest. *De verb. sign.* fr. 269 Lindsay.
61. "Divinities such as Apollo, Cybele, Aesculapius and Isis were certainly of foreign origin, but, like foreign aristocracies or subjugated peoples, these received citizenship, becoming fully Roman: it is not therefore possible to distinguish them from their gods and their cults" (Scheid 1989, 653).
62. Verg. *Aen.* 12.823ff.

> sermonem Ausonii patrium moresque tenebunt
> utque est nomen erit. commixti corpore tantum
> subsident Teucri. morem ritusque sacrorum
> adiciam, faciamque omnis uno ore Latinos.[63]

The Ausonians (i.e., the Latins) will maintain their language and their customs (*mores*); and their name shall remain the same. The Teucrians (i.e., the Trojans) will remain only in the corporeal mixing. I will add the *mos* and the religious rites, and I will make them all equal, Latins, in physical aspect.

Jupiter decides that the descendants of this mixed marriage will maintain the traditional *mores* of Latium without additions or modifications from the Trojans. Furthermore, he will limit the Trojan "presence" in their offspring to a secondary, "genetic" component, guaranteeing that their physical appearance will exhibit authentically Latin—rather than Trojan—features. This is to say that the new race will have an unmistakably Latin identity.

Such great care for preserving the Latins' original identity nevertheless presents a concession to the Trojans: they will be authorized to introduce among the traditional customs of the Latins their own religious *mos*. This, in fact, is the specific mission entrusted to Aeneas in the poem: "to bring his gods to Latium."[64] The descendants of the Trojans and the Latins, despite possessing an undeniably Latin identity, will have *mores* differentiated along a temporal scale. In general, their customs will be in line with the traditions of their Latin forefathers, whereas their religious *mos* will be "new," belonging to a class that Festus would not have hesitated to call *peregrinum*.[65] The status of this Latin identity created by Jupiter is particularly interesting when considered from the perspective of a reader contemporary to Vergil. For this reader of the *Aeneid,* the religious *mos* that was so new and strange at the moment of its introduction into Latium is in fact a venerable *mos*, the very foundation of Roman religion and therefore part of the *mos maiorum*. Could a Roman ever *not* consider "father Aeneas" among his *maiores*, and consider the religious *mos* introduced by him new and strange? The Roman reader of Vergil here confronts not just one kind of *mos maiorum*, but two—differently scaled in time, but both fundamental in the definition of his own cultural identity: the Latin *mores* that existed before Aeneas' arrival in Latium, and

---

63. Verg. *Aen.* 834ff.
64. Vergil declares this from the beginning of the poem (cf. Verg. *Aen.* 1.6, *inferre deos Latio*) and Aeneas repeats it a few lines above those we have cited (12.192): *sacra deosque dabo.*
65. Interesting Servius' comment on Verg. *Aen.* 836, on the 'addition' of the Trojan religious *mos: verum est: nam sacra matris deum Romani Phrygio more coluerunt.* According to the commentator, the Romans "really" observed a foreign custom in their religious rites, venerating Magna Mater according to a custom that was Phrygian, not Roman.

those posterior to that arrival. Here, we are again up against the same paradox that the Athenians had to struggle with when they wanted to know the "true" custom of the ancestors. The fact is that the definition of *mos maiorum* is relative and a function of temporal development. A *mos* that is "new" at the moment of its appearance will just as easily become part of the *mos maiorum* once it has become established with time.

Negotiation of *Mos Maiorum*

Beyond the effects of the temporal dimension, *mos maiorum* is not well defined because customs do not exist in a world apart. They interact with the life of the community on the basis of the function they are called upon to fulfill. This community—especially if it is a large community, open and in continual expansion (as Rome was, beginning with the period of the conquests)—will of course be infused with various tensions and conflicts. The contours of the *mos maiorum* will inevitably feel these tensions, particularly when incidental interests and conflicts of power also enter into play, transforming the *mos maiorum* at the very least into a subject of interpretation.[66]

We may now look at some examples taken from a political context. In 20 B.C.E., the proconsul L. Cornelius Lentulus requested a triumph on his return from Spain.[67] The Senate responded that Lentulus' deeds merited this honor in their own right, but no *exemplum* passed down by the *maiores* existed of anyone ever celebrating a triumph who had not been dictator, consul or praetor. Having held none of these positions, Lentulus was denied his request. However, in consideration of the deeds he had accomplished, the Senate conceded to Lentulus a "minor" form of triumph, the ovation. But the tribune Tiberius Sempronius Longus had no trouble demonstrating that even the concession of an ovation would be contrary to *mos maiorum*. In such a case, as we can see, the Senate was ready both to assert and to silence the *mos maiorum* by applying it only halfway. To find a way out of a difficult situation (one specifically connected with the present life of the community), the most conservative institution of the *res publica* was ready to negotiate with the past and with the *mos maiorum*.

Even a vigorous defender of *mos maiorum* such as Cicero did not hesitate to do the same thing for reasons of political opportunity, rather presumptuously in fact. In his oration *On the Command of Gnaeus Pompeius,* Quintus Catulus had expressed his disapproval of the proposal to confer full powers

---

66. Syme 1974, 155, "This [the *mos maiorum*] was not a code of constitutional law. . . ."
67. Liv. *AUC.* 31.20; cf. Rech 1936, 37ff.

on Pompey, and had done so deploying the classic argument *ne quid novi fiat contra exempla atque instituta maiorum* ("lest anything new be done against the examples and institutions of our forefathers").[68] However, Cicero's rhetorical art allowed him to defend this transgression with an arguably very artificial justification. He claimed that this contravention of *mos maiorum* was permissible because Pompey's political career had always been based on the same kind of violations of custom. In fact, each and every office held by Pompey had had something *inauditum,* something *inusitatum,* something *singulare,* something *incredibile* about it: why then assert *mos maiorum* in this case, when it had not been asserted in the rest? Even if in the prudent form of a *praeteritio* (*non dicam hoc loco*), Cicero affirms:

> maiores nostri in pace consuetudini, in bello utilitati paruisse, semper ad novos casus temporum novorum consiliorum rationes accommodasse.[69]

> If, in matters of peace, our forefathers were always preoccupied for custom, in war they minded utility, and always adapted the parameters of innovative plans to the circumstances produced by new events.

Cicero then cites a number of examples from the military and political careers of Scipio and Marius to strengthen his position, explicitly theorizing the possibility of negotiation with *mos maiorum.* He goes so far as to attribute to the *maiores* themselves this fluid and "opportunistic" attitude towards the traditional *mos,* claiming that they by their own behavior paradoxically authorize Pompey's transgression of *mos maiorum.* That is to say, on one hand, the ancestors prescribe the *mos,* but on the other, they guarantee the possibility of violating it precisely because of their own *mos.* We would be hard pressed to find a better example of the fluidity and flexibility of *mos maiorum.*

This tendency to negotiate with the *mos maiorum* provides an opportunity to reflect upon the contradiction within the Roman community itself that arises in the era of the great expansions and becomes more acute in the period

---

68. Cic. *Manil.* 60ff. For an analysis of these two cases—that of Lentulus and that of Pompey—cf. Rech 1936, 37. The author begins from the presupposition that the *mos maiorum* was an absolutely stable foundation, so much so to consider that the cases referring to it "were not so contradictory as might seem" (cf. 13). Consequently, he uses these examples not to show the possible conflict within the *mos maiorum,* but simply to reveal how at Rome the political and juridical procedure was based often on the mechanism of "precedent." In general, it needs to be said that often people went overboard, especially in the archaic period, making *mos maiorum* an absolute and adamantine law. Compare claims like that of Le Bras 1959, 417–20, esp. 420: "au dessus, planent les *mores,* plus étouffantes qu'aucune chape de lois."

69. Cic. *Manil.* 60.

leading up to the Augustan restoration. In fact, if Roman society was in continual transformation during this time, Roman culture, at least officially, persisted in looking for its behavioral parameters in ancestral *mos*. This tension within Roman society—a tension between present and past, between innovation and adaptation—is well known. However, to define it better, we might employ the categories of "hot" and "cold" with which Claude Lévi-Strauss demarcates the opposition between two types of culture: those that accept their history and, by interiorizing it, transform it into a positive mechanism (hot societies); and those that stubbornly refuse to accept their history and, by setting in motion elaborate strategies, attempt to reduce time's influence upon them as much as possible (cold societies.)[70] Within this schema, Rome appears (at least from a certain moment) to be an objectively "hot"—in fact, very "hot"—society that wishes at all costs it were "cold." Roman society was a society that based its own power and well being on expansion and change, while pretending that *mos* did not change and continuing to respect the rules imposed by the *maiores*. In such situations, a relationship with the past and with ancestral customs must necessarily be contractual.

THE ORALITY OF *MOS MAIORUM*

As we have seen in the preceding paragraphs, the fact that at Rome the customs of the ancestors were poorly defined is a consequence of the interaction of *mos maiorum* with both the temporal dimension and the situational context. But this fluidity is intrinsic to *mos maiorum* for a much more concrete reason, as well: the way in which it was preserved and passed on. This brings us to consider, by way of conclusion, a fundamental aspect of *mos maiorum*: its position in the "cultural memory" of Roman society—understanding by this expression the "external memory" of the Romans, their objectified and shared memory that made a true social patrimony of traditional laws, rites, behaviors, prescriptions and so forth.[71]

In a community that makes ample use of writing, the conservation of cultural memory will be entrusted in good part to the letters of the alphabet. This was obviously the case at Rome, where forms of what has been called "display writing" (*tituli*, law tables and so on) guaranteed that cultural memory retained a certain vitality in the internal communication of the city.[72] Yet writing had a very marginal role in the conservation and the transmis-

---

70. Lévi-Strauss, 1964, 254ff. and 1978, 63ff.
71. I use the expression "cultural memory" (*kulturelle Gedächtnis*) in the sense given to it by Assmann 1997.
72. Pucci 1992, 233–314, esp. 240ff.

sion of *mos maiorum* at Rome, the "text" of which was inexistent. It was not stored or displayed anywhere. In fact, the *mos maiorum* was not committed to any fixed form of writing, but was a purely oral creation. Latin authors frequently make it clear that *mos* lay outside the dominion of writing. Cicero says that *propria legis et ea quae scripta sunt et ea quae sine litteris aut gentium iure aut maiorum more retinentur* ("both the written rules and those that are conserved not in alphabetic characters but by the right of the peoples and by the customs of the ancients are part of the law").[73] *Mos maiorum* is a law in every respect, therefore—only that it was not written down anywhere, as in the case of laws true and proper. A commentator of Vergil—as a good grammarian, always sensitive to wordplay—employed the figure of assonance in order to clarify the contradiction inherent in *mos* as a "law" that remained outside the dominion of writing: *mos est lex quidam vivendi nullo vinculo adstricta, id est lex non scripta* ("*mos* is a law of living that is not bound by any chain, that it is, it is not written").[74] Similarly Isidore: *mos est vetustate probata consuetudo, sive lex non scripta. nam lex a legendo vocata, quia scripta est* ("*mos* is a custom that has withstood the test of time, or an unwritten law. In fact, the law is called so from the act of reading (*a legendo*), because it is written").[75]

Evidence for the Roman cultural perception of ancestral *mos* appears explicit about the oral nature of traditional custom. Its conservation and its transmission are not entrusted to the letters of the alphabet. *Mos* is not written and *mos* is not read. Given our almost exaggerated written perspective on Roman culture (since we know it exclusively through texts), this oral nature of *mos maiorum* may be surprising at first. What about literary production—was this not the principal method of conserving and transmitting the ancient *mos*? Obviously from the time when Rome began to have a literary tradition this too contributed to keeping its memory alive. But we should keep in mind at least two peculiar aspects of the relationship between *mos maiorum* and written literature. The first is that this type of transmission—leaving apart works destined for theatrical production—was necessary limited to the affluent and educated classes. We should not think that all Romans entrenched themselves in the knowledge of *mos maiorum* through Ennius' *Annales* or Livy's history. The second is that these works, even when they speak of ancient *mos*, were not expressly composed for that purpose. Customs are recorded in the form of stories, exemplary deeds and famous sayings, all inserted into the framework of historical narrations or poetic creations that ultimately speak of something else entirely. When *mos*

---

73. Cic. *Part. orat.* 130.
74. Servius in Aen. 6.316.
75. Isid. *Etym.* 2.10.1–2; cf. 5.3.2–3.

maiorum is transmitted through literature, it is not in the form of an explicit collection of precepts (like Erasmus' *De Civitate Morum Puerilium*, Della Casa's *Galateo* or Emily Post's *Etiquette*), but indirectly, through the mention of deeds and stories that function as examples of those *mores*. To cite only a single example: When Ennius wrote his famous verse *moribus antiquis res stat Romana virisque*, certainly he was asserting—and to almost oracular effect—the value of ancient *mos* as the foundation of Roman society.[76] However, this was within a work dedicated not to cataloging the *boni mores* one by one, but to telling the history of Rome. By the single events that mark the fortune of the city, by the behavior of exemplary characters, and by the deeds accomplished by the heroes of the past, the educated Roman reader was encouraged to remember the ancient *mos*. Yet this was essentially an inferential mechanism—recalling a behavioral model through an exemplary deed or event—rather than a direct codification of customs in writing.

To return to the oral character of the *mos maiorum*, to its image as the Romans themselves transmit it: How was ancestral tradition conserved and transmitted at Rome? This function, which had important implications for social life, was fulfilled above all by a system of practices that was preserved in the collective memory of the Romans due to a continual process of recapitulation. Here are some examples of these practices, touching upon various levels of social life:

- the use of *exempla* in deliberative contexts. Quintilian recalls the persuasive power possessed by an *exemplum*, that is, by *rei gestae aut ut gestae . . . commemoratio*, ("the remembrance of a deed or something considered as such"). To this definition he added cases such as *iure occisus est Saturninus sicut Gracchi* ("Saturninus was killed justly, like the Gracchi") or *Brutus occidit liberos proditionem molientis, Manlius virtutem filii morte multavit* ("Brutus killed his sons who were plotting treachery, Manlius punished his son's valor with death").[77] Particularly relevant from our point of view is the "commemorative function" (*commemoratio*, not *narratio*) attributed to *exempla*. An *exemplum* of the *mos maiorum* brought to mind a "memory." This was a "sign" capable of evoking a much greater cultural meaning through the utterance of an extremely synthetic phrase.

---

76. Enn. *Ann.* fr. 156 Skutsch. The "oracular" nature of the verse was noted by Cicero (cited by August. *Civ.* 2.31).

77. Quint. *Inst. orat.* 5.11.6–7. For the persuasive value of the *exempla maiorum*, cf. statements such as Cic. *De orat.* 2.335, *qui ad dignitatem impellit, maiorum exempla . . . colliget.* For the relationship between *exempla* and *mos maiorum*, see Mencacci 1996.

- the attachment of various aristocratic groups to particular family traditions and those of the nobility in general.[78] In *De Officiis*, when Cicero describes the fourth *persona*—i.e., the role that every person voluntary chooses in the community—he underscores the importance of imitation: *quorum vero patres aut maiores aliqua gloria praestiterunt, ii student plerumque eodem in genere laudis excellere* ("Those whose fathers or forefathers distinguished themselves with some glory often try to make a name for themselves in the same area").[79]

- within aristocratic tradition, a commemorative function of particular importance as far as the *mos maiorum* is concerned is that served by funerary practices. The procession of the *imagines maiorum*, featuring members of the family wearing not only masks depicting the faces of their ancestors, but also garments relating to their honors and their deeds, revived memories of great personages of the past and their behavior.[80]

- the education of the young. In this regard, the behavior of Horace's father, for example, is clear: in educating his son, he was content to *traditum ab antiquis morem servare* ("preserve the custom handed down by the ancients").[81]

- the Senate's customary repetition of procedure, a practice in which the oral tradition of the entire body, scrupulously adopted and observed by newly co-opted members, intertwined with private traditions maintained by the most important families.[82]

- finally, the topography of the city itself. It could function as a mechanism for the conservation and reiteration of *mos maiorum*, a phenomenon that is known from other cultural traditions as well.[83] On this (perhaps less familiar) "topographical" aspect of Roman cultural memory, we may tarry a little longer.

We may think, for example, of the famous episodes of Augustan literature, such as the archaeological tour that Propertius gives to his guest Horus in the first elegy of his fourth book. In these lines, the evocation of

---

78. Rech 1936, 26.

79. Cic. *Off.* 1.116; cf. 117. This passage is mentioned by Mencacci 2001; see also her reflections on the clever appropriation of the collective *maiores*—the great men of the past—as personal *maiores* by Cicero, a *novus homo*, and therefore, deprived of specific family *mores* to imitate.

80. Polyb. *Hist.* 6.53; the relationship between the aristocratic funeral and ancient *mores* can be seen also in Cic. *De orat.* 2.225. Cf. Bettini 1991a, 190ff.

81. Hor. *Sat.* 1.4.17. Other examples of this type are in Rech 1936, 74ff.

82. Rech 1936, 35ff.

83. Cf. Assmann 1997, 33ff.

Chapter 3. Mos, Mores and Mos Maiorum 117

Rome's ancient topography is repeatedly interspersed with praise of ancient customs that these places bring to mind, and with criticism of contemporary customs.[84] The function that these exemplary "places" fulfill—the cultural transmission and a kind of "localization" of *mores*—is known outside of literary invention, as well. In Cicero's defense of Milo, he recalls how the very fact that his client had killed Clodius along the via Appia—built by Clodius' ancestor, Appius Claudius—played to his disadvantage: *nisi forte . . . eo mors atrocior erit P. Clodi quo is in monumentis maiorum suorum sit interfectus, hoc enim ab istis saepe dicitur* ("Unless perhaps . . . the death of Publius Clodius is considered particularly horrible, since he was killed among the *monumenta* of one of his ancestors. For this is often said by them").[85] The Via Appia is emphatically culturalized: more than a public work, the road is a *monumentum* (literally, "that which calls to mind") recalling the behavior of an ancestor.[86] Consequently, Milo's enemies could deploy the topography of a homicide as an argument aggravating the defendant's position. Naturally, Cicero's rhetorical ability immediately hit upon a method of counterargument, on the same topographical basis: along the Via Appia, Clodius himself had killed Marcus Papirius—an act symbolizing just how different Clodius was from his ancestor who had built that road.[87]

At Rome, the cultural memory of *mos maiorum* is put into practice through reference to a series of "figures of memory"—concrete images that belong to the collective memory and that function as "signs" capable of calling to mind some behavior to follow.[88] In these figures of memory—whether they are deeds of the past, *exempla*, places, rituals or images—the foundational behavior of the Roman community coalesces and the evocation of these symbolic figures permits its realization within social communication. In Roman culture, the "rules" of *mos maiorum* are not fixed in explicit formulas (as with the written *lex*) but must be "extracted" each time from the practices, places and *exempla* that someone can recall, constantly appealing to memory. Linguistically speaking, *mos maiorum* exists not in the form of definite and specific utterances (as the case would be of a law code), but in the form of generative patterns that furnish only the coordinates along

---

84. Prop. *Carm.* 1.1ff.
85. Cic. *Mil.* 17.
86. Places in the city could function also as *monumenta* of negative behaviors, as well as of positive behaviors: e.g., the *vicus sceleratus*, named so because there Tullia ran over the body of her father Servius Tullius with a cart (Paul. Diac. *Ep.* 451 [Lindsay]). Cf. also Jaeger 1997.
87. Cic. *Mil.* 18.
88. The expression "figure of memory" comes from Assmann 1997, 10ff., who reformulates in this way the "*images-souvenirs*" of Halbwachs 1952, 16ff. Although Assmann's reflections are centered on Egypt, Israel and Greece, the entire chapter dedicated to "cultural memory" (5–58) offers some very interesting cues for reflection on the Roman cultural tradition.

which the selection and realization of a specific utterance may be made. In pronouncing the phrase "the *mos maiorum* states that . . . " it is not possible to cite a written text that contains the rule, but only to appeal to a certain "figure of memory" that constitutes the nucleus of the utterance's meaning.

Inasmuch as *mos maiorum* pertains to the domain of memory and orality, then, it may appear fluid and poorly defined. Faced with an explicit question like that of the Athenians—"but which is the 'true' *mos maiorum*?"—it is impossible to give an answer: first of all because one cannot cite any text as the basis for distinguishing what is authentic and what is spurious. For this reason, the only possible answer is "the best"—i.e., the custom that seems most opportune, most in agreement with justice, nature or whatever other parameter of judgment is invoked in a particular circumstance. What will weigh most heavily in the choice of such parameters is, of course, the force of the groups or of those individuals who make appeal to *mos maiorum*, the historical or social context in which this appeal takes place and so on. The "text" of the *mos maiorum* is ensconced in the Roman collective memory. It is a recollection, a habit, a complex of forms realized each time through social practice. But *mos maiorum*—like all creations belonging to the sphere of memory rather than writing—always entails the possibility that none exists: memory, we know, implies forgetfulness.[89] It also entails the possibility of being continuously recreated in a different form, since memory provides not clear-cut formulations but kernels of information that may be realized differently each time they are recalled.

Let us summarize what we have said so far about the "flexibility" of *mos maiorum* at Rome. We have seen that its fluidity derives from the fact that ancestral customs are strictly influenced by the passing of time (the dialectic between *consuetudo* and *desuetudo*, the stratification of various *consuetudines*), by interaction with the present life of the community (the necessity of negotiation with traditional customs) and, finally, by being an oral tradition bound not to written texts but to "figures of memory" that range from *exempla* to places in the city, from *imagines* of the ancestors to ritualized practices. This last feature of *mos maiorum*—its existence in the form of "figures of memory"—lends itself well to recapping the other two characteristics. Since they belong to the world of memory and orality, these figures of memory depend precisely upon time and their relationship to the

---

89. Obviously, written texts can also fall into oblivion, when they are no longer in circulation within a culture: "When [texts] are no longer used, they become a tomb rather than a container of meaning, and only the interpreter can revivify that sense through the hermeneutic art and by commentary" (Assmann 1997, 62ff.). The difference is that a text that is no longer in circulation, provided that it is conserved, can be revived, as an infinite number of examples from our own cultural tradition show. A forgotten "memory," however, is lost forever.

social dynamic. In fact, when a community's cultural memory maintains its collective form without becoming a written text, its permanence will inevitably be tied to the preservation of what Maurice Halbwachs called "social frameworks"[90]—reference frameworks that, in the collective memory and internal communication of a community, guarantee the cultural meaning of individual figures of memory. When these "social frameworks" change—either with the passing of time or because the demands of the present drive the community's behavior in another direction—the perception of the *mos maiorum* will also change. When they disappear completely the *mos maiorum* will also be forgotten.

Majority *Mores:* Ethnocentric and Moralistic Framework

These reflections on *mos maiorum* have brought us slightly off track from the theme we have been exploring: the modalities in which a certain group defines its *mores,* based on an established *consensus.* We were saying that when the group defining the *mores* is identified with the entire community, this is the scenario of "majority" *mores*—cases in which particular behaviors, as Quintilian says, *persuasione etiam si non omnium hominum, eius tamen civitatis aut gentis, in qua res agitur, in mores recepta sunt* ("have been accepted into the *mores* on the basis of a conviction if not of all men then at least of the city or of the people among whom the case develops").[91] We can now return to Sosia where we left him, as he was describing the battle of Amphitryon's army against the Teleboans and the legions positioned *more nostro et modo.* The presence of the possessive adjective *nostro* is very important. It reveals that when a definition of *mos* is found in a context involving the entire collective, the subject identifies with the group and assumes its point of view: "If I am a Roman and I am speaking of Roman *mores,* of course I will say that 'we' do things like this, that 'we' have these *mores.*" Speaking of *mores* established by the ancestors, the subject tends to identify with this group and to assume its point of view. Consequently, a definition of the national *mores* instituted by the *maiores* can function "contrastively": in other words, a definition of the *mores* can be used not only to identify the group that recognizes itself in these *mores,* but also to contrast it with others. Obviously, this is a way of identifying the group to which the subject belongs ("'we' are *not* like this"). When a scenario of "majority" *mores*

---

90. The expression belongs to the theory of Halbwachs 1952, but we use it through the reformulation of Assmann 1997, 10ff.

91. Quint. *Inst. orat.* 5.10.13. Quintilian speaks here of the *certa,* of things "beyond question" on which an argument may be based.

assumes a contrastive aspect, there are two possible frameworks: in the first, there is a contrast with a group external to the one with which the subject identifies; in the second, with a group (or a single person) internal to the subject's own group.

In the first framework—contrasting the *mores* of the group with which the subject identifies to others'—we return to the situation analyzed by Nepos, where there was a contrast between "our" *mores* and the *mores* practiced by other peoples. If this comparison is made without any sense of cultural relativism (as happens most frequently), we end up with a series of ethnocentric statements. When he describes the tactics of "our" army, Sosia's contrast of the tactical *mores* of his own group and the enemy's is very neutral. He limits himself to saying that "we" position our troops *more nostro et modo,* while the enemy does the same thing their way. But there is a thin line between this and saying something like "We position our troops in our way, which is far superior to that barbarous manner in which the enemy stations its troops."

When ethnocentrism rears its ugly head, we encounter disdainful remarks about others—as when Cato, apparently viewing foreign peoples from the same moralistic perspective as he views the Roman community, claims that the Ligurians *inliterati mendacesque sunt et vera minus meminere* ("are illiterate liars, incapable of conceiving the truth").[92] Often, however, ethnocentric statements regarding the *mores* of other communities are indirect or partial. Here the examples become more interesting. In Plautus' *Casina*, when Lysidamus is about to consummate his presumed "marriage," the "bride" (actually the slave Calinus in drag) says to him: *ubi tu es, qui colere mores Massiliensis postulas?* ("where do you think you are, that you would want to practice the *mores* of the Massillians?")[93] The practice of passive homosexuality (which the Romans considered unacceptable in most instances)[94] is here defined by reference to the customs of a community—the Massillians—that had the reputation of being effeminate.[95] Calinus does not say explicitly, "We Romans do not participate in such obscenities," but rather, "Where is he who wants to behave like the Marseillians?" But the first statement is implicit in the second: Lysidamus and the audience must simply assume the first. Likewise, when Valerius Maximus narrates the punishment that the Carthaginians inflicted upon Attilius Regulus, he comments that *(dei) Carthaginienses moribus suis uti passi sunt,* ("[the gods] permitted the

---

92. Cat. *Orig.* fr. 31 Peter.
93. Plaut. *Cas.* 963.
94. It is sufficient to recall the discussion in Cantarella 1995, 129ff.
95. Cf. Athen. *Deipn.* 12.523c.

Carthaginians to practice their customs"),[96] appealing to the entrenched Roman belief that the Carthaginians were cruel and lacking in generosity. In this case, too, what is presumed is a phrase such as "Roman *mores*—'our' *mores*—are much better than those of the Carthaginians." Ethnocentrism operates like this very frequently—i.e., through assumptions of implicit statements behind explicit statements. In the same way, when Caesar writes that the Helvetians *moribus suis Orgetorigem ex vinclis causam dicere coegerunt* ("compelled Orgetorix to defend his case while still in chains, according to their custom"),[97] his ethnocentrism is again indirect. One cannot deny that Caesar is giving an objective ethnographic fact on the juridical practices of the Helvetians. At the same time, however, behind the phrase *suis moribus* (in reference to the Helvetians), it is difficult to ignore the point of view of a Roman who thinks "'we' certainly do not permit that someone accused of a crime should have to give his defense while in chains" (and therefore, that the Helvetians are barbarians).

Now to the second framework: contrasting the *mores* of the group with which the subject identifies to the *mores* of groups (or individuals) internal to the community itself. This occurs any time someone belonging to the community is accused of not respecting *mos maiorum*, working upon him some mechanism of exclusion. If the first framework (contrast with external groups) often assumes the form of ethnocentrism, this second framework (contrast with groups or individuals internal to the principal group) tends instead to assume the form of moralism. Operating within this second framework, in fact, the subject presupposes or professes to stand on the side of the "old" national *mores* and to represent them better than other members of the same community, who are accused of having forsaken them. This is the typical Roman moralism: *o tempora, o mores!* Such attitudes can be deployed profitably for ideological ends as well, as many statements of Sallust reveal—or (as we have already seen in the case of *mos maiorum*) to resolve conflicts of power internal to the city to the advantage of a certain group, especially in periods of great political disturbance.[98] As stated above, in cases like these the normative value and the perlocutionary linguistic function that characterize the appeal to *mos maiorum* in Roman culture comes very nicely into view. Let us examine only two of the many possible examples of this second, moralistic framework.

---

96. Val. Max. 1.1.14.
97. Caes. *BG.* 1.4.1.
98. From this point of view, a simple quantitative fact seems very interesting: the great majority of materials concerning *mos/mores* come from Cicero. Even without the help of the *TLL* (which in any case confirms this observation), Rech (1936, 23) had already shown this; cf. Roloff 1967, 274–322.

When, in 92 B.C.E., the censors Gnaeus Domitius Ahenobarbus and Lucius Licinius Crassus suppressed the teaching of rhetoric at Rome, they proclaimed as follows:

> renuntiatum est nobis esse homines qui novum genus disciplinae instituerunt. . . . maiores nostri quae liberos suos discere et quos in ludos itare vellent instituerunt. haec nova, quae praeter consuetudinem ac morem maiorum fiunt, neque placent neque recta videntur.[99]

> It has been brought to our attention that some persons have instituted at Rome a new type of instruction. . . . Our forefathers have already decided what their children should learn and what schools they should attend. We do not like these innovations, which go against all habits and customs of the ancestors, nor do they seem just.

The group made up of the rhetoricians who work in the city of Rome is censured by the magistrates, because their teaching does not respect ancestral *mos* in matters scholastic. Consequently, the rhetoricians are sentenced to "exclusion" from the community. The censors say, as it were, "You cannot take part in 'us'; the group with which we identify does not recognize you as belonging to it." Of course, the same mechanism of moralistic exclusion from a group can also be directed against a single person. When Sallust describes the arrival of corruption in Rome, he writes:

> huc accedebat, quod L. Sulla exercitum, quem in Asiam ductaverat, quo sibi fidum faceret, contra morem maiorum luxuriose nimisque liberaliter habuerat.[100]

> In addition, Lucius Sulla, in order to make the army that he had led into Asia more faithful, treated it with too great liberality and made it live in luxury, against the mos maiorum.

Sulla's behavior is reprehensible, since contrary to traditional custom. He is censured because the manner in which he treated his army allowed vice and luxury to enter Rome, and so on him falls a similar sentence of "exclusion" from the community with which Sallust identifies.

---

99. Suet. *De rhet.* 25.1; Aul. Gell. *NA.* 15.11.2.
100. Sal. *Cat.* 11.5.2.

Minority *Mores*

Let us review what we have seen so far. To respond to our initial question—"What is the group that, through its own *consensus*, defines the *mores?*"—we proposed two possible scenarios: the first involving "majority" (i.e., collective) and the second "minority" *mores* (i.e., those belonging to a minor group inside the community itself). We have already outlined the first scenario, deducing that in cases like these the group that reaches a *consensus* on the *mores*, consolidating it in time, is the collective itself, or is represented by the *maiores*. We have also seen that when a contrast is created with different *mores*, this "majority"-type scenario will further divide into two frameworks involving some mechanism of exclusion either of external groups (ethnocentrism) or internal groups (moralism).

On to the second scenario involving *mores* that belong not to the entire community but to minor groups internal to it. Here the argument necessarily becomes more uneven. In the case of collective customs, we were dealing with a well-defined group: the community in its entirety. Making some judgment of his own or others' *mores*, the subject assumes (or pretends to assume) the point of view of the entire community. On the contrary, in the case of "minority" groups the subject necessarily assumes a partial point of view. The process seems to function like this: within the larger community, a polarity arises between two groups, and someone, identifying with one of the two groups, defines the *mores* of the other negatively. In other words, this second scenario entails not so much a process of simple identification of the group ("we" do this) as one of contrast with another group ("others" do this and they are wrong to do so). Frequently the group with which the subject identifies is not made explicit, but has to be identified through assumption, just as we saw in the cases of ethnocentrism analyzed above. Here, too, it is best to begin with some examples.

It was night when our friend Sosia disembarked from the ship and headed toward his master's house: *qui me audacior est homo aut qui confidentior / iuventutis mores qui sciam, qui hoc noctis ambulem?* ("What man is braver and more confident than I, who, knowing the customs of the young, walk around at this hour of night?")[101] Giving his (negative) opinion on the customs of the Roman youth of his day, Sosia establishes a polarity between two groups: one explicit, the *iuvenes*, and one implicit, the "elders," with whom he identifies. In other words, to define the *mores* of a "minority" group consisting of *iuvenes*, Sosia appeals to the *consensus* of another minority group equally internal to the Roman community, that of the "elders," whose

---

101. Plaut. *Am.* 154.

point of view he implicitly assumes. Elsewhere, the *consensus* of the elders against the young may be invoked explicitly—for example, when one old man addresses another in order to win his solidarity in the negative assessment of the customs of "today's" youth. In this way, a small group of *senes* is created—a metonymy of the entire group of elders that hold a monopoly on good morals—to judge the customs of the youth.

In Plautus' *Bacchides,* the pedagogue Lydus addresses the *senex* Philoxenus like this: *eademne erat haec disciplina tibi, quom tu adulescens eras?* ("When you were young, did you have the same education [as the youth of today]?")[102] Certainly not, he goes on, because in your time everyone went to the gym in the morning, everyone went running and wrestled and did not fool around playing lovers' games with prostitutes! Philoxenus responds: *alii, Lyde, nunc sunt mores* ("Customs have changed, Lydus!")[103] "I know only too well that they have changed," Lydus replies, "because once young men used to obey their tutors until they entered upon their political careers. Today, if you slap a child of not even seven years, he'll break the table over your head." In this Plautine scene, the pedagogue solicits the *consensus* of the other old man in order to express his own negative judgment on the customs of "today's" youth. Together, these two *senes* represent a minority group of old men contrasted with another minority group (the young) through their judgment of *mores.*

This polarity between the old and the young can be presented symmetrically, as well. In this case, the situation is unexpectedly reversed. At one point, Horace invites the *puer* not to despise joy and love *donec virenti canities abest / morosa* ("as long as tardy old age is far from your green age").[104] In Porphyry's note to this line, we read the following comment on the expression *morosa: morosa canities, id est senectus difficilis* ("*morosa canities,* that is, inflexible old age").[105] Again, a polarity is created between the minority

---

102. Plaut. *Bacch.* 421ff.; Philoxenus does not actually offer Lydus the complicity that the pedagogue asks of him.

103. Plaut. *Bacch.* 437. Lydus' tirade in the *Bacchides* could merit a longer analysis, since here he does not limit himself only to lamenting the decadence of customs among the youth, but seeks also to identify the reasons for such decadence. He imputes the cause to the bad education and bad example that *parentes* give to their children. The situation is analogus to that of chs. 28 and 29 of Tac. *Dial. de orat.,* where Messalla interprets the decadence of morals on the basis of the fact that mothers do not breast-feed their children anymore but entrust this job to wet-nurses, while parents are the first to give their children bad examples of *dicacitas, lascivia* and so forth. In cases like this, above and beyond the polarity "the young" *versus* "the elderly" is another, within the group of "the elderly": the good elderly *versus* the bad elderly, or the elderly/the elderly *versus* the eldery/the young, in so far as these last display the same vices as the young.

104. Hor. *Carm.* 1.9.18.

105. Porphyr. in Hor. *Carm.* 1.9.18 (p. 38 Havthal). On the *morositas* of the elderly, see Cic. *De senec.* 65.

group of the young and the minority group of the elderly—only this time, the directionality of the contrast is reversed. Horace assumes the point of view of the minority group of the young in order to (negatively) define old age as *morosa* ("inflexible"). The point of view assumed in this assessment is not unlike that taken by Catullus when he invites Lesbia to make love with him, holding of no account the *rumores . . . senum severiorum* ("the grumblings of too severe old men").[106] In the conflict between the young and the old, there exist two symmetrical points of view on the *mores* practiced respectively by the two groups. It is enough that the minority group of reference—that with which the subject identifies in his definition of the *mores*—be inverted, for one of the two points of view to find the chance to express itself.

There are other polarities, regarding different groups. In the prologue to Plautus' *Truculentus*, the behavior of the courtesan Phronesium is described in this way: the woman tries to squeeze her lovers dry, *poscendo atque auferendo, ut mos est mulierum; / nam omnes id faciunt, quom se amari intellegunt* ("asking and taking, as is the custom of women; in fact, they all do this when they realize that they are loved").[107] Here, the polarity is perhaps only the most classic: that between "men" and "women." The minority group with which the subject identifies is that of "men," who claim the right to define (always negatively) the customs of that other group, "women." The seventh book of Vergil's *Aeneid* provides another example, even if the categories have shifted slightly. Queen Amata's speech is introduced by these words: *solito matrum de more locuta est* ("she spoke according to the habitual *mos* of mothers").[108] Here, the polarity is not between "men" and "women," but between "fathers" and "mothers." The group with which the observer identifies is obviously that of the "fathers," who define the customs of the "mothers" through an opposition. According to Vergil, a *pater* would have spoken in a manner differently than Amata, who is a *mater*.

Naturally, we could multiply these examples. Again in the prologue of the *Truculentus*, when it is said of Phronesium that *haec huius saecli in se mores possidet* ("she perfectly incarnates the *mores* of our times"),[109] the polarity introduced is between "those of today" and "those of earlier times." The group to which the observer subscribes is obviously "those of earlier times," who, by their *consensus*, had in the past formulated *boni mores*, customs, in the opinion of the observer, neglected by the present *saeculum*. Of course, this last example has many points of contact with the "moralistic"

---

106. Cat. *Carm.* 5.2ff., *rumoresque senum severiorum / omnes unius aestimemus assis*.
107. Plaut. *Truc.* 16ff.
108. Verg. *Aen.* 7.357.
109. Plaut. *Truc.* 13; cf. also 284, *hoc saeculum moribus quibus siet*.

type examined in the preceding scenario (exclusion from the community of groups or of individuals because their *mores* diverge from the *mos maiorum*). At the same time, however, there also exist some rather unexpected, indeed quite curious groups. In Plautus' *Trinummus,* Lysiteles declares that *amor . . . mores hominum moros ac morosos facit* ("love makes men's *mores* stupid and intractable").[110] This time the polarity is between "people in love" and "people not in love." The subject, identifying himself with the group of those "not in love," gives his assessment—and it is negative!—of those belonging to the first, "in love" group.

In all the examples we have seen, the community that frames the various polarities is "the Romans." From time to time, this greater community can be divided into "minority" groups that try to assert their own customs over others.' The characteristic traits of this kind of scenario are a partiality and mutability of the points of view. The same person, in fact, can take on the point of view of the young to pass judgment on the *mores* of the elderly, and some years later, or simply in a different context, the point of view of the elderly in order to describe the *mores* of the young. Again, the same person can assume the point of view of "men" to speak against "women" or of "those in love" to speak against "those not in love" or, conversely, of "those not in love" to speak against "those in love." Of course, in this last case, everything depends on the whims of Cupid. In other cases, however, things will depend instead on the age or gender of the subject or the context. In some circumstances, the subject will actually be able to take on not one but two points of view, and therefore to identify with two groups of reference simultaneously. This is the case of Juvenal when he utters the famous phrase: *quid quod et antiquis uxor de moribus illi / quaeritur? o medici, nimiam pertundite venam* ("what to say of the fact that he also has the courage to seek a wife with old-fashioned customs? Doctors! Give him a blood-letting! [Because he's crazy!]")[111] The speaker assumes simultaneously the point of view of "men" speaking against "women" (wives have bad customs) and that of "those of earlier times" speaking against "those living now" (women were better before).

Wisdom: Internal Cultural Relativism and the Theater of Life

There are some particularly interesting cases in which the subject tries to free himself from this polarizing and contrastive mechanism in order to

---

110. Plaut. *Trin.* 669.
111. Juv. *Sat.* 6.45.

create a kind of cultural relativism within the community itself. Ennius describes Servilius' "ideal companion"—a wise and prudent man whose counsel one would seek when making an important decision—as someone who *mores veteresque novosque tenentem, / multorum veterum leges divomque hominumque, / prudentem* . . . ("knows both new and old customs, many laws of the ancients, of men and of gods, and who is prudent . . . ").[112] This perfect man who would make the ideal counselor is someone who "knows both new and old customs" and who consequently knows how to act. That is, in the polarity between customs "of yesteryear" and those "of today," Servilius' advisor does not identify with either. He takes no position. As a wise, prudent man and as a good politician, he prefers knowledge of customs to moralism about customs. We might say that Servilius' companion professes a cultural relativism like Herodotus' and Nepos', except that he applies it not to customs practiced by different communities, but to different customs present within his own community. This is the opposite attitude to that found in the examples cited above, where we saw elderly men criticizing the customs of the young in the name of those of "the good old times." Such behaviors are founded upon a strong identification with the group to which one belongs, producing a strongly moralistic attitude. The behavior of Servilius' companion, on the other hand, is founded upon something that not only has little to do with moralism, but is often opposed to it: wisdom.

This relativistic wisdom about *mores* invites a final example, which we introduce in order to suggest a sphere in which the theme of "reflection upon *mores*" inevitably undergoes some slippage: the theater. I am referring in particular to the similarity between human life and the theater, which "wise men" of all periods have employed in the inevitably skeptical and relativistic conviction that the world is nothing but a stage where people play their "parts" (which, precisely because they are "parts," should not be taken too seriously, especially in the conflicts that occur between them.) In Horace's *Ars Poetica,* explaining how to stage a good drama, the poet recommends that *aetatis cuiusque notandi sunt tibi mores* ("you must look well to the specific customs of each age").[113] A description of the *mores* appropriate to the different stages of life then follows: those of the young man inclined to vice and prodigality, those of the mature adult seeking wealth and friendship, those of the avaricious old man and the *laudator temporis acti / se puero, castigator censorque minorum* ("admirer of times past, when he was a child, castigator and chastiser of those younger than him").

---

112. Enn. *Ann.* 283ff. Skutsch.
113. Hor. *Ars* 156ff. The Horation typology of the *mores* that characterize the individual phases of life is naturally longer and more detailed than the summary that we have given here.

The interesting aspect of Horace's typology resides not so much in his catalog of diverse *ēthē* characteristic of the various *hēlikiai* or age-classes, as in the way in which he articulates them. We might expect Horace, in creating a typology of characters, to depict their various *mores* as occurring simultaneously—or, at least, outside of any temporal dimension. Instead, he describes the various types of customs in succession: *first* the young man is a certain way, *then* his customs change when he matures, and *finally* he reaches old age and they change again.[114] Horace does not speak of distinct *personae* that recite different parts on the same stage together, but describes the experiences of a single individual who assumes different customs as he advances in age and experiences changes in the condition of his own existence. The theater of the world (where characters of different ages and therefore of different *mores* play their parts) shades imperceptibly into the theater of individual existence. There, new "roles" are played with the inevitable passing of the years, and so new *mores* are adopted. A vision of this kind, laying bare the differences and conflicts between various "minority" *mores* within the experience of one and the same person, unavoidably gives the impression that none of these *mores* is better than the rest in an absolute sense—or, at least, that the focal point for reflection on *mores* does not rest here. In fact, we are not far from the spirit that motivated Darius' experiment. Asserting that each age class is inevitably prey to its own *mores,* like asserting that each community could never renounce its own traditions, affirms the notion that no age class, like no community, can claim to have a monopoly on morality. A skeptical conclusion, yes—but one of profound wisdom.

Mores and Auctoritas

It would be mistaken to define *mos* or *mores* as a monolithic and absolute block, therefore. Originally, *mos* is simply an attitude—a *iudicium animi,* a *sententia*—arising from a unique occasion and morphing into a real social practice only at the end of a long process. This transformation occurs after a certain group has reached a *consensus* upon it, and once this *consensus* has been confirmed in time as a *consuetudo* (which at Rome bears the mask of the *maiores*). But even when this *consuetudo* has been established and the *mos* has finally become a collective phenomenon, the *mores* continue to

---

114. Cf. Hor. *Ars* 158, *qui voces iam scit puer;* 161, *tandem custode remoto;* 166, *conversis studiis;* 169, *multa senem circumveniunt incommode;* cf. the note of Kiessling and Heinze 1914, 319, according to which, the Horation exposition "gibt sich statt als ein Kapitel der Poetik als ein Kapitel der Psychologie, als seine selbständige Entwicklung der *mores cuiusque aetatis* . . . wie sie der einzelne im Verlauf seines Lebens durchläuft."

remain fluid and diverse—fluid, because even *mos maiorum* is not a definite model, but a nucleus that generates behaviors; diverse, because *mores* are defined through a game of contrasts between one community and another or between different groups within the same community. This is why there are certain "wise" people who are able to escape the polarities between different *mores* and reach a state of cultural relativism, whether "external" (Herodotus, Nepos) or "internal" (Servilius' companion, Horace). In other words, even the collective *mores* remain an occasional creation, and on each occasion their definition depends on the group whose *consensus* one appeals to and with which one identifies. Paraphrasing Terence, we might say: *tot societates, tot sententiae, suos cuique mos.*

The occasional character of the *mores* (as well as their plurality) does not imply, however, that their affirmation is left to chance. Quite the opposite. When a group or an individual defines a *mos*, a very precise rule comes into operation, made up of the social force that this group or individual possesses. Employing the Romans' own terminology, everything depends on the *auctoritas* enjoyed by the followers of a certain *mos*.[115] Individuals might enjoy this kind of *auctoritas*, as in the case of Caesar: his individual *mos* of reciting a *carmen* before getting on a chariot was accepted by the entire community. Or, it might belong to political groups and organs of the *res publica*. In fact, at Rome there was an explicit institutional "authority" in the field of *mores*: the two *censores*, whose specific duty was to enforce the observance of morality. The *censores* also had the power to punish deviation: simply recall the case mentioned above of the censors Gnaeus Domitius Ahenobarbus and Lucius Licinius Crassus, who repressed rhetorical teaching at Rome because it was contrary to *mos maiorum*. But outside of institutions and the dynamics of politics, the determination of *mores* turned equally on the "authority" held by the groups that defined them. In fact, in a hierarchical society such as Rome, the role of *auctoritates* in the definition of the *mores* crops up again at the levels of "gender" and "age class." At Rome, the group composed of men is always stronger than that composed of women; therefore, in any contrast of *mores* women will always have the worst of it (also in the sense that the point of view of women is only very rarely represented in the texts that we possess). For a similar reason, we may expect that the *mores* of "the young" will always have difficult asserting themselves against those of "the elderly."

But beyond the fact that the different groups competing for control of "morality" enjoy different degrees of *auctoritas*, one thing is sure: both *mos*

---

115. For the dynamics of "authority" in the determination of social relationships, above all as regards the authority of "he who speaks," cf. Lincoln 2000, with Greek and Roman examples, and Bettini 2000.

and *mores* represent a network of more or less achievable possibilities very often in conflict with one another. There is not one single *mos*. Instead, there are as many *mores* as there are groups to define them. And it is upon these possibilities—these "thousand manners of living," one may wish to say with Montaigne—that the life of the Roman community was constructed.

FOUR

Face to Face in Ancient Rome
The Vocabulary of Physical Appearance in Latin

On several occasions, Jean-Pierre Vernant has guided us through the world of images and imitations within ancient Greek culture. At the same time, the studies of Françoise Frontisi have permitted us to understand how the Greeks unified in a single image—*to prosōpon*—two notions that remain distinct in our culture: the mask and the face.[1] With regard to ancient Roman culture, however, very little has been said along these lines, although the Romans had to confront problems similar to those faced by the Greeks: on one hand, the need to define what images are; one the other, the need to describe themselves and their own appearance. In this chapter, I would like begin sketching out a possible "anthropology of physical appearance" in the Roman world. To do so, we will focus primarily on the words used in Latin to describe a person's appearance.

Two preliminary remarks. First: in this as in so many other cases, we will be dealing with cultural representations that are not entirely coherent. In other words, the terms and cultural models that we are about to examine do not fit neatly into a single, internally consistent "theory": there is no single, overarching representation of the face or physical appearance that accommodates every mode of representation employed by the Romans.

---

1. The contributions of Vernant and Frontisi towards this topic may be found in different places, beginning with Vernant 1975; Vernant and Frontisi 1983, 53–69; Vernant 1975, 31–58; Frontisi 1988, on which see Vernant 1995, 310–15; and Frontisi 1991b, 131–58. see also Vernant 1988, 211–32.

Indeed, the terminology that refers to physical appearance is a frequently shifting field, suggesting different metaphorical possibilities and different expressive "intentions." (This is the same principle we observed in Roman cultural representation of time and physical space, with their corresponding vocabulary).[2] Sometimes perspectives on the face and "person" change and nothing dictates that these perspectives will be of the same order, or that they will interact on the same level. However, this is probably something we should expect from any cultural configuration of broad relevance and wide-ranging significance within a society.

Second: The question of physical appearance and above all of the "face" should not be reduced to a simple problem of anatomy.[3] A person's face, countenance, physique and build are meaningful in ways far beyond their intrinsic "natural" significance, so to speak. These features of the human body have an extremely specific cultural value. Taken together, they form a fundamental aspect of "the person": its identity. In fact, the ability to recognize someone (to be able to say, "This is Gaius") and the ability to be recognized (to be able to say, "I am Titius," and being accepted as such) both depend to a great degree on physical appearance. This is particularly true of ancient societies, where methods of identification we take for granted today—pictures, identification cards, passports, fingerprints and even DNA—did not exist. As a result, when we consider how the ancient Romans "saw" someone's appearance, face and physique, we cannot separate the analysis of these terms from the anthropological and cultural problem *par excellence*, identity.

Aspect and Sight

So let us see. Vernant and Frontisi have surely taught us how to look at the Greeks "face to face." For the Greeks, the face—*to prosōpon*—was something above all subject to sight. Better yet, it was something designated by a term derived directly from "sight" (*op-*). In defining this vitally important part of the body, the Greeks valorized a relationship between "seeing" and simultaneously "being seen": *to prosōpon* is the "face to face" presence of an individual who, in order to define his own identity, models himself on others in a relationship of complete visual reciprocity. The same tendency to understand the face in terms of "sight" is apparent also in the terms *ops* or *eidos*, both derived from the roots related to "seeing" and once again

---

2. Cf. Bettini 1991a.

3. Even if the two fields coincide in part: this explains why some, though not all of the terms that we will analyze here have been dealt with also by André 1991, 27ff.

used to designate a person's physical appearance. Equally interesting is the Greek expression *dusōpia*, literally "bad face," signifying an excess of shame or deference. Plutarch dedicated one of the essays in his *Moralia* to this personality defect. In his definition, *dusōpia* is a kind of exaggerated shyness "that reaches the point of not being able to look someone in the eye (*antiblepein*) when they ask for something."[4] Even in the case of excessive timidity, then, the face (*-ōpia*) is involved; here, in the reciprocal exchange of gazes—the act of *antiblepein*—one actually loses face. It is clear that in Greece "the face" was defined by and perceived within the sphere of visual interaction. We may then ask how the Romans and how the Latin language responded to this same problem.

In Latin, too, there was an important term denoting physical appearance taken from the field of "sight" and "seeing": *species*. This substantive was derived from the same root that also appears in the rare verb *specio* ("to watch, observe") as well as in its many compound forms (e.g., *respicio, conspicio, perspicio*), the nouns *speculum* ("mirror") and *specula* ("look-out point") and so on. *Species* could signify the ability "to see," but it is rare in this sense.[5] Far more often, it meant "appearance" (the capacity "to be seen.") In this second sense, *species* covers an enormous field of reference, ranging from "appearance" in the most general sense (of people or things), to "apparition,"[6] "image" (natural or artificial), "beauty" and the philosophical "species." The range of meanings covered by *species* includes that of Greek *eidōlon* and *eidos* (which the Latin word regularly translates),[7] but extends far beyond these more narrowly defined Greek terms. *Species* is a term of very broad application, therefore, and is not limited by any means to a person's face or individual features. And so it cannot be the term we are after, at least if we are trying to understand what is distinctive about the Roman definition of "the face" and "appearance."

Likewise in the case of *aspectus*, another word belonging to the family of *specio*. *Aspectus* is properly derived from *aspicio* ("to look") and has both the active sense of "look" or "gaze" and the passive sense of "appearance."[8] Once again, we find a "visual" term not limited specifically to "the face" or "countenance," but to "appearance" in the most general sense (of things, people or animals). In fact, it is interesting to note that when reference is made to the appearance of the face, the single term *aspectus* does not suffice: a hendiadys

---

4. Plut. *De vit. pud.* 1.528e.
5. Cf. Ernout-Meillet 1965, s.v. *specio;* Lucr. *De re. nat.* 4.242, 5.722; Vitr. *De arch.* 5.9, 3.4, 9.2.
6. Negri 1984, 58ff.; Stramaglia 1998, 29ff.
7. Cf. Ernout-Meillet 1965, s.v. *specio*.
8. Cf. *TLL* II, 801–2.

such as *aspectus et os* or *vultus et aspectus* must be used.⁹ This demonstrates that *aspectus* by itself is inadequate for indicating the human face. It meant "appearance" in a very general sense: "being looked at" or "the ability to be looked at"—understood as a kind of quality belonging to all visible objects, not only to the human face. In this sense, the range of meanings attributed to *aspectus* is quite similar to that of *species*.¹⁰

In light of the vocabularies of the Romance languages, we might reasonably have hoped to discover something more specific in the visual sphere. Words like Italian *viso* and French *visage* suggest that the Romans, like the Greeks, privileged the visual dimension in their definition of the face by referring to it with the word *visus*. But this would be an error of perspective: in Latin, the term *visus* was used in the strict sense of "the ability to see" or, passively, the "vision" that one sees. It never meant "face." The face as "sight," as something that can "look" and "be looked at" at the same time, is evidently a cultural model that postdates classical Latin.¹¹ How did the Romans characterize the face, then? Put another way, what did the Romans "see" when they looked at each other, face to face?

A Face That Speaks

An answer is not far to seek: above all, the Romans saw a mouth. The word *os* is the most common expression in Latin for "the face," and comparative evidence within Indo-European shows that the primary meaning of *os* is "mouth."¹² The Latin word *os* in the sense of "face" is a metonymic extension of the word's original meaning, then. In Benveniste's terminology, we could say that Latin derives the designation "face" from its signification "mouth." But why this choice precisely?

The Mouth That Speaks and the Mouth That Eats

Anatomically speaking, the mouth is certainly an important part of the face. However, it is not the only important part of the face, and it is not neces-

---

9. Quint. *Inst. orat.*, 6.3.26, *aspectus et habitus oris non inurbanus;* Tac. *Ann.* 14.10, *vultu et aspectu terrere legiones.*

10. The close relationship between the two terms was clearly felt by the Romans: cf. Aul. Gell. *NA.* 13.30, . . . *ab aspectu species et a fingendo figura.*

11. Blaise 1954, s.v. records the sense of "face" for *visus* in *Itinerarium a Burdigala Hierusalem usque*, p. 20, 15 (4th c. C.E.).

12. Cf. Ernout-Meillet 1965, s.v. *os*; André 1991, 56ff.

sarily the part of the face that first catches our attention. If *os* eventually comes to occupy the entire semantic space of "the face," overshadowing all other facial features, the explanation must lie more in the cultural value of *os* than in the purely anatomical meaning of the "mouth." In Latin, *os* has strong connotations; it evokes a capacity that chiefly distinguishes human beings from other animate creatures: language.[13] For Latin speakers, the connection between *os* and words such as *oro* or *orator* was probably immediately recognizable.[14] But even ignoring etymological speculation, such common idioms as *in ore esse* ("to be much spoken of"), *uno ore* ("by general agreement") and *aperire ora* ("to speak") leave little doubt about the relationship between *os* and *oro*. Likewise the great number of passages in which *os* is used in the sense of "discourse, speech," "the sound of the voice" or "pronunciation."[15]

Os is first and foremost "speech."[16] We may suggest, therefore, that for the Romans "the face" corresponded to the mouth insofar as it manifested the ability to speak. The mouth is the speaking part of the face. As such, it overshadowed everything else in defining "facial appearance." The specifically "verbal" value of the human face becomes clearer if we compare *os* with the word in Latin used to designate an animal's "snout" or "beak": *rostrum*. The term *rostrum* was also originally used simply of the mouth, but was almost "invasively" extended to indicate the rest of the face. But to what kind of "mouth" does the word *rostrum* refer? Derived from the verb *rodo* ("to chew"), *rostrum* is therefore "the mouth that eats." *Rostrum* is the mouth insofar as it "chews" (*rodit*).[17] In other words, an animal's mouth is exclusively an organ destined to chew food. Animals are considered dumb beasts, which know only how to eat and nothing more. For this reason, their facial appearance is understood exclusively in terms of "eating."[18] This is not the case with human beings. The human mouth stands for the whole face

---

13. See, e.g., Cic. *Leg.* 1.9.27, *moderationem vocis, orationis vim, quae conciliatrix est humanae maxime societatis*.
14. Var. *Ling. Lat.* 6.76, *oro ab ore;* Enn. *Scaen.* 306 Vahlen², *quam tibi ex ore orationem duriter dictis dedit;* etc. Cf. Ernout-Meillet 1965. s.v. *oro*.
15. Cf. *TLL* IX, 2, 1081–1082 Tessner.
16. Cf. Ernout-Meillet 1965, s.vv. *os* and *oro*.
17. Ernout-Meillet 1965, s.v. *rodo;* André 1991, 36.
18. In cases of comic, familiar, or joking language where *rostrum* is used to indicate a man's face, the "eating" characteristic of this type of 'mouth' is made explicitly obvious: cf., e.g., Plaut. *Men.* 89, *apud mensam plenam homini rostrum deliges*. Elsewhere what is emphasized is the gross and animal-like nature of the *rostrum*, as at Lucilius fr. 1121 Marx, *baronum ac rupicum [= rusticorum] squarrosa, incondita rostra*. On the fact that *rostrum* (according to *consuetudo*) was a word considered inappropriate for designating a man's face, but was in any case used for this purpose in particular contexts, see the evidence of Non. Marcell. *De comp. doctr.* 455ff. Lindsay.

because of its relationship with *oratio* and *orator*.[19] Above all, the human mouth is a mouth that speaks.

Identity in Walking and Talking

Representations and terms that define bodily appearance cannot be separated from their cultural content—that is, from their capacity to define identity. It will be opportune to recall, therefore, that, in general, the voice and speech play a decisive role in defining identity, as well. To observe this process, we will have to look at some moments when someone's identity is put into crisis, since uncertainty tends to bring to light the (usually tacitly understood) features used in identification. In general, these are stories of duplicates or "doubles," in which someone falsely assumes another person's identity, imitating that person's physical features and other traits.

Morpheus, the god of dreams, could perform expert imitations of another's *figura* in order to deceive dreamers.[20] Ovid tells us:

> non illo quisquam sollertius alter
> exprimit incessus vultumque sonumque loquendi;
> adicit et vestes et consuetissima cuique
> verba. . . .[21]

> No one was better than Morpheus at imitating someone's gait, face, and the sound of their voice, as well as their clothes and most personal expressions.

Ovid's description of "identity theft" is extremely interesting, since it reveals the specific elements that the Romans considered to be identifying features: the gait, the face and the sound of the voice. Below, we will consider the way in which the *vultus* was able to express someone's identity and how the voice served as an instrument of identification. But now we may open a brief parenthesis to analyze another situation in which the *gressus* or *incessus* are listed as traits capable of defining identity.

In the first book of the *Aeneid*, Cupid adopts the likeness of Iulus to

---

19. Pliny (*Nat. hist.* 11.138) asserts that *os* was used not only for human beings but also for animals (*facies homini tantum, ceteris os aut rostra*); the same in Carisius, *Grammatici Latini* 390.28.13 Keil, *vultus proprie hominis, os omnium*. In actual fact, *os* is used very infrequently to designate the "face" of animals (cf. the passages in *TLL* IX, 2, 1089, 30–38 Zimmermann). Note that this often happens when an author is speaking of a human being transformed into an animal (Io) or of a divinity with animal-like features (Anubis) or of mythic beasts (Phoenix), etc.
20. Ov. *Met.* 11.633ff.
21. Ov. *Met.* 11.635ff.

better deceive Dido and make her fall in love with Aeneas. Here we see Cupid at work: *gressu gaudens incedit Iuli* ("he walks in happily with Iulus' step").[22] Imitating Iulus' gait forms an inseparable part of the trick and Cupid's alteration of identity. Likewise, the goddess Iris takes on the identity of the old woman Beroe, but is then unmasked by her *gressus:* evidently, Iris continued to walk with a goddess' bearing, failing to fool anyone who observed her carefully.[23] The gods, as we know, walk differently than mortals do: *vera incessu patuit dea* ("the goddess was revealed by her walk"), as Vergil says of Venus.[24] Elsewhere, someone's manner of walking serves as a way to express family identity, guaranteeing, for example, the relationship between father and son. Andromache, looking at her son Astyanax, sees in him the features of her dead husband: *hos vultus meus / habuit Hector, talis incessu fuit, habituque talis* ("this is the same face that my Hector had; this was his way of walking and his personality").[25] *Gressus* is also a factor involved in the creation of a "living ghost" (the typical expedient, since Homer's *Iliad*, for rescuing a hero in distress). When Juno must fashion a "substitute" of Aeneas in order to fool Turnus, she begins with a creature formed of cloud and then *dat sine mente sonum gressusque effingit euntis* ("she gives him a voice without mind and she feigns Aeneas' way of walking").[26]

But to return to the specific problem we were discussing: the power of the mouth and of speech in identifying someone. It is particularly interesting that Ovid's Morpheus, master of counterfeit identities, is acquainted with the art of imitating not simply the "voice" but also the "most characteristic expressions of each person." In identifying someone, all the components of the act of speaking play a role: vocal quality and lexical choice, as well as the most characteristic features of their diction. Recall that at Vespasian's funeral "an *archimimus* named Favor depicted the emperor's person and imitated his dress, what he did and what he said while he was alive."[27] Here, someone wishing to assume another person's identity is concerned above all with reproducing their linguistic idiosyncrasies—just as Ovid's Morpheus, in order to better deceive Halcyon, the wife of Ceyx, not only uses the dead man's words, but also *adicit . . . vocem . . . quam coniugis illa / crederet esse sui* ("adds a voice that the woman would believe to be her husband's").[28]

---

22. Verg. *Aen.* 1.689.
23. Verg. *Aen.* 5.646ff.
24. Verg. *Aen.* 1.405.
25. Sen. *Tr.* 464ff.
26. Verg. *Aen.* 10.640; Cf. Hom. *Il.* 5.164ff.; Sil. Ital. *Pun.* 17.523ff.
27. Suet. *Vesp.* 19, *in funere Favor archimimus personam eius ferens imitansque, ut est mos, facta ac dicta vivi.* For the imitation of the voice in caricature, see below, n. 148.
28. Ov. *Met.* 10.671ff.

Moreover, the *vox,* like the *incessus,* was capable of defining not only individual identity but also that of a family or group. Indeed, it could confirm that a person was an authentic member of a particular lineage: Lucretius, in a passage dealing with the "genetics" of resemblance, attributes to Venus the ability to reproduce in the descendants of a family line the *maiorumque . . . vultus, vocesque comasque* ("the face of their ancestors, their voice, and their hair").[29] Someone's way of speaking, therefore, with its phonetic peculiarities and individual lexical choices, was a powerful contribution to their identity. As Pliny said: *vox in homine magnam vultus habet partem. agnoscimus ea prius quam cernamus non aliter quam oculis* ("In man, the voice plays an important part in the face. By means of the voice, we are able to recognize someone before we even see them, recognizing someone as we do with our eyes").[30]

Someone's voice makes them recognizable. It produces their identity. Very likely these are the cultural models that gave the face/mouth its meaning at Rome. With this term—*os*—the Romans designated "the face" not only by appealing to that most human capacity—language—but by evoking above all a "verbal quality" that made a major contribution to the definition of someone's identity (in conjunction with the facial expression, the gait, and so on). Someone's voice, their pronunciation of words and their typical expressions constituted a true and proper "speaking icon," located in the face/mouth—the *os.*

In this perspective, comparing Roman with Greek culture becomes very interesting. As mentioned above, in the Greek world, what appears to be the decisive factor in defining the face is the visual component. For the Greeks, the face was *prosōpon.* For the Romans, on the other hand, the face was understood as a "mouth" and as "speech." Pliny is explicit: "the voice plays an important part in the face." In this light, the relationship that the Romans have with the *persona* ("mask") seems indicative. *Persona* is, of course, the Latin equivalent of Greek *prosōpon,* which, as we have said, designates both "the face" and "mask." The word *persona,* in fact, was associated with the verb *persono* ("I speak through, I resound").[31] According to the interpretation of Gavius Bassus, *quoniam . . . indumentum illud oris clarescere et resonare vocem facit, ob eam causam persona dicta est* ("because this apparel for the face makes the voice clearer and more sonorous, it is called *persona*").[32]

For the Greeks, the mask—like the face—belonged in the dimension of *visuality.* For the Romans, it seems to have been instead a matter of *orality.*

---

29. Lucr. *De re. nat.* 4.1224.

30. Plin. *Nat. hist.* 11.271.

31. The relationship is obviously impossible due to the difference in quantity of the -*o*-. Cf. Ernout-Meillet 1965, s.v. *persona.*

32. Aul. Gell. *NA.* 5.7.2.

Once again, in order to define someone's "facial identity," Roman culture valued the act of speaking above that of seeing. "The mask" was conceived as an object that made sound, just as the face was a "mouth" and the voice identified the face. At Rome, identity was conveyed above all by the act of speaking. Servius declared this explicitly: people, he said, "recognize each other by means of their speech (*se sermone cognoscunt*)."[33]

An Interior Face

In addition to *os*—"the face that speaks"—another word, and the cultural dimension it represents, is crucial to the description of "appearance" at Rome: *vultus*. In many cases, this word functions simply as a synonym of *os*, denoting "the face." Elsewhere, a difference between the words *vultus* and *os* is perceptible. Livy, for example, describes Appius Claudius' intransigence like this: *idem habitus oris, eadem contumacia in vultu* ("he did not change the expression of his *os*, he did not change the haughtiness of his *vultus*").[34]

If, as regards *os*, Livy emphasizes the immutability of the man's general expression (the *habitus* of his face), his description as regards *vultus* underscores the presence of an emotion—the arrogance characteristic of the Claudii—that finds expression in the face. Our analysis of what *vultus* meant to the ancient Romans will focus on this, then: the expression of "interiority."

An Interior Face That the Greeks Do Not Have

Cicero demonstrates himself particularly proud of the word *vultus*, when he writes: is, *qui appellatur vultus, qui nullo in animante esse praeter hominem potest, indicat mores, cuius vim Graeci norunt, nomen omnino non habent* ("this thing that is called vultus and which is not found in any creature except human beings, indicates a person's character: the Greeks understand what the vultus is, but they have no corresponding word for it whatsoever").[35]

According to Cicero, animals do not have a *vultus*, it being exclusive to human beings.[36] Moreover, the Greeks did not have a word adequate for

---

33. Servius Auctus in *Ecl.* 4.60, *sicut enim maiores se sermone cognoscunt, ita infantes parentes risu se indicant agnoscere*. The reference is to the theme of recognition between the newborn and his parents, which, according to tradition, was supposed to happen through the "laugh."
34. Liv. *AUC.* 2.61.1.
35. Cic. *Leg.* 1.9.27.
36. Cicero seems to be correct. In fact, in the few cases that *vultus* is used for animals, it is really a matter of human beings transformed into animals: Verg. *Aen.* 7.20 (men changed into animals by Circe); Ov. *Fast.* 2.177ff. (Callisto changed into a bear); Sen. *Oed.* 761 (Acteon changed into a

expressing the meaning conveyed by Latin *vultus*. This is precious comparative evidence that Greek authors seem to confirm, at least indirectly. Aristotle, for example, says that a corpse cannot have a true and proper *prosōpon* except through a kind of homonymy, since "there is no *prosōpon* if there is no *psuchē*." It is difficult to shake off the impression that Aristotle is struggling from a lack of terminology, since he is compelled to employ a single word to describe both the living and expressive face of a human being (the person endowed with a *psuchē*) and the dead and inexpressive face of a cadaver.[37] Not so with the Latin *vultus*, which, at least according to Cicero, encompasses a very specific semantic and cultural space: *vultus . . . indicat mores*. The *vultus* is a vehicle for expressing personality traits and internal emotions. Servius even maintains that *vultus . . . pro mentis qualitate formatur* ("the *vultus* is shaped in accordance with the quality of the soul").[38] The grammarian Eugraphius clarifies the point when he says that *vultus . . . animi motu facies ad tempus aptata* ("the *vultus* . . . is the face assumed according to the motions of the soul").[39] Isidore, with his etymological vision of culture, links the origin of the word *vultus* to the word *voluntas*, of which the *vultus* would then be an external manifestation.[40] In expressing someone's *voluntas*, the *vultus* is assigned the task of expressing the emotions of the soul (Incidentally, this is a derivation that some modern scholars have tried to revive from time to time).[41] Quintilian is also quite explicit. In fact, as the professor of rhetoric explains, the *caput* plays a determining role in *actio*, especially as regards *significatio*.[42] And within the *caput* (itself such an important part of the human body)

> dominatur autem maxime vultus. hoc supplices, hoc minaces, hoc blandi . . . sumus, hoc pendent homines, hunc intuentur, hic spectatur etiam antequam dicimus: hoc quosdam amamus, quosdam odimus, hoc plura intellegimus, hic est saepe pro omnibus verbis.

> the *vultus* is the most important part. By means of the face we beseech, we threaten, we appear innocuous. . . . Men rely on this, this is what they look at and this is what is looked at before someone even begins to speak. Because

---

stag); Apul. *Met.* 6.26 (Lucius changed into an ass). Cf. above, n. 19 for the analogous case of *os* used of animals in the case of human beings transformed into beasts.

37. Arist. *De gen. anim.* 734b.
38. Serv. in *Aen.* 1.683.
39. Eugraph. in Ter. *Andr.* 119 Wessner.
40. Isid. *Etym.* 11.34, *vultus vero dictus, eo quod per eum animi voluntas ostenditur.*
41. On the etymology of *vultus*, cf. Cohen 1979, 337–44 (inclining towards *vel- of *volvo*); cf. André 1991, 36.
42. Quint. *Inst. orat.* 11.69 and 72. Cf. now Dupont 2000, 122ff.

of the face, we love some people, while we hate others; it is by means of the face that we understand many things, and the face is often worth more than all the words taken together.

The *vultus* is the central focus of interpersonal communication. This part of the head becomes a locus of hints and signs, to the point of functioning as a true and proper "language" that people can use to decipher the feelings and intentions at work in another person's soul.

This situation has a number of interesting consequences. In particular, it confirms our idea that, in addition to *os*, there was a word in Latin referring to the face directly related to the sphere of interiority. The word *vultus* designated someone's external appearance in relation to the internal—not only as "the 'face,'" but also as a vehicle for their *mores* and *mens*. *Vultus* was an expression of the soul. For this reason, Latin *vultus* can be used both in the singular and plural to refer to an individual's face:[43] *vultus* is not a fixed "image" but a changing expression. In fact, *vultus* designates a set of dispositions connected with something that is variable by nature: the "inner life" of the person. Cicero, in a letter to Cornificius, commends Cherippus for not only reporting Cornificius' emotions and words to him, but describing his individual expressions in detail: *vultus mehercule tuos mihi expressit omnes, non solum animum ac verba pertulit* ("he has truly revealed all the expressions of your face ["the faces which you make," he might have said], in addition to sharing your feelings and your words").[44]

As the expression of internal emotions, the *vultus* is necessarily "shifting." Recommending that the orator avoid a defect of voice and appearance the Greeks called *monotonia*, Quintilian makes the following observation: *nonne ad singulas paene distinctiones, quamvis in eadem facie, tamen quasi vultus mutandus est?* ("even if the face remains the same, should there not be variety for each portion of the speech, changing like the *vultus?*").[45] The *vultus* is supposed to modulate the *facies* in a potentially infinite series of expressions whose variety reinforces and comments upon the speech, according to its development, transitions and nuances. The *facies* does not change, however.[46] The *vultus* is mutable and, as such, poses a number of problems for literary description, as may well be imagined. Literary texts often have the task of representing—by means of the written word—the various expres-

---

43. The use of the plural of *vultus* is specifically underscored by Quintilian (*Inst. orat.* 8.6.28) in his discussion of figures: *est etiam huic tropo quaedam cum synecdoche vicinia; nam, cum dico vultus hominis pro vultu, dico pluraliter quod singulare est*.
44. Cic. *Ad fam.* 12.30.3.
45. Quint. *Inst. orat.* 11.3.47.
46. On this, see below, 148–49.

sions that people may assume as the external manifestation of what is in their souls. To do so, texts have no choice but to transform the shifting variability of the *vultus* into an equally varied series of adjectives. To take the tragedies of Seneca as only one example, there the word *vultus* is accompanied by over twenty different adjectives.[47]

As with *os*, so too with *vultus* a comparison with Greek culture is in order. This comparison is in fact suggested by a native informant—Cicero, who has already explained to us that the Greeks did not have a word corresponding to Latin *vultus*. A difference does exist between the two cultures: If in Greek "the face" (*to prosōpon*) is primarily "something for seeing," in Latin *vultus* is something opposed to the dimension of visuality. The *vultus* is not something "to see," but something "to infer." The *vultus* does not presume an open gaze, but glimpses, glances and signs.

Once again Cicero helps us understand the meaning of *vultus* for the Romans. In forensic activity, he says, it is essential to cultivate a careful and scrupulous attention to detail (*diligentia*): *ut vultus . . . perspiciamus omnis, qui sensus animi plerumque indicant, diligentia est* ("diligence is being able to perceive all expressions [*vultus*], which generally reveals the feelings of the soul").[48] It is not enough simply to look (*re-spicere*) at the *vultus* in order to understand it; one must *per-spicere*—that is, employ a penetrating stare somehow capable of overcoming the barrier of exteriority. The prefix *pre-* is crucial. "The face" does not reveal itself to a superficial glance; instead, it requires visual penetration. The fact is, in the cultural configuration presupposed by the Latin word *vultus*, the face takes on a decidedly semiotic value, functioning as a collection of signs referring to the individual feelings of the conscience or to specific personality traits. The *vultus* is not an image to contemplate but a sign to interpret. Semiotically, inside comes out. The "face" in front of us, as the expression of an otherwise invisible internal condition, refers elsewhere. This is something very different from the visual immediacy of the Greek *prosōpon*.

In this light, it is not surprising that in the practice of physiognomy the analyst's attention is attracted precisely to the *vultus*. In fact, in the physiognomic treatise of the so-called Anonymus Latinus, we read:

> omnis vultus cum est plenus et crassus, ignavum significat et voluptatibus deditum, deductus cogitatorem, subdulum, timidum, astutum asseverat. vultus parvus parvum et angustum ingenium, enormis stultitiam et ignaviam testatur.[49]

---

47. *Trux, superbus, obscurus, pallens, dubius, subdolus, torvus, ferox*, etc.
48. Cic. *De orat.* 2.148.
49. Anonymus Latinus, *De Physiognomonia* 50 (in Raina 1993).

Whenever the *vultus* is full and fleshy this means that the person is lazy and pleasure-seeking; when the face is thin and drawn-out, it indicates a thinker, someone who is tricky, shy and clever. A small face indicates a small and narrow character; a large face indicates stupidity and sloth.

In the corresponding section of the treatise attributed to Pseudo-Aristotle, the Greek text uses the word *prosōpon*:[50] Cicero has already explained that the Greeks did not have a wide range of choices when it came to speaking about the face. Since the discussion involves unmistakably physical characteristics of the face ("fleshy" and "full," "thin" and so forth), we may have expected the Latin text to employ *facies* instead of *vultus*. As we will describe below, *facies* designates the face as a "natural" set of features—the characteristics of its basic anatomical structure.[51] Evidently for the anonymous author of the physiognomy, however, the kind of face that was interesting from the point of view of physiognomic analysis was *vultus*. In the Roman cultural tradition, it is *vultus* that fulfills the semiotic function of the face; it is *vultus* that is traditionally associated with the dialectic of inside/outside and with externalizing the "inner world" through signs. At Rome, the physiognomists' "face"—that is, the semiotic face—was, of course, the *vultus*.

Vultus *and* Oculi: *The Seat of the Soul*

We can now try to "locate" Latin *vultus* as we did earlier for *os*. If, for the Romans, "the face" (*os*) corresponded to the lower portion of the face where the mouth is located, *vultus* seems instead to involve the upper portion where the eyes are. In many cases, the word *vultus* appears to designate what we might call "visual capacity" and indeed also the eyes. Lucretius, enumerating a series of natural portents, tarries on the description of monstrous beings that lack mouths and eyes: *muta sine ore etiam, sine voltu caeca reperta* ("creatures that are silent without *os,* and blind without *voltus*").[52] The absence of *os* renders these monsters mute and their lack of *vultus* renders them blind. Undoubtedly, the word *vultus* means "eyes" here. So too in Seneca's *Hercules Oetaeus:* Alcmena, in the final scene of the tragedy, confronts the apotheosis of Hercules and asks herself if what she has seen really is her son: *fallor an vultus putat / vidisse natum?* ("Am I mistaken or do my eyes (*vultus*) think that they have seen my son?").[53] Once again, *vultus* clearly

---

50. Pseudo-Aristotele, *Physiognomika* 811b5 (in Raina 1993).
51. See below, 151–54.
52. Lucr. *De re. nat.* 5.841.
53. Sen. *Herc. Oet.* 1977ff.

refers to the "sight" of the eyes.[54] We may therefore conclude that when the Romans said *vultus,* they focused on the upper part of the face and not the lower (as when they said *os*). The face/mouth is therefore opposed to the face/eyes. But how is it that the eyes are involved in defining of the "face" of interiority?

The answer to this question is not unexpected. We need only recall the famous passage in which Pliny describes the powers of the eyes:

> neque ulla ex parte maiora animi indicia cunctis animalibus, sed homini maxime, id est miserationis, clementiae, odii. . . . profecto in oculis animus habitat. . . . animo autem videmus, animo cernimus: oculi ceu vasa quaedam visibilem eius partem accipiunt atque trasmittunt.[55]

> In all animals, but especially in human beings, there is no part of the body that conveys more signs of the state of the soul, that is, signs of sympathy, forgiveness, hatred. . . . There is no doubt that the soul resides in the eyes. . . . With the soul, we are able to see, we discern with the soul: but it is the eyes that receive and transmit this visual force, like vases.

The eyes, where the soul "resides," are a kind of window between a person's inside and outside—a privileged channel through which *indicia* are transmitted—making it possible for a person's soul to be deciphered. This is why *vultus,* localized around the eyes, points precisely towards a person's "interior," serving as its means of signification. Quintilian explicitly confirms that, as part of the *vultus,* it is the eyes that act as the "window into the soul": *in ipso vultu plurimum valent oculi, per quos maxime animus emanat* ("in the *vultus,* the eyes are most important; the soul emerges through the eyes most of all").[56]

Vultus, Frons *and* Supercilia

It is not quite correct to identify the *vultus* with the eyes, however, since the eyes do not appear to constitute the entire *vultus* in Roman culture. Cicero,

---

54. The same happens with the hallucinations of Oedipus (Sen. *Phoen.* 42ff.) when he relives the horrible experience of being blinded in the form of an attack by his father's ghost against his already hollow eyes: *en ecce, inanes manibus infestis petit / foditque vultus.*

55. Plin. *Nat. hist.* 11.145ff. The topos of the eyes as a place in which a man's interior life is made visible occurs also in physiognomic treatises: cf. Anonymus Latinus, *De Physiognomonia* 10 (in Raina 1993).

56. Quint. *Inst. orat.* 11.3.75.

in the same passage where he praises the virtues of the word *vultus,* expressly distinguishes the eyes and *vultus*. The former are able to reveal *quem ad modum animo affecti simus*—i.e., our feelings—whereas the *vultus* "reveals the traits of our character (*indicat mores*)."[57] *Vultus* and *oculi* are not exactly identical: rather, it seems that *vultus,* although localized in the eyes, can be identified more generally with the entire upper part of the face. Consider the way in which Cicero attacks Piso, condemning him for his deceptive and lying behavior towards his fellow citizens:

> oculi supercilia frons vultus denique totus, qui sermo quidam tacitus mentis est, hic in fraudem homines impulit, hic eos quibus erat ignotus decepit, fefellit, induxit.[58]

The eyes, the eyebrows, the forehead, in short, the entire *vultus,* which constitutes something like a silent language of the mind, is what has dragged the others into his trap; it is his *vultus* which has tricked them, deceiving and entangling those who were not familiar with the man.

Once again, the *vultus* is identified as a place of semiosis, where a person's "interiority" is revealed—like a real, albeit soundless "language" of the mind. Yet the *vultus* consists not only of the eyes (although they are mentioned first), but also of two other significant parts of the face: the eyebrows and the forehead. In the Roman cultural tradition, these two parts of the body function as a kind of semiotic interface with a person's "interiority," just as the eyes do. In fact, the Romans considered the *frons* and the *supercilia* a source of expressive power. For example, Pliny tells us:

> frons et aliis, sed homini tantum tristitiae, hilaritatis, clementiae, severitatis index. in assensu eius supercilia homini et pariter et alterna mobilia. et in his pars animi: negamus iis, annuimus. haec maxime indicant fastum, superbiam. aliubi conceptaculum, sed hic sedem habet; in corde nascitur, huc subit, hic pendet. nihil altius simul abruptiusque invenit in corpore, ubi solitaria esset.[59]

Other animals also have a forehead, but only in human beings is the forehand able to indicate sadness, joy, pity, severity. In the moment of assent, the eyebrows move both in unison and alternately. A part of the soul also

---

57. Cic. *Leg.* 1.26, *et oculi nimis arguti, quem ad modum animo affecti simus, loquuntur, et is, qui appellatur vultus, qui nullo in animante esse praeter hominem potest, indicat mores.*
58. Cic. *Pis.* 1.1.
59. Plin. *Nat. hist.* 11.138.

resides in the eyebrows: we use the eyebrows to deny something, we use the eyebrows to indicate assent. It is above all in the eyebrows that we can see pride and boastfulness. This feeling does not arise in the eyebrows, but the eyebrows are where it resides: it actually arises in the heart and from there it rises up and then hangs there in the eyebrows, because there is no other place in the body so steep and high, a place which that feeling of pride can have all to itself.

The forehead and the eyebrows are another, equally semiotic region of the human face. Like the eyes, these parts of the face can function as a kind of *index* revealing a person's inner emotions. In fact, the communicative function of the *frons* (as of the eyes and the *vultus* more generally) is made clear in a number of proverbial expressions.[60] The *supercilium* was also proverbial for being able to reveal involuntary impulses which could be read as divinatory signs.[61] The word could also be used as a synonym for pride or severity,[62] just as the adjective *superciliosus* could refer to an extremely severe or austere character.[63] Pliny, in a passage dealing with physiognomy, refers explicitly to the signifying virtues of both the forehead and the eyebrows as means of assessing a person's character from the features of his or her face.[64] Quintilian, too, as a meticulous teacher of *actio*, carefully noted that *multum et superciliis agitur, nam et oculos formant aliquatenus et fronti imperant* ("a great deal happens in the eyebrows, because they mark out to a certain degree the shape of the eyes and they rule the forehead").[65] Quintilian's testimony becomes all the more intriguing, however, when he describes the trick that comic actors employ better to express the emotions of the soul, despite the rigidity of the masks they wear:

> pater ille, cuius praecipue partes sunt, quia interim concitatus interim lenis est, altero erecto altero composito est supercilio, atque id ostendere maxime latus actoribus moris est quod cum iis quas agunt partibus congruat.[66]

---

60. Cf. Cic. *Att.* 14.3b.1, *non enim solum ex oratione, sed etiam ex vultu et oculis et fronte, ut aiunt, meum erga te amorem perspicere potuisses*. Other examples in Otto 1890, 130 and 147. Cf. also Lamacchia 1976, 957–86, above all as regards shame and "impudence."

61. Cf. Plaut. *Pseud.* 107, *supercilium mihi salit;* Otto 1890, 335. See also the meaning that Pliny (*Nat. hist.* 11.145) attributes to *conivere*, or the action of "squinting the eyelids."

62. Cf. e.g., Cic. *Leg. agr.* 2.93 and *Post red. in sen.* 7.16; etc.

63. Cf. Sen. *Ep.* 123.11.

64. Plin. *Nat. hist.* 11.275 (from Pompeius Trogus); on the eyebrows, cf. Arist. *De nat. anim.* 1.12.491b; Pseudo-Aristotele, *Physiognomonika* 29.812b (in Raina 1993); Anonymus Latinus, *De physiognomonia* 18 (in Raina 1993).

65. Quint. *Inst. orat.* 11.3.78.

66. Quint. *Inst. orat.* 11.3.74.

The father, who has the main role, is sometimes enraged and at other times is calm, so he has an eyebrow that is raised and an eyebrow that is lowered, and the actors turn the side of the mask to the audience that is better suited to the particular lines that they are reciting at the moment.

Codified in the tradition of the theatrical mask, the position of the eyebrow is a sign that instantaneously expresses an emotional state. By showing one side of the mask or the other—the angry side, with its eyebrow raised, or the calm side, with its eyebrow lowered—the actor uses the *supercilium* as a true and proper sign of the fixed polarities between which the comic *pater*'s emotional state oscillates.

Before concluding this discussion of the eyebrows, we must of course cite the words of Charles Le Brun, the *premier peintre* of the court of Louis XIV and one of the great experts on the features of the human form and their expressive power. In his *Conférence . . . sur l'expression générale et particulière*, published in 1698, Le Brun writes:

> Just as we said that the gland situated in the center of the brain is the place where the soul gathers the images of the passions, the eyebrow is the place in all the face where the passions can best be recognized, although many have said instead that this happens in the eyes.

Le Brun's treatise is accompanied by a series of illustrations, drawn by the artist himself, beginning with a depiction of "Tranquility"—a kind of "zero grade" of the human soul—which formed the basis for the other emotions: *l'Admiration, l'Etonnement, l'Attention, le Mépris* and so on. As we flip through these various illustrations, it is impossible to overlook the special attention Le Brun devoted to the eyebrows in altering the expression of the "schematic" face. Varying the length, inclination and shape of the *supercilium*, he clearly attributed great importance to it as a part of the face that reveals the "passions."[67]

Let us then return to *vultus* and to the problem with which we began: where *vultus* is "located." *Vultus,* the major focal point of which is the eyes (and indeed often tending to be identified with the eyes), nevertheless extends to include other parts of the face such as the forehead and the eyebrows, which are likewise endowed with the power to express a person's inner state. In short, it seems that *vultus* is generally understood by the Romans to be the upper portion of the face and that this region is considered by Roman culture to transmit the emotions of the soul.

---

67. Le Brun 1992.

The Face That Deceives and the Vultus/*Mask*

In *De Oratore,* Cicero discusses a variety of comic effects, including the humor of shameless imitation—such as when Crassus caricatures his opponent Gnaeus Domitius Ahenobarbus by exclaiming *per tuam nobilitatem, per vestram familiam* ("by your noble descent, by your family line"), thus provoking the audience's laughter.[68] According to Cicero, the comic effects of caricature are achieved by means of *vocis ac vultus imitatio* ("imitation of the voice and face"). As with the voice, then, it was possible to imitate the *vultus* so as to induce laughter (The Romans were well aware of how annoying such caricatures could be for the butt of the joke).[69] In caricature, the *vultus* is imitated in order to inspire laughter—that is, with the intention of revealing the identity of the person against whom the comic attack is directed. *Depravata imitatio* therefore presupposes the "recognizability" of this person and that the caricature will be deciphered immediately; otherwise, the comic effect would not work.[70]

It is also possible to imitate the *vultus* in such a way that masks the fact of "imitation"—not to provoke laughter, but to deceive the "audience." In a passage we have already cited in part, Servius makes a very interesting observation in this regard. The grammarian has been commenting on one of the most famous instances of "the double" in Roman literature: when Cupid mimics Ascanius' physical features in order to make Dido fall in love with Aeneas. Vergil has Venus give her son the following instructions: *tu faciem illius noctem non amplius unam / falle dolo, et notos pueri puer indue vultus* ("use your tricks to counterfeit the face [*facies*] of Ascanius for not more than one night and, boy that you are, put on the familiar face [*vultus*] of that boy").[71] Servius remarks: *faciem pro vultu posuit. nullus enim faciem alterius potest accipere, sed vultum, qui pro mentis qualitate formatur. unde infra est 'et notos pueri puer indue vultus'* ("Vergil has used the word *facies* in the place of the word *vultus.* In fact, no one would ever put on the *facies* of someone else: but they could assume someone else's *vultus* because it is shaped in relation to the qualities of the mind. This is why Vergil says later, 'and, boy that you are, put on the familiar face [*vultus*] of that boy'").

Apparently, it was possible to imitate someone's *vultus* but not their *facies.*[72] This imitation was possible because the shape of the *vultus* derived

---

68. Cic. *De orat.* 2, 242.
69. Sen. *De const.* 2.17, *quid quod offendimur, si quis sermonem nostrum imitatur, si quis incessum, si quis vitium aliquod corporis aut linguae exprimit?*
70. The issue of caricature obviously also interested Freud 1972a, 178 and 186.
71. Verg. *Aen.* 1.683ff.
72. This *differentia* in relation to the *vultus* is frequently repeated by the grammarians and

from an inner state or moral condition, and because it was considered distinct from someone's "natural" bodily features. *Vultus* is thus implicated in a cultural sphere of great interest: deception. Indeed, precisely because the face functions as a kind of semiotic "interface" that reveals a person's interior state, feelings and emotions, it can also be used in deception, giving a false impression of what that person "really" feels. Lying, after all, is also a form of semiosis. It is clear that *vultus* can be faked: for example, Cicero encourages the idea that true glory cannot be achieved *ficto non modo sermone, sed etiam vultu* ("either by lying words or by a lying face").[73] He also denounces Staienus—full of "nothing but fraud and falsehood"—for his *fictos simulatosque vultus* ("false and simulated expressions").[74] Even more interesting in this regard is Cicero's denunciation of Piso, which we have already had a chance to mention: *oculi supercilia frons vultus denique totus, qui sermo quidam tacitus mentis est, hic in fraudem homines impulit, hic eos quibus erat ignotus decepit, fefellit, induxit* ("the eyes, the eyebrows, the forehead, in short, the entire *vultus*, which is something like a silent language of the mind, is what has dragged the others into his trap; it is his *vultus* that has tricked them, deceiving and entangling those who were not familiar with the man").[75]

The *vultus*, because it is a "silent language" that allows the mind to convey its inward state, can be used to transmit true as well as false messages. Because, as Quintilian writes, "people rely on [the *vultus*], they look at it, they see it even before someone begins to speak . . . so that the *vultus* is often worth more than all the words taken together," liars employ this recognized "language of the mind" in their deceptions. People rely on observation of the *vultus* in order to decipher someone's sentiments and intentions. Cicero therefore attributes a kind of moral responsibility to the face: falsifying the *vultus*, as Piso did, is an utterly reprehensible act. In fact, the *vultus* was traditionally considered the locus of sincerity. The face speaks and provides independent evidence of a person's will and intentions. "An anxious face can reveal a great deal (*multa sed trepidus solet / detegere vultus*)," Seneca's Atreus says.[76] The chorus of his *Hercules Oetaeus* remarks: "Even if you would deny it, your face declares whatever you are hiding (*licet ipsa neges / vultus loquitur quodcumque tegis*)."[77]

---

commentators (see below, 160–61, in regard to *forma*).

73. Cic. *Off.* 2.12.43.

74. Cic. *Clu.* 72. Another case of simulation of the *vultus* can be found in Stat. *Theb.* 7.739, with Jupiter *simulans Halicamona vultu.*

75. Cic. *Pis.* 1.1. On this passage, see the excellent analysis of Ricottilli 2000, 56ff.

76. Sen. *Thy.* 330ff.

77. Sen. *Herc. Oet.* 704ff.

Using the face in deception is particularly reprehensible because within the system of cultural expectations, *vultus* is considered an even more direct and sincere "language" than the spoken word—unable to be falsified, because involuntary and independent of a person's willful control.[78]

A liar's efforts are not always successful, of course. It is possible for the falsification of the *vultus* to be flawed; as a result, the audience may manage to decipher what is "really" going on. Vergil provides an interesting example of this situation in the fifth book of the *Aeneid*. The goddess Iris, in order to convince the Trojan women to set fire to their ships, puts aside her own *facies* and divine *vestis*, taking on the appearance of the old woman Beroe in every detail (*fit Beroe* ["she becomes Beroe"]).[79] After making her impassioned speech to the Trojan women, the false Beroe hurls a firebrand at the ships—to the dismay of the Trojan women who are standing there. But the old woman Pyrgo, nurse to Priam's sons, does not fall for the goddess' trick:

> non Beroe vobis . . .
> . . . divini signa decoris
> ardentesque notate oculos, qui spiritus illi,
> qui vultus vocisque sonus vel gressus eunti.[80]

> Women, this is not Beroe . . . look at the signs of divine beauty, the fire in her eyes, her spirit, her face and the sound of her voice and the way in which she walks.

As we know, someone's voice and gait are powerful markers of identity. But evidently Iris is not as talented as Cupid: she has failed to imitate Beroe's voice and gait perfectly. She is also betrayed by her eyes (whose ardor betrays a *spiritus* an old woman could not possibly possess) and by her *vultus*—the silent language of the mind, which transmitted involuntary and therefore sincere signals that she was not human. And old Pirgo noticed.

The possibility of falsifying one's own *vultus* and transforming it into a deceptive sign invites us to reflect upon the words Vergil uses in describing Cupid's "simulation" of Iulus: *et notos pueri puer indue vultus* ("and, boy that you are, put on the familiar face of that boy").[81] The verb the poet employs

---

78. This seems to be the reason why, in some cases, the *vultus* functions as an identificatory element of the person, capabling of making it recognizable: so, for example, in Sen. *Oed.* 840, the title-character asks the old Corinthius: *refersne nomen aut vultum senis?* In Sen. *Herc. Fur.* 1016ff., Megara, confronted with Hercules' madness, exclaims: *natus hic voltus tuos / habitusque reddit.*
79. Verg. *Aen.* 5.619ff.
80. Verg. *Aen.* 5.646ff.
81. Verg. *Aen.* 5.646ff.

here—*induere*—clearly refers to "putting something on," as if Cupid had put a sort of mask over his face. The expression *induere vultum* (or *vultūs*) is used elsewhere to indicate the act of making facial expressions.[82] Seneca says quite clearly: *indue dissimilem animo tuo vultum* ("put on a face that does not match your spirit").[83]

Thanks to the image of "putting on" a *vultus*, we recognize that this word covers the same range of meaning as *persona*. To the extent that it can be imitated and even falsified, *vultus* operates noticeably at odds with its own "transparent" character. The enigmatic, tangled ways of the human heart and its capacity to experience—and at the same time to counterfeit—sincere passions allows *vultus* to function in the same manner as *persona*—that is, as an *index*, as a way to reach the depths of someone's soul or as a screen for deception. And so we return once again to the *prosōpon* and to its double sense, both "face" and "mask"—although we have reached it by an entirely different route than that followed by the Greeks. If the Greeks associated the face and the mask as purely *exterior* phenomena, subject to the reciprocity of the gaze, the Romans associated them through their capacity to reveal "interiorities," real or falsified, through a series of signs.

The Natural Face

We now come to another—probably long anticipated—point in our journey. Since we have been speaking about the "face," it was only a matter of time before we would have to deal with *facies*. This word designates both "the face" in particular and "physical appearance" in a more general sense. We have already encountered this term in Servius' observation that it is possible to imitate *vultus*, but not *facies*. Why should this be the case? The origin of the word *facies* itself may provide an answer to this question. Both Varro and Aulus Gellius posit a relationship between *facies* and the verb *facio*. As Varro states:

> proprio nomine dicitur facere a facie, qui rei quam facit imponit faciem. ut fictor cum dicit 'fingo' figuram imponit, quod dicit formo, formam, sic cum dicit 'facio' faciem imponit.[84]

---

82. Cf., e.g., Sen. *Med.* 751, *pessimos induta vultus* and *Ben.* 2.2.2, *itaque laetus facit et induit sibi animi sui vultum* (*gerere* or *ferre vultum* could also be used in this sort of situation: Liv. *AUC.* 42.62.11; Sen. *Agam.* 950).
83. Sen. *Polyb.* 6.4.
84. Var. *Ling. Lat.* 6.78.

The verb *facere* derives from *facies*, because the person who makes something gives it a *facies*. Just as the *fictor*, when he says '*fingo*,' gives a *figura* to something; or when he says '*formo*,' gives a *forma* to something, so when he says '*facio*' he gives something a *facies*.

Deriving the verb from the abstract noun, Varro takes the opposite approach to what we would probably do; but the relationship between the two terms is clear. Similarly, Aulus Gellius, in a long and interesting chapter on the uses of the word *facies*, explains:

facies . . . forma omnis et modus et factura quaedam corporis totius a faciendo dicta, ut ab aspectu species et a fingendo figura.[85]

Facies is the complete conformity and measure and making of the entire body: it derives from the verb *facere*, just as the word *species* derives from *aspectus* and *figura* from *fingere*.

It seems that the word *facies* denotes "the face" (or "bodily appearance" more generally) via a metaphor similar to Italian *fattezze* ("features") or English "build." *Facies* refers to the physical traits of the face—the specific way in which the face or the entire person is "made." In other words, *facies* belongs to the natural order and exists independently of a person's impulses or emotions. As Isidore says, *facies simpliciter accipitur de uniuscuiusque naturali aspectu, vultus autem animorum qualitatem significant* ("the *facies* is simply understood from each person's natural appearance, while the *vultus* indicates the qualities of the soul").[86]

This is why in a world still unacquainted with plastic surgery the *facies* cannot be falsified or forged. The *facies* comes from nature. Presumably, no one can so alter his own features so that they match another's—unless, of course, he happens to be a god, like Mercury who takes on the appearance of Sosia in Plautus' *Amphitruo* or the goddess Iris who sets aside her own *facies* in order to "become" Beroe (even if the *vultus* manifested upon her *facies* eventually betrays her). Precisely because it forms a "natural" part of physical appearance—that is, the inimitable arrangement of facial features—*facies* bears the burden of verifying identity. This is why Morpheus, disguised as Ceyx, shouts at the wretched Halcyon: *agnoscis Ceyca, miserrima coniunx? / an mea mutata est facies nece? respice, nosce* ("do you recognize your Ceyx, my miserable wife? Or is my *facies* so altered by death? Look carefully, recognize

---

85. Aul. Gell. *NA*. 13.30.
86. Isid. *Etym*. 11.1.34. On the difference between "facial gesturing" and *facies*, cf. the analysis of Ricottilli 2000, 35ff.

me").⁸⁷ *Facies* defines the link between the person and their capacity to be recognized.

Naturally, there are cases in which human beings (and not only divine beings like Iris) are able to alter their *facies*, even if incompletely. This is true of women who use cosmetics to make themselves more beautiful, for example. In Ovid's treatment of this topic, the poet shows with what *cura* the *puellae* of the Augustan age are able to *commendare* their *facies* with cosmetics.⁸⁸ Ovid justifies this feminine cosmetic *cultus* with an interesting simile, comparing it to the *cultus* that nature receives through agricultural practice: weeds are replaced by the fruits of Ceres. Therefore, if civilization is born out of the *cultus* of nature, how can one deny *cultus* to the female face?⁸⁹

Traditional Roman morals, however, characterized women's cosmetics in far less ennobling terms. In Plautus' *Mostellaria*, the young Philematium, in a long toilette scene, asks the old woman Scapha to hand her some *purpurissum* ("rouge"). The old woman refuses to give it to her: *non do . . . nova pictura interpolare vis opus lepidissimum?* ("I'm not going to give it to you: do you want to paint over what is already a masterpiece?").⁹⁰

The face of a woman—especially that of a beautiful woman—is like the canvas of a great master: to cover it with cosmetics would be like ruining a painting with new colors. The word *interpolare* used by Plautus is quite interesting.⁹¹ Scapha will use the same word again later, in adjectival form, to describe old women who try to beautify themselves with perfumes and cosmetics—only to obtain effects so ghastly as to merit inclusion in Jonathan Swift's notoriously misogynistic *Lady's Dressing Room*. As Scapha exclaims, *nam istae veteres, quae se unguentis unctitant, interpoles, vetulae, edentulae* ("look at those old women who smear themselves with lotions, these *interpoles*, these toothless hags").⁹² The word *interpolare* is a technical term of the *fullones*, who used this technique to restore the appearance of old clothes.⁹³ According to Plautus, the female *facies* is not like a piece of clothing that can be "touched up." The face should be left as is; nature should be given her due. Similarly, Pliny the Elder did not want women to use false eyelashes because, as he says, *alia de causa hoc natura dederat* ("it was not for this

---

87. Ov. *Met.* 11.658ff.
88. Ov. *Med. fac.* 1, *discite quae faciem commendet cura, puellae*.
89. On the use of this cultural metaphor in Ovid, see the note of Lazzeroni 1994, 63ff. On *cultus* and the birth of our modern concept of "culture," cf. Oniga 1993, 123–45.
90. Plaut. *Most.* 261ff.
91. Cf. Ernout-Meillet 1965, s.v. *interpolo*.
92. Plaut. *Most.* 274.
93. Non. Marcell. *De comp. doctr.* 34.1 Lindsay.

purpose that nature gave them eyelashes").[94] Moralists always know what Nature is—and know even better what Nature has prescribed!

The Recognizable Face and Personal Identity

Ovid's false Ceyx demonstrates what an important factor *facies* is in determining someone's identity: "Do you recognize your Ceyx, my miserable wife? Or is my *facies* so altered by death? Look carefully, recognize me." Isidore is explicit in connecting *facies* with what we would define as "identity":[95] *facies dicta ab effigie. ibi est enim tota figura hominis et uniuscuiusque personae cognitio* ("the word *facies* is from *effigies:* this is where the entire figure of a man is located—that is to say, the means of recognizing each person"). In another passage, he states that *facies dicta est, eo quod notitiam faciat hominis* ("we say *facies* because it makes [*faciat*] someone recognizable").[96] As usual, Isidore's etymological explanation strikes us as fanciful. But by insisting on this relationship between the *facies* and the *notitia* or *cognitio hominis,* Isidore provides us with some very precious evidence.

Notitia and *cognitio hominis* are Latin phrases equivalent in function to the modern notion of "identity." If we were to translate Isidore's words into a more modern idiom, we might be tempted to say, "*Facies* defines a person's identity." In doing so, however, we would be ignoring the slow and laborious process that leads to the modern notion of identity. Born out of philosophical reflection, this cultural configuration supposes that it is the characteristic of "permanence"—always "being the same" (*idem, identitas*) in different phases and contexts—that defines someone's or something's identity. With Isidore's evidence, we find ourselves not at the philosophical but a social—or "civic"—stage of identity. The quality of "sameness" ("intrinsicness," so to speak) is not considered a feature that defines someone's identity.[97] Rather, identity is simply the ability to be recognized by others. "Identity" is *notitia* or *cognitio* by others, who, in recognizing us, affirm that we are who we are, or, in *not* recognizing us, deny us our own identity.

In Latin, *cognitio* in fact refers to the recognition of someone or something that is already known to us, often covering the same semantic space as Greek *anagnōrisis*. As such, *cognitio* of someone—recognizing him or her—functions as a kind of guarantee of identity. To give just one example:

---

94. Plin. *Nat. hist.* 11.154.
95. Isid. *Etym.* 1133.
96. Isid. *Diff.* 2.52.
97. Naturally, this does not mean that the permanence, and above all the presence, of the past in the form of memories, do not subjectively play a part in personal identification; see above, 117–19.

when Hyginus tells the story of Theseus, he describes the test of recognition to which Aegeus subjects his son Theseus: *cum posset eum lapidem allevare et gladium patris tollere, ibi fore indicium cognitionis filii* ("if he should be able to raise the stone and lift his father's sword, this would be the proof of his son's identity"). Theseus, by accomplishing this task, provides what we would call "proof of identity" as the son of Aegeus.[98] *Notitia*, the other ancient Latin term pertaining to identity, expresses the idea of "renown" or "cognizance." Pyramus and Thisbe, the two famous lovers of Ovid's story, lived in neighboring houses along the wall built by Semiramis: *notitiam primosque gradus vicinia fecit* ("their closeness created cognizance and motivated the first steps"). *Notitia* means that two people "know one another"—that they recognize one another's faces whenever they meet.[99]

When Isidore speaks of *cognitio* or *notitia hominis*, "identity" is placed on the level of recognition. External recognition guarantees that someone really is that person. An intriguing scene of Plautus' *Stichus* provides additional evidence for this "recognition" model of identity. A *pater* discusses with his two daughters the qualities most valued in a woman: when Antipho asks *quae mulier videtur tibi sapientissuma?* ("which woman seems to you the most wise?"), his daughter Panegyris answers, *quae tamen, quom res secundae sunt, se poterit gnoscere* ("she who, when things go well, can be recognized as herself").[100] At Rome, what we would define as the ability to maintain one's identity in all circumstances corresponds to the ability to be recognized.[101] Seneca tells us something interesting in this regard, as well. Speaking of mirrors, Seneca insists that they were invented *ut homo ipse se nosset, multa ex hoc consecuturus, primum sui notitiam* ("so that a person could know himself and thus procure many advantages: first and foremost cognizance of himself").[102] The mirror furnishes man his "recognizability"—we would say his identity.

The manifestation of personal identity through a process of recognition

---

98. Hyg. *Fab.* 37. For *cognitio* as the equivalent of *anagnōrisis*, cf. also Ter. *Eun.* 921, *ibo intro, de cognitione ut certum sciam;* Hyg. *Fab.* 122, *cognitione facta . . . Mycenas venerunt*; 126, *cognitio Ulixes*; etc. *Cognitio* means, therefore, "to become familiar with, frequent"; cf. e.g. Cic. *Arch.* 5, *itaque hunc omnes . . . cognitione atque hospitio dignum existimarunt*; Petr. *Sat.* 132, *paenitentiam agere sermonis mei coepi . . . quod oblitus verecundiae meae cum ea parte corporis verba contulerim, quam ne ad cognitionem quidem amittere severioris notae homines solerent.* Cf. *TLL* III, 1483, 18–44 Lambertz. Moreover, see Isid. *Diff.* 1.89, *inter cognitionem et agnitionem quidam sic distinguunt, quod cognitio eorum sit quae ante non scivimus et ea postea scire permittimur, agnitio vero eorum, quae prius scientes, deinceps scire desivimus eorumque postea recordamur.*

99. Ov. *Met.* 4.59; cf. also *Ep. ex Pont.* 4.8.48ff., *virtus / notitiam serae posteritatis habet*; 3.1.49, *exposuit mea me populo fortuna videndum / et plus notitiae, quam fuit ante, dedit;* Nep. *De excell. duc.* 94, *hi propter notitiam sunt intromissi;* Ter. *Heaut.* 1.1.1, *quamquam haec inter nos nupera notitia est.*

100. Plaut. *Stich.* 123ff.

101. On the theme of "keeping contact with oneself" (*respicere*) as a support for one's own identity, cf. Bettini 1991c, 122ff.

102. Sen. *Nat. quaest.* 1.17.4.

plays a role in other aspects of Roman social life, as well. For example, the function of the *agnitor* is to "acknowledge" and therefore guarantee the authenticity of a sealed document. Once again, the process of identification occurs through a form of direct personal recognition. When Quintilian describes the care that the *patronus* must give to examining the documentation for a case, he warns his students: *denique linum ruptum atque turbatam ceram aut sine agnitore signa frequenter invenies* ("it often happens that the cord might be broken or that the wax is altered or the seals are not attested by an *agnitor*").[103] The *agnitor* is a key figure; his function involves the validation and identification of *signa*, just as *cognitio* or *notitia* involves the validation of someone's identity. Both are accomplished through another individual.

Another example from Plautus demonstrates just how much personal identity in ancient Rome depended on recognition by others. In the *Miles Gloriosus*, Sceledrus and Palaestrio are not recognized by the girl Philocomasium, although the two of them recognize her perfectly well. It is precisely what we would define again as the "identity" of the two heroes that is at stake:

> PHIL. quis tu homo es aut mecum quid est negoti?
> SCEL. me rogas, hem, qui sim? PHIL. quin ego hoc rogem quod nesciam?
> PAL. quis ego sum igitur, si hunc ignoras? PHIL. mihi odiosus, quisquis es,
> et tu et hic. SCEL. non nos novisti? PHIL. neutrum SCEL. metuo maxume.
> PAL. quid metuis? SCEL. enim ne nos <nosmet> perdiderimus uspiam:
> nam nec te neque me novisse ait haec. PAL. persectari hic volo,
> sceledre, nos nostri an alieni simus, ne dum quispiam
> nos vicinorum imprudentis aliquis immutaverit.
> SCEL. certe equidem noster sum. PAL. et pol ego.[104]

> PHIL. And you: who are you? What do you have to do with me?
> SCEL. What? You're asking me who I am? PHIL. Why shouldn't I, seeing as I don't know you?
> PAL. Who am I then, if you don't recognize him? PHIL. Whoever you are, I don't like you: you and him both. SCEL. You don't recognize us? PHIL. Neither one. SCEL. Now I really am afraid.
> PAL. What are you afraid of? SCEL. I am afraid that we have lost ourselves somewhere, since she says she doesn't know either of us, not you, and not me either. PAL. I'd really like to figure this out, Sceledrus: are we ours any-

---

103. Sen. *Nat. quaest.* 12.8.13.
104. Plaut. *Mil.* 425ff. In fact, Palaestrio had early made an agreement with Philocomasium to pretend not to recognize them, to throw Sceledrus into doubt.

more, or someone else's? I wouldn't want for one of our neighbors to have
secretly changed us without our knowing it.
SCEL. Of course we are ours. PAL. Me too, by Pollux!

Seeing that Philocomasium does not recognize either him or Palaestrio, Sceledrus is afraid that they have "lost themselves" somewhere. Palaestrio raises the stakes, wondering if by some chance they have not "lost possession" of themselves, transformed unawares by one of the neighbors and consequently no longer recognizable by their acquintances. This lack of recognition—a loss of *notitia*—corresponds in every way to what we would call "loss of identity."

Naturally, such examples may be multiplied. Take, for example, the paradoxical adventures of the emperor Jovinianus in the *Gesta Romanorum*. The emperor has lost his own identity, replaced by an angel as divine punishment for his arrogant behavior. The tribulations of Jovinianus involve being chased out of his own court, being rejected by his friends and even being attacked by his own dog. In short, the emperor is systematically "not recognized" by those who were once closest to him. This drama of lost identity is expressed through the loss of the emperor's *notitia*, the same word used by Isidore when he located the possibility of being recognized in the *facies*. Jovinianus has lost his own "recognizance"; here too we might easily say, his "identity."[105]

Realistic Faces, Togate Statues

In the course of our analysis, we have encountered at least three different linguistic and cultural manifestations of the Roman "face": *os*, the "speaking" face; *vultus*, the face as "interiority"; and *facies*, the "natural" face. In all three, we have seen the wealth of connotations they presuppose. Let us pause for a moment to reflect on this. It is quite striking from how many perspectives "the face" is considered in Roman culture. All this linguistic attention will certainly prove interesting for an anthropology of images. In fact, it is difficult to avoid imagining that some relationship exists between the importance attributed to the face in the Latin language and two quite idiosyncratic aspects of Roman culture: the *ius imaginum* on one hand and the practice of portraiture on the other.

As we know, Roman aristocratic tradition kept alive the memory of ancestors' "faces" through a complicated ritual involving wax masks, the

---

105. Oesterley 1872, ch. 59 (51), 360ff.: cf. 362, 4; 15; 26; 364, 36 (*noticia hominis*).

imagines maiorum. These masks, modeled after the features of deceased relatives, were a sort of iconographic archive of the family's physical features. They were normally kept in cabinets made specifically for this purpose and placed in the *atrium* of the house. When a family member died, the masks were taken down and worn by those participating in the funeral procession. Thus, the family's ancestors, wearing the insignia and uniforms of the offices they had held in life, were able to walk the streets of Rome once again, accompanying their deceased progeny to their final resting place.[106] The Roman nobility attributed a tremendous cultural importance (at once genealogical, political and religious) to the face in the form of the *expressi cera vultus* of their *maiores*.[107]

The same may be said for the role played by the portrait in Roman artistic culture. In fact, the practice of portraiture—both a public and a family ritual—focused primarily on the face, which was represented in the most realistic detail, taking care to express the subject's "inner self" and character.[108] It appears that in the form of the funeral *imago* and the portrait, Roman cultural practice was as equally concerned with "the face" as the Latin language, with its wealth of expressions and "takes" on facial appearance. For the Romans, the face appears to have been an object of central cultural importance. The face was looked at, reflected in language, and reproduced by art. But why were the Romans so interested in the face?

This question inevitably leads us into a Roman anthropology of the body—a subject on which there is much work yet to be done. But let us try, for a moment, to picture the figure who stands at the center of Roman life, who was the object of so much attention, and who—in reality, or in the ideological representation of reality—performed the actual functioning of Roman *civitas:* the adult Roman male, the *civis*. Before us is a man completely covered by a *toga*—a form of clothing so strongly marked both in terms of Roman identity and "belonging" that it served as a true and proper "uniforme de la citoyenneté."[109] The toga constructs the body of the citizen in the manner of a ritual garment, transforming him into a sort of living statue:[110] a *statua togata,* we might say, just like the togate statues that the Romans themselves used to set up.[111] In his rejection of nudity and in his solemn (even obsessive) concern with arranging the flowing toga, the *civis*

---

106. Bettini 1991c, 179ff.; Flower 1996, 91ff.
107. Plin. *Nat. hist.* 35.6.
108. Cf. e.g. the classic analysis of Bianchi Bandinelli 1976, 71ff. who rightly made an important connection between Roman portraiture and the use of the *imagines maiorum.*
109. Dupont 1989, 290.
110. Barghop 1996, 81–87.
111. Plin. *Nat. hist.* 34.18.

Romanus did not put any part of his body on display—with the exception of the face, of course.[112]

It was thus upon the citizen's face that attention inevitably was placed, both in terms of the words used to discuss and describe the face and the cultural practices focusing upon the face. Others—those who grant us, in the form of *notitia* or *cognitio*, our identity; those who gaze at the politician, the father, the *orator* and so forth in order to recognize who they are and to read their character—necessarily gaze upon the face. Likewise, it is the face in the form of a wax mask that its wearer takes care to coordinate with the appropriate type of toga—and nothing else—that identifies an ancestor. Again, "the face" identifies someone in a portrait, an image that "realistically" portrays their physical features and the inclinations of their character.

The Manufactured Face

Let us return to Latin *facies*. As we have already seen, *facies* is a rather transparent derivate of *facio*. Moreover, Roman authors who analyze the meaning of this term regularly turn to metaphors taken from the artistic domain—the world of the *fictor*, of *fingere*, *figura* and *formare*. In other words, the metaphorical field used to describe someone's bodily or facial appearance (*facies*) clearly corresponds to that of manufacturing, in the sense of "forming" or "creating" something. In this regard, the clear relationship that Aulus Gellius posits between *facies* and *factura* is very interesting: "the *facies* is the complete conformity and measure and make up (*factura*) of the entire body: it derives, in fact, from *facere*."[113] *Factura* is obviously derived from the field of manufacture, and can also be applied to bodily appearance. Therefore, it is as if someone's appearance/*facies* were defined through the image of an object made and shaped by someone else. As anticipated, the set of terms and cultural representations used by the Romans to describe bodily appearance cannot be described by a single model. We have already seen that "the face" was considered a mouth (*os*) and a window to the inner self (*vultus*.) Now, it seems that "the face" (*facies*) is "manufactured." This aspect of the problem deserves further exploration, for there are many terms in Latin for "physical appearance" taken from this metaphorical field.

---

112. Cf. Bettini 1999b, 8–21.
113. Aul. Gell. *NA*. 13.30; cf. also Non. Marcell. *De comp. doctr.* 52 Lindsay, *a factura corporis facies;* Marius Victorinus, *Rhetorica* 1.5, *qualitas . . . si dicas cuius generis vestis, cuius generis factura;* Oribasius, *Synopsis ad Eustathium filium* 5.45, *parva factura capitis;* cf. *TLL* VI, 1, 142–144 Hey.

Consider the word *forma*. This term has an extensive and complex range of uses, with meanings ramifying in a number of different directions. To complicate matters further, the etymological origin of the word *forma* is not altogether certain.[114] An analysis of the full semantic range covered by *forma* would be an undertaking quite disproportionate to our aims here, but we can be certain of the fact that *forma* was used by the Romans to refer to "physical appearance."[115] In fact, the ancient lexicographers seem to have attributed to *forma* the same characteristics as they did to *facies:* it is something natural and stable, opposed to the personal "interiority" and variability of *vultus*. So Donatus: *forma immobilis est et naturalis, vultus et movetur et fingitur* ("the *forma* is unmoving and natural, while the *vultus* moves and can be simulated")[116] and *vultum sibi fingere multi possunt, formam nemo* ("many people can fake their *vultus,* but no one can fake their *forma*").[117] The previously cited *scholion* of Eugraphius is in accordance: *forma naturalis facies est, vultus vero animi motu facies ad tempus aptata* ("*forma* is natural appearance, while *vultus* indicates an expression temporarily assumed according to the motions of the soul").[118]

Forma is perceived as being very close to *facies* ("the face" defined as something "fashioned" or "made"). We should emphasize, however, that the principal meaning of the word *forma* is very concrete: it denotes the "mold" used both to produce coins and to model wax or shape cheese.[119] Once again, physical appearance (*forma*) is associated with a concrete operation of manufacture: producing shapes with a mold. *Forma* has very nearly the same meaning of "physical appearance" as *facies*. Indeed, we have already seen that the Romans themselves perceived these two modes of designating physical appearance—*facies* and *forma*—as very similar to and even interchangeable with one another.

The relationship between "the manufactured" and "bodily appearance"

---

114. Cf. Ernout-Meillet 1965, s.v. *forma*; on its possible relationship with Etruscan, cf. Bonfante 1987, 37–38. Ancient etymologies made a connection between *forma* and the notion of "heat" (likely because of the existence of an adjective *formus*, "hot"): cf. Donat. in Ter. *Phor.* 1078 Wessner, *fornum veteres ignem et calorem quendam quasi fervorem dixerunt, et ideo fornaces, forcipes, formam et formosos . . . ; exstinguerent: bene est. quia forma calor; et forma ab igne et calore dicta es.*

115. Cf. *TLL* VI, 1, 1065–87 (esp. 1069, 15ff.).

116. Donat. in Ter. Andr. 119 Wessner.

117. Donat. in Ter. Andr. 120 Wessner.

118. Eugraph. in Ter. Andr. 119 Wessner.

119. Cf. *TLL* VI, 1, 104, 43ff.: *Lex Rubria, CIL* I2.592.2.2, *pecunia . . . signata forma p(ublica) P(opuli) R(omani);* Col. *De re rust.* 7.8.3, *(caseus) in calathos vel formas tranferendus est;* Plin. *Nat. hist.* 35.153, *cera . . . in eam formam gypsi;* etc. Cf. the observations of Ernout-Meillet 1965, s.v. *forma*, who in their semantic analysis of the word place the concrete meaning of "mold" at *the* beginning of the process.

becomes even clearer when we consider the term *figura*.[120] This word was also commonly used to mean "bodily appearance" or "semblance," particularly in the generic sense of "shape."[121] For example, in Ovid's *Heroides*, Ariadne laments the fact that her *figura* could not attract the attention of faithless Theseus: *di facerent ut me summa de puppe videres: / movisset vultus maesta figura tuos* ("If only the gods had made it so that you would see me from up on the stern of the ship! My desolate appearance would have moved even your eyes").[122] Theseus sails away aboard his ship—if only Ariadne's sad silhouette, now vanishing in the distance, had managed to catch his eye! What is important for our analysis is that the ancient sources recognized a relationship between *figura* and the sphere of *fingere*, the activity of the *figulus* or *fictor*. As Isidore tells us: *figura est, cum impressione alicuius imago exprimitur, veluti si cera ex anulo effigiem sumat aut si figulus in argillam manum vultumque aliquem imprimat et fingendo figuram faciat* ("a *figura* is an image created by means of an impression, as when a shape is pressed into the wax with a signet ring, or when a potter presses his hand into clay or sculpts someone's face and creates a *figura* by means of an act of *fingere*").[123] The same idea could also be formulated this way: *figura artis est opus, forma naturae bonum* ("*figura* comes from art, whereas *forma* is a gift of nature").[124]

Yet even without the speculations of ancient lexicographers, there is no doubt as to the relationship between *figura* and the root **fig-* of *fingo*.[125] The author of the *Panegyric of Messalla* explicitly plays on the relationship between *fingo* and *figura* when he imagines a kind of metaphoric afterlife: *mutata figura / ... me finget equum* ("my altered shape ... will make me a horse").[126] Once again, *figura* corresponds to the act of "creating" or "making." In this case, what the image refers to is much more specific than was the case for *forma*: the sphere of *fingere*, in fact, instantly evokes the art of modeling in clay, of sculpting, of painting—of creating artificial images in general. An expression such as *figura* can help us understand, therefore, what specific cultural model stands behind words like *facies, factura* and *forma:* the manufacture of images. In other words, we may hypothesize that the Romans, seeking a way to represent themselves in terms of physical appear-

---

120. Cf. *TLL* VI, 1, 722–738 Bauer.
121. Cf. e.g. Cic. *Nat. deor.* 1.32.90, *hoc dico, non ab hominibus formae figuram venisse ad deos*; Cic. *Verr.* 4.36.89, *eum multo magis figura et lineamenta hospitae delectabant*; etc.
122. Ov. *Her.* 10.133ff.
123. Isid. *Diff.* 1.528.
124. Isid. *Diff.* 7.530.5.
125. Note that the suffix *-ura* is joined here not to the theme of the verbal adjective, as usually occurs, but directly to the root: not *fictura* (hardly attested) but *figura*. Cf. Ernout-Meillet 1965, s.v. *figura*.
126. *Corpus Tibullianum, Panegyricus ad Messallam* 206ff.

ance and "outward show," had recourse to their experience with artificial images.

The Human Form as Artificial Image

This impression seems to find confirmation in other words of the same type. Consider *statura,* for example. This word is derived from *status* ("standing, standing on one's feet") and is built with the suffix *-ura* (the same as in *fig-ura*), which, as we know, denotes an abstract verbal idea "put into practice."[127] *Statura* therefore properly designates the way in which a person puts into practice his ability to stand up—his *habitus,* the specific way in which he inserts himself into the space that surrounds him. This "bodily coordination" is also decisive in determining the specific features of someone's physical appearance. Witness the following conversation between Hanno and Milphio in Plautus' *Poenulus:*

> HA. sed earum nutrix qua sit facie mihi expedi.
> MI. statura hau magna, corpore aquilo. HA. ipsa ea est. [128]

> HA. But tell me what their nurse looked like.
> MI. She was not large in stature, and was darkly colored. HA. That's her!

What immediately strikes us in this bit of rapid-fire dialogue is the fact that *statura* is able to create identity by distinguishing one person from another. The same thing occurs in Cicero's *Philippics,* when the orator declares: *velim mihi dicas Lucius Turselius qua facie fuerit, qua statura* ("I would like for you to describe the Lucius Turselius' appearance and *statura*").[129] *Statura* is again seen as a quality that contributes substantially to someone's identity, on par with *facies.*

Because *statura* is such an important personal trait, it may be qualified in various ways. It can be *parva, commoda, quadrata* and even *tantula;* its *gracilitudo* may be emphasized or its capacity to *excedere* just measure (*iusta*), and so on.[130] *Statura* refers to a person's appearance in terms of the spatial dimension of verticality, underscoring the specific "bearing" of someone's

---

127. *Cursus > cursura, quaestus > quaestura, status > statura.* On substantives in *-ura,* cf. the classic study of Benveniste 1948, 101ff.
128. Plaut. *Poen.* 1111ff.
129. Cic. *Philipp.* 2.16.
130. *Rhet. ad Her.* 4.33 (*parva*); Plaut. *As.,* 401 (*commoda*); Plin. *Nat. hist.* 34.65; Caes. *BG.* 2.30 (*tantula*); Suet. *Tib.* 68 (*statura quae iustam excedat*).

body as a distinctive feature of their appearance. But it is not simply how they look; it is also how they stand and what they are like. In this sense, it is difficult to escape making an analogy with *statua,* one of the words used in Latin to designate plastic images "in the round."[131] From the perspective of "verticality"—of *statura*—a human being "stands up" like a *statua*. Once again, the models used in the representation of human physical appearance intersect with the world of artificial images.

While *statura* is oriented towards "verticality," *lineamentum* refers to the characteristics of the body itself, to the distinctive elements of its physical features: its "lines." Cicero speaks of a woman's *figura* and *lineamenta*.[132] In another passage, he uses these words to praise the beauty of the human figure in general: *quae compositio membrorum, quae conformatio lineamentorum, quae figura, quae species humana potest esse pulchrior?* ("What arrangement of parts, what congruity of features, what shape, what aspect could be more lovely than that of the human body?").[133]

In a discussion of human physiognomy and the divine wisdom revealed therein, Minucius Felix makes a very interesting distinction between *figura* and *lineamenta:*

> magis mirum est eadem figura omnibus [hominibus], sed quaedam unicuique lineamenta deflexa; sic et similes universi videmur et inter se dissimiles invenimur.[134]

> Even more remarkable is the fact that people all have the same *figura,* but each one still has his or her own *lineamenta*. Therefore, we all have a similar appearance, but we are found to be different from one another.

According to Minucius, *lineamenta* bear the burden of expressing individual identity, while *figura* (which, as we know, embraces a more general semantic space) seems instead to be a marker of what we might call "species identity." From the point of view that interests us here—the relationship between human appearance and artificial images—it is interesting to note, however, that *lineamenta* is also commonly used to refer to the "contours" of artistic images, such as paintings and sculptures.[135] No doubt, the original sphere

---

131. On the relationship between *statua, signum* and *imago* see Pucci 1991, 107–29.
132. Cic. *Verr.* 4.89.
133. Cic. *Nat. deor.* 1.47.
134. Min. Fel. *Oct.* 18.1.
135. Cf. *TLL* VII, 2, 1438–1440 Bader (esp. 1439, 77ff.); cf. e.g. Cic. *Nat. deor.* 1.27.75, *cedo mihi istorum adumbratorum deorum lineamenta atque formas*; Cic. *Verr.* 2.4.98 (*operum lineamenta*); Val. Max. 3.7, ext. 4, *vultum Iovis Olympii . . . eboris lineamentis . . . amplexus.*

of reference of *lineamenta* is precisely that of artificial images: the "features" evoked to represent the shape of the human form, even of an individual, are understood as the "lines" drawn by an artist in the process of creating an image. Here, we recognize the same metaphorical extension between these two fields that we have already seen.

Remaining within the sphere of *fingere,* an analogous metaphorical process occurs with the word *effigies*—a term we have already seen in our discussion of *facies. Effigies* primarily designates an artificial image, but it equally designates the contours of the human form, just as *figura* does.[136] Pliny declares:

> in facie vultuque nostro cum sint decem aut paulo plura membra, nullas duas in tot milibus hominum indiscretas effigies existere, quod ars nulla in paucis numero praestet adfectando.[137]

> Although our face and aspect consist of just ten parts, or just a few more, there are not two faces, two effigies, which are identical among all the thousands of people in the world: this is a result that no art would be able to achieve even a much smaller number of creations.

Something similar occurs with the much more complicated word *filum.* As may still be seen with English "filament," *filum* is "a thread."[138] Metaphorically, however, *filum* becomes *deducta res quaeque ad tenuitatem* ("anything drawn out and thin")[139] and may therefore refer to the edge of a sword or the extremely thin shape that characterizes the end of a blade.[140] What is interesting for our purposes is that the word *filum* was used (by Lucretius) to refer to something more or less equivalent to our "contour." For example, he uses this term to refer to the shape of elements, the image of the sun, objects whose appearance blurs with distance and the appearance of fires in the sky.[141] This metaphor—the "filament" (*filum*) reduced to an almost imperceptible thinness—is well suited to define the extremely subtle outline of a shape and, above all, an image. For this reason, *filum*—and here we return to the field that interests us—could be used to describe external

---

136. Cf. *TLL* V, 2, 180–84.
137. Plin. *Nat. hist* 7.8; cf. Stat. *Silv.* 2.1.191.
138. Cf. *TLL* VI, 1, 760–764 Lackenbacher (but the internal organization of this lemma leaves much to be desired).
139. Non. Marcell. *De comp. doctr.* 313.12 Lindsay.
140. Enn. *Ann.* 239 Skutsch.
141. Lucr. *De re. nat.* 2.341, 4.88, 5.571, 589.

appearance.¹⁴² It would seem that in these cases, *filum* is almost an equivalent of French "silhouette," meaning the outline of a person's body. Varro, speaking of human resemblance, puts it like this: *eo similiores sunt* (sc. *homines) qui facie quoque paene eadem, habitu corporis, filo* ("This is why there is more similarity between people who share the same face, the same bodily deportment, the same silhouette").¹⁴³ Having the same *filum* suggests resemblance as much as having the same *facies*. In the same way, Aulus Gellius describes the art of physiognomy in these terms: *mores naturasque hominum coniectatione quadam, de oris et vultus ingenio, deque totius corporis filo atque habitu sciscitari* ("It detects the character and the nature of people by means of conjecture, based on the characteristics of the face and of its expression, from bodily deportment and from the contour of the entire body").¹⁴⁴

There is no explicit ancient evidence that *filum*, in the sense of "contour," "was employed above all in the language of the artists"¹⁴⁵—although this is a reasonable hypothesis. What is certain, however, is that *filum* in this sense easily slips towards the world of images. Arnobius rebukes the pagans for wanting to imprison divinity in human form: *at vero vos deos parum est formarum quod amplectimini mensione, filo et adterminatis humano* ("but to you it seems no great thing to constrain the gods into dimensions of these forms, and to limit them with a human contour").¹⁴⁶ Lamenting the pagan practice of using prostitutes as models for depicting goddesses, he also wrote that *omni cura studioque certabant* [sc. *artifices*] *filum capitis prostituti Cythereia in simulacra traducere* ("with great care and attention the artists compete to transfer the outline of a prostitute's face onto their images of Venus").¹⁴⁷ As in the case of English "profile," Latin *filum* appears to oscillate between the world of real physical features and that of artificial images.

The Art of Images: A Way to "Think" the Face?

The convergence of so many terms—*facies, factura, forma, figura, statura, effigies, lineamentum, filum*—in a single direction confirms the idea that Roman

---

142. Cf. *TLL* VI, 1, 763, 66ff. The word seems to have a certain specialization in the field of female physical appearance: cf. Plaut. *Merc.* 755, *satis scitum filum mulieris*; Lucilius fr. 816 Marx, *surge mulier, duc te—filum non malum* (a fragment of Lucilius cited by Non. Marcell. *De comp. doctr.* 313.16 Lindsay to give an example of *filum, oris lineamentum*); Aul. Gell. *NA.* 14.4, *forma atque filo virginali;* Apul. *Met.* 4.23, *virginem filo liberalem;* etc.
143. Var. *Ling. Lat.* 10.4.
144. Aul. Gell. *NA.* 1.9.2.
145. Thus Ernout-Meillet 1965, s.v. *filum.*
146. Arnob. *Ad nat.* 3.13.
147. Arnob. *Ad nat.* 6.13 (the example chosen is that of the famous prostitute Phryne).

culture borrowed heavily from the domain of artistic practice in representing the human body. The world of artificial images supplied the Romans with a metaphor for conceptualizing physical appearance. "The person," conceived less as the subject of action, responsibility, feelings and so forth, than as the pure "appearance" of a face or body, is transformed into an image. This observation might also prove useful from the perspective of historical psychology, since it illustrates a further aspect of what image making means in the development of a culture. It is as if the artistic process served not simply to imitate the body, but also to understand it. As Cicero observed, "people are not able to think about the gods without the construction of artificial images that were themselves made by other people."[148] Indeed, it is as if people are not able to understand themselves—as "figures," in their pure exterior physicality—without the production of replicas of other people. Reproducing the features of the human form makes it possible to distill from the complex whole of a person a single set of features and forms defining their appearance and, at the same time, to endow these features with a specific value. Naturally, this is a process with deep anthropological roots—and as such, transcultural character. Indeed, we continue to speak of a person's "profile" and "features," the "lines" and "shape" of their face.

Alienated from the Self and from the person as a whole, "bodily appearance" becomes imagistic. Here, it is difficult not to think again of Sosia's words in Plautus' *Amphitruo*, when he sees his own person and identity stolen from him by the god Mercury. This is what he thinks to himself about the strange events that have befallen him:

> certe edepol, cum illum contemplo et formam cognosco meam,
> quem ad modum ego sum—saepe in speculum inspexi—nimis similest mei.[149]

> By Pollux, it's true: when I look and recognize my own form, the way that I am—I've looked at myself in the mirror often enough—he is entirely similar to me.

Sosia knows that he has a particular shape. He is familiar with and recognizes it—and that *other* person looks amazingly like him. But Sosia soon reaches another, more desperate conclusion—and it is very close to the subject we have been discussing:

---

148. Cic. *Nat. deor.* 2.45, *ut nisi figuris hominum constitutis nihil possint de dis imortalibus cogitare.*
149. Plaut. *Am.* 441ff.

hic quidem omnem imaginem meam quae antehac fuerat possidet.[150]

That man has taken possession of the entire image that used to be mine.

Seeing himself reflected in another who has a form very much like his own, Sosia discovers that his physical appearance is in fact an *imago*, purely an "image." Separated from him and scrutinized as an object of fear or comfort, Sosia's own "person" is fixed in a form that has neither inside nor outside—like an actual image, be it painted or sculpted, whose very essence consists exclusively in its "appearance." We are very near the psychological mechanisms that we earlier attempted to describe to explain why the description of the human form takes so much of its terminology from the domain of artificial images.

Immobility and Motion

We have reached the end. Before concluding, however, I would like to take the discussion a little further, from the point of view of the cultural model to which we have so frequently referred: identity. We know that the face, like physical appearance in general, creates identity: but in what form, exactly? What cultural features did the Romans consider pertinent to this end? First, we must observe that somatic identity in ancient Rome was not so much a matter of "being seen" by others, depending instead on characteristics that were in some sense intrinsic to the subject. We have seen, in fact, that visual expressions such as *species* or *aspectus* are highly generic terms and are not used specifically in regard to the face or the body. Rather, they refer in the most general sense to the appearance of anything visible to the eye. For the Romans, facial and somatic identity were instead a matter of terms such as *os, vultus, facies, figura* and so on. This terminology is drawn from a variety of different metaphorical fields (and we noted that representations of physical appearance in Latin are not always interchangeable), but alike in the fact that they lack a visual dimension.

Within this set of characteristics there seem to be two basic models at work. On one hand, a model deriving from the domain of artificial images, representing physical appearance and in particular the face as something "fashioned" or "made:" *facies, figura, statura, lineamentum* and so on. The other model is represented by the words *os* and *vultus*. At this point, we can better define this model as deriving from the category of "movement." Both

---

150. Plaut. *Am.* 458.

os and *vultus* make physical mobility a pertinent feature of the human face: *os* represents the face as "speaking," while *vultus* represents the face as a shifting "disposition" bound to the individual's inner state (and actually able to be imitated or falsified). If we accept the popular derivation of *vultus* from the word family of *volvo*, then etymologically speaking *vultus* already expresses this feature of "mobility."[151] In other words, it seems that in identifying a person Latin speakers attribute an important role to those parts of the face that moved.

This is hardly surprising, given that other "moving" parts of the face were considered capable of conveying someone's sentiments and personality. This is true of the eyes, the forehead, and—above all—the eyebrows. Even if these are incapable of overshadowing other facial features and of designating the face or countenance by themselves—as *os* and *vultus* do—nevertheless they are parts of the face that possess a strong identificatory power in the Roman cultural encyclopedia. If we turn from the face to the body as a whole, it is worth noting again that *gressus* was also considered highly characteristic of the individual. As such, it played a critical role in all cases of "doubling" and "impersonation."[152] But also in the case of *gressus* identity is established through that which "moves," that which marks someone as definitely "living."

It is perhaps not unreasonable, then, to conclude that a person's somatic and facial identity in ancient Rome oscillated between the two poles of "immobility" and "movement"—the image as something "fashioned" and the person as a "living being." At different times, the person may be identified by his more spiritual and specifically human "moving" characteristics, or by those that derive from the fixity of a *factura*. To speak about a person and to define "who he is" in terms of his appearance means to emphasize both his nature as a fixed image and his specifically "living" and "mobile" features. To identify someone means on the one hand to assimilate that person to an immobile statue or a manufactured figure and on the other to emphasize that person's resources as a living, constantly changing creature. The image that moves, the statue that speaks, the "natural" *facies* that changes its expression, a human being's physical "person"—his "being there" on the stage of the world—unrelentingly poses this linguistic challenge to culture: "describe me."

---

151. Cf. Cohen 1979.

152. Perhaps the importance of the gait in identification also has something to do with the "centralité" (Dupont 1989, 290) of the use of the toga at Rome? When the entire body is covered, only someone's gait—their "way of walking"—gives the onlooker some hint for determining that person's identity.

PART 3

Doubles and Images

FIVE

Sosia and His Substitute
Thinking the Double at Rome

The war against the Teleboans is over. The slave Sosia, on his way to Thebes from a rather improbable *portus Persicus*, has just disembarked at an even more incredible *portus Thebanus*—the geographic fantasies (or inconsistencies) of a great comic mind. He heads towards the house of his master Amphitryon, the great general, in order to inform Alcmena, the mistress of the house, of the army's return. It is night and, lantern in hand, he complains—like any good comic slave worth his salt (and in lyric meter, no less)—about the life he is compelled to lead under his master. Then, under the pretext of preparing himself mentally for the account he will give to his mistress, he recites what is perhaps the most delightful passage of archaic *epos* that has survived in Roman literature: the description of the battle won by Amphitryon.[1] This would already suffice for the opening scene of a Plautine comedy; but night gives no sign of waning and in front of the house stands a strange man. *Non placet*, remarks Sosia.[2]

So it happens that a rather banal turn of phrase bears the burden of introducing an encounter that is central not only to the plot of this comedy, but to the history of our own culture. Sosia, with his lantern in hand, is in fact the first character in the history of Western literature to experience the

---

1. Only an excess of national pride could have driven Jouanny (1962, 888) to define this Plautine description of the battle a "monologue fastidieux" that Molière would finally work into the "style de théâtre." Cf. Oniga 1985, 113–208 and 1991.
2. Plaut. *Am.* 292.

unenviable fate of encountering his own Double (his *sosia,* as is still said in Italian today)—someone who looks just like and pretends to be him.³

Telepathy and Determinant *Omina*

Is Sosia's encounter with "himself" really such a unique event? After all, one may think of the theme of identical twins (another favorite of Plautus) and of the countless misadventures that occur, in the *Menaechmi* and elsewhere, when two indistinguishable brothers switch roles and functions on the same stage. Are these not also cases of "doubled" identity? Indeed, there are many points of contact between these two types of plot; but the differences between them far outweigh any similarities. In the *Menaechmi,* the mechanism of the plot is based on a perfect resemblance between two brothers that amazes (or fools) everyone around them, causing them—each unaware of the other's existence—to experience a series of bizarre adventures. In the case of Sosia and his rival Mercury/Sosia, their perfect resemblance does not result in any kind of confusion; rather, one of the two characters ends up being suppressed—supplanted—by the other. Again, the typical misunderstandings of the so-called "comedy of errors" are founded upon the existence of two characters of identical appearance in the same place. The trick of the plot demands that these characters do not come into direct contact with one another, at least for some time. Only in this way is it possible for others to mix them up and for them to be mixed up, with all the comic results we are familiar with. Needless to say, when the look-alikes finally encounter one another, the misunderstandings are resolved and the comedy naturally comes to a close.⁴

In *Amphitruo,* things proceed in exactly the reverse order. It is at the beginning of the play, and not at its end, that the look-alikes meet, and there are no misunderstandings of any kind. Quite the opposite. One of

---

3. Unless we also consider such cases as the famous "living image" (*empnoun eidolon*) that, according to Eur. *Hel.* 31ff., Hera is supposed to have substituted for Helen on her voyage to Troy in the company of Paris: but in this case there is no "encounter." Better yet the story of Hercules exchanging blows with a statue that represents him (Apoll. *Bibl.* 2.6.3; Hesychius of Alexandria π 2576, s.v. *plēxanta kai plēgeenta,* III, 346 Schmidt; Paus. 9.11.4; Eustatius ad Hom. *Il.* 11.749 [van der Valk 1971, 882, 38]; cf. Brillante 1988, 23). As for Greek precedents for the story of Amphitryon, unfortunately there remains too little for an accurate assessment of the way in which the encounter of Amphitryon with Zeus/Amphitryon was developed there (on the Greek forerunners to the Plautine comedy, cf. Stärk 1982, 275ff.; Raccanelli 1987. Concerning the "double" more generally, the last few years have seen a number of noteworthy studies, especially Dolezel 1985, 463–72; but above all Fusillo 1998, in which many of the modern literary works on the "double" that appear in this paper are analyzed.

4. Bettini 1991b.

the two characters immediately bursts into a brusque and absolute declaration—"you are not *you*, but *I* am!"—and punctuates this assertion with his fists. What Sosia experiences is not what usually befalls someone in comic cases of mistaken identity; in fact, his personal identity is not mistaken but immediately and violently commandeered.[5] On that seemingly endless night before the door of his master's house, Sosia is deprived of his very identity: his name, his appearance, his existence. *Ubi ego perii? . . . an egomet me illic reliqui, si forte oblitus sum?*[6] Sosia is "dead"; he has been "left behind somewhere" and "forgotten"; he no longer has a place in this world.

Sosia's absurd encounter with his Double—the most incredible kind of encounter that can occur—is staged by Plautus with exquisite care. Between the two Doubles a kind of telepathy is established, not only permitting Mercury to know, in the minutest detail, all that Sosia has done up to that point, but—even more remarkably—bringing the unsuspecting Sosia to predict what he is about to experience at the hands of Mercury/Sosia.[7] Freud, in his analysis of E. T. A. Hoffmann's *The Devil's Elixirs,* remarked that the motif of the Double and the two "identical" characters is marked "by mental processes leaping from one of these characters to another—by what we should call telepathy—so that the one possesses knowledge, feelings and experience in common with the other."[8] Freud's observation is crucial to understanding how the plot of the Double operates. To adapt it to a worldview closer to that of Plautus' culture and his audience, we might say that from the very opening lines of the play, Sosia, although completely unaware of it, produces a series of *omina* that anticipate what his *alter ego* is about to do. In some way, these *omina* actually bring about what eventually does unfold.[9] So, for example, before he even encounters Mercury/Sosia lying in wait for him before the house, Sosia declares:

> sum vero verna verbero: numero mihi in mentem fuit
> dis advenientem gratias pro meritis agere atque alloqui?
> ne illi edepol, si merito meo referre studeant gratiam,
> aliquem hominem alligent, qui mihi advenienti os occillet probe.[10]

---

5. From this point of view, the adventures of the Menaechmi in Plautus' comedy of the same name are exemplary (cf. again Bettini 1991b, 37ff.): for the distinction between the "simultaneous" and the "exclusive double," cf. Dolezel 1985.

6. Plaut. *Am.* 455ff. Frequently in the remainder of the play reference is made to the theme of "being elsewhere."

7. Plaut. *Am.* 410ff. Cf. Fusillo 1998, 138, who interprets Mercury's omniscience in the form of Sosia's superego, which unmasks the slave's transgressions. On the *argumenta* adopted by Mercury in order to convince Sosia, see below, 240–41.

8. Freud 1977a, 95–97.

9. For this cultural model, typical of the cultures of antiquity, cf. Bayet 1971, 44ff.

10. Plaut. *Am.* 180ff.

"Such a slave I am for the scourge: when I arrived here, did it cross my mind to thank the gods for the favors they have granted me, and to address them in prayer? Yes indeed, by Pollux, if they wanted to bestow upon me the favor I deserve, they'd have to send somebody to punch my lights out the moment I arrived!"

In a moment, Mercury will, in fact, beat Sosia senseless. Sosia's telepathic *omen* will actually come true. The same thing happens a few lines later, when Sosia overhears Mercury making boastful threats aside about having already bested four men:

. . . formido male
ne hic ego nomen meum commutem, et Quintus fiam e Sosia.
quattuor viros sopori se dedisse hic autumat:
metuo ne numerum augeam illum.[11]

I've got a very bad feeling that I'm about to change my name from Sosia to Quintus ("the Fifth"). He says that he's already put four men to bed: I'm afraid I'm going to rack up that number.

The idea of "changing names" seems only to be a joke based on the fact that in Latin the word *quintus* (in the sense of the "fifth" in a series of men laid low by Mercury) can function also as a proper name, Quintus. Momentarily, however, Sosia will discover that he really is going to have to give up his name, when it is taken from him by his Double. Once again, Sosia's telepathic *omen* is destined to come true: the "doubled" person perceives what his Double has in store for him. But the issue of Sosia's *nomen*, like that of his *imago*, merits a closer look.

A Name, a Figure and a Lantern

While someone's name is the conventional label for that person (and as such, stable and inalienable), their outward appearance is a natural sign of their identity—incontrovertible proof that they are that person and no other. In the confrontation with his Double, Sosia is attacked on two fronts. Thus, he becomes someone bearing the name "Nobody,"[12] first in the stranger's predictions about his identity:

---

11. Plaut. *Am.* 304ff. On this kind of "prediction" by Sosia, frequent in the scenes that we are analyzing, cf. also the (rather disappointing) observations of Forehand 1971, 633ff.

12. On this kind of word-play, besides the well-known episode of Odysseus and Polyphemus, there is also the story of the man who had himself called "Self" in Thompson 1966², K 602.1.

Chapter 5. Sosia and His Substitute

nescioquem loqui autumat, mihi certo nomen Sosiae est.[13]

He says that "I-don't-know-who" is speaking; just as well, since my name is Sosia!

and then as a sign of his total submission:

MERC. qui nunc vocare? SO. nemo nisi quem iusseris.[14]

MERC. What's your name, then? SO. I'm nobody, unless you tell me otherwise.

Immediately following, Sosia becomes someone with a name merely *similar* to his real name:

MERC. Amphitryonis te esse aiebas Sosiam. SO. Peccaveram: nam Amphitryonis socium ne me esse volui dicere.[15]

MERC. You said you were Sosia, Amphitryon's slave.
SO. Obviously I was mistaken . . . I meant to say that I am his ally (*socium*)—yes, that's it!

Sosia's *nomen*, which guarantees his personal identity, reels under the physical blows that the Double lands upon the person it represents. Linguistic invention desperately attempts to fill the void with more or less paradoxical strategies, such as trying to make the indefinite pronoun *nemo* serve the unambiguous function of a proper name or trying to counter the treacheries of physical resemblance with cunning verbal similarities (*socius*, not *Sosia*). But in the end even language must yield: The mutual pact between the name "Sosia" and the person it previously represented—Amphitryon's slave, the one with the lantern in his hand—has been rendered null and void.

If denying someone their name is a matter of mere words (obviously helped if accompanied by blows), in the case of "appearance"—*forma* or *imago*—things are much more complicated. It is not enough simply to say that you possess someone's appearance; you must actually take it on. However, Mercury has undeniably assumed Sosia's appearance in each and every detail. At first, he is represented as someone "terribly similar" to Sosia,[16] then as so similar to Sosia that not even Sosia seems "so like himself as he does"[17]

---

13. Plaut. *Am.* 332.
14. Plaut. *Am.* 382.
15. Plaut. *Am.* 383ff.
16. Plaut. *Am.* 442.
17. Cf. the *repetitio cum varietate* of *nimis similest mei* (Plaut. *Am.* 442) in *tam consimilest atque*

in bodily form, in stature, in attire—in everything, that is. Finally, Mercury "possesses the complete *imago*" that used to belong to Sosia.[18] Slowly but surely, the resemblance between the two becomes more pronounced, until eventually it morphs into the theft of Sosia's "image." As best they can, Plautus' linguistic resources (with a difficult blend of fantasy) attempt to describe this extraordinary experience.

The discussion between the two goes on for quite a while, since Sosia requires some time to be convinced that Mercury/Sosia is so like him that he (Mercury) now actually *is* him (the true Sosia, Amphitryon's slave). However, we must take into account that a certain object has been playing a central role during this long sequence: the lantern Sosia holds in his hand when he enters and that he continues to hold throughout the scene. This lantern has always been present on stage, if inconspicuously (Molière would transform it into a kind of mannequin to which Sosia could address his famous description of the battle, as if to Alcmena herself).[19]

Likely, in the course of the heated debate between Sosia and Mercury/Sosia, the former, growing ever more incredulous, repeatedly brought the lantern near to the other's face in order to verify that they really were indistinguishable. This was in fact the case. No doubt this was the precise scenographic purpose of the lantern in Sosia's possession.[20] When Poe's William Wilson decides to find out what really is going on with that other "William Wilson" (who, since arriving on campus on the same day and having the same name and mannerisms, has been disrupting his life as a student), the first thing that he does is to obtain a lamp. Holding it steady, he enters the other's room, lifts the bed curtains and casts the lamplight upon his face: "I looked;—" he says, "and a numbness, an iciness of feeling instantly pervaded my frame. . . . Were these—*these* the lineaments of William Wilson?" Yes, his very own—identical! The story has reached the crucial moment in which the existent of the Double is discovered and a "lamp" is necessary for the

---

ego (443), accentuating the extraordinariness of the "resemblance." In fact, it is probably the case that *tam consimilest atque ego* is not a simple equivalent of *consimilis mei* (Ussing 1875, 277, for example, interpreted it in this way), but a brachyology for *tam consimilis est (mei) atque ego (sum consimilis mei)* ("he resembles me as much as I resemble myself"). The linguistic elaboration of resemblance ends at 446 with an equally overwrought expression, *nihil hoc similist similius* ("there is nothing more similar than this similarity").

18. Plaut. *Am.* 458.

19. The *Sosias* of von Kleist's *Amphitryon* will do the same thing. For the relationships between Plautus, Molière and Kleist, cf. Mantinband and Passage 1974, 109ff. On the fortunes of the *Amphitruo* in general, cf. Lindberger 1956; Jauss 1979, 213ff.; Bertini 1981, 307ff.

20. Beyond the obvious indication to the audience that the scene occurs at night (thus Cutt 1970, 145).

task.²¹ Hastily abandoning the room, William Wilson extinguished the light. Perhaps Sosia, defeated and deprived of himself, did the same.

The Substitute and Sosia's Identity

Before abandoning the field, however, Sosia attempts to react; he attempts to assert his ownership of and confidence in his own identity against the other's ambitions. The form of Sosia's defensive argumentation is quite interesting:

> quid, malum, non sum ego servos Amphitruonis Sosia?
> nonne hac noctu nostra navis huc ex Portu Persico
> venit, quae me advexit? non me huc erus misit meus?
> nonne ego nunc sto ante aedis nostras? non mi est lanterna in manu?
> non loquor, non vigilo? nonne hic homo modo me pugnis contudit?
> fecit hercle, nam etiam mi misero nunc malae dolunt.
> quid igitur ego dubito, aut quor non intro eo in nostram domum?²²

Curses, am I not Sosia, Amphitryon's slave? Did our ship not sail tonight from the Persian Port? Was I not on board that ship? Did my master not send me here? Do I not find myself now outside our house? Do I not have a lamp in my hand? Am I not speaking? Am I not awake? Did that man not beat me with his fists just now? He did indeed and my cheeks are still smarting for it! Why therefore do I have my doubts (*quid igitur ego dubito*)? Why don't I just go on into our house?

Philosophers, Memory and the Mirror

The *igitur* with which Sosia concludes his speech and the *dubito* following immediately thereupon—"Why therefore do I have my doubts?"—deserve careful examination.²³ *Igitur* is a philosophical conjunction and by using it to cap his long catalog of questions, Sosia seeks to find a logical conclu-

---

21. Poe 1992. Cf. Ziolkowsky 1977, 175ff.; Passage 1954, 13ff. (esp. for the relationship between Dostoyevsky's *The Double* and Romantic literature on the same theme). A lantern also appears in the long-awaited recognition scene between Mattia Pascal and his relatives in Luigi Pirandello's novel *The Late Mattia Pascal*. On the lantern as a disconcerting object often connected with the world of spirits, cf. Romaldo 1994, 31ff.
22. Plaut. *Am.* 403ff. On these lines, cf. Barnes 1957, 19ff.
23. I think *dubito* has here the sense of "being in doubt" rather than that of "hesitating." Cf. *TLL* V, 1, 2082, 55ff. (Accius fr. 191 Ribbeck³ and Pacuvius fr. 50 Ribbeck³).

sion to everything he has been saying. He then feels authorized to be more self-assured and to approach Amphitryon's house (although obviously the other Sosia will prevent him from reaching it). The development of Sosia's argumentation is striking in that it seems to be a kind of comic predecessor of the famous Cartesian *cogito*. Sosia's *igitur*, like Descartes' *ergo*, is based on an affirmation of "existence" by someone who finds himself in a state of uncertainty—even if for reasons much more unusual than those that drove Descartes to his "method of doubt." In fact, this curious analogy between the comic slave's joke and one of the most famous aphorisms in the history of philosophy did not escape Giambattista Vico.[24] Sosia's discourse is a philosophical one. It should be no wonder, then, that this comedy about the victorious general and his slave would be transformed in the Middle Ages into that of the student returning from Athens (i.e., Paris) after completing his studies in philosophy, a comedy in which even Amphitryon's slave (Geta, not Sosia anymore) is transformed into a logician.[25] Of course, because the story of Amphitryon turned on a conspicuously philosophical argument, this transformation of roles was already in some sense implicit in the structure of the narrative. Discussing "identity" is the bread and butter of philosophers; sooner or later, they were going to be imported directly into the plot.

But on what grounds does Sosia draw his confident conclusion? To what does Sosia appeal in order to dispel his misgivings about not being "himself"? He relies on recent (but not too recent) events and experiences (the ship, his arrival, the order given to him by his master), his awareness of his own "presence" (here, in front of the house), the continuity of his own actions (carrying the lamp) and hearing himself speak (not in a dream, but in reality). He even appeals to the beatings he has suffered and to the pain that he still feels: even the self-irony of the *verbero*, the whipping boy of Roman *palliatae*, forms part of the dossier of evidence proving Sosia's existence. Beyond the theatrical comedy, however, this long list provides us with an intriguing catalog of what a Roman in the late third or early second century B.C.E. might consider the core or substance of his own identity and

---

24. On Plaut. *Am.* 447, *sed quom cogito, equidem certo idem sum qui semper fui*, Vico constructed a polemical argument against Descartes' *cogito*, to show that the self-awareness to which Descartes appealed is not knowledge, and does not require the learned considerations of a philosopher, if even an uncouth comic slave could formulate it. Vico readapted the verse rendering it much more suitable to his polemic (but very much less suited to the text and meter): *sed quom cogito, equidem certo sum ac semper fui*. Removing *idem* and *qui*, the statement acquires a much more general, Cartesian relevance (Vico 1968, 139. Cf. Corsano 1974, 140ff.) Doubtless, however, that between Descartes and the myth of Amphitryon there is a kind of elective affinity: its influence has been hypothesized on Rotrou's *Les Sosies* and on Molière's *Amphitryon* (Fusillo 1998, 88ff.).

25. Cf. Vitale di Blois, *Geta* 157ff. and 257ff. (= Bertini 1980, 141ff.; cf. 257ff.).

"presence." This moment of crisis provokes awareness of the Self and mobilizes the features that serve to identify it. It compels Plautus to list in detail what would be invoked in such a crisis in order to confirm one's own identity with a confident, concluding *igitur.*

What we find in Sosia's speech is frankly what we would expect from anyone in the same situation. His appeal to experiences of the past (but of the recent past), to his direct perception of his own identity, to the continuity of his actions, and so on, all seem to belong to a rather standard set of reactions. From this point of view, they recall an almost transcultural code of behavior. Memory of the Self is a universal basis for identity.[26] A Chinese story told by Leibniz (the problem of identity certainly brings philosophers out of the woodwork!) provides a perfect example:

> Suppose that some individual could suddenly become King of China on condition, however, of forgetting what he had been, as though being born again, would it not amount to the same practically, or as far as the effects could be perceived, as if the individual were annihilated and a king of China were the same instant created in his place? The individual would have no reason to desire this.[27]

Whoever retains the memory of who he is *is* himself; whoever has lost that memory has also lost himself.

But let us return to Sosia's reasoning. From someone who finds himself unexpectedly confronting his own "mirror image," we might expect at least a hint of the presence or the powers of—precisely—the *mirror,* an object that in our own culture and literary tradition regularly accompanies the arrival of the Double. Sosia does in fact refer to "the mirror" when he finally accepts the fact that the man he has encountered before his master's house is "terribly similar" to him.

> certe edepol, quom illum contemplo et formam cognosco meam,
> quem ad modum ego sum (saepe in speculum inspexi), nimis similest mei;
> itidem habet petasum ac vestitum: tam consimilest atque ego;
> sura, pes, statura, tonsus, oculi, nasum vel labra,
> malae, mentum, barba, collus: totus.[28]

---

26. Jervis 1984, 36ff.
27. Leibniz 2003, 58.
28. Plaut. *Am.* 441ff. There is no need to reiterate how important the "mirror" is in the finale of "William Wilson," for example; in chapters six and seven of Dostoyevsky's *The Double;* in G. de Maupassant's *Le Horla* and so forth. See also Rank 1914, esp. 69ff., and Fusillo 1998, 63.

I swear by Pollux, when I look at him and recognize my form, the way that I am (since I've often seen myself in the mirror), he is terribly similar to me; he has the same hat and clothes, he is as similar to me as I am to myself: leg, foot, stature, haircut, eyes, nose, lips, cheeks, chin, beard, neck: everything.

Then as now, the mirror was closely linked to the category of "personal identity."[29] It is not surprising, therefore, to find it mentioned by someone who needs to confirm his own external appearance. We should also keep in mind that in ancient cultures the mirror was endowed with remarkable powers: it was believed capable of preserving (by means of *sumpatheia*) some part of the nature of what was reflected on its surface[30] and revealing the "true" nature of the person reflected upon it.[31] Elsewhere, the mirror is imagined to be able to actually "capture" the figure of the person looking into it, so that it could be carried around and admired by others.[32] All this only reinforces the association between the mirror's reflecting surface and the active presence of the person's Double. Could it be that Sosia happened to mention "the mirror" precisely because it was thought capable not only of reflecting and confirming a person's figure, but also of stealing it? Whatever the case, it is also necessary to mention that the mirror's magical powers are not only part of the ancient cultural horizon, but also of modern literature. It is needless to recall the numerous Romantic stories that focus on the theme of the Double and all the characters who famously lose their shadows[33] or reflected images.[34] As a means of confirming identity, or as a dangerous threat to individuality, the mirror is yet another element of the transcultural code. The centuries do not seem to have changed or to have reduced its enigmatic powers.

I Feel Like "One of Us"

More specific details emerge as Plautus reminds us of the fact that Sosia is

---

29. Not only because of its obvious use in day-to-day life, but also because of the object's metaphorical development: cf., e.g., the so-called "philosopher's mirror" that noble men often use to remind themselves of *themselves* and to follow the path of justice (cf. Sen. *Nat. quaest.* 1.17.2ff.; Phaed. *Fab.* 3.8.14ff., etc.). As we know, Apul. *Apol.* 14 is dedicated to the "mirror" and its use.

30. Arist. *Somn.* 2.459b26; Proclus in Pl. *Resp.* 2.290.10k.

31. Paul. Silent. *Anth. Pal.* 5.266: if a man bitten by a rabid dog looks at himself in the mirror, the reflection he sees is of the animal.

32. Stat. *Silv.* 3.4.93ff. Cf. Guidorizzi 1991, 31ff.; Bettini 1999a, 113ff.

33. As in the famous *Peter Schlemihls wundersame Geschichte* by von Chamisso (in Jaager-Grassi and Mazzucchetti 1989).

34. See in particular *Die Geschichte vom verlornen Spiegelbilde* in Hoffmann 1984, where the "character" Peter Schlemihl also appears.

not a minor bureaucrat in Czarist Russia, like Golyadkin of Dostoyevsky's *The Double,* nor a young college graduate like Poe's William Wilson: he is a Roman slave. Moreover, Sosia's social role determines—rather decisively—the course that his reasoning takes through his loss of identity. Cultural models now cease to be generic and transcultural, and the distinct contours of the culture to which the character on stage belongs begin to appear.

Let us begin with the way in which Sosia expresses himself. Sosia's language will provide the evidence we need to understand the models within which he situates his sense of Self. He says to Mercury/Sosia:

certe edepol numquam me alienabis quin noster siem;
nec nobis praeter me alius quisquamst servos Sosia.[35]

I swear by Pollux, you are never going to get me to change ownership (*me alienabis*), so that I won't belong to this house any more (*quin noster siem*). Here among us there is no other slave named Sosia besides me.

The verb *alienare* has the technical meaning of "to transfer property to someone else." Sosia understands that his Double intends to dispossess him of "himself." To describe this detachment from his Self, Sosia uses a rather curious expression: "You are not going to stop me in any way from being *ours.*" What does he mean when he says "ours"? Certainly, when language attempts to describe loss of identity, a certain amount of disarray is to be expected in the normal lines of discourse and in particular in use of the personal pronouns. If someone cannot say *ego* in reference to himself anymore, but only in reference to his interlocutor, the larger network of personal pronouns will obviously also break down. For example, Sosia says of his Double a few lines later:

neque lact' lactis magis est simile quam ille ego similest mei.[36]

There is no milk more like milk than *that* "I" is like *me.*

In any other context, it would be senseless to talk about an *ego* qualified by an *ille* (which is *similis mei* to boot!) But here we are speaking about loss of identity (or at least about split identity): such a breakdown in the rules that govern the use of the personal pronouns is entirely comprehensible, therefore—even natural. Given that, it might be more understandable if

---

35. Plaut. *Am.* 399ff.
36. Plaut. *Am.* 601; cf. also 607: AMPH. *quis te verberavit?* SO. *ego memet (verberavi), qui nunc sum domi* "AMPH. Who hit you? SO. I hit himself, the 'I' that is still at home."

Sosia had feared to be no longer *meus*—already a sufficient play on the personal pronouns and adjectives. Why then does he describe himself as *noster*?

It is possible that Sosia employs *noster* as a simple equivalent of *meus*, without any further connotation.[37] Yet the larger context seems to orient our interpretation in another direction. In the very next line, the slave declares, "Here among *us* there is no other slave named Sosia besides *me*." Sosia has in mind a *nos* corresponding to the family group to which he belongs, a family physically embodied in the house in front of him, which he would like to enter. This *nos* to which Sosia refers gives us a clue to the meaning of his declared alienation "from us" rather than "from me." We should keep in mind that Sosia is not a free man: he is a slave, and his way of understanding his current situation is appropriate (and peculiar) to that condition. Sosia's very identity as a slave in fact corresponds to the group of people to which he belongs (Amphitryon's *familia*); he is united with the others just by being under the power of the same master. This must be why Sosia, in responding to Mercury/Sosia, expresses himself with the word *noster* and not *meus;* it is as if he were saying, "If you are asserting that I am not Sosia, you are trying to dispossess me not from *me* but from *us,* from the group with which I identify, headed by my master." Sosia, the slave, possesses a strongly marked group identity. Later, when Amphitryon will declare that he too no longer knows who he really is and is in danger of undergoing a similar moment of self-dispossession, the category of "you," rather than that broader category of "we," will be employed:

> Amphitruo es profecto, cave sis tu te usu perduis.[38]

> Of course you are Amphitryon; be careful that you (*tu*) do not lose control of yourself (*te*).

The master enjoys "possession (*usus*) of himself" and in order to maintain his own identity he has to make sure that his *te* remains in possession of his *tu*. He has no need to appeal to a larger group identity. Sosia, on the other hand, in order to remain "himself," has to avoid being *alienatus* from "us."

The importance of the category "slave" for understanding the specific way in which Sosia thinks and describes his loss of identity may also be seen

---

37. Thus perhaps, in an analogous situation, the *noster* of Sceledrus in Plaut. *Mil.* 433: *certe equidem noster sum,* "I certainly am 'one of us.'" But we cannot exclude that also here dominates the sense of "group identity" characterizing the slave (Brix 1884, 59 and 69 seems inclined towards this interpretation).

38. Plaut. *Am.* 845.

in the concluding words of this scene. When Sosia, defeated by his Double's arguments, yields to Mercury/Sosia, he says:

> ibo ad portum atque haec uti sunt facta ero dicam meo;
> nisi etiam is quoque me ignorabit: quod ille faxit Iuppiter,
> ut ego hodie raso capite calvos capiam pilleum.[39]

> I will go to the port and tell my master what has happened: unless he also doesn't recognize me! May Jupiter grant exactly that, so that today I might shave my head and wear the freedman's cap on my bald head!

The fact that this joke appears in such a prominent position at the very end of the scene makes it all the more important (though in any case it would be well worth our attention). "If my master doesn't recognize me," says Sosia, "that will be a great piece of good luck. It means that I will cut my hair and take the freedman's cap and that I will finally be a free man!"[40] This is a humorous metaphor about changing identity: Sosia produces a *Witz* by making an analogy between "no longer being himself" and "no longer being a slave." Yet, if Sosia is able to take advantage of such an analogy, we must conclude that, for a Roman slave, passing from the condition of slave to that of freedman was perceived as a true and proper change of identity. In this transformation, the slave became a different person, no longer identifiable with his former self. This should not surprise us. Sosia himself emphasizes the ceremonial aspect of this change of status as a "rite of passage": cutting the hair[41] and donning the *pileus,* the freedman's cap.[42] We know that after his emancipation, a slave changed not only his attire (now wearing the citizen's toga) but also his name.[43] For Sosia, then, this longed-for transformation from *servus* to *liber* functions as a frame of reference that is good for thinking his experience of "no longer being himself." The condition of "not being recognized" within the family group finds an unexpected outlet in the Roman ritual of *manumissio.* Golyadkin or William Wilson would not have been able to comfort himself with thoughts of this

---

39. Plaut. *Am.* 460ff.
40. Cf. Plaut. *Men.* 1025ff., where the first Menaechmus, who "does not recognize" the slave Messenio, declares him free.
41. Cf. Polyb. *Hist.* 30.19.3; Liv. *AUC.* 45.44.19. The hair was cut also after surviving a shipwreck (Nonius Marcellinus [*De comp. doctr.* 848 Lindsay] relates the two practices): cf. Grondona 1980, 54ff.
42. On the *pi(l)leus,* cf. Samter 1894, 535ff.
43. Cf. Lecrivain's 1904 article on "*Libertus, Libertinus*" in Daremberg and Saglio 1877–1919, III, 2, 1200ff.

kind. But when the Roman slave ponders his identity and its transformation, he does so according to Roman cultural categories.

Thinking the Double at Rome

Sosia the slave understands his own identity and the loss of identity he has suffered in a manner consistent with his social and cultural role. We find here the first substantial difference between the way in which Plautus develops the theme of the Double and the way in which modern writers have depicted their various doubles or *Doppelgänger*. What other differences might there be? It is now time to concentrate our attention on the (quite real) possibility that, for Sosia—that is to say, for Plautus, his audience and the culture that they shared—the experience of being doubled could be couched in anthropological categories quite different from those which modern culture would employ in similar contexts.

Plautus provides us with some precious information in this regard, once again at the end of the scene, when the incredible encounter between the Doubles has ended and the slave is about to make his exit. At this point, Sosia no longer feels, as he earlier did, the need to defend his identity (he has now definitively lost it) so much as to describe how all this could have happened. The way in which Sosia tries to explain (better, to understand) what has happened to him reveals just how different he is. Indeed, resorting to a frame of reference that explains this exceptional experience in a way that makes sense to himself and to others, Sosia seems very far removed from the intellectual horizons of modern culture. He thinks his loss of identity in a radically different manner from what we see in Dostoyevsky *The Double* or Poe's "William Wilson." We will need to resist the temptation to make parallels with eighteenth century or modern literature, then.[44] The Double as theorized by Otto Rank—a fragile Viennese creature hovering between narcissism and death—does not help us understand the anxieties of the Plautine slave. The stage upon which Sosia and his substitute tread shows itself for what it really is—a very Roman stage—and the steps that reverberate there are unlike those of Heine's *Doppelgänger* ("You *Doppelgänger*, you pale

---

44. Besides the two stories of Poe and Dostoyevsky, of nineteenth-century literary production we must also cite, at least, the works of E. T. A. Hoffmann centered on the theme of the double: the already-mentioned "Story of the Lost Reflection," in *A New Year's Eve Adventure* IV (this story gained particular popularity through Offenbach's operatic version in *The Tales of Hoffmann*); *Lebensansichten des Katers Murr; Die Brautwahl* in *Die Serapionsbrüder* V; and the entire *Die Elixiere des Teufels*. Many valuable literary references may be found in the classic work (Rank 1914) and obviously in Fusillo 1998, 104ff. and 263ff.

companion . . . ").⁴⁵ Although Franz Schubert has set this "double-going" to a score that leaves a lasting impression,⁴⁶ for the time being we must force ourselves to forget it.

At the end of his implausible encounter, Sosia lists—in the form of self-interrogation, speculation and joking—a set of cultural models that frequently offer analogies with or links to the theme of the Double or the loss of identity:

> abeo potius. Di immortales, obsecro vostram fidem,
> ubi ego perii? ubi immutatus sum? ubi ego formam perdidi?
> an egomet me illic reliqui, si forte oblitus fui?
> nam hicquidem omnem imaginem meam, quae antehac fuerat, possidet.
> vivo fit quod numquam quisquam mortuo faciet mihi.⁴⁷

> But I'll go. Immortal gods, I beseech you, where did I meet my end? Where was I transformed? Where did I lose my identity? Or was I left behind back there, and forgot what happened? Because it's clear that this man here has my entire appearance, the appearance that used to be mine. Something is happening to me while I'm alive that nobody would have done for me if I died!

A point-by-point commentary on these lines will enable us to understand two crucial models that Plautus' culture (and his characters) could employ for thinking an encounter with the Double: the "magic of transformation" and the "aristocratic double."

The Magic of Transformation: Immutatus *and* Versipellis

The first question that Sosia asks himself is, "Where did I meet my end?"— literally, "Where did *I die?*" The expression *perii*, like the invocation of the gods which precedes it, covers perhaps too many negative psychological situations (especially in Plautine comedy, where it occurs hundreds of times) to be considered anything but generic. Yet the addition of *ubi* gives the

---

45. Heine 1993, 167.
46. F. Schubert, *Der Doppelgänger,* in *Schwanengesant* 13. In the piano part of the *lied,* two voices differing by an octave intertwine, violating a well-known rule of composition: but this harmonic doubling evokes the "doubled going" of the *Doppelgänger.*
47. Plaut. *Am.* 455ff. The entire sequence that we are dealing with here disappears in Molière's reworking (522ff.), where Sosia, bested by Mercury, limits himself to noting that it would be prudent to leave. Apparently, a Roman slave's musings on the "double" would not have had great interest for the French audience of the time.

conventional expression a striking specificity. Evidently, Sosia perceives his loss of self and identity as "having died somewhere." If someone has been substituted by another "himself," it is effectively as if he has died. There was a moment and a place in which Sosia himself unknowingly "died." Dostoyevsky's Golyadkin is also obsessed by the Double who causes him so much trouble at the office: the "other" Golyadkin. Anton Antonovich tells him that his maternal aunt saw her own Double *before dying*.[48] The Double recalls death and this connection perhaps reflects popular belief.[49] The general interpretive framework in which we should read the association between the Double on one hand and Death on the other is probably furnished by beliefs in the existence of *psuchai, imagines, simulacra* and so on, which faithfully reproduce the features of the deceased in the form of a ghostly apparition or shade. There is no need to repeat well-known examples.[50] Since someone's ghost normally bears their features, it is easy to imagine that an encounter with someone who has an identical external appearance would provoke thoughts of death: If that other being has an *imago* identical to my own, is it not perhaps my ghost, and therefore am I myself not dead?

The second question that Sosia addresses to himself is perhaps more interesting still: "Where was I transformed?" This translation does not do justice to the specific qualities of the highly Plautine verb *immutari*.[51] The expression signifies "being transformed" by means of magical powers but also alludes to "loss of ownership," making it a term that lacks direct equivalents, demanding periphrasis.

The basic sense of *immutare* in Plautus is that of "altering" and "changing," as when Jupiter himself says to the audience:

Amphitruo fio et vestitum immuto meum.[52]

---

48. Cited by Harden in Dostoyevsky 1985, 68. This edition has the advantage of containing both the redactions of 1846 and 1866, along with an appendix of other notes by Dostoyevsky as he planned a final revision. (In chapter VI, there are interesting divergences between the two versions, precisely as concerns the importance of the 'mirror').

49. Cf. Passage 1954, 17.

50. Cf. e.g., Hom. *Il.* 23.65ff. (Patroclus' *psuchē*); Verg. *Aen.* 4.654 (Creusa's *imago*), etc. Cf. Vernant 1990, 34ff. and 1991, 3ff.

51. Physical transformation recurs two times in the *Amphitruo* (here and at 846) and once at *Miles Gloriosus* 432. According to Eugrafius ad Ter. *Andr.* 242, the difference between *commuto* and *immuto* is of the quantitative/qualitative type: *motus species sunt 'commutatio' et 'immutatio,' et est illud circa quantitatem, istuc circa qualitatem, ut si quis ex parvo magno factus sit commutatus, si quis ex nigro albus immutatus dicitur* ("*commutatio* and *immutatio* are two kinds of transformation, and the first concerns quantity while the second concerns quality, such that if someone is changed from big to small, he has been *commutatus*, but if someone is changed from black to white, he is said to have been *immutatus*"). But *commuto* is often also used to indicate "transformation" as metamorphosis: cf. *TLL* III, 1987ff.; on *mutare* in Ovid, cf. Anderson 1963, 1–27.

52. Plaut. *Am.* 866.

I become Amphitryon and change (*immuto*) my clothes.

In Sosia's case, his *immutatio* does not involve merely a change of clothes, but an alteration of his actual physical appearance and his personal identity, as well: *ubi formam perdidi?* he goes on to say. Being *immutatus* has caused him to lose his own *forma*, because the "other" Sosia has usurped *omnem imaginem meam*, as the "real" Sosia says. It is already considerably clear from the context that the process of *immutare* implies magic, so there is no need to reiterate that shapeshifting (expressed in Latin by verbs such as *muto, commuto* and *immuto*) was one of the forms of ancient magic that its practitioners were most eager to realize.[53] Moreover, the magical quality of *immutatus* seems confirmed by a passage we have already seen. Amphitryon and Sosia are speaking, but this time it is the great general who fears that he has lost himself:

AM. delenitus sum profecto, ita ut me qui sim nesciam.
SO. Amphitruo es profecto, cave sis ne tu te usu perduis.
ita nunc homines immutantur, postquam peregre advenimus.[54]

AM. I am so beside myself at this point that I no longer know who I am.
SO. You are Amphitryon, of course: just be careful that you do not lose control of yourself. Men sure seem to have changed (*immutantur*) since we came back from our travels.

Amphitryon no longer knows "who he is," and this sensation derives from the fact that he feels *delenitus* (a rare word that denotes the condition of someone who has gone out of his mind because he has been "bewitched").[55] Sosia, inviting his master not to "lose control of himself," reveals that a few too many "transformations" have occurred since their return. This is very interesting: here, the mention of being *immutatus* is explicitly accompanied by that of "ownership," a possession at risk of being lost.

The magical connotations of the verb *immutare* and its connection to "loss of ownership" are even clearer in a passage of *Miles Gloriosus*,[56] the

---

53. On *muto* cf. e.g. Verg. *Ecl.* 8.70; Ov. *Met.* 9.81, etc.; on *commuto* cf. e.g. Hyg. *Fab.* 125, etc. On *immuto,* cf. n. 59 below.
54. Plaut. *Am.* 844ff.
55. Cf. the note of Oniga 1985 on 844.
56. To understand the text, it may perhaps be useful to briefly go over the the plot of the comedy. The young Pleusicles is in love with the courtesan Philocomasium, now in possession of the soldier Pyrgopolynices. The soldier has given her an apartment, and is having the slave Sceledrus keep watch on her. The clever Palaestrio—Pleusicles' old and faithful slave—now also in the possession of the soldier on account of an accident at sea, has made a hole in the wall of the house

most intriguing evidence that we have from Plautus for the anthropological significance of *immutatio*. Here the young woman Philocomasium pretends not to know either Sceledrus or Palaestrio, men with whom she is in fact only too well acquainted:

> PHIL. quis tu homo es aut mecum quid est negoti?
> SCEL. me rogas, hem, qui sim? PHIL. quin ego hoc rogem quod nesciam?
> PAL. quis ego sum igitur, si hunc ignoras? PHIL. mihi odiosus, quisquis es, et tu et hic. SCEL. non nos novisti? PHIL. neutrum SCEL. metuo maxume.
> PAL. quid metuis? scel. enim ne nos <nosmet> perdiderimus uspiam:
> nam nec te neque me novisse ait haec. pal. persectari hic volo,
> sceledre, nos nostri an alieni simus, ne dum quispiam
> nos vicinorum imprudentis aliquis immutaverit.
> SCEL. certe equidem noster sum. pal. et pol ego.[57]

> PHIL. And you: who are you? What have you got to do with me?
> SCEL. What? You're asking me who I am? PHIL. Why shouldn't I, seeing as I don't know you?
> PAL. Who am I then, if you don't recognize him? PHIL. Whoever you are, I don't like you: you and him both. SCEL. You don't recognize us? PHIL. Neither one. SCEL. Now I really am afraid.
> PAL. What are you afraid of? SCEL. I am afraid that we have lost ourselves somewhere, since she says she doesn't know either of us, not you, and not me either. PAL. I'd really like to figure this out, Sceledrus: are we ours anymore, or someone else's? I wouldn't want for one of our neighbors to have secretly changed us without our knowing it.
> SCEL. Of course we are ours. PAL. Me too, by Pollux!

Because Philocomasium recognizes neither Sceledrus nor Palaestrio, Sceledrus is afraid that they both have "lost themselves somewhere." Palaestrio raises the stakes, wondering if one of their neighbors have not by chance transformed them (*immutati*)—"changed us without our knowing it." Evidently, he assumes that there could be some *vicinus* endowed with magical powers, some sorcerer able to cause those around him to undergo a

---

that borders on that of an old man, Periplectomenus, perfect for Pleusicles and his girlfriend. In this way, the two lovers can meet each other with some frequency. But Sceledrus, mounting the roof, sees Philocomasium next door in the arms of her lover. At that point there is real need of a comic strategem, which Palaestrio hits upon: he will make Sceledrus believe that he has seen not Philocomasium but her twin sister. Naturally, the girl must also play her part, and she pretends not to recognize either Palestrio or Sceledrus.

57. Plaut. *Am.* 425ff.

metamorphosis. It is worth noting that once again the person who undegoes a process of *immutari* also suffers "loss of ownership" of himself. Sceledrus is afraid *ne nos nosmet perdiderimus*, and Palaestrio explains that if they have been *immutati*, they now "belong to someone else" (*alieni*) and no longer "to ourselves" (*nostri*). To *immutare* someone entails—at least in Plautus' linguistic-cultural outlook—changing his external appearance and "taking possession" of him.

The features of the magical metamorphosis connected with loss of ownership surely must also characterize the meaning of the term *immutatus* outside of the text of Plautus and belong more generally to the terminology and beliefs of ancient magic. In fact, some interesting evidence from beyond the Plautine corpus reveals the same strict interdependence between transformation and loss of ownership: here, however, *immutatio* concerns the magical transformation not of people, but of objects. The evidence in question comes from a *tabella defixionis*, one of those curious little tablets on which magical curses, formulas and prayers were inscribed, to be turned against someone's enemies or some other hated person. This context provides further confirmation that the expression *immutare* belongs strictly to the sphere of magic. The tablet reads:

> Dea Ataecina Turibrig(ensis), per tuam maiestatem te rogo oro obsecro uti vindices quot mihi furti factum est quisquis mihi imudavit involavit minusve fecit eas [res] qiss tunicas VI [. . . pae]nula lintea II in[dus]ium.[58]
>
> O goddess Ataecina of Turobriga! By your majesty I beg, beseech and implore you to vindicate what was taken from me: someone has changed (*imudavit*), stolen or concealed the things which are listed here: six tunics, two linen cloaks, a lady's dress . . .

The tablet's author addresses himself to the goddess Ataecina as the victim of theft and wardrobe damages. Because the tablet speaks explicitly of robbery, we can be sure of the fact that the context is of "loss of ownership." What the petitioner asks for is to be helped in recovering not only what "someone" (*quisquis*) has "robbed" (*involavit*) and "concealed" (*minus . . . fecit*) from him, but specifically what that someone has "changed" (*imudavit*). The inscriber of the tablet thus assumes that the disappearance of his clothes might be due not sinply to what could be called "normal" theft but to a sort of "magical transformation."[59] Someone had the power to "seize pos-

---

58. *CIL* II, 462, Lusitania (Audollent 1967, 177ff.). On *imudavit* = *immutavit*, cf. Niedermann 1918, 68.
59. Jeanneret 1918, 124, gave this *immutare* a rather unhappy interpretation: "immutare . . .

session" of those clothes, taking them away from their legitimate owner by "transforming" them (thus rendering them unrecognizable). The type of theft evoked in the *tabella* may in fact recall the well known "magical transference of crops" from one field to another (*fruges excantare, alienam segetem pellicere*), mentioned in the Twelve Tables.[60]

Let us return to Sosia *immutatus*. Sosia suspects he has been the victim of a metamorphosis and consequently that he has lost his *forma*. Clearly, the cultural model invoked here is that of "magical transformation" and in particular that of the "loss of ownership" that accompanies such a change. Like Palaestrio, Sosia confronts the possibility that he is living in a magical world where supernatural metamorphoses can take place and where it is possible to end up in someone else's power as the result of transformation.[61] Might Sosia "feel" like Lucius in the moment he becomes a donkey, having smeared himself with the mysterious ointment offered to him by Photis?[62] Or like one of Odysseus' companions transformed into an animal by Circe and subjugated to the witch's terrifying powers?

This parallel with the way in which Circe's magic is described in the *Odyssey* may be useful (from a linguistic point of view, as well) for understanding the twofold process evoked by Sosia in his reference to *immutatio* (the magical transformation and the subject's loss of self-ownership). Circe has the power to subdue her guests by means of enchantment (the expression used by Homer explicitly emphasizes the submission of the victims through the magical act):[63] she gives them a powerful magical potion and turns them into animals. Accordingly, Odysseus' companions—now changed into pigs—appear to be completely under Circe's power, "having

---

signifie à l'origine 'changer, alterer, trasformer,' et dans notre texte 'soustraire, voler.' Il se pourrait que cette restriction de sens eut lieu en vertu d'un euphémisme ironique, analogue à celui qui attribue au verbe *faire* le sens de 'voler' dans le néologisme du français populaire: *on m'a fait ma montre.*"

60. Fr. 8.7–8 Schoell. On these two texts, cf. Beckmann 1928, 5ff., with much relevant evidence; and Tupet 1986, 2610ff.

61. Lucius, having reached *media loca Thessaliae*, is convinced that *nec fuit illa civitate quod aspiciens id esse crederem, quod esset, sed omnia prorsus ferali murmure in aliam effigiem traslata*, "Nor was there anything in that city that I, upon seeing it, believed that it was what it was, but I believed every creature and object to have assumed a form different from that which it had before, on account of some wicked enchantment" (Apul. *Met.* 2.1).

62. Apul. *Met.* 3.24. On the *commutationes hominum*, cf. also the valuable evidence of August. *Civ.* 18.17–18.

63. Hom. *Od.* 10.213: *katethēlxen*, from *katathelgein* ("to subject by enchantment"). For the interpretation of this verb, cf. Lucian, *Adversus indoctum et libros multos ementem* 12 where the verb is used to indicate the power of transformation possessed by Orpheus' lyre over animals and objects. For ancient explanations of the Homeric passage, see Hayman 1873, 150 *ad loc*. Cf. also Page 1973, 55ff.

forgotten their homeland" and "shut inside the pigsty."[64] Naturally, in the context of the *Odyssey*, "forgetting the homeland" means losing the most defining characteristic of identity. Odysseus' companions "are no longer themselves," in terms of both their personal self-awareness and the impulses that normally characterize their behavior. We have already seen the fundamental role played by memory in the definition of identity. In the same way, Hermes explains to Odysseus that Circe possesses the incredible power of contriving wicked tricks against him, "rendering him weak and impotent."[65] Magical transformation appears again to entail the weakness and submission of the victim. The hero's loss of power is actually imagined to occur at the precise moment in which, having been lured into the bedroom by the shrewd enchantress, he finds himself "naked" (*apogumnothenta*) and greatly exposed to witch's magical powers of transformation.[66]

Returning to Sosia. The way in which Sosia interprets his loss of appearance and identity involves a realization that another—Mercury/Sosia—now has complete possession of the *imago* that formerly belonged to him. At the same time, the identity he was so sure of possessing has now been denied to him. To explain this improbable event, he imagines that he has been transformed into someone else, someone different than he was before. Sosia thus emphasizes what for us is only one aspect of the encounter with the Double: loss of identity, the fact of no longer being recognizable as himself. For this reason, he feels that he has been transformed into another person.

Plautus' text enables us to reconstruct another part of the model: the terminology that expresses the active appropriation of someone else's identity—in other words, the situation of Mercury, who "took possession" of Sosia, or of Jupiter, who assumes upon himself the identity of Amphitryon.[67] There is another character explicitly evoked in *Amphitruo*, complementary to *immutatus Sosia:* the fearsome *versipellis*. Mercury uses this term to describe the behavior of his father Jupiter as he assumes the appearance of Amphitryon:

in Amphitruonis vortit sese imaginem
omnesque eum censent esse servi qui vident:
ita vorsipellem se facit quando lubet.[68]

---
64. Hom. *Od.* 10.236ff., "The effect of the potion must be supposed to be, to unman them entirely, and disable them from resisting or evading the stroke of the wand" (Hayman 1873, 152 *ad loc.*).
65. Hom. *Od.* 10.301 (cf. also 341), *kakon kai anēnora*.
66. In the expression *anēnora* ("unmanly"), Hayman 1873, 158, sees the possibility of an allusion to the loss of human form that Odysseus would have endured.
67. For the distribution of this motif in folkloric tales, cf. Thompson 1967, D 40ff.
68. Plaut. *Am.* 121ff.

He changed himself into the spitting image of Amphitryon and all the slaves who see him think that it is him: so he makes himself into a shape-shifter when he wants to.

Versipellis ("shapeshifter," literally, "skin-changer") is the term used of sorcerers who magically change their outward appearance, werewolves[69] and Thessalian witches.[70] Describing Jupiter in this way, Mercury curiously compares the king of the gods to less august figures, such as the witch Pamphyle in Apuleius, who could transform herself into any other being.[71] The expression *versipellis* reveals the other side of the coin, then. Passive loss of identity exists in tandem with active transformation in the form of a forcible appropriation of some other or someone else's identity. Someone capable of taking on a new identity is a "skin-changer," while he who unwittingly suffers such a loss is *immutatus*. Taken together, the *immutatus* on one side and the *versipellis* on the other constitute a single paradigm. In this light, the fact that we find both ways of framing the experience of "doubling" within the same text certainly merits our attention.

Losing Oneself in Oblivion

We have not yet finished with the series of questions that Sosia asks himself, however. *Ubi immutatus sum?* he has just asked, and "Where did I lose my *forma?*" The questions form a clear sequence of events: the loss of his *forma* is a consequence of the *immutatio* he has undergone. And then: "Or perhaps I was left behind somewhere, and forgot what happened?" Because this question follows what is for us, at least, the rather unusual assertion about *immutatio*, this new explanation offered by Sosia for his loss of identity risks being overlooked or dismissed as obvious. But it is not obvious.

First, we need to ascertain where that *illic* is in which Sosia believes he "was left behind." The word order suggests that this adverb should be understood in relation to *ubi*, which precedes it—that (undefined) place where Sosia had been *immutatus* and where he lost his *forma*.[72] Sosia describes a rather strange condition: leaving himself somewhere and then forgetting all

---

69. Called precisely *versipellis*: Plin. *Nat. hist.* 8.50; Petr. *Sat.* 62.13.

70. These too are called *versipelles*: Apul. *Met.* 2.22. Metamorphosis through "changing skin" is found in numerous stories of folklore (cf. Thompson 1967, 530ff.), while "inside-out fur" frequently functions as an attribute of demonic characters or tricksters: cf. e.g., Gogol's *Evenings on a Farm Near Dikanka* and Borghi Cedrini 1989, 112, etc.

71. Apul. *Met.* 3.21. At 1043, Amphitryon will define Jupiter as *Thessalus veneficus*, as someone who has upset the mind of his family.

72. Fusillo (1998, 65) interprets this *illic* as actually referring to the underworld.

about it. It may be possible to compare Sceledrus' preoccupation in *Miles Gloriosus* that "he has lost possession of himself *somewhere*." Here, too, the context hinges on an *immutatio* and the expression "lost possession of himself somewhere" closely resembles "being left behind" in an undefined place and "forgetting" at the same time. In both cases, the *place* where the metamorphosis occurs seems to be imagined as a location that is not only hard to specify but in fact impossible to remember.

The motif of "forgetting" in connection with magical metamorphosis again permits a parallel with the Circe episode of Homer's *Odyssey*. This episode confirms that the element of "oblivion" forms part of the ancient paradigm of magical transformation. Odysseus' companions, whom Circe has turned into pigs, are characterized precisely as "having forgotten their homeland,"[73] like those who eat the lotus flowers.[74] In Homer, much as with the *immutatio* and the loss of *forma* that Sosia has suffered, transformation appears to imply oblivion and forgetting one's former life. Indeed, even an analogy with the souls of the Dead who "forget" their own past after drinking the waters of Lethe appears highly suggestive in this light;[75] in this case as well a total transformation of state, order and identity entails forgetting one's previous condition.

But Sosia's "transformation" is much worse than the (already miserable) condition that Odysseus' companions suffer through Circe's enchantments. Sosia imagines not merely that he is *immutatus*, not merely that he has forgotten himself, but that he has forgotten his true *self* in some *place* that he cannot locate. It is rather difficult for us, with our cultural categories, to follow Sosia's reasoning. But we must conclude from what he says that his magical world contains the possibility of "leaving oneself," fully forgetful of the fact, in the hands of someone else who takes possession of that Self through the very act of transformation. When someone is denied their identity, their thoughts take refuge in the possibility that their "true" person has been deposited somewhere else, and that instead some kind of substitute roams about whom no one is willing to believe. Sosia seems to think that it is possible for someone to exist vicariously in one place, while "they" (the "real" person) are actually somewhere else. We might think here of Vergil's *Aeneid*, when Venus makes Cupid take on the appearance of the young Ascanius so that Dido, taking him in her arms, might be more easily enflamed by love. Where is the "real" Ascanius, meanwhile? "He is asleep, hidden on high Cythera or Idalium, lest he discover the trick and somehow intervene."[76]

---

73. Hom. *Od.* 10.236.
74. Hom. *Od.* 9.102. Parallels in Hayman 1873, II, 86; Page 1973,15ff.
75. Cf. e.g. Verg. *Aen.* 6.715.
76. Verg. *Aen.* 1.680ff. Around Sosia's opinion could be collected a constellation of beliefs and

Ascanius, deprived of his identity, "lies asleep" in some remote and out-of-the-way place. This "disorientation" threatening one's faith in one's personal identity is likely very different from what affects modern man in analogous cases of "doubling," but it is just as frightening. There is the threat of "losing" and "forgetting" oneself somewhere and of going about in the world in some other form. Is the life you are leading only a proxy for what is happening somewhere else to your "true" Self, lost and enslaved through some magical event of which you have no recollection whatsoever?

The Death of Metamorphosis and the Modern Double

The anthropological framework employed by Sosia in interpreting his unfortunate situation—magical metamorphosis—is specific to and characteristic of the culture to which he belongs. Moreover, it is entirely alien to our modern notion of "doubling." This is already quite clear from Plautus' text. But just how little our own cultural conception of "doubling" involves metamorphosis (and therefore just how differently Sosia *thinks* his loss of identity) is confirmed by a parallel that is all the more intriguing because taken from the world of dreams.

Artemidorus of Daldis devotes a long chapter of his book *The Interpretation of Dreams* to detailing a typology of "dreams of metamorphosis," giving their various symbolic meanings.[77] Dreams in which the human body appears deformed, altered, changed into some animal form and so on, are cited with great frequency in this work:[78] evidently, the dream of metamorphosis formed a significant part of the ancient dream experience. In fact, metamorphosis was not simply a mythological or literary motif (as in Ovid's *Metamorphoses*, the poets who figure in the paraphrases of Antoninus Liberalis and Apuleius' *Golden Ass*), but an active cultural model—so much a lived experience for the general populace that it furnished abundant material for dreams. This is not surprising, since magic played an important role in this

---

stories—some certainly different in content, but presupposing an analogous "doubling." Cf. e.g. the stories of magic in which a character killed by witches receives an artificial prolongation of his own life until he finds a second, more "definitive" death, as in the story of Socrates told in Apul. *Met.* 1.2ff.; or the story of the child whom witches "substitute" with a straw doll in Petr. *Sat.* 63.8. In this light, we should recall also the famous "living image" of Helen that Hera sent into the arms of Paris, while the true Helen was in Egypt (Eur. *Hel.* 31ff.; cf. Stesichorus fr. 192P = Bowra 1973 and above all Gentili 1989, 166ff.). In Greece, a dream also seems to presume the possibility of a real doubling and of a real experience 'outside' the person (cf. Guidorizzi 1988, xiiiff.). After Tylor 1871 and through the famous work of Rohde 1890–1894, the various forms of experience of the "double" were often located, as we know, at the origin of the notion of the "soul."

77. Artem. 1.50.
78. Cf. Artem. 1.20, 1.24, 5.39, 5.63, etc.

world. But does metamorphosis form part of the modern dream experience? Apparently not, at least according to the observations of George Devereux. Drawing on his own experience as a psychoanalyst, Devereux concluded that this type of dream occurs only in psychotic subjects—and very infrequently even in those cases.[79] Metamorphosis no longer seems to feature in modern dreaming, nor to contribute material to contemporary dreamers. Although the possibility of being transformed into something else presented itself concretely to ancient cultural perception, it is decidedly rare for us. And this confirms that Sosia, in his attempt to somehow justify the existence of his "substitute," employs a psychological category as intimately bound up in his own culture as it is foreign to our own.

Apart from this indirect evidence, it is nevertheless clear that magical transformation is not even a minimally relevant feature of the various stories of "doubles" found in later literature. If we really want to find a modern parallel for the way in which Sosia thinks his Double, we will have to look not to the classic "mirror-doubles" already cited—"William Wilson" and *The Double*—but to the transformations undergone by Dr. Jekyll. In other words, the way in which Plautus presents Sosia's encounter with Sosia corresponds not to the typical story of the Double or *Doppelgänger*, but to a modern story that holds a rather strange position in respect of other literature dealing with this theme. Once modern science has claimed for itself all the power of "changing" people (or at any rate believes that it has achieved this terrifying capability), what Sosia attributed exclusively to the powers of magic must happen "rationally." It is again possible to become someone else: Dr. Jekyll becomes Mr. Hyde. Scientist though he might have been, the good doctor becomes a frightful *versipellis*.

In the classic Romantic encounter with the Substitute, there is no trace of magical transformation, which contributes to the particular atmosphere of these stories. Yet magic, even when it is frightening, is nevertheless a form of explanation for everything that does not seem explicable. It is possible, in other words, that the absence of magical transformation from the reference framework of the modern "double" makes this phenomenon even more ambiguous and anxiety-provoking. Lacking the "way out" offered to Sosia's culture by magic, modern reason remains prisoner to the enigma and the Substitute can crystallize all of its frightening absurdity. To a mentality that willingly admits the existence of magic, William Wilson would have been an *immutatus* and the other, his Double, would have been a dangerous *versipellis*. But now? To free ourselves from the thought of the Double, there

---

79. Devereux 1976, xxvff. On this, and generally on the relationship between dream imagines and cultural paradigms, see Guidorizzi 1988, viiff.

remains nothing but to reveal (quite awkwardly) its artificial nature (as sometimes Hoffmann's characters may do)[80] or to eliminate this freak of nature by destroying it, as we find in Poe's story, in Hoffmann and elsewhere.[81] Between the two pretenders to a single identity (the two halves of a split personality) arises the pitiless war of attrition that notoriously characterizes most of modern literary production concerned with the theme of the Double.[82]

In our culture, Reason does not easily yield. The provocation caused by the literary existence of the Double is too violent: someone has to catch this enigmatic creature and bring it in line, without killing it. What Sosia perceived as magic is therefore turned into mental sickness, the pathological projection of an apparition. Psychoanalysis ("dissection of the soul," as Thomas Mann called it in *The Magic Mountain*)[83] would cleverly transfer into the *interior* world of man what for ancient culture was essentially an *external* transformation.[84] Anatomized by the capable hands of the analyst, the unconscious would finally reveal the "truth" of *immutatio* and the *versipellis*.

Imagines Maiorum and the Aristocratic Double

Let us finally return to Sosia on his mental journey through the world of the Double. When he has finished interrogating himself, the slave permits himself another joke:

> nam hicquidem omnem imaginem meam, quae antehac fuerat, possidet.
> vivo fit mihi quod numquam quisquam mortuo faciet mihi.[85]

> It's clear that this man here has my entire appearance, the appearance that used to be mine. Something is happening to me while I'm alive that nobody would do for me if I died!

Here we find once again and in the clearest possible terms a connection between the Double and Death. But a more precise description of Sosia's

---

80. Thus the adventure of Johannes Kreisler, victim of an optical illusion created by Meister Abraham with the help of mirrors (Hoffmann's *Lebensansichten des Katers Murr*).

81. The story of *The Devil's Elixirs* is based precisely on the perennial contest between Medardus and Viktorinus, while Kreisler, too, before realizing that he is the victim of an optical illusion, insistently asks Meister Abraham to "kill" his malignant *Doppelgänger*. The same desire of killing the double is found also in Maupassant's *Le Horla*.

82. Cf. Passage 1954, 26.

83. "Seelenzergliederung" (Mann 1998).

84. The psychological literature on the literary "double" is vast: besides the well-known work of Rank 1914, cf. more recently also Tymms 1949; Rogers 1970; Keppler 1972; Funari 1986, etc.

85. Plaut. *Am.* 458ff.

thought (or rather of the chain of associations that underlies his *Witz*) will show that, from an anthropological point of view, the cultural context to which he is now referring is more specific and more marked than anything we have looked at so far.

The content of the joke is this: Sosia refers explicitly to the *imagines maiorum* that played a part in the funerary practice of noble Roman families. "If that man possesses my entire *imago*," reasons Sosia, "then something is happening to me in life that would never happen to me even in death—that is, I have at my disposal an image of myself separate from me." Sosia, who is a slave, would certainly never have had the right to a procession of *imagines* on the day of his funeral. But that is precisely what is happening to him now, and while he is still alive.[86]

In Sosia's thinking, for someone to encounter another who has taken on his exterior *imago*, is equivalent to meeting someone, in life, who is in possession of his own funeral *imago*. Apparently, these images of the ancestors, carried in procession at the noble Roman funeral, constitute another anthropological model good for thinking the Double. Sosia's joke is therefore a precious piece of evidence for exploring the anthropological significance of the *imagines maiorum*, a cultural model of extreme importance for the Romans.[87] In fact, this joke implies that the funeral *imago* could be thought of not just as a simple effigy but as a full-fledged "double" of the deceased. Let us see if we can confirm this with evidence from other sources. This will be a good way to examine these texts from a new and unusual point of view.[88]

Ancient descriptions of funeral *imagines* tell us that they are wax reproductions of the faces of the dead, and that these reproductions are supposed to be "extremely similar" to the person who has died.[89] Normally, the *imagines* are kept in special cabinets in the atrium of the Roman house. When some member of the family dies, these masks are taken out and worn by the family members who most closely resemble (in build and so forth) the person whose *imago* they are wearing. These individuals are also dressed in clothing appropriate to the office and status of the dead person, and don the regalia and signs of their public honors.[90] Such images are then "performed" and

---

86. The explanation of Pylades, according to whom the text is referring to the *ludi funebres* with a joking allusion to the expression *ludos facere* (cf. Plaut. *Most.* 427ff.), does not seem to me very likely: the text orients us quite differently. The word *imago* has just been given, as being "possessed" by Mercury/Sosia: and this clearly alludes to "wearing" the funeral masks.
87. Bettini 1991c, 169ff.
88. For relevant bibliography, see Bettini 1991c, 169ff; *Croisille* 1985, 135ff. The literary sources that discuss the *imagines maiorum* have been collected by Lahusen 1984, 128ff. (including some texts which quite frankly seem to have little to do with the images of the ancestors); Flower 1996, 91ff.
89. Polyb. *Hist.* 6.35.5.
90. Cf. above all Polyb. *Hist.* 6.53ff.; Diod. *Hist.* 31.25.2.

in their performance they evoke the presence of dead ancestors. Polybius, describing the noble Roman funeral with some emotion, remarks: "How can one not be moved, seeing the images of men famous for their virtues, gathered together and, so to speak, living and moving?"[91] The *imagines* are "doubles" of the deceased. Far more than mere figures that resemble them, they are actual substitutes for the dead.

Diodorus Siculus, speaking of the funeral of Lucius Aemilius Paulus, adds a further observation of some relevance: "Among the Romans, those who were especially noble or who were famous because of their ancestors . . . were accompanied all their life by *mimētai* who carefully studied their bearing and any peculiarities in their appearance."[92] Who are these *mimētai?* The author simply may be referring to those artists who studied the features of the rich and famous in order to reproduce them in works of art. But given that *mimētēs* properly means "mime, actor," Diodorus instead may be referring to the practice of mimes who studied the behavior and features of the rich and famous in order to then actually impersonate them. This latter interpretation appears to be confirmed by a much later Roman source. Suetonius tells us that at the funeral of Vespasian "an *archimimus* named Favor depicted the emperor's person and imitated his dress, what he did and what he said while he was alive."[93] Suetonius states explicitly that this occurred "according to custom" (*mos*): the presence of the mime at the emperor's funeral was not an *ad hoc* invention, but a regular element of this ritual. Moreover, the *archimimus* mentioned by Suetonius closely approximates the *mimētēs* who, according to Diodorus, accompanied an aristocrat in order to learn to imitate his bearing and idiosyncratic features. Some peculiar information given to us by Pliny the Elder, however, gives us a further hint of the active presence of these *mimetai* attached to noble Romans.

In the section of his work dedicated to the powers (and the peculiarities) of resemblance, Pliny cites five cases of noble Romans whose physical similarity to an actor or mime was so great that their *cognomen* derived directly from this fact.[94] A Scipio was called *Salvitto,* a Lentulus was called *Spinther,* a Metellus was called *Pamphilus,* a Curio was called *Burbuleius* and Messalla Censorius was called *Menogenes,* all because there was an actor or a mime

---

91. Polyb. *Hist.* 6.53.10.

92. Diod. *Hist.* 31.25.2.

93. Suet. *Vesp.* 19, *in funere . . . archimimus personam eius ferens imitansque, ut est mos, facta ac dicta vivi.* Not much credit was given to Diodorus in Zadoks and Jitta 1932, 25, according to whom this "mimic" use could not be dated as far back in time as Diodorus wished: but no reason is given why.

94. Plin. *Nat. hist.* 7.53ff. In fact there are six cases, if any importance is given to the addition that is found in the margin of the *Leidensis Lipsi* n. 7 at 7.55, where Agrippinus is said to be indistinguishable from the mime Parides.

of that name bearing a striking resemblance to each of them. Furthermore, Pliny tells us that the orator Lucius Plancus passed on his *cognomen* to the actor Rubrius for the same reason: i.e., the extraordinary *similitudo* between them. Pliny's continual mention of resemblances between famous Romans and *histriones* or *mimi* is striking. Might we hypothesize that these extraordinary *similitudines* were recorded with such great care precisely because the actors or mimes were in actual fact the *mimētai* attached to these nobles to study their bearing and particular way of speaking? This would explain the migration of *cognomina* from one to the other, to signal, in a certain sense, the interchangeability between those two people, that one was the *alter ego* of the other.

What a strange fate for physical resemblance![95] Someone who looks like a Roman noble and who possesses the mime's skill of augmenting or emphasizing this natural similitude is attracted into that noble's orbit, to become almost his Double. Read in the context of Vespasian's *archimimus* and the other actors who greatly "resembled" some aristocrat, the information given to us by Diodorus about *mimētai* seems to demonstrate that for the Roman *nobilis*, his own funeral representation—his *imago*—began to take shape during his own lifetime. Accompanied by a *mimētēs* who strove to acquire all the peculiarities of his appearance (so that they could be faithfully reproduced upon his death), the Roman aristocrat inevitably must have imagined his own death in the form of the Double.[96]

Sosia was not mistaken, then. A doubling of identity could be represented by the *imago funebris* (or, at any rate, in the form of aristocratic death). Death appears closely associated with the sphere of the Double. Sosia the slave joked about a solemn object—the *imago*—that may never have been within his reach, but he knew the significance of the cultural and psychological category to which it referred. There is therefore something very profound about the *Witz* with which the Plautine slave, almost with a shrug of the shoulders, frees himself from a phantom that in all likelihood would never have concerned him, had not Plautus' imagination arranged that unexpected and unpleasant encounter for him before his master's door.

---

95. Bettini 1999a, 205–6.
96. For the category of the "double" in archaic Greek culture (the *kolossos* or "substitute" of the dead man and of his *psuchē*), cf. the famous study of Vernant (1965b).

SIX

Ghosts of Exile

Doubles and Nostalgia in Vergil's *Parva Troia*

Aeneas, at Carthage, is telling his story. He has reached the moment when the Trojan exiles disembark at Epirus, a long journey and several failures now behind them. Already, Aeneas has tried to found a city on the coast of Thrace that would bear his name—Aeneades—but the appalling prodigy of Polydorus' blood compelled them to flee in all possible haste.[1] After receiving what seemed to be an unambiguous revelation at Delos, he had attempted to found another city called Pergamea on Crete, but a dream-vision of the Penates drove the exiles to depart once again, leaving only a small group behind.[2] Finally they reached the coast of Epirus, where Aeneas hears some truly unexpected news:

> hic incredibilis rerum fama occupat aures,
> Priamiden Helenum Graias regnare per urbes
> coniugio Aeacidae Pyrrhi sceptrisque potitum,
> et patrio Andromachen iterum cessisse marito.[3]

Here the unbelievable rumor of events reaches his ears, that Helenus, son of Priam, is ruling over Greek cities, in possession of the bride and scepter of Aeacidean Pyrrhus and that Andromache is once again bestowed upon a husband of her own race.

---

1. Verg. *Aen.* 3.17ff.
2. Verg. *Aen.* 3.132ff.
3. Verg. *Aen.* 3.294ff.

As it turns out, Helenus, son of Priam and brother of Hector, has inherited Neoptolemus' kingdom and wed Andromache—in a marriage that immediately catches our attention because of the anthropological as well as literary-interpretive questions it raises.

Andromache's "Levirate"

In Aeneas' account, a rather unusual expression describes the marriage between Helenus and Andromache: *patrio . . . iterum cessisse marito* ("once again bestowed upon a husband of her own race"). The adjective *patrius* seems to indicate that Andromache, once the slave and concubine of the Greek Pyrrhus, has again become the wife of a Trojan—of a man from among her "native" people. Servius, however, reminds us that Andromache actually came from Thebes in Asia Minor, making the adjective *patrius* rather inappropriate: strictly speaking, neither Hector nor Helenus belong to Andromache's actual *patria*, because Andromache herself is not originally Trojan.[4] Servius' observations often tend to be pedantic, and this observation easily applies to this comment, as well. Vergil might simply have been somewhat imprecise or perhaps he forgot Andromache's Theban origins, unconsciously identifying her as a Trojan because the most significant events of her life occurred at Troy.[5] But even if—or, precisely because—the expression is a *lapsus*, we should examine the implications of the adjective *patrius* more closely. Returning to Servius' gloss, we discover that the commentator, having raised the problem, immediately suggests an interesting solution:

> aut certe secundum ius locutus est, quia uxor viri domicilium sequitur, iuncta ergo Hectori facta Troiana est.[6]

> Or he expressed himself in legal terminology, because the wife follows her husband's place of domicile; therefore, having married Hector, she became Trojan.

Andromache, then, by virtue of marrying a Trojan, becomes a Trojan herself. She identifies with the group she joins, severing all ties to her group of origin. After her marriage to Hector, the young bride from Thebes acquires

---

4. Serv. in *Aen.* 3.297, *'patrio marito' atqui Thebana fuit de Thebis Phrygiis*. See also the note of Williams 1962 and that of Cova 1994, *ad loc.*
5. Cova 1994, *ad loc.*, " . . . the reader understands it [the expression *patrius*] more easily in psychological and sentimental terms."
6. Cova 1994, *ad loc.*

a Trojan identity that she will never relinquish, assimilated completely to her husband's lineage. The model assumed here does not differ much from the Roman marriage practice involving the husband's *conventio in manum*, whereby his new bride abandons all connections to her "family of orientation" and actually becomes an *agnata* of her husband, fully adopting the identity of his lineage.[7] Andromache has likewise lost herself, so to speak, becoming part of the lineage to which her husband belongs.

The adjective *patrius* is central to the characterization of Andromache, revealing a very precise perspective on the identity of the woman whom Aeneas is about to meet. From the moment she enters the picture, Hector's widow is represented as a woman who in every way "belongs" to the city of Troy. In fact, the development of this episode confirms that Andromache, despite her marriage to Pyrrhus and events subsequent to this event, is still entirely defined by her Trojan role as "Hector's wife." The expression *patrio . . . marito* unmistakably alerts the reader to the meaning the poet wishes to convey. The adjective already embodies Andromache's entire identity.

Reading further in Servius (who holds some other interesting observations in store for us), we learn that Vergil's use of the verb *cessisse* is also quite unusual. Servius, of course, does not fail to comment upon this:

> nam et 'cessisse' de iure est, cedi enim hereditas dicitur . . . [sic ait, ut dicimus: ex hereditate paterna illud mihi cessit].[8]

> *Cessisse* in fact belongs to legal terminology, because an inheritance is said to "come to" (*cedi*) . . . [His words echo our expression: "this came to me through paternal heredity"].

We are apparently dealing with a sort of "transfer" along hereditary lines—a wedding resulting from the fact that Helenus, the brother of Andromache's dead husband, Hector, has in some sense "inherited" his widow.[9] Helenus and Andromache's marriage appears substantially to be a "levirate marriage"—a custom followed by many cultures around the world in which a dead man's brother marries his widow. In fact, such marriages are often conceived precisely as an "inheritance" within the overall transfer of the

---

7. Cf. Corbett 1969, 68–90 and Treggiari 1991, 28–32.

8. Serv. in Aen. 3.297. In citations from Servius' commentary, the parts set off in brackets belong to Servius Auctus.

9. For the use of *cedere* as a legal term, see Williams 1962 on 3.297, comparing 3.333ff. (*regnorum reddita cessit / pars Heleno*) and 12.17 (*cedat Lavinia coniunx*).

dead man's property.¹⁰ Moreover, Helenus, as Hector's younger brother,¹¹ is an ideal candidate to inherit his widow, since typologically it is the younger brother (and not the elder) who is designated as the levirate husband.¹²

This is not the motivation that Vergil offers for this marriage between brother- and sister-in-law, however. Andromache later explains to Aeneas that "Pyrrhus gave me, a slave, to his slave Helenus (*me famulo famulamque Heleno transmisit habendam*)."¹³ The marriage was therefore a result of Pyrrhus' wish to make an arrangement between two people who belonged to him, rather than an application of hereditary custom.¹⁴ But described in this way, Andromache's wedding seems more a commercial transaction (*transmisit habendam*) than an actual marriage.¹⁵ More than anything else, the Vergilian expression *cessisse*—especially in connection with a husband defined as *patrius*—attributes to the matrimonial process a strong sense of automaticity.

The choice of this expression—as also of *patrius*—has important consequences for the characterization of the individual Aeneas is about to meet. This characterization is also quite consistent. Andromache, marrying her husband's brother in a sort of levirate, has in some sense reproduced—almost unavoidably (*cessisse*)—her own past. She is again the bride of a Trojan, again the bride of a son of Priam, who marries her as if inheriting a piece of family property. After so many misfortunes, Andromache has returned to the role that best defines her: the Trojan wife of a son of Priam. In this, she reestablishes the bond that Hector's death had broken.

But Helenus is not Hector. At best, he is a substitute, a stand-in for Hector, and not a particularly brilliant one at that.¹⁶ In his famous poem *Le cygne*, Baudelaire describes Andromache's wedding with a remark worthy of Racine: "veuve d'Hector, hélas, et femme d'Hélénus."¹⁷ With its morose

---

10. On this topic, it is sufficient to refer to the famous discussion in Frazer 1918, 263–341. For the levirate as inheritance, see in particular 338–39.

11. Hector is Priam's first-born son: Apoll. *Bibl.* 3.12.5; Scholia ad Iliadem 22.229b (p. 314 Erbse).

12. Frazer 1918, 295ff.

13. Verg. *Aen.* 3.329.

14. Servius ad loc.: *erili voluntate, non lege coniugii* [*vel quia inter captivos matrimonii fides non stabat*]: *unde et habendam dixit*. For the interpretation of *famulus* (weaker than *servus*), see Cova 1994, ad loc.; for *coniugium* between two *famuli*, see Cova 1994,1.

15. Cf. the note of Williams 1962, ad loc.; Cova 1994,1.

16. In the tradition of the "Trojan legend," Helenus is a decidedly ambiguous character: cf. Perret 1942, 217–19 and Cova 1994, xlvi–xlviii. Given the precedents, it is no wonder that Vergil's Helenus should turn out to be a character at the very least "farblos" (as in the characterization of Heinze 1982, 106). For a general discussion of the characterization of Helenus in Vergil, see the discussion in Cova 1994, xlviii–liii.

17. *Le cygne* 40 in Baudelaire 1976, 85–87 and 1003–9. Naturally, the relationship between the episode in Vergil and *Le cygne* has been the object of much study: we cite here only Nelson 1961, 332ff.; Barchiesi 1975, 481ff; Bernardelli 1976, 625ff. The entry "Baudelaire" in Macchia 1984, 469–71 is also very useful.

and enigmatic irony, that single line of verse is worth a thousand pages of criticism: Andromache's new marriage reproduces the past, that much is clear—but it reproduces the past in a reduced and degraded form. Furthermore, everything in the city built by the Trojan exiles in Epirus reproduces the past in this way, as we shall soon see. Andromache's levirate marriage to Helenus perfectly matches the closed world of the "little Troy" that Aeneas is about to enter.

The Encounter

Aeneas is overcome by an irrepressible desire to speak with Helenus and with this in mind he sets out from the harbor where his ships have docked.[18] Needless to say, chance happenings and coincidences—particularly in literary works—are hardly ever accidental and this is no exception. Reaching the city, Aeneas runs into Andromache who "happens" to be celebrating the anniversary of Hector's death:

> sollemnis cum forte dapes et tristia dona
> ante urbem in luco falsi Simoentis ad undam
> libabat cineri Andromache manisque vocabat
> Hectoreum ad tumulum, viridi quem caespite inanem
> et geminas, causam lacrimis, sacraverat aras.[19]
>
> In the grove before the city by the banks of a false Simoïs, Andromache was by chance offering libations, solemn banquets and sad gifts to the ashes, invoking the *Manes* at the tomb of Hector, which, though empty, she had consecrated with green turf and two altars, a cause for tears.

What a coincidence! The arrival of the Trojans happens to occur on a significant date—the anniversary of the great hero's death. Circumstances conspire to make this event even more exceptional. Aeneas' encounter with Andromache has an almost dreamlike quality: on "that very day" Aeneas meets Andromache. But where? By Hector's tomb, we are told—which is obviously

---

18. Verg. *Aen.* 3.298ff. Regarding *miroque incensum pectore amore*, cf. the observations of Williams 1962, "a strong phrase suggesting the overwhelming longing of the exile to meet his old friend." This is revived by Mackie 1988, 69, who, unfortunately, does not develop it further.

19. Verg. *Aen.* 3.301ff. For the interpretation of *sollemnis* in this context, in addition to Servius' gloss on this line, cf. the observations of Grimm 1967, 151ff. For the possibility that the *geminae arae* on which the sacrifice is being performed mark a particular emphasis in the ceremony, see Fowler 1917, 163ff.

"empty" (*inanem*), because we are not at Troy. Yet can we be so sure? The tomb stands "in front of the city," just as the cremation of Hector's corpse took place precisely "in front of the city" and was followed by the erection of a tomb (the true tomb that housed the urn containing the hero's remains).[20] And then there is the river, the "false Simoïs" on whose banks stands that tomb where Andromache performs her sacrifice.

These are Aeneas' words, let us not forget—the story that Aeneas himself is telling to Dido (and which, presumably, has utterly enthralled her—for biographical reasons, if nothing else).[21] The question then arises: How does Aeneas know that the stream is a "false Simoïs?"[22] He still has not spoken with anyone; all he has seen so far is a widow of noble carriage engrossed in her ritual. There is only one possible answer: the stream must resemble the Trojan Simoïs so much that Aeneas instantly recognizes it. In this moment lies the key to this encounter's dreamlike quality, I believe; otherwise Baudelaire would not have chosen this phrase—*falsi Simoentis ad undam*—as the epigraph to his poem.[23] Aeneas encounters Andromache just as she is performing a sacrifice at Hector's tomb and this tomb not only stands "in front of the city" like the "real" tomb of Hector but also is situated so as to resemble that Trojan place *par excellence.* It is as if Andromache were standing in front of a theatrical backdrop that reproduced Troy and its landscape in every detail—just as the audience of Puccini's *Madame Butterfly* instantly recognizes Mount Fujiyama in the background. But we are not at the theater; at least so far as we know, these characters are not "performing" this story—they are living it.

The narrative turns to Andromache's reaction upon recognizing Aeneas. It is an equally disturbing scene:

> ut me conspexit venientem et Troia circum
> arma amens vidit, magnis exterrita monstris,
> deriguit visu in medio; calor ossa reliquit.

---

20. Cf. Hom. *Il.* 24.778ff. Also in Sen. *Tr.* 483ff., Hector's *tumulus* is imagined to be in front of the city.

21. Given that Dido, like Andromache, is a widow, we cannot exclude the possibility that this characteristic of the story's addressee affects the strategy of the text. A certain contrast is indeed established between Andromache's obsessive devotion for her dead husband and the imminent oblivion to which Dido will consign Sychaeus' memory, although the queen of Carthage also remains a desperate prisoner of the shadow of the past. A detailed comparison between the two heroines can be found in Starry West 1983, 257ff. (e.g., 263, Dido has a cenotaph of her husband and looks after it much as Andromache does).

22. The critics appear to have accepted without question this affirmation by Aeneas (e.g., Nelson 1961, 334, "There, in a grove outside the city, by the waters of a mock Simoïs").

23. Thus in the first edition of *Le cygne,* published in *La Causerie* (1860); cf. Pichois' critical note in the Pléiade edition (Baudelaire 1976, 1008).

> Labitur et longo vix tandem tempore fatur:
> verane te facies, verus mihi nuntius adfers,
> nate dea? vivisne? aut si lux alma recessit,
> Hector ubi est? dixit lacrimasque effudit et omnem
> implevit clamore locum.[24]

> When she caught sight of me approaching and, mad, saw all around her Trojan arms, frightened by such great portents straightened up in the middle of her seeing and went cold. She faints, and after a long time manages to speak: "Is your face true, does a true messenger come to me, oh son of a goddess? Are you alive? Or if the loving light has receded, where is Hector?" She spoke and poured out tears and filled the entire place with her lament.

In that "Trojan place," Andromache sees herself surrounded by "Trojan arms"—and Aeneas advances toward her. She is terrified; for her, Aeneas' Trojans are not men but *magna . . . monstra*.[25]

Andromache naturally would have been greatly surprised to see Aeneas again. But this still does not explain why she would consider these new arrivals *monstra*. Servius Auctus provides us with an interesting hint in this regard: *aut certe 'monstris' quod tunc advenerat Aeneas cum illa manes invocaret et eum crederet esse defunctum* ("or *monstris* is used because Aeneas turned up just at the point when she was invoking the *manes,* and because she believed him dead").[26] Andromache has been sacrificing to a dead man; the unexpected apparition of Aeneas, therefore, can only have come from the Underworld. Servius' commentary adds yet another clue, this time of a religious nature: *lucum ut supra diximus numquam ponit sine religione. nam in ipsis habitant manes piorum, qui lares viales sunt* ("as we said above, he [sc. Vergil] never uses *lucus* without a religious connotation. And here in fact live the *manes* of the most pious men, the *Lares viales*").[27] And further on: *nam et inferis sacrificat et in luco ubi habitant manes* ("In fact she is sacrificing to the infernal gods, and she does this in a grove, where the *manes* live").[28] Andromache sacrifices to the Dead in a place where the souls of the Dead are supposed to reside. If we put any stock in the ancient scholiasts, Andromache is fully justified in believing these living beings are ghosts.

---

24. Verg. *Aen.* 3.306ff.
25. Andromache shows here the typical symptoms of that petrifying Vergilian horror: cf. also 3.259ff., *subita gelidus formidine sanguis / deriguit; cecidere animi* (the Harpies) and 7.446ff.: *at iuveni oranti subitus tremor occupat artus / deriguere oculi* (Allecto the appearing to Turnus).
26. Servius in Aen. 3.306.
27. Servius in Aen. 3.302.
28. Servius in Aen. 3.311.

The reflections of ancient exegesis, however well founded, may lead us to overlook an interesting aspect of this encounter. Andromache encounters a living man—Aeneas—and immediately wonders whether he is not a ghost.[29] Furthermore, when confronted by the apparent *revenant* of a person she knows well, she suddenly thinks of someone else: Hector, her husband. She immediately asks about him and then bursts into tears.[30] Aeneas may well have been disappointed by this reception; Andromache all but ignores him, asking only if he is alive or dead. Her thoughts race back to Hector. She sees a living man, and thinks he is dead. She sees Aeneas, and looks for Hector. We now begin to realize that for Andromache—who has married her husband's brother—the world is populated only by "doubles" and "substitutes." More precisely, for Andromache the Living served as substitutes for the Dead, and for one dead man in particular: Hector. Helenus fulfills this function, "representing" his older brother in his role as husband and brother-in-law. Aeneas also fulfills this function, suggesting Hector's presence by his appearance. And all this takes place beside a tomb that stands "in front of the city," on the banks of a river that immediately recalls the Simoïs of Troy.

Aeneas explains himself and reassures Andromache. He too makes inquiries, and she recounts to him—albeit very discretely—her past. Then she begins again to ask:

> sed tibi qui cursum venti, quae fata dedere?
> aut quis ignarum nostris deus adpulit oris?
> quid puer Ascanius? superatne? et vescitur aura,
> quem tibi iam Troia . . .
> ecqua tamen puero est amissae cura parentis?
> ecquid in antiquum virtutem animosque viriles
> et pater Aeneas et avunculus excitat Hector?[31]

> But what course did the winds give you, what fates? Or what god drove you unknowingly to our shores? What of the boy Ascanius? Does he yet live?

---

29. Based on this scene, Vergilian scholarship has repeatedly interpreted Helenus and Andromache's *parva Troia* as an actual world of the "living dead" (cf. Nelson 1961; Bright 1981, 40ff.; Quint 1982, 30ff; Starry West 1983, 258–59), often with fascinating results. On the relationship between the dimension of the "past" in which Andromache has enclosed herself and the Aeneas' "living reality" which "rudely breaks upon it," there are some excellent observations in Grimm 1967, 155.

30. For the ancient exegesis of this passage, it is worth citing evidence from Donatus in Ter. *Andr.* 245, '*amatorie nominato exsiluit in gemitus.*' sic Vergilius: *aut si lux alma recessit / Hector ubi est?* Andromache's lament was therefore understood in relation to her feelings of love (cf. Barabino et al. 1994).

31. Verg. *Aen.* 3.337ff.

> And does he still breathe, he whom for you Troy already . . . ? Does the boy still recall his lost mother? And do his father Aeneas and uncle Hector still urge him on to that ancient valor and manly courage?

Now it is Ascanius who occupies Andromache's thoughts, if only for a moment. She knows not if the boy is alive or dead (for Aeneas has not replied) and immediately her thoughts jump to the boy's dead mother, Creusa: does he still remember her? This is followed by a very human and quite motherly preoccupation to discover what the boy Ascanius "is like." Yet even this sentiment takes a sudden and unexpected turn—not so much because of Andromache's focus on the boy's manly and warlike *animus* (we might expect this from an epic heroine, after all), but because it again marks his—that is, Hector's—obsessive reappearance. Does the memory of "Uncle Hector" urge the boy on to manly exploits? Andromache seems able to think only of the Dead and of one dead man in particular.

Let us pause a moment to consider this seemingly banal expression, *avunculus Hector*. Servius tells us that some considered the word *avunculus* ("maternal uncle") too "humble" for an epic poem.[32] In terms of style and genre, the ancient critics may well have been correct; but they were certainly wrong as regards the poem's substance.[33] In fact, this word permits us to understand Andromache's reaction and to follow the twists and turns of her reasoning. Creusa, Aeneas' wife and Ascanius' mother, was also a daughter of Priam, a sister of Hector.[34] For this reason, Vergil can call Hector the *avunculus* ("maternal uncle") of Ascanius. This gives us a glimpse into Andromache's way of thinking and the reason for her intense preoccupation with the memory of Ascanius' dead mother: the boy reminds her of Creusa because Creusa was the sister of Hector, and Hector is at the center of her thoughts.[35] And Hector—right on schedule—makes another appearance in the lines immediately following, now cast as the boy's *avunculus*. As this game of Doubles and Substitutes proceeds at an ever more disturbing pace, there is no one among the Living who does not remind Andromache of the Dead. But Vergil (that is, Aeneas, at Dido's palace) has not yet told us where exactly—i.e., in what city?—Andromache is now living.

---

32. Serv. in Aen. 3.343, *quidam 'avunculus' humiliter in heroico carmine dictum accipiunt*. On the linguistic interpretation of *avunculus*, see Bettini 1991a, 39–46.

33. According to Williams 1962, ad loc., only "the faithful" Silius Italicus (*Pun.* 3.248) dared to use the word again in an epic poem.

34. Cf. Apoll. *Bibl.* 3.12.1.

35. Andromache's thoughts and emotions follow a particularly winding course; a different, but not incompatible, interpretation is provided in Feldman 1958, 362ff. and Witton 1960, 171ff. Heinze (1982, 107 n. 1) finds an elegant Greek parallel for Andromache's recollection of Creusa in Eur. *Hec.* 992.

The City

Helenus has arrived. But this son of Priam is not like his wife, the widow Andromache. He instantly "recognizes his fellow countrymen" and is "delighted" to take them to the city. Helenus also weeps, of course, but his are tears of joy. Aeneas proceeds toward the city:

> procedo et parvam Troiam simulataque magnis
> Pergama et arentem Xanthi cognomine rivum
> agnosco Scaeaeque amplector limina portae.
> nec non et Teucri socia simul urbe fruuntur.
> illos porticibus rex accipiebat in amplis:
> aulai medio libabant pocula Bacchi
> impositisque auro dapibus paterasque tenebant.[36]

> I advance and recognize there a miniature Troy and Pergamus in imitation of the great originals, and a dry river that has the name of Xanthus and I embrace the threshold of a Scaean gate. With me, the Teucrians, too, enjoy this familiar city. The king welcomed them in the wide portico, and in the middle of the hall they poured out cups of wine, and held their bowls when the banquet was served on gold.

More doubles. It is not only that Hector's (empty) tomb stands in the same position it had occupied at Troy, near a stream resembling the Simoïs: this simulation of Troy involves the whole city. And this *Troia* is a true and proper Troy, though it is *parva*.[37] There is Pergamus, only smaller, along with a Scaean Gate and even that other Trojan river, the Xanthus, although this one is *arens,* an impoverished image of the "great deep-eddying river" that flowed through Homer's Ilium.[38]

Helenus and his exiles have reconstructed Troy. That is to say, they have succeeded in doing what Aeneas has already twice attempted—unsuccessfully—to do by founding the cities of Aeneades and Pergamea. He will attempt to do this once more, pursuing his dream of a *Troia recidiva* on Italian soil,[39] until the pact between Jupiter and Juno will finally prevent him

---

36. Verg. *Aen.* 3.349ff.
37. In contrast with the *superbum Ilium* of 3.2ff.; cf. Cova 1994,1.
38. Hom. *Il.* 20.73. The parallel is cited by Conington and Nettleship (1894, *ad loc.*) and is repeated by Williams 1962, *ad loc.* Incidentally, the "ruisseau sans eau" in which Baudelaire's swan attempts—in vain—to bathe (*Le cygne* 20) probably owes something to Vergil's *arens Xanthus.*
39. A stock topic of Vergilian scholarship: cf. Heinze 1982, 82ff.; Otis 1964, 251ff.; and most recently Labate 1991, esp. 180–84.

from realizing his dream and force him to resign himself to the sad conclusion that Troy is gone forever.[40] Helenus, however, has not had to suffer the injunctions of an unjust fate and has therefore been able to reconstruct in each and every detail the city he has lost. In fact, even if only for a moment, Aeneas yields to the lure of this simulacrum. He "embraces" the threshold of the Scaean Gate, just as if he had actually returned home.[41] The duplicity is as patent as it is perfect: Aeneas recognizes (*agnosco*) the "true" Troy in the guise of this false one.[42]

The *parva Troia* built by Helenus and Andromache is a truly singular creation for which it is difficult to find parallels in ancient literature.[43] In fact, this episode seems so thoroughly "modern" that it begs to be interpreted in the framework of the so-called "literary anticipation." To some critics, it has even suggested a sort of (ambiguous) sympathy for all that is hopelessly "anachronistic"—a sympathy destined to make a profound mark upon our literary culture.[44] Others discovered an excellent parallel, comparing the rebuilt Troy to Goethe's young Werther "who had a jacket tailored to match the jacket of his memories."[45] This *parva Troia,* a place of the past and of memories—and therefore also an overpowering invitation to forget[46]—was something extremely new in ancient literature. Yet it is as if all the materials used in its construction were somehow already there. This, paradoxically, is why the episode makes such a strong impression. The false Troy of Buthrotum corresponds to a kind of magical *bricolage,*[47] a kaleidoscope of preexisting cultural fragments which, fused together, produce an effect of extraordinary novelty. Let us review them in order, itemizing the individual

---

40. Verg. *Aen.* 12.819ff. Cf. Fenik 1960, 20–31 and 143–44; Suerbaum 1967, 176ff.; and above all Feeney 1984, 179ff.; etc.

41. Servius in Aen. 3.351, *quasi ad Troiam pervenisset.* Cf. Val. Flacc. *Arg.* 1.676; Sen. *Agam.* 392ff.; and also Verg. *Aen.* 2.490, where the Trojan women, terrified of the Greeks who have invaded their city, *amplexaeque tenent postes.*

42. Cf. Cova 1994, *ad loc.*

43. For Cova 1994, li, the episode is a "page of surrealistic poetry."

44. Greene (1986, 211) aptly comments that in this episode "the *Aeneid* displays an awareness of tragic anachronism that Vergil's culture did not formulate discursively, and as the central classic of Western civilization it inscribed this awareness, this ambivalent sympathy, upon our whole tradition."

45. Thus Orlando 1993, 337, discussing Goethe's *Sorrows of Young Werther* 4.4. In what is certainly one of the most important books of literary criticism to have appeared in Italian in the past ten years, Orlando develops the specific category of the "discarded literary object," distinguishing the Vergilian situation from other, more recent varieties, such as that found in Rousseau: "the capacity to recognize in objects what we could call a passage of time perceived individually, thus imbuing those objects with a pathetic satisfaction, was something beyond the reach of both Vergil and Shakespeare."

46. On the topic of "not remembering," see especially Quint 1982.

47. I use the term here in the sense given to it by Lévi-Strauss 1964.

Chapter 6. Ghosts of Exile 211

fragments that tradition bestowed upon the *bricoleur* and examining how Vergil put them to original use in this episode.

We can begin with the substance of the story. That Helenus had settled at Buthrotum and that Aeneas encountered him there was part of the Trojan legend prior to Vergil. We also know that there were many "Troys" in that part of the world, and that Buthrotum itself was known as "Troy."[48] In this sense, Vergil did not invent this stage of Aeneas' journey out of whole cloth, as he did other episodes throughout the third book.[49] He follows a specific tradition; it is only that in Vergil's new version this legendary location, already associated with Helenus and with Troy, has become a second "Troy." It is identical in every respect to the Troy that once stood upon the Dardanelles. This is what makes the episode a magnificent literary invention rather than a tedious reprise of tradition.[50]

The same can be said of Helenus and Andromache's decision to rebuild their lost city. Again, there is apparently nothing new here: Aeneas himself has attempted to rebuild Troy and will attempt to do so again.[51] Horace's Juno will analyze this behavior for its psychological and cultural motivations, interpreting it as an excess of *pietas* on Aeneas' part for his lost *patria*.[52] According to Servius, it was common practice for all exiles to reconstruct cities modeled upon those they had left behind:

> novimus enim hanc fuisse consuetudinem, ut advenae patriae suae imaginem sibi redderent, ut effigiem Xanthi Troiamque videtis.[53]

---

48. See Perret 1942, 214 and 229–31 and Lloyd 1957b, 385–86 (see following note); Lloyd 1957a is of minor interest in this regard; Galinsky 1969, 45 and 112 (on the tradition that Andromache and Aeneas were slaves at the court of Neoptolemus); Biraschi 1982, 278–91 (on the possibility that the Trojan legend contributed in two different ways to Epirus' cultural heritage). See also the overview in Cova 1994, xliii–xlviii. For Buthrotum as a Roman colony, see Ooteghem 1937, 8–13 (a summary of Ugolini 1937). See also Ugolini 1932.

49. Cf. Lloyd 1957b, which marks an important point in the interpretation of Book 3's relationship to the Trojan legend. Here, we find the idea that Vergil invented the theme of a "progressive divine revelation to Aeneas of his destiny" as a main thread capable of organizing the body of earlier legends into a coherent "voyage of Aeneas." See also Anderson 1994, 40–41. On the narrative structure of book 3, see also the comprehensive study of Cova 1992, 87ff.

50. That the episode at Buthrotum clearly represents "the poetical climax of the book" (Lloyd 1957b, 392) has been asserted more than once in Vergilian scholarship (cf., e.g., Putnam 1980, esp. 7). Cova (1992, 106) provides some interesting "quantitative" observations on the relationship between the effective duration of the stops at Actium and at Buthrotum, and the number of verses in which the two episodes are respectively developed.

51. Quint (1982, 34; see also 31) speaks of an actual "parade of replica Troys."

52. Hor. *Carm.* 3.3.57ff., *sed bellicosis fata Quiritibus / hac lege dico, ne nimium pii / rebusque fidentes avitae / tecta velint reparare Troiae.* For a general interpretation of the Horatian poem, see Fraenkel 1993.

53. Serv. in Aen. 10.60.

We know in fact that there was the custom that foreigners recreated the image of their own homeland, as you see Troy and a copy of the Xanthus river.

We should consider quite seriously what Servius says here, particularly as regards Troy. As an elegant study by Domenico Musti has shown, Greek colonization efforts did in fact frequently aspire to build "a city similar to Troy," especially whenever the landscape offered a hill, two rivers and an elevated position for a citadel.[54]

Moreover, the ancient world supplies us with other examples of cities that were in some sense "doubled." Josephus informs us that when Antiochus Epiphanes conquered Jerusalem and drove out the supporters of Ptolemy VI, the high priest Onias fled to the king-in-exile, and "obtaining from him a site in the *nome* of Heliopolis, he built a small town (*polichnē*) modeled after Jerusalem and a temple resembling ours."[55] But even Onias' "little Jerusalem"—an architectural simulation created as part of a political strategy driven by hostility and spite—cannot compare to Helenus and Andromache's city. Neither this little Jerusalem nor the "cities similar to Troy" in the Greek tradition could boast of being inhabited by a noble widow who had married her brother-in-law and who tended at every turn to see the Dead among the Living. Vergil's *parva Troia* is something far more unsettling than the simple imitation of a city that exists elsewhere. It is a piece of the past come alive, inhabited by people who come from that past. Above all, it is inhabited by the ghosts of those who perished long ago (or, at least, who seem to have done so).

Helenus and Andromache's Troy is not a "city similar to Troy." It is the Double of that ruined city in each and every respect. It has everything that Troy once had: rivers, buildings and people. This is something radically different from the practice, attested by Servius, that "newcomers construct for themselves an image of their own fatherland" (*ut advenae patriae suae imaginem sibi redderent*). It is one thing for exiles to imitate a city that continues to exist elsewhere, even if they have been compelled to abandon it. It is something else entirely to build the simulacrum of a city that no longer exists. The difference between these two ways of "doubling" a city parallels that between someone who simply keeps his sweetheart's picture in his

---

54. Musti 1988, 95–122; Martin (1975, 232) would have us suppose that we have evidence in Thuc. *Hist.* 6.2.6 for a Phoenician custom of building their new foundation on the model of their metropolis, but this is not what the text says.

55. Joseph. *Bell. Iud.* 1.33. Josephus often returns to the city built by Onias, altering his account somewhat in each instance: cf. Joseph. *Ant. Iud.* 12.387ff.; 13.62ff.; 13.285; 20.236ff.

wallet and Admetus, who keeps a statue of Alcestis in his marriage bed and treats that statue as a full fledged substitute for his lost wife. The image of a person or of a city realized *in praesentia* is one thing, a Double constructed *in absentia* is something altogether different.

This mention of Admetus suggests another point for reflection. We have before us another cultural fragment that Vergil's *bricolage* employs in a completely unexpected way. We often find stories in ancient literature based on the presence of a "substitute," a *simulacrum* or a double of some absent person: from the ghost of Protesilaus consoling Laodamia to the statue of Alcestis that Admetus kept in his bed; from the *eidōlon* of Helen to the woman whom Nero chose to be his concubine because—it was said—she greatly resembled his mother Agrippina, and so forth.[56] Those stories, however, involve individuals represented or replaced by others who resemble them, by ghosts or by painted or sculpted images—not, that is, with the Double of an entire city. The more we reflect upon it, the stranger this Vergilian invention of a *parva Troia* seems. If Andromache had simply been a loving wife, like Laodamia, she would have commissioned a portrait of Hector. Instead, she and Helenus have built a reconstruction of the entire city.

In Deterioribus

Unfortunately, because of its very nature as a Double, another fundamental feature marks Helenus and Andromache's *parva Troia:* its inadequacy—and by this I mean a melancholy wanting that prevents it from ever fully replacing the original. In order to focus on this aspect of the problem, Augustine's analysis of resemblance in his *Soliloquia*—i.e., what he says about the specific nature of Doubles and about the "images" of real things—will prove helpful.[57] As Augustine explains, similarities can be divided into two

---

56. Bettini 1999a, 12–38 and 230.
57. August. *Solil.* 2.10ff., ratio *dicimus item falsam arborem quam pictam videmus, et falsam faciem quae de speculo redditur, et falsum turrium motum navigantibus falsamque infractionem remi nihil ob aliud nisi quod verisimilia sunt.* augustinus *fateor.* rat. *ita et in geminis fallimur, et in ovis, et in sigillis uno anulo impressis et <in> ceteris talibus.* aug. *sequor omnino, atque concedo.* rat. *similitudo igitur rerum, quod ad oculos pertinet, mater est falsistatis.* aug. *negare non possum.* rat. *sed haec omnis silva, nisi me fallit, in duo genera dividi potest. nam partim aequalibus in rebus, partim vero in deterioribus est. aequalia sunt, quando tam hoc illi quam illud huic simile dicimus, ut de geminis dictum est, vel de impressionibus anuli. in deterioribus autem quando illud quod deterius est, simile esse dicimus meliori. quis enim in speculum attendat, et recte dicat se esse illi imagini similem, ac non potius illam sibi?* . . . *natura gignendo vel resultando similitudines deteriores facit. gignendo, cum parentibus similes nascuntur; resultando, ut de speculis cuiuscemodi* . . . *iam vero animantium opera sunt in picturis, et huiuscemodi quibusque figmentis: in quo genere includi etiam illa possunt, si tamen fiunt, quae demones*

types: those that demonstrate a kind of "equal resemblance" (*in aequalibus*) and those that demonstrate a kind of "worse resemblance" (*in deterioribus*). Resemblances *in aequalibus* apply when we can say of two things that "*this* resembles *that* as much as *that* resembles *this*—as in the case of twins or impressions made from the same ring." Resemblance *in aequalibus* does not involve a model and its copy, therefore: there is no "before and after" in either hierarchical or temporal terms. The resemblance is reciprocal and works both ways. Resemblance *in deterioribus*, on the other hand, applies when "we say that something which is inferior to some other thing resembles that other, better thing. Who in his right mind would ever stand in front of a mirror and say that he resembles the image rather than that the image resembles *him?*" Resemblance *in deterioribus* refers to situations, then, in which we know exactly who is imitating and who is being imitated, what resembles and what—so to speak—"is resembled."

Resemblance *in deterioribus*—the more common and widespread type—is naturally what interests the philosopher. Augustine therefore proceeds to make a further division, distinguishing two subtypes: the first involves sensory perception (optical illusions, nocturnal visions) and the second involves "real" things. The second subtype is further subdivided into resemblances produced by nature and those produced by animate beings: "nature produces resemblances *in deterioribus* by generation or by reflection: by generation, as when children are born who resemble their parents; by reflection, as in any sort of mirror." As for those produced by animate beings, these obviously include "paintings and depictions of all sorts."

In cases of resemblance *in deterioribus*, therefore, one element stands in a relationship of inadequacy or disproportionality to the other. A painter can never hope to make a substitute for reality; his copy is inevitably inferior to the original. This is precisely what has happened in the case of Helenus and Andromache's Troy, as we can see from the way in which Vergil describes the city. It is Troy, but "small" (*parva*). *This* Pergamon can only be "in imitation of the great original" (*simulataque magnis*). *This* Xanthus running through the city is "dry" (*arens*) and *this* Simoïs is "false" (*falsus*). Likewise, Hector's tomb is inescapably "empty" (*inanis*) and Andromache's husband, although he is Hector's brother, can only ever be himself: Helenus. The *parva Troia* of Epirus is a Troy *in deterioribus*, a fact that its inhabitants would probably be quick to admit. But would Andromache be willing to make such an admission, when she has made these Doubles—these ghosts—the very meaning of her existence?

---

faciunt. I give the text in Hörmann 1986, 58–59. Not all of the editor's choices are commendable; cf. the observations of Bouhot and Madec 1987, 332ff. Cf. also Gilson 1943, 275–82.

Resemblances

Helenus, responding to Aeneas' questions, tells the hero at some length—in over a hundred lines of admonitions and geographical details—of the destiny that awaits him. Helenus is ever the soothsayer and epic poems have their narrative demands. But time is pressing and Anchises has decided to depart.[58] It is the moment to bid farewell. Andromache brings some gifts for the departing guests—robes embroidered with gold and a Phrygian cloak for the young Ascanius, among other things:

> accipe et haec, manuum tibi quae monumenta mearum
> sint, puer, et longum Andromachae testentur amorem,
> coniugis Hectoreae; cape dona extrema tuorum,
> o mihi sola mei super Astyanactis imago!
> Sic oculos, sic ille manus, sic ora ferebat;
> et nunc aequali tecum pubesceret aevo.[59]

> Take this, too, boy, to be a remembrance of my hands and witness of the long-reaching love of Andromache, wife of Hector. Take these last gifts of your people, you who for me are the last remaining image of my Astyanax! He had eyes, hands and a face like yours; and he would have been grown up with you, equal in years.

For Andromache, these gifts for Ascanius are not merely gifts: they are *monumenta*.[60] That is, they are meant to "make him remember her" (*moneo/monumentum*). Putting on these garments, Ascanius will immediately think of another, just as Andromache's own thoughts turn to Hector at every moment. Andromache is preoccupied not only with her own ghosts and memories, but also with others'. Not even her manner of speech—the very words she uses—can resist her melancholy fixation on the past; in this, she is unwavering. When she speaks to Ascanius, the bride of Helenus even refers to herself as "Hector's wife." The center of her being and her thoughts remains steadily focused on the dead hero.[61] Andromache, several times a

---

58. Otis (1964, 261) insists on the contrast between Aeneas—a young man, yet one attracted by the nostalgia of the *parva Troia*—and Anchises—who is near to death, but directed towards the future. On the contrast in general between the staticity of the "miniature Troy" and the impulse given by the practical demands of the voyage, cf. Di Cesare 1974, 68.

59. Verg. *Aen.* 3.486ff.

60. On these *monumenta*, see the brief observations of Nelson 1961, 335. The commentators (Williams 1962 and Cova 1994) note the reference to Hom. *Od.* 15.126 (Helen to Telemachus on his departure from Sparta).

61. On this characteristic of Andromache, see the discussion of Cova 1994, li.

mother, several times a bride, is always Hector's widow: in this moment of self-definition, she can find no better description for herself than *coniunx Hectorea*.⁶² Then, following an all too familiar pattern, Andromache suddenly invokes another dead person, someone whom the image of the living Ascanius calls to mind: her son Astyanax, of whom Ascanius is the one remaining *imago*, as we have seen.

Andromache's identity is fixed forever. Whatever may have befallen her in the past or may befall her in the future, she will only ever be the great hero's widow and the mother of his lost son. Racine observed:

> Most of those who have heard of Andromache know her only as the widow of Hector and the mother of Astyanax. They cannot reconcile themselves to her loving another husband and another son. And I doubt that Andromache's tears would have made the impression they made on the spirit of my spectators, if they had been shed for another son than the one she had by Hector.⁶³

We are already well acquainted with Andromache's tendency to "double" things—not only buildings and landscapes, but also people, as she continually discovers the Dead among the Living. In this case, however, her tendency has become—if possible—even more unambiguous. Here, Ascanius is literally defined as Astyanax's *imago* and in her melancholy fantasy the dead boy's mother even finds tangible support and concrete evidence for this hallucination:⁶⁴ Ascanius has the same eyes, face and hands as her dead son—or better, of his dead cousin. We should not forget that the "resemblance" between Ascanius and Astyanax involves kinship: Creusa, Ascanius' mother, was the sister of Hector, Astyanax's father. Their resemblance must

---

62. Regarding this expression, Servius notes: *dictum est hoc habita ratione personae cum qua loquebatur, ac si diceret, 'uxoris avunculi tui.'* It is true: this is the expression with which Andromache could have used in addressing Ascanius, if this were a normal conversation between aunt and nephew—but above all if she were not obsessed by the memory of "her" Hector and by the desire to cite his name at all costs.

63. See the *Seconde Préface* to Racine 1950, 243. Incidentally, in this sense Racine anticipated the observations that Heinze (1982, 107) would dedicate to Vergil's Andromache. In the characterization of Andromache purely as the "veuve d'Hector," Racine is even more radical than Vergil. As Knight (1950, 267) noted, the French poet cites numerous lines of the Vergilian episode in his *Préface* (i.e., 3.292–93, 301, 303–5, 320–27, 330–32), but omits ("à dessein"?) those in which Andromache narrates to Aeneas her wedding with Helenus (3.329, *me famulam famuloque Heleno transmisit habendam*). Elsewhere, in his marginal note to Hom. *Il.* 6.425, Racine had explicitly remarked that Andromache was "Reine, et non point concubine" (see the valuable contribution of Rossi 1994, 87–88, where we have found also the observation of Knight mentioned above).

64. According to Grimm 1967, 161, here Andromache is "close to self-hypnotism"; Heinze (1982, 107) sees in this remembrance of Astyanax "einer der tiefst empfundenen Züge in Vergils Gedicht."

therefore obey the rules of kinship, an issue we should briefly consider at this point.

Another Andromache—that of Seneca's *Trojan Women*—uses the following words to describe Astyanax's appearance:

> o nate, magni certa progenies patris
> . . .
> > veteris . . . suboles sanguinis nimium inclita
> > nimiumque patris similis. hos vultus meus
> > habebat Hector, talis incessu fuit
> > habituque talis, sic tulit fortis manus,
> > sic celsus umeris, fronte sic torva minax
> > cervice fusam dissipans iacta comam.⁶⁵

> My son, sure descendant of a great father . . . too celebrated offspring of an ancient race, and too like your father. Hector had this same face, this same gait, this same carriage, these same strong hands. His shoulders were like yours; on his furrowed brow the same threatening look, when he let down his hair with a shake of his head.

Astyanax is the very portrait of his father Hector. According to a logic hardly unique to Roman culture, a son reproduces his father's physical features in every detail, thus providing reliable evidence of his legitimacy.⁶⁶ The physical features in which Seneca's Andromache sees Astyanax's resemblance to Hector are very nearly those in which Vergil's Andromache sees Ascanius' resemblance to Astyanax: his face, his eyes, his hands. But there is a difference. For Seneca's Andromache, it is the son—Astyanax—that reproduces the father's features. Here, Ascanius reproduces his cousin Astyanax's appearance. In Seneca, we are dealing with the usual resemblance along vertical lines from father to son, while in Vergil the resemblance is oblique, or better, "horizontal." How to justify this resemblance? Why should Ascanius be the *imago* of Astyanax? There can only be one answer—and, as usual, that answer lies in the figure of Hector. If Astyanax resembles his father Hector, and if Ascanius in turn resembles not so much his father as his uncle

---

65. Sen. *Tr.* 461ff. In comparison with Verg. *Aen.* 3.490ff., *sic oculos, sic ille manus,* Vergilian commentators (from De la Cerda 1612, 344, to Cova 1994) have traditionally cited Hom. *Od.* 4.149ff. (Menelaus remarking on the similarities between Telemachus and Odysseus). To this Homeric comparison De la Cerda added another, which, however, was ignored by other commentators: Stat. *Ach.* 1.330ff., *sic ergo gradus, sic ora manusque nate feres* (Thetis teaches her son to walk like a girl).

66. Bettini 1999a, 211–39.

(again Hector), this explains how Aeneas' son could be the *imago* of his dead cousin. But we must always assume that mediating this relationship is the man whom Andromache continues to keep at the center of her thoughts and of her identity.

Resemblances are arbitrary, as we know: everyone sees what they wish to see. If Andromache projects onto Ascanius both the image of her son and (most probably) that of her husband, another woman in love—Dido—projects the image of Aeneas onto Ascanius:

> sola . . . illum absens absentem auditque videtque
> aut gremio Ascanium, genitoris imagine capta
> detinet, infandum si fallere possit amorem.[67]

> She hears and sees him though they are not together, or she holds Ascanius in her lap, enraptured by the image of his father, if thus she might beguile her love unspeakable.

Although he will have to wait until he reaches Carthage, Aeneas will finally be granted the paternal satisfaction of seeing his own image (rather than someone else's) reflected in his son. This is not the only time that Dido is fooled by love's hallucinations, however.

We need to make one last observation before leaving Andromache. This would ideally concern her vision (which, unfortunately, Vergil does not describe); but at the very least it will regard her tendency to hallucinate the missing in place of those who are actually present before her. At least according to the medical principles of previous centuries, Andromache could probably be diagnosed as suffering from the illness of "nostalgia." This word—*nostalgia*—merits a brief, preliminary discussion. The Romans did not know the term. Nor, despite appearances, is it an ancient Greek term—although it is a (quite legitimate) combination of two words in that language. It was not until the end of the seventeenth century that the Swiss doctor Johannes Hofer, in a dissertation written at the young age of nineteen, gave this fortunate name to a frequently fatal illness afflicting Swiss soldiers far from home.[68] "Nostalgia" was the acute grief caused by longing to return home (or, as Kant keenly observed, by the illusion that this is what one longs for—when, in fact, the nostalgic person actually longs for the childhood he

---

67. Verg. *Aen.* 4.82ff.

68. Hofer 1688 (republished under the title of *De Pothopatridalgia* by Zwinger in 1710 in his *Fasciculus Dissertationum Medicarum Selectiorum,* systematically replacing "nostalgia" with "pothopatridalgia"; but Zwinger's term did not catch on). Hofer's text is translated in the excellent book edited by Prete (1992, 45–59).

spent in his native land, something he can never regain even by returning home).⁶⁹ In the case of Vergil's Andromache, it is even more intriguing to mention the remarks of A. von Haller, who observed that "one of the first symptoms is to hear the voices of beloved persons in the voices of those with whom one happens to be conversing."⁷⁰ And F. G. Boisseau makes what is perhaps the most striking observation: "I could compare the look in the eye of a person suffering from nostalgia only to that of a tender mother who has recently lost a darling child and who suffers this loss in silence, but all the while experiencing a violent grief."⁷¹ Andromache, the mother of the dead Astyanax "sees" the images of her beloved family members in others. The look in her eye would have told us this. This perhaps would have sufficed for the good doctor Boisseau to diagnose her as "nostalgic." But what if *parva Troia* in its entirety—the landscape, the buildings, and the ghosts who dwell there—were nothing but an invention of nostalgia?

Nostalgia, Mother of Images

Even if the Romans did not have a specific term for "nostalgia," they did have the word *desiderium*—meaning, like *pothos* in Greek, the soulful longing that one feels for everything that has been lost forever. But *desiderium*, it seems, was connected with the creation of images. Seneca notes that images have the power to mollify *desiderium* for those who are absent:

> imagines nobis amicorum absentium iucundae sunt quae memoriam renovant et desiderium [absentiae] falso atque inani solacio levant.⁷²

> Images of our absent friends please us because they renew our remembrance of them, and they alleviate our longing with empty and inconsistent relief.

At the same time, according to Pliny, the force of *desiderium* is so great that it can actually generate images of unfamiliar faces: *pariuntque desideria non traditos vultus, sicut in Homero evenit* ("they give birth to the image of unfamiliar faces, as happened in the case of Homer").⁷³ I have pursued this

---

69. E. Kant, "Anthropology From a Pragmatic Point of View" (cited by Prete 1992, 66).
70. *"Nostalgia"* in *Supplément aux Dictionnaires des Sciences, des Arts et de Métiers* VI, Livorno 1779 (cited and trans. by Prete 1992, 64).
71. "Nostalgia," in *Encyclopédie Méthodique: Médicine* X, Paris 1821 (cited and translated by Prete 1992, 81).
72. Sen. *Ep.* 40.1. Cf. also 84.8.
73. Plin. *Nat. hist.* 35.9.

topic at some length elsewhere, collecting many examples in which the loss of a loved one leads directly to the creation of an image.[74] There is no point in covering that ground again, therefore—even if the nostalgic Andromache, with her hypermnesic *imagines* and resemblances, invites us to do so. From this point of view, however, it will prove even more interesting to consider Aeneas' parting words to Andromache:

> vivite felices, quibus est fortuna peracta
> iam sua; nos alia ex aliis in fata vocamur.
> vobis parta quies; nullum maris aequor arandum,
> arva neque Ausoniae semper cedentia retro
> quaerenda. effigiem Xanthi Troiamque videtis
> quam vestrae fecere manus. . . . [75]

Live happy, you whose fate is already fulfilled; we are tossed from one fate to another. You have found peace. You have no expanse of sea to traverse, nor the ever-retreating fields of Ausonia to seek. You see the images of Xanthus and of Troy, made by your own hands.

If a slightly off topic comment is permitted, the sense of *felices* here is rather difficult to understand. Andromache, at least, does not appear to be very happy, obsessed as she is with her ghosts; living in the Double of a destroyed city might provide some consolation or relief—but certainly not happiness.[76] But Aeneas considers Helenus and his companions to have already reached the end of their wanderings: their *quies* is assured. As he pays his respects, Aeneas explicitly emphasizes the fact that their *fortuna* is *peracta* ("fulfilled"). Yet, as we know, the fate of the Living is always unfolding, whereas that of the Dead is "fulfilled."[77] The happiness of Helenus and his companions is, then, only a vague semblance of happiness, such as might be expected at the end—the true end—not only of all suffering, but also of any possible change of condition.

Aeneas' farewell to those who remain suggests one further observation. The manner in which he addresses them—that is, the way in which he defines the *parva Troia* that he is about to leave behind—introduces a theme

---

74. Bettini 1999a, 10–12 and 51–53.

75. Verg. *Aen.* 493ff.

76. To certain critics Aeneas' exclamation has seemed ironic: cf. Nelson 1961, 335 ("compassionate irony"); Grimm 1967, 161; Starry West 1983, 259. For the theme of "consolation" offered by images, cf. again Bettini 1999a, 52–53.

77. I owe this observation to A. A. Long; cf. Conington and Nettleship 1894, ad loc., on the *quies* in which Helenus' companions live as the "quiet of the dead." Cf. Starry West 1983, 259.

we have been anticipating for some time now: images. In Aeneas' words, those who remain do not "inhabit" the city they have built: they simply "see" Troy and they "see" what is only a copy of the river Xanthus (*effigiem Xanthi Troiamque videtis / quam vestrae fecere manus*). Sometimes the choice of a single word conveys more than a hundred lines of description or ten paragraphs of analysis. This *parva Troia* is something "to see," just as an image is seen—and the river Xanthus that runs beside it is specifically defined as such: an *effigies,* a copy that the exiles have "constructed" with their own hands along with the rest of this Troy, just as one makes an image of an absent person. Helenus and the exiles thus find themselves in the same position as the Corinthian potter who, to console his grief-stricken daughter, made an image for her of her lost fiancé; or the father of the *Book of Wisdom* who was so devastated by the loss of his son that he had a statue made of him[78]—"et bien des autres encor," as Baudelaire would say to extend an already long list.[79] Like the Corinthian potter's daughter or the Biblical father, the Trojans console themselves for their irreparable loss by contemplating the image of something that no longer exists.

Images thus make their well timed entrance into an episode whose very structure—with its insistence on substitutes, shadows and similarities—has predicted their appearance all along. Now we can see what this *parva Troia* really is: an *effigies* built by the hands of its inhabitants as a consolation for the *desiderium* that afflicts them. If that is the case—if this Double of the destroyed city is a monument erected to nostalgia and to remembrance—we can draw yet one more conclusion. It is often easy to forget the deeper anthropological meaning that was (and still is) implied by erecting a statue or by devotion to someone's image. When Admetus swears to his wife Alcestis that he will keep a statue of her in their marriage bed, treating it (her?) as if it (she?) were still alive, he is making a vow that he will remain absolutely faithful to it (her)—much like the faithful lover keeps his sweetheart's picture in his wallet. The image itself embodies fidelity and respect for a relationship. The history of culture provides frequent examples of images employed precisely as "sacralizing objects," concrete pledges of a vow that must be faithfully observed. The image is a pact. Elsewhere I have covered this topic as well.[80] Here, we can simply note that even in contemporary culture, the act of erecting a statue to someone (a king, a minister, a dictator) explicitly signals "faithfulness" to that person's memory and that that pact is, and will be, respected—at least until the act of demolishing the image openly violates this contract, breaking the bonds of former attachment.

---

78. Bettini 1999a, 51–3.
79. Again Baudelaire's *Le cygne* 52.
80. Bettini 1999a, 60–68.

Helenus' companions, the makers of the most incredible *effigies* ever known—the Double of an entire city—expressly demonstrate with this "product of their own hands" that they were still faithful to their country of origin. This fidelity involves choosing a "Trojan" place in which to live and the laborious reconstruction of a gate, a citadel, a tomb in front of the city, as well as choosing a king who was the king's son, a husband for Andromache who was her husband's brother. And to crown it all, a nostalgic queen suffering from hypermnesia, living in the past and imagining the Dead whenever she encounters the Living. The Trojans are not only nostalgic. They are citizens still faithful–perhaps too faithful—to their country and to their vanished city. But what sort of citizen is Aeneas?

Exiles

According to René de Chateaubriand, there are two ways to preserve the memory of one's own country while in exile and to satisfy what he calls "instinct de la patrie."[81] Obviously this is an ersatz satisfaction, a fantasy, because the only way to truly placate this instinct would be to go back home. But very often this is simply not possible. Fortunately, however, "the heart is expert in deception," as Chateaubriand explains:

> Sometimes it is a cottage which is arranged like the paternal habitation; sometimes it is a wood, a valley, a hill, on which we bestow some of the sweet names of our native land. Andromache gives the name of Sïmois to a brook. And what a moving object is this tiny stream, which recalls the idea of a mighty river in her native country! Far from the soil which gave us birth, nature appears to somehow diminished, the shadow of that which we have lost. Another trick of the instinctive love of country is to grant great value to an object of little intrinsic worth, but which comes from our native land, and which we have brought with us into exile. The soul seems to linger upon even inanimate things which share our destiny; part of our lives remains attached to the bed where our good fortune lay, and still more to that on which our misfortune rested.

These remarks could already stand as a marvelous commentary on Vergil's *parva Troia* and its nostalgic "tromperies." Chateaubriand's observation that the "false Simoïs" is characterized by "nature diminuée" is extremely subtle:

---

81. De Chateaubriand 1966, 187–88 *Génie du Christianisme* 1.5.14). According to Bernardelli 1976, this passage of Chateaubriand should be counted among the "sources" of Baudelaire's *Le cygne* along with the Vergilian episode.

in the eyes of the exile, even unsuspecting Nature—which can only ever be like unto itself—becomes the shadow of the "truer" Nature of one's home. But Chateaubriand's words are even more remarkable from the perspective of a potential theory of exilic identity. In fact, Chateaubriand's thinking may justifiably be considered a "first draft" of such a theory, since the "instinct de la patrie" to which he refers is surely nothing other than a transposition in Romantic terms of what we would define as the problem of lost or negated identity. Far from his own country, far from the land and the city that identify him within a precise system of reference, the exile attempts to reestablish his own sense of belonging through the "tromperies" of an image or of an object brought from his native land. We might also redefine these two symbolic modes of reestablishing lost identity (searching for similarities or becoming attached to an object) in more modern terms, such as metaphor (a city "resembling" Troy, a figure for the vanished city) and metonymy (a piece of the distant homeland, a fragment once in contact with that lost world). We might also rouse the figure of Frazer with his "analogical" or "sympathetic" magic (an image that resembles the faithless lover) opposed to "contagious" magic (a lock of that lover's hair). The heart of the matter remains the same, however. Andromache will always belong to the first category, and Aeneas, through no choice of his own, to the second. This is certainly a point worth emphasizing.

Aeneas will not be allowed to re-establish his own Trojan identity through an analogous reconstruction of the city he has lost. He is not able to resort to the "tromperies" of images and ersatz names. Each time that he attempts to do so, in fact, someone or something—Fate, in short—opposes him. Aeneas does bring something with him from Troy, however: the Penates.[82] This is an object of great value and surely not an insignificant piece of Troy. But the Penates nevertheless belong to that category of things that Chateaubriand would assign to a second order: connections made not by means of images, but through concrete objects. The Penates represent Troy not metaphorically, but metonymically. The Trojan identity they embody does not belong to the "sympathetic" type, but operates by means of "contact." Aeneas is able to define his own identity insofar as he is the possessor of a distinctively "Trojan" object.

Aeneas' difficulty is that he believes he belongs to the first category, when in fact he belongs to the second. As we know, Aeneas wants to rebuild Troy. He has already tried to do so and will try to do so again. Ultimately, this is not what lies in store for him, however. Unlike Helenus and Andromache,

---

82. Cf. Verg. *Aen.* 2.11ff., *feror exul in altum / cum sociis gnatoque Penatibus cum magnis dis*. They are entrusted to him by the shade of Hector at 2.293, *sacra suosque tibi commendat Troia Penates: / hos cape fatorum comites, his moenia quaere / magna pererrato statues quae denique ponto*.

Aeneas will not be able to "reduplicate" his lost homeland. A very different fate awaits him: he must utterly lose his own *patria* in order to receive a new one. Juno's—and to some extent also Jupiter's—will is that he become a kind of "disappearing" or "vanishing" exile who forsakes not only the reconstruction of his own city, but the preservation of his own national identity as well. He will give up his own language, his own customs, the very name and even the physical traits of his people.[83] Far from rebuilding Troy in Italy, the Trojans will lose their very selves and will take on the name of "Latins." Luckily, they still have the Penates; and this sacred object, the very heart of the city, will in some sense preserve their identity. But the rest will be lost. This is the complete opposite of Helenus' Trojans, who are metaphorical to the point of improbability. They are makers of Doubles who suffer from an excess of identity, as it were: they are too Trojan and their lives are a sort of endless experience of nostalgia. They are consumed entirely by remembrance. Aeneas and his companions, on the other hand, must undergo a radical curtailment of their identity. Their future demands that they forget themselves and give up contact with the very city that gave birth to them. They must abandon their language and their customs and accept amnesia. At the end of the war, in the merger of the warring peoples, Juno stipulates precisely that.

IF GREAT WORKS of literature such as the *Aeneid* present characters and themes that extend well beyond the stories that they tell, and if the culture of the past can (and should) be used to anticipate what happens in the present, then we may end this discussion. Vergil's *parva Troia* and above all the visit that Aeneas makes there figure the two possible extremes of the exile's experience: On one side, a nostalgic obsession with one's own identity; on the other, detachment, amnesia and forced assimilation. On one side, the "Little Italy" that we find in so many American cities, the "Chinatown" guarded by gates adorned with lanterns, the miniature St. Peter's Basilica in a Montreal square; on the other, ethnic surnames altered beyond recognition, native languages unused and forgotten, shame for one's own physical features.[84] On one side, the construction of Doubles *in deterioribus,* admittedly inadequate, but still able to sustain *desiderium* and a memory of the past; on the other, the obliteration of identity—until one day an object emerges from the back of a desk drawer, forgotten but still moving in the fullness of its meaning: a German-made razor, an Italian bottle opener, the Penates.

---

83. Verg. *Aen.* 12.819ff.

84. On the difficulties created by the actual "somatic image" in an ethnically diverse population, see the overview in Thompson 1989, 11–24.

SEVEN

Death and Its Double

Imagines, Ridiculum and *Honos* in the
Roman Aristocratic Funeral

We have already had the opportunity to observe that in ancient Rome the aristocratic funeral offered the opportunity for an extraordinary display of "doubles." The *veterum instituta* ("institutions of the ancients"), as they were called by Tacitus, required that an *effigies* of the dead should rest on the coffin, in plain sight.[1] Moreover, the *imagines* of the ancestors, according to an extremely impressive and touching ceremonial, were carried behind the coffin in funerary procession. What we learn from ancient descriptions (in particular those of Polybius) is that the *imagines maiorum* were wax images reproducing the faces of the ancestors and that these reproductions bore a "striking resemblance" to the deceased.[2]

As we have mentioned, the *imagines* were normally stored in wooden shrines in the atrium of the house, but on the day of the funeral of a family member, they were uncovered and worn by those who most closely resembled (both in size and carriage) the dead person whose *imago* they were

---

1. Tac. *Ann.* 3.5, *praepositam toro effigiem.* I am following the text of the manuscripts, and not the correction by Muretus, *propositam,* accepted by almost all editors. Not only do I think there is no need to correct the text, but I also believe that the correction spoils the subtlety of the original sense. As demonstrated by Benveniste 1966, 132ff., the Latin prefix *prae* generally indicates a forward, leading position, in the sense of "prominent," "in plain sight": in this case, Tacitus probably intended that the *effigies* of the deceased were to be "the most visibile" among the objects placed on the funerary bed, catching everybody's attention.

2. Polyb. *Hist.* 6.53.5. The bibliography concerning the *imagines maiorum* in Rome is quite vast: see Bettini 1991c and Flower 1996, 91ff.

wearing.³ Furthermore, these men would dress up in clothes appropriate to the social rank that the deceased enjoyed during life, and were accompanied by the signs of his distinction.⁴ In this way, the images were "performed," playing a performative role that consisted in arousing once again the presence of the dead ancestors. And we know how Polybius reacted to the Roman aristocratic funeral: "How can one not be moved, seeing the images of men famous for their virtues, gathered together and, so to speak, living and moving?"⁵ The *imagines* were not simply figures that both in features and in complexion resembled the deceased, but they were truly and effectively their Doubles. During a funeral, a family's ancestors were really "there," returning from the world beyond in order to escort the recently deceased to the grave and accompany him as he joined the *lignée* of the Dead. As Pliny remarked with almost epic simplicity, "Each dead person was always surrounded by all the deceased members of his family, all those who had lived before him."⁶

The funerary "double" played a particularly impressive role on the occasion of Julius Caesar's death. We are told that "somebody raised above the bier an image of Caesar himself made of wax. . . . The image was turned round and round by a mechanical device, showing the twenty three wounds in all parts of the body and the face, that had been dealt to him so brutally."⁷ The *effigies* of the deceased is still placed well in sight on the coffin, in observance of the *veterum instituta;* but according to the dramatic character of the public performance that takes place around the body, the funerary image assumes the uncanny form of a wax automaton.

With funeral practices of the imperial period, the ceremonial importance of funerary "doubles" increased dramatically. During Augustus' funeral, as many as three *imagines* of the deceased emperor were displayed alongside those of his ancestors. The body was hidden in a coffin within a chariot, but externally, well visible, there was a wax image of the emperor adorned with triumphal garments, another in gold and a third (probably also in gold) carried on a triumphal chariot in procession.⁸ Since this was the funeral of the first emperor of Rome, it is evident that the tradition was at the same time respected and multiplied: not one, but actually three *effigies* of the deceased were visible at the funeral. To a certain extent, the following principle was observed: the more distinguished the deceased, the more solemn the funeral and the greater the number of the *imagines* around his coffin,

---

3. See above, 197–98.
4. See in particular Polyb. *Hist.* 6.53ff.; Diod. Sic. *Bibl. hist.* 31.25.2.
5. Polyb. *Hist.* 53.10.
6. Plin. *Nat. hist.* 35.6.
7. App. *Hist. Rom.* 2.147.
8. Dio Cass. *Hist. Rom.* 56.34.

in a play of reflections that could transformed "doubles" even into "triples." The importance of such images at funerals reached its peak when, however, the emperor's funerary ceremony assumed the form of the so-called *funus imaginarium* (beginning with Pertinax and Septimius Severus).[9] In these cases, the deceased emperor was granted not one, but two funerary rites: the first regarded the departed person's actual corpse, while the second regarded his wax statue. Before being solemnly burned, this statue was put on public display for seven days and a sort of ritual pantomime moved around this effigy involving doctors, senators, knights, groups of women and of young boys and so on.[10] So there is little doubt that the noble and imperial Roman funeral was characterized by the category of the Double: without *imagines*, without the visible imitations of the deceased, these ceremonies would have made no sense at all.

Let us continue with our analysis. Dionysius of Halicarnassus provides us with some uniquely interesting information. The author, drawing upon the lost work of the Roman annalist Fabius Pictor, describes a *pompa circensis*.[11] He explains that, in addition to other groups, a number of armed dancers also took part in the procession, continuing as follows:

> Just behind them were dancers who impersonated satyrs performing the Greek dance called *sicinnis*. Those who represented the Sileni were dressed in shaggy tunics that some called *chortaioi*, and cloaks made with different types of flowers; those representing satyrs, on the other hand, wore girdles and goatskins and their heads were covered with manes that stood upright and other similar things. These mocked and mimicked the serious movements of those who preceded them, teasing them and turning them into laughter.

Then Dionysius provides the information that—from our perspective—is the most interesting. He introduces it as his own personal experience (*eidon*, "I have seen"):

---

9. The expression *funus imaginarium* in the sense of funeral celebrated for an image comes from *Scriptores Historiae Augustae, Pertinax* 15.1, *funus imaginarium ei [sc. Pertinaci] et censorium ductum est*.

10. Herodianus, *Ab excessu divi Marci* 4.2.1ff., with regard to the funerals of Septimius Severus; Dio Cass. *Hist. Rom.* 74.4.1ff., who declares he witnessed the funerals of Pertinax. Cf. *Scriptores Historiae Augustae, Severus* 7.8, *funus deinde censorium Pertinacis imagini duxit*; *Pertinax* 15.1, funus imaginarium ei et censorium ductum est. The *funus imaginarium* of the Roman emperor obviously recalls the theme of the "king's two bodies" in Kantoriwicz 1957; with regard to the Italian Renaissance, see also Ricci 1998, with bibliographical references successive to Kantoriwicz's book. For the *funus imaginarium* see in particular Dupont 1986b and Pucci 1997.

11. Dion. Hal. *Ant. Rom.* 7.72.10ff. (= Fabius Pictor fr. 20F Beck & Walter); see in particular Bernstein 1998, 254ff.

Even at the funerals of illustrious people I have seen, alongside the rest of the procession (*pompa*) preceding the funerary chariot [the author is obviously referring to the parade of the *imagines maiorum*], bands of dancers impersonating satyrs who preceded the bier dancing the *sicinnis*, and this occurred in particular at the funerals of the rich.[12]

Together with the solemnity of the funerary procession preceding the coffin, it was also possible to see groups of satyrs dressed up in eccentric clothes dancing the *sicinnis*. We may presume by analogy that they imitated and mocked the behavior of the serious part of the procession. Furthermore, according to Dionysius' description, the position of the satyrs within the procession was clearly before the coffin—that is to say, together with the solemn group of *imagines*. A strange mixture—the *imagines maiorum* performed by people representing in their attire the different *dignitates* of the ancestors, and the satyrs skipping and jumping while dancing their characteristic *sicinnis*. Granted the seriousness and the almost epic solemnity characterizing the procession of *imagines* during the Roman funeral, the contextual presence of a definitively comic double during the rite is surprising. In fact, we may have doubts as to the veracity of the information transmitted by Dionysius. Or, at any rate, we may find it difficult to believe that the *sicinnis* dancers mocked the "serious" members of the parade by turning them into objects of laughter (as they did with the armed dancers who preceded them in the parade of the *ludi magni*). Yet what other purpose could the dancers have served, if not to arouse laughter, dressed, as they were, as satyrs wearing girdles and goatskins, their heads covered with bristling manes?

There is other evidence for the role of imitation and the comic spirit during the funerals of illustrious people, e.g., the presence of an *archimimus* named Favor at Vespasian's funeral, as reported by Suetonius. Here, we may add some more explicit information regarding the reproduction of the "events and sayings" of the deceased during his lifetime, for Suetonius also reports what Favor actually said during the emperor's funeral procession: "Having asked the procurators in the presence of everybody, how much his funeral procession would cost and hearing that it would cost a hundred thousand sesterces, he exclaimed: 'give me a hundred sesterces and then you can fling me into the Tiber!'"[13] These words pronounced by Favor must have been an imitation—or better, a comical caricature—of Vespasian's character and of the *dicta* that he used to pronounce during his lifetime.

---

12. This sentence of Dionysius is considered no more than an "interpolation" by scholars interested only in reconstructing the lost text of Fabius Pictor (so explicitly Bernstein 1998, 261 n. 190); however, for our purposes Dionysius' personal testimony deserves particular attention.

13. Suet. *Vesp.* 19.2.

Suetonius also informs us that Vespasian was notoriously greedy,[14] an aspect of character that Favor's joke highlights explicitly. Furthermore, we know that the deceased emperor loved "witty remarks, even if rather coarse and covetous."[15] In particular, he used to "make jokes regarding unmentionable gains, in order to diminish or cancel their hatefulness, turning them into jokes by word play." Once again according to Suetonius, Vespasian famously joked with his son Titus, who had found fault with the emperor for contriving a tax on public toilets: "He held some money from the first payment received and he asked his son 'whether its odor was offensive,' and to his son's negative reply he rejoined, 'and yet, it comes from urine!'"[16] Favor's pronouncement—"give me a hundred sesterces and then you can fling me into the Tiber!"—is a witty remark explicitly concerning greed and is based on the rather disgusting possibility of making money off death and funerals. But apparently this is the kind of thing that Vespasian casually uttered during his lifetime!

The person speaking is not Favor, but Vespasian, the deceased. In other words, Favor has identified himself with Vespasian completely: he is his living Double. The only difference is that this living Double is not designed to stir the emotions or to encourage virtue, as occurred in front of the *imagines* of the ancestors, effigies of the deceased or the wax body of the emperor. Instead, the Double selects "sayings and facts" regarding the deceased with the express purpose of causing laughter. Needless to say, from our cultural perspective, for a dead person to utter "Give me a hundred and then you can do away with this procession and fling me into the Tiber!" is a truly exceptional occurrence.

Let us continue describing the relationship between mimes and comic doubles on the one hand, and the aristocratic funeral on the other. Again, Diodorus Siculus' remarks on the funeral of Lucius Aemilius Paulus are of particular interest. We have reported a portion of this passage above, but its importance for understanding the role of "doubles" in funerary practice justifies its repetition here in full:

> Among the Romans, those who were especially noble or who were famous because of their ancestors for are portrayed after death in images (*eidolōpoiountai*). This is done according to resemblances in traits and physical characteristics, and they were accompanied all their life by *mimētai* who carefully studied their bearing (*poreia*) and any peculiarities in their appearance (*tas kata meros idiotētas tēs emphaseos*). Similarly, each of the

---

14. Suet. *Vesp.* 16.1
15. Suet. *Vesp.* 22.1.
16. Suet. *Vesp.* 22.1, 23.1

ancestors marches past [the coffin] with clothing and such signs of distinction that those observing them can understand from their appearance the grade of honors they have reached and which position they have attained in the city.[17]

Although the text is incomplete (it is in fact an excerpt by Photius of the works by Diodorus), the allusion to funerary practice is clear: reference is being made to the parade of *imagines* and to the custom of accompanying them with the clothes and *insignia* that distinguished the rank of each deceased person. Particularly interesting, however, is the mention of *mimētai* who follow Roman aristocrats "all their life" and who "carefully studied their bearing (*poreia*) and any peculiarities in their appearance." But, once again, who were these *mimētai*? Perhaps here we can answer this question more fully than our earlier discussion permitted. As suggested previously, Diodorus' mention of the custom of *mimētai* "representing" Roman nobles after death may lead us to think that they were simply "artists" or "sculptors." However, this interpretation is problematic for two reasons.

First, in Greek, *mimētēs* appears never to have the meaning "sculptor" or "figurative artist." This idea is designated by terms such as *plastēs, andriantopoios, agalmatopoios*, or, more specifically, by *grapheus/graphikos, zōgraphos* and so forth to indicate a painter. On the other hand, the noun *mimētēs* was consistently employed to denote an "imitator" (as well as in the negative sense of "forger"), or in any case, to denote the artist as a mime who gave life to certain characters, either as an "actor" or as "poet."[18] Even Diodorus, who uses this term on two other occasions, assigns it the standard meaning of a person who uses his own body to imitate another's behavior.[19] If elsewhere Diodorus employs the term *mimētēs* in its effective and common meaning, there seems to be no reason why he should have to force its meaning when talking about the Roman nobility.

Second, Diodorus says that these *mimētai* "carefully studied their bearing (*poreia*)." Why would a sculptor or any artist for that matter, charged with reproducing the features of the deceased, need precise details about the way in which he walked? All he would need was to perform a careful study of the features of the face and body. But an "imitator," an "actor" who

---

17. Diod. Sic. *Bibl. hist.* 31.25.2.
18. Cf. Liddell-Scott-Jones 1940, s. v.
19. In the former case, *mimētēs* is referred to the architect Perilaus, when he was invited by Phalaris to "play the part" of the convict imprisoned in the famous bull, later to be burnt himself (9.19.16ff.); in the latter case, it is stated that the soldiers generally "imitate the behavior (*mimētai genesthai*) of the commanding officers" (29.6.2): in both cases, it is clearly a question of "imitating" someone not by reproducing his features, as a figurative artist would be doing, but of impersonating or reproducing his behavior.

endeavors to personify another human being, will be interested in the way he walks (which, we now know, represents for the Romans a fundamental trait of identity). For this reason, when someone wishes to be mistaken for another, he or she imitates the other's *gressus* or *incessus*. As we have seen, this is precisely Cupid's method in the *Aeneid*, when he adopts the appearance of Ascanius in order to fool Dido into falling in love with Aeneas. If someone's way of walking is something that must be imitated by anyone wishing to pretend to be that person, it seems clear that the *mimētai* were nothing other than "impersonators," according to the correct meaning of the word *mimētēs*. They were actors—mimes—who studied their subjects in detail, because they would have to personify them in the future.[20] Interpreting Diodorus' passage in this way (and surely there can be no other way to interpret it), what he tells us coincides perfectly with Suetonius' description analyzed above.

The reader will also recall what Pliny the Elder said about the active presence of *mimētai* in the company of Roman nobles.[21] Finally, an inscription found not far from the tomb of the Scipiones at Vigna Codini likely provides further evidence for the *mimētai*:

Caesaris lusor
mutus et argutus imitator
Ti. Caesaris Augusti qui
primus invenit causidicos imitari

Caesar's jester, speechless and expressive imitator of Tiberius Caesar Augustus, who was the first to invent the art of imitating lawyers.[22]

Tiberius' *lusor*—evidently a "jester," an actor; at any rate, someone involved in entertaining the emperor—is represented as dumb (*mutus*). It is not clear, however, if this was a natural defect or a precise artistic choice. At the same time, we are told that this personage was also *argutus*—an allusion to the actor's nonverbal expressiveness, his ability to convey "meanings" despite his dumbness. This is a meaning of the Latin adjective *argutus* in other contexts; for example, the eyes are described as *arguti* when they are able to reveal even the deepest feelings without words.[23] Even a person's hands can be described

---

20. F. R. Walton in the Loeb edition of Diodorus (11.377), "actors."
21. In fact, there may have been seven. If we are to give any importance to the note added in the margin of the Plinian manuscript named *Leidensis Lipsi* n. 7 (cf. 7.55 *in fine*): see the note by Schilling 1977, 151. See also Bettini 1999a, 204ff.
22. *ILS* 5225 = *CIL* VI 4886; see Purcell 1999, 181–93. (I wish to thank my friend Giuseppe Pucci, who pointed out this interesting work to me.)
23. Cic. *Leg.* 1.9.27, *oculi nimis arguti, quemadmodum animo affecti simus, loquuntur* ("eyes

as *argutae* when they are particularly expressive in gesture.[24] Thus, the imperial *lusor* was *argutus:* he was able to "make himself understood" even though he was dumb. Let us now examine the exact function of this *lusor*.

The text of the inscription tells us that he was an *imitator*, a "mime" who had introduced a particularly fortunate type of imitation: of "lawyers." From our point of view, the genitive that follows the word *imitator* is particularly revealing. Of course, this genitive may indicate that the *lusor* "belonged" to the emperor as part of his family group.[25] However, we cannot exclude the possibility that he was an "imitator of Tiberius Caesar Augustus," meaning that among his duties was to be the emperor's *mimētēs*. In other words, this inscription may provide further information about those who were attached to famous people and who "carefully studied their bearing and any peculiarities in their appearance," in order to represent them at the time of their death according to the *mos* mentioned by Suetonius.[26] However we wish to interpret the syntagm *imitator Ti. Caesaris Augusti*, this inscription proves the presence of mimes at the imperial court and their close association with the person of the emperor.

At this point, some further reflection. The *mimētai* who studied Roman aristocrats in order to be able to impersonate them were something like "guardian angels." Aristocrats endured careful "observation" by their imitators, like the constant surveillance undertaken by defendants of their accusers, according to a Roman *lex* recalled by Plutarch.[27] Unlike the "watchman" peering over the accuser's shoulder, however, the *mimētēs* did not only keep an eye on what the Roman aristocrat was doing. The *mimētēs* conducted his observation in order to reproduce his study. As I have said, accompanied by a *mimētēs* who strove to acquire all the peculiarities of his appearance (to be faithfully reproduced upon his death), the Roman aristocrat inevitably must have imagined his own death in the form of his "double." The connection is reciprocal, then: the Double signified Death, and seeing one's own Double was an immediate reminder of aristocratic Death. Doubled after death by an *imago* that was "extremely similar" and "performed," doubled while still among the living by a *mimētēs* who followed him everywhere, the Roman

---

which are very expressive reveal the afflictions of the soul").

24. Aul. Gell. *NA*. 1.5, *manus argutae admodum et gestuosae* ("very expressive hands and prone to gesticulate"); Cicero (*De orat.* 3.59.218) expressly recommends that the *manus* of the orator should be *minus arguta, digitis subsequens verba, non exprimens* ("be less expressive [than the actor's hand], and should not express the words but accompany them with the movement of the hands").

25. So Purcell 1999, 181–83.

26. This hypothesis is also advanced by Purcell, but with no reference to the *mimētai* mentioned by Dio.

27. Plut. *Cat. min.*, 21, 5, "under a particular law the defendant placed a guard day and night next to the accuser, so as to control the evidence he was collecting and preparing for his accusation."

aristocrat was distinguished from the common citizen for this extraordinary reason: he directly and personally experienced the Double, recognizing that it represented honor and prestige. No doubt he must also have perceived the presentiment of death that its presence evoked.

There is no need to emphasize how powerful and intense the phenomenon of "doubling" was in Roman funerary ceremonies. The presence of the Double ranged from the parade of the *imagines maiorum* to the exhibited images of the deceased, the wax body of the emperor, the satyrs imitating the "serious" part of the procession and the *mimētai* who studied the behavior of the aristocrats to become, after death, their (comical) living substitutes. As already remarked, the presence of "doubles" at the aristocratic or imperial funeral is so constant that this ceremony would have been practically inconceivable without the presence of "doubles."

This means, however, that the ordinary relation that seems to exist in almost all cultures between the loss of a beloved person on the one hand and the production of images on the other is insufficient to explain the phenomenon of "doubling" in this particular context. We are fully aware that images are often the result of *pothos, desiderium* and nostalgia, while funerary doubling seems to function as a rigid and "cold" substitution of the deceased.[28] But in the case of Roman aristocratic funerary practice, the emphasis on this theme is so strong that we cannot but think there must have been something more specific connected with the cultural models of Roman tradition than some general relation between Death and the Double. What, then, was the real meaning, at Rome, of the connection between the Double on one hand and the aristocratic funeral on the other?

Let us try to answer this question by examining the problem from a different perspective—that of those who were without *imagines* at their funerals. First, poor citizens, whose burial reflected their manner of living: their corpses were thrown onto a *lecticula* or placed into a small *arca* or *sandapila*, barely covered by an old *toga* and then buried outside the Esquiline, where *vespillones* ("grave robbers") would take care of them.[29] In the case of the poor, then, there was no *pompa* and there were no *imagines*. More interesting from our point of view is the ancient Roman custom that Nero appealed to in order to legitimize the haste with which Britannicus was buried.[30] Tacitus reports:

---

28. As regards the category of "double" in archaic Greek culture (the *kolossos*, equivalent to the dead and his *psuchē*) see Vernant 1965b and Bettini 1999a, 12–15.

29. Tac. *Hist.* 3.67; Hor. *Sat.* 1.8.9; Luc. *Bell. civ.* 8.736; Suet. *Domit.* 17; Juv. *Sat.* 3.172; 8.175; Mart. *Ep.* 2.81, etc. See Toynbee 1971, 42ff.; but the evidence recorded by the author is rather slim.

30. Tac. *Ann.* 13.17.

> nox eadem necem Britannici et rogum coniunxit, proviso ante funebri paratu, qui modicus fuit. in campo tamen Martis sepultus est . . . festinationem exsequiarum edicto Caesar defendit, id a maioribus institutum referens, subtrahere oculis acerba funera neque laudationibus aut pompa detinere. ceterum et sibi amisso fratris auxilio reliquas spes in re publica sitas, et tanto magis fovendum patribus populoque principem, qui unus superesset e familia summum ad fastigium genita.

> A single night brought together the death of Britannicus and the pyre of his dead body. The preparations of his obsequies were made in advance and were of a humble type. He was buried in the Campus Martius. . . . His rapid funeral rites were justified by Caesar with an edict appealing to a custom of the ancestors (*maioribus institutum*), according to which the funerals of the dead were to be dispensed with as soon as possible, without lingering on funerary *laudationes* or any type of *pompa*. But for himself, as he was deprived of a brother's aid, the remainder of his hopes were placed in the Republic, trusting that both the nobility and the common man would be only more supportive of a ruler who was the last vestige of a family born to the heights of power.

This traditional practice, confirmed by a passage of Cicero's *Pro Cluentio*,[31] is extremely interesting. Owing to his social position and to his family origins, the young Britannicus was certainly entitled to a ceremonial funeral rich in *imagines*. But Nero, who wanted to avoid excessive publicity of the boy's death, appealed to an *institutum* of the *maiores* that discouraged protracting the funerals of *acerbi*, depriving them of *laudationes* and funerary *pompa*. Why then were *acerbi*—even those of the upper classes—not entitled to *imagines* and to the "double" funerary rites normally characterizing aristocratic funerary practice (being placed instead on the same level as the poor)? What did these two categories have in common? Likely, the absence of images and other funerary rites during the funerals of both the poor and the *acerbi* points to the profound meaning of the Double in the aristocratic funeral, when its appearance was so "visible" and powerful.

At Rome, *ius imaginum*—the right to keep *imagines* of one's ancestors—was not granted to everyone. This right was instead the exclusive

---

31. Cic. *Cluen.* 9.28 (a child). Not only did funerals of *impuberes* take place at night, but the bier was *preceded* by torches and wax candles (Serv. in Aen. 11.143; Sen. *De tran. anim.*, 11.7; *De brev. vit.* 20.6). Since we know that, during aristocratic funerary processions, the *imagines maiorum* were placed in front of the coffin (Hor. *Ep.* 8.11; Sil. Ital. *Pun.* 10.566f.; Tac. *Ann.* 3.76; see Bettini 1991c, 297 n. 4), it would almost seem that the torches and wax candles were taking the place of funerary *imagines*.

prerogative of those who counted among their ancestors one who had held a curule magistracy.³² This custom helps explain the social and cultural meaning of *imagines* of the deceased. Simultaneously, *imagines* functioned as a pledge and as a sign of *honos*. The possession of *imagines* and the possibility of displaying them in public during a funeral meant that a family had obtained *honores*. As Florence Dupont states, "le droit aux images est la seule façon d'être noble à Rome," the right of possessing that "gloire institutionelle que se dit en latin *honos*."³³ Besides, we have already seen that the one thing *imagines maiorum* were able to (even ostentatiously) express were the specific *honores* attained by the ancestors. The possibility of "doubling" or of being "doubled" was felt by Romans to be closely associated with the notion of *honos*. This relates not only to funerary *imagines*, however: the word that constantly occurs in texts dealing with the question of erecting a statue to somebody is in fact *honos*. To cite only two examples: When Cicero speaks about the statues that were awarded to four Roman ambassadors killed by Lars Tolumnius, he exclaims *iustus honos* ("just honor!"); and on the statue awarded to Gnaeus Octavius who was murdered on a mission to King Antiochus, the orator comments, "The senate erected a statue to him, which was designed to honor (*honestare*) his lineage for many years."³⁴ In other words, even in the case of erecting statues the notion of "doubling" by means of images seems to be interchangeable with that of *honos*.

The anthropological context in which the incredible presence of images takes place during aristocratic funerals is therefore represented by *honos*. In Roman culture, possession of an image "transmitting the memory of man," in Pliny's words, implied the tangible and explicit recognition of *honos*.³⁵ How could a poor plebeian or a young boy ever be entitled to *honos*, if he had not yet been able to give a sense to his life? A young *acerbus*, even one of good family, was unable to carry out any of the enterprises that might in the future grant him the *honos* of an *imago*. This was, of course, a reason for great sorrow.³⁶ He could not be "doubled" during funerals. He could not even have with him "the people of his family," as Pliny calls them, in the form of *imagines maiorum*. In the Roman funeral, Death and its Double meet at one particular point: *honos*, taking the concrete form of images.

---

32. Mommsen 1969, 436ff.; Flower 1996, 53ff.
33. Dupont 1986b, 244.
34. Cic. *Philipp.* 9.2.4–5; 9.1, 3; Plin. *Nat. hist.* 34.17, 21, 25; Sen. *Ep.* 64.9.
35. Plin. *Nat. hist.* 34.17.
36. In an inscription dedicated to young Cornelius Scipio (Degrassi 1963, I, 312), who died approximately at the age of twenty around the year 175 B.C.E., we can read: *quoiei vita defecit, non honos honore*: what this young Cornelius would have needed to achieve *honores* was not virtuous behavior, but *life*.

Let us tarry a moment on the absence of "doubles" during aristocratic funerals. Tacitus narrates that at the funeral of Cassius' wife, *imagines* of Brutus and Cassius ("whose presence was made visible by their very absence," Tacitus wryly observes) were not allowed to pass by.[37] Parading the images of Caesar's murderers in a funeral procession would have been inconvenient; their presence would have been "disgraceful" to the family. In this as in other cases, the extremely delicate relationship between funerary images on one hand and the reputation and good name of the family on the other is clear. The same relationship between *imago* and *honos* may also be observed in the even more dramatic practice of *damnatio memoriae*, which consisted in removing the images of the condemned from public display.[38]

In our study of "doubles" and their particular meaning in aristocratic funerary practice, we must not overlook an important feature whose presence is perhaps the most disconcerting in the context of such rituals: derision and laughter. This topic will permit us some final reflections.

Like the *mimētai* studying the Roman aristocrat in order to mock his vocal and physical idiosyncracies, there is no doubt that the satyrs dancing the *sicinnis*, imitating and mocking the funerary ceremony in which they take part, constitute a type of "double" quite different from the one represented by the *imagines maiorum* and other funerary statues. This is the kind of "doubling" that Cicero probably would have included in the category of *ridiculum*. In fact, in the *De Oratore*, Cicero evokes the existence of a *genus* of jokes that "consisted in imitation (*imitatio*) and is always ridiculous. We [sc. orators] can only make use of them in passing, infrequently and speedily, otherwise this is completely inelegant."[39] The orator employs *depravata imitatio*—caricature—to create difficulties for his opponent by mocking him. According to Cicero, this grotesque effect is achieved by means of *vocis ac vultus imitatio* ("imitation of the voice and *vultus*"). But also apart from caricature, simple *imitatio* of a person can produce irritation. Seneca was apparently well aware of its effects: "What about the fact that we feel offended when someone imitates the way in which we speak or walk, if someone reproduces the way in which we speak or any of our physical aspects?"[40]

We realize, therefore, that in aristocratic funerals—and even before, thanks to the constant presence of the *mimētai*—the relationship between the Roman noble (or indeed the emperor himself) and his Double was a relationship characterized by mockery. But how to explain this curious ten-

---

37. Tac. *Ann.* 3.76, *praefulgebant . . . eo ipso quod . . . non visebantur.*
38. Varner 2004.
39. Cic. *De orat.* 2.252
40. Sen. *De const.* 17.2, *quid quod offendimur, si quis sermonem nostrum imitatur, si quis incessum, si quis vitium aliquod corporis aut linguae exprimit?*

sion between solemn and dramatic "doubling" on one hand and derisory and insulting "doubling" on the other? The imitation and "roasting"—so to speak—of important figures such as the emperor was a traditional practice at Rome. This form of abuse was not only tolerated, but actually encouraged. Purcell confirms and emphasizes this with some very interesting examples and arguments.[41] However, in the case of aristocratic and imperial funerary practice, this strange and unusual interlacing appears once again capable of being referred to the same concept of *honos* that represents the anthropological framework in which to situate the "solemn" series of aristocratic Doubles.

Dionysius of Halicarnassus understood that, because of their similar nature, a link could be drawn between the presence of bands of satyrs in solemn contexts (such as the *pompa circensis* and aristocratic funerals) and the practice of "mockery, raillery and fun-making" during another solemn ceremony: the triumph.[42] In ancient Rome, this practice is recorded as dating back to the times of Scipio Africanus, if not earlier.[43] It is almost as if in Roman culture the solemn celebration of a citizen could not take place without the act of mockery. In this respect, the triumph is truly emblematic. The attainment of a triumph and the accompanying ceremony represented an extremely important *honos* for the person in question. At the same time, we know that during this ceremony soldiers were allowed to satirize their commanders freely and sarcastically. The same ambivalence can be observed in the aristocratic funeral: even the *honos* of the funerary *pompa*—the final recognition bestowed upon a noble citizen who had played an important role in the life of the city—implied the practice of *ridiculum*. In the case of the triumph, this was expressed in the form of verbal jokes and satirical elements, while in the case of the aristocratic funeral this was expressed through the language of images, typical of the funerary *honos*. Funerary "doubling" thus took the shape of *depravata imitatio* and the funeral ceremony became a play of mirrors, reflecting both solemn and comic doubling. The *funus gentilicium*, representing the climax and most important moment in the life of an aristocrat, was therefore grounded in a balance between elevation and degradation. This may seem strange to us, but it is typical of Roman culture. In the "dialogue" between the *imagines maiorum* accompanied by all the grave representations of their *dignitas*, on one hand, and the clownish mimes pillorying the deceased, on the other, Doubles in Rome spoke the same language: the language of *honos*.

---

41. Purcell 1999, 186.
42. Dion. Hal. *Ant. Rom.* 7.72.11.
43. Purcell 1999, 186.

EIGHT

Argumentum

The universe of the novel, and of the *Satyricon* in particular, is governed by coincidence. Encolpius and Giton board a ship and—what a coincidence!—the ship's captain is none other than their enemy, Lichas. Of course, by the time they realize this, it is already too late. But what to do? Toss themselves into the sea? Hide themselves in a sack, hoping that when they reach port their friend Eumolpus will carry them down to safety, hidden amongst the luggage? Instead, Eumolpus convinces them to shave off their hair and cover their faces with *stigmata* as if they were two fugitive slaves, since, he reasons, such a transformation would render them unrecognizable. But as things turn out, Eumolpus' solution is the worst they could have found—for in fact cutting one's hair during a sea voyage is a sign of bad luck. So when another passenger observes them occupied in this inauspicious task, he denounces them to the captain (who in the meantime has seen in a dream exactly whom he has been transporting aboard his ship). Charged with bringing misfortune upon the ship and its crew, the two stowaways are hauled before Lichas who—of course—recognizes them. Eumolpus, therefore, finding himself and his companions in dire straits, attempts to defend his two friends, maintaining with great cheek that they boarded the ship deliberately, in order to beg pardon for their previous misbehavior. But Encolpius and Giton's unfortunate attempt to disguise themselves instantly convinces Lichas that they had not, in fact, boarded the ship for this purpose.

noli, inquit, causam confundere . . . si ultro venerunt, cur nudavere crinibus capita? vultum enim qui permutat, fraudem parat, non satisfactionem.[1]

"Don't try to disrupt the proceedings!" he said. "If they came on their own accord, why did they cut their hair? When someone alters his appearance, he intends to deceive, not to render satisfaction."

Eumolpus does not throw in the towel so easily. At this point, the ship has already been transformed into a courtroom—or better yet, into a school of rhetoric—and he attempts to *resolvere* Lichas' *declamatio* with the following rebuttal:

intellego . . . nihil magis obesse iuvenibus miseris quam quod nocte deposuerunt capillos: hoc argumento incidisse in navem videntur, non venisse.[2]

I am fully aware that nothing harms the case of these poor young men more than the fact that at some point on the night in question they did away with their hair. Based on this *argumentum*, it would appear that they stumbled upon this ship by accident, rather than coming aboard by express purpose.

The "Inferential" Sign

Eumolpus and Giton's freshly-shaven heads are an *argumentum*—for now we can say the "proof"[3]—of the fact that they boarded the ship not to seek pardon from Lichas, but simply because they did not know that he was its captain. Eumolpus realizes that Encolpius and Giton's intentions when they boarded the ship can be "inferred" from this: They must have come on board by chance, not to seek pardon from its captain—otherwise, once they were aboard and understood (heavens!) where they were, they would not have cut off their hair to avoid being recognized. Eumolpus has studied his rhetoric well and employs the correct terminology: Quintilian tells us that the *natura omnium argumentorum* is in fact *ut sit ratio per ea quae certa sunt fidem dubiis adferens*[4] ("to be a *ratio* capable of providing certainty to that which is doubt-

---

1. Petr. *Sat.* 107.7ff.
2. Petr. *Sat.* 107.12.
3. The "argument" of this chapter—namely, the Latin word *argumentum*—is extremely vast. In these pages, I do not intend to exhaust the subject, which would have necessitated a detailed discussion of a huge number of passages, but rather to indicate a possible route through some uses of this word, above all those that are less well known. For a general discussion of *argumentum*, its most recurrent meanings and the principal biographical references, see Lumpe 1984, 299ff.
4. Quint. *Inst. orat.* 5.10.8ff. Cf. also 5.10.11, *ergo cum sit argumentum ratio probationem*

ful by means of what is certain"). In order to fulfill this function—i.e., to give certainty to that which is doubtful by means of that which is certain—*argumentum* has an inferential structure: it is a sign understood "as a single perceivable phenomenon, which refers to a fact not directly knowable."[5] In the "trial" sketched out by Petronius, two opinions are contrasted, and it is in doubt whether Encolpius and Giton got on board the ship to seek pardon from Lichas (as Eumolpus sustains) or if they happened upon it by chance (as Lichas argues). The act of cutting their hair functions as a *ratio* capable of "providing certainty" to that which is "in doubt" by means of what is "certain": it is an *argumentum* in every respect, therefore.

Everyday Inferences and Metaphors of *Argumentum*

The inferential mechanism underlying *argumentum* is clear in uses of this term.[6] As an example, we may take an amusing scene of Plautus' *Truculentus* in which the soldier Stratophanes receives news from the slave girl Astaphium that her mistress, the courtesan Phronesium, has given birth. In actual matter of fact, it is all a ruse: Phronesium has procured herself a baby from another mother and intends to pass it off as the soldier's child. Stratophanes wants more than anything to believe that the child is his: *ehem, ecquid mei similest?* ("My! Does he look like me at all?") he asks. Astaphium is quick with an answer: *rogas? / quin ubi natust machaeram et clipeum poscebat sibi?* ("Do you need to ask? He was not born but a moment when he asked for a sword and shield"). Stratophanes has no doubt about it at that point: *meus est, scio iam de argumentis* ("Yes, he's mine; I'm sure of it from the *argumenta*").[7] If a newborn immediately asks for a shield and a sword, it means that he is Stratophanes' son: it is possible to "infer" from these *argumenta* who the child's father is and to have proof of its paternity.

Something similar happens in *Amphitruo,* when Sosia must confront the aggression of his double, the god Mercury, who has taken on his identity in every respect (appearance, stature, bearing and so forth). Mercury/Sosia is trying to convince the unlucky slave that *he* is the real Sosia. The battle is hard-fought indeed, because Mercury/Sosia, being a god, knows all the

---

praestans, qua colligitur aliud per aliud, et quae quod esset dubium per id quod dubium non est confirmat, necesse est esse aliquid in causa quod probatione non egeat, "consequently, since *argumentum* is a *ratio* of probatory nature, through which one thing is inferred by means of another, and through which that which is in doubt is confirmed by that which is certain, it is necessary that in the case something exists that does not in its own turn require proving."

5. See Manetti 1987, 205ff., in reference to the *Rhetorica ad Herennium.*
6. Cf. *TLL* II, 542, 73ff.
7. Plaut. *Truc.* 504ff.

most hidden secrets of the real Sosia's life and uses them as proof of the fact that he is the "real" Sosia. It is already an ordeal when the true Sosia, now desperate, asks Mercury/Sosia to tell him what he was doing in his tent while the rest of the army was fighting against the army of Pterelaus: *victus sum, si dixeris* ("I'm done for, if you can tell me"), he declares.[8] But Mercury/Sosia does not even bat an eyelid: he recounts that in the tent there was a barrel of wine and that filling a bottle from it, he drank the entire thing. Sosia has lost and Mercury/Sosia remarks: *quid nunc? vincon' argumentis te non esse Sosiam?* ("And so? Have I won or not, with these *argumenta* that you are not Sosia?")[9] The mechanismis are the same. A certain element (the knowledge of what happened privately in the tent during the battle) functions as a sign from which one can infer a certain conclusion, an inference that can then be used as proof for substantiating that which is not certain in itself precisely by means of that which is.

As the evidence of Plautus shows, the use of *argumentum* in the sense of "inferential sign" or "proof" is not the exclusive patrimony of orators and lawyers. It is also part of the common language and boasts of quite ancient testimony. This should come as no surprise, since what *argumentum* expresses—inference through signs, and the use of that inference as proof in situations of uncertainty—is a necessary part not only of forensic activity but also of life in general. Naturally, orators and lawyers give us the best "metalinguistic" analyses of the term.[10] Yet, even more interesting than these precise definitions are certain images that they employ to describe the nature of *argumentum*. Take two passages of Cicero, for example: *argumentum . . . rerum vox est, naturae vestigium, veritatis nota* ("*Argumentum* is a voice of things, an imprint left by nature, a mark of truth")[11] and *haec causa ab argumentis, a coniectura, ab iis signis, quibus veritas inlustrari solet, ad testis*

---

8. Plaut. *Am.* 427ff.
9. Plaut. *Am.* 433.
10. For Quintilian, cf. above, n. 4. See also *Rhet. ad Herenn.* 2.8, *argumentum est, per quod res coarguitur certioribus argumentis et magis firma suspicione* ("*argumentum* is that through which the accusation is confirmed with surer arguments and more certain suspicions"). The examples offered are interesting: *si tumore et livore decoloratum corpus est mortui, significant eum veneno necatum* ("if the corpse is discolored by bloating or lividity, this means that the subject was poisoned"). The inferential structure appears to be expressed, in fact, through the classic instrument of the hypothetic period (Manetti 1987, 206); see also Calboli's (1969, 231ff.) note *ad loc.* See also Cic. *Top.* 2.8, *esse . . . argumentum . . . rationem quae rei dubiae faciat fidem* ("an *argumentum* is . . . a ratio that gives certainty to something in doubt"). Boethius commented in his commentary on Cicero's *Topica* that *argumentum . . . est, quod rem arguti id est probat, nihil vero probari nisi dubium potest* ("an *argumentum* is something that *arguit* or that furnishes a proof: but something cannot be proven unless it is in doubt") (Migne 1844, 64, 1048). And Isidore (*Etym.* 18.15.5) insisted on the hypothetical and "investigative" nature of the word: *argumentum . . . sola investigatione invenit veritatem* ("an *argumentum* discovers the truth only through investigation"), etc.
11. Cic. *Scaur.* 16.

tota reducta est ("This case has boiled down entirely to the testimony of witnesses—away with *argumenta,* hypothesis and those signs by which the truth is normally illustrated!")[12] Eloquent metaphors indeed: an *argumentum* is a kind of "voice of things," an "imprint of nature." Through an *argumentum,* truth is revealed by means of a "sign," or "receives light" from it. Ciceronian representation is no doubt rich in figures for defining *argumentum,*[13] but always the same attribute is emphasized: the ability to communicate a meaning that would otherwise remain unexpressed (the voice of things, the imprint of nature, the mark of truth) or to offer something the possibility of "being illustrated," of "standing out." This final image, in fact, presents considerations of particular interest.

An Inference Is a Flash

Let us look at the relationship between *argumentum* and the verb to which it is related: *arguo*. In the very first instance, this verb means *ostendere, patefacere, manifestare*[14] and so presupposes, in a certain sense, a process of "revelation." Its semantic connection with *argumentum* is clear, since *argumentum* (the inferential sign) also presupposes a kind of revelation. As we have seen, the *argumentum* employed by Astaphium in persuading the soldier Stratophanes (the fact that the child "asked for a sword and shield" as soon as it was born) implies the revelation that the child is, in fact, *his* son and not someone else's. An *argumentum,* then, realizes the process of *arguere,* actually producing the revelation that the verb implies.

Of course, this is precisely the semantic quality that substantives in *-men/-mentum* have: they are "des réalités concrètes ou abstraites qui, en quelque sort, enferment en elles le procès, soit qu'elles tirent leur existence du procès (type resultatif) soit qu'elles se manifestent par l'exercice de ce procès (type actif)."[15] *Argumentum* gets its quality precisely from the process of *arguere;* its very existence implies this. Therefore, we may analyze some of the many cases in which the revelation realized by the verb *arguo* presupposes the existence of a "medium," something through which this process is realized. Seneca, for example, says the following in reference to the Minotaur: *scelus . . . matris arguit vultu truci ambiguus infans* ("The ambiguous child revealed its mother's guilt by its grim visage").[16] Pasiphae's guilt is revealed

---

12. Cic. *Cael.* 66.
13. Vasaly 1993, 209ff.
14. *TLL* II, 551, 19.
15. Perret 1961, 256.
16. Sen. *Phaed.* 692ff.

by the Minotaur's "grim visage"; otherwise, it would never have been known. Vergil uses *arguo* in the same way in his rather sententious hemistich *degeneres animos timor arguit* ("Their fear revealed their base character").[17] It is their fear that allows the baseness of their character, normally imperceptible, to be revealed. A "grim visage" and fear, therefore, can fairly be defined *argumenta*, since they realize the process of *arguere*, since it is possible to infer from them the guilt of *bestialitas* in the first case and baseness of character in the second. That is to say, any element (a grim visage, fear) that has the ability to *arguere* what is immediately indiscernible (hidden culpability, the depths of human nature) functions as an *argumentum*.

Let us explore this problem a little further. In fact, let us try to determine if there is a more fundamental meaning from which these particular "designations"[18] of *arguo* and *argumentum* (i.e., "to reveal, demonstrate," and so on) are derived. One way to go about this is to examine how the adjective *argūtus*[19] is used, since it is likewise related to *arguo*.[20] As it turns out, in many cases the adjective *argūtus* indicates that which "strikes" the senses with particular force.[21] When it is used in reference to auditory perception, for instance, *argūtus* accompanies the mention of a clear or penetrating sound. A tongue,[22] a pipe,[23] a swan's song[24] and so on, may all be said to be *argūtus*. Likewise with visual impressions: the eyes may be called *arguti* in reference to their capacity to reveal the feelings of the soul,[25] just as the hands may be called *argutae* in reference to their expressiveness when gesticulating.[26] Evidently, hands and eyes may "strike the attention" or somehow "stand out" in the same way that the sound of a reed pipe and a swan's song do. The same is true also for smell and taste: the aroma of oil may be *argūtus*[27] (we might say "sharp" or "penetrating"), just as the flavor of pears and figs

---

17. Verg. *Aen.* 4.13.
18. I use the terminology of Benveniste 1974, I, 5 and 80.
19. On the uses of this very useful adjective the survey of Iodice Martino 1986, 34ff.
20. Ernout and Meillet 1965, 46, s.v. *arguo*. Cf. the series such as *status, statuo, statū-tus; tribus, tribuo, tribū-tus; cornū, cornū-tus*.
21. Cf. *TLL* II, 557, 48ff.
22. Naevius, *Tragediarum Fragmenta*, fr. 25 Ribbeck[3], *argutis linguis* ("with tongues that make themselves heard").
23. Verg. *Georg.* 7.24, *arguta . . . fistula* ("a loud flute").
24. Verg. *Georg.* 9.36, *argutos inter strepere anser olores* ("a duck that quacks among the swans of resonant song").
25. Cic. *Leg.* 1.9.27, *oculi nimis arguti, quamadmodum animo affecti simus, loquuntur* ("very expressive eyes communicate the affections of the heart").
26. Aul. Gell. *NA.* 1.5, *manus argutae admodum et gestuosae* ("very expressive hands inclined to gesticulate"). Cicero (*De orat.* 3.59.218) recounts that the *manus* of the orator is *minus arguta, digitis subsequens verba, non exprimens* ("less expressive than that of the actor and accompanies the words with the movement of the fingers, but does not express them").
27. Plin. *Nat. hist.* 15.18.

may be *argūtus*[28] (we would say "strong" or "sharp"). *Argūtus*, therefore, corresponds to the ability to strike the attention, to stand out, to be distinct.

It is worth examining the problem from an etymological point of view as well. *Arguo, argūmentum, argūtus* are surely related to a form **argus*, meaning "clarity" or "clearness"—the same root **arg-* that we find in Greek *argos* ("clear, shining") and in Hittite *hargi* ("clear, white").[29] In Latin, *argentum* ("shining metal") and *argilla* ("white earth") are also from this root.[30] The form in *-u-*, as in **argu-*, which forms the basis of *argu-o, argu-mentum* and *argu-tus*, appears in Greek *argu-ros* ("silver, shining metal").[31] The etymological meaning of this group of words seems to rest, then, in the image of clarity, of radiance. We can therefore explain why the adjective *argūtus* implies the notion of being sharp, penetrating and standing out. The original image is that of a "flash" of light that stands out from its surroundings and strikes the attention because of its brightness. But there is another consequence of this that interests us more directly. We know now that the ability possessed by words like *arguo* and *argumentum* to reveal something hidden is expressed through the image of a flash of light striking the attention, and Cicero, as we have seen, represented *argumentum* as a kind of "voice of things," an "imprint of nature." He was convinced that through an *argumentum* the truth is revealed by means of a "sign" or that from it the truth "receives light"—all images quite close to the original etymological meaning of the word. In short, when one adopts an *argumentum*—the *ratio per ea quae certa sunt fidem dubiis aderens*[32]—a kind of flash is produced. An inference is a light that goes on, a beam of light that comes out of the darkness and strikes the attention.

Iconographic Inference

Other specific uses of *argumentum* as "inference" are of particular interest in the history of the Roman intellectual lexicon: for example, those connected with iconography and the other figural arts, where *argumentum* is used to define a type of symbolic communication. In this regard, Pliny, in the last books of his *Natural History*, provides us with some of the best examples. Parrhasius was becoming famous for his representations of the people of Athens:

---

28. Palladius 3.25.4 and 4.10.26.
29. Ernout-Meillet 1965, s.vv. *argumentum* and *arguo*.
30. Ernout-Meillet 1965, s.vv. *argentum* and *argilla*.
31. Ernout-Meillet 1965, s.v. *argentum*.
32. Quint. *Inst. orat.* 5.10.8ff.

Chapter 8. Argumentum

> pinxit demon Atheniensium argumento quoque ingenioso. ostendebat namque varium iracundum iniustum inconstantem, eundem exorabilem clementem misericordem; gloriosum . . . excelsum umilem, ferocem fugacemque et omnia pariter.³³

> He painted the Athenian people making use of an ingenious *argumentum*. In fact, he represented it as flighty, irascible, unjust, inconstant, but at the same time embracing, indulgent, pitying; proud . . . sublime, humble, fierce and cheap, all in the same measure.

Wishing to represent the changeable nature of the Athenian people, Parrhasius resorted to an ingenious expedient, capturing in a single image several faces that expressed a variety of contrasting psychological dispositions.³⁴ Pliny defines this "pictorial device"³⁵ as an *argumentum*, and indeed we remain always in the realm of inference. In order to paint "something that is difficult to make concrete"³⁶—the shifting nature of a people's character—Parrhasius availed himself of a complex of signs from which it was possible to infer what he wished to express.

Again according to Pliny, the artist Nealces does something similar when he finds himself needing to communicate something that would be difficult to express with the normal techniques of painting:

> cum proelium navale Persarum et Aegyptiorum pinxisset, quod in Nilo, cuius est aqua maris similis, factum volebat intellegi, argumento declaravit quod arte non poterat: asellum enim bibentem in litore pinxit et crocodilum insidiantem ei.³⁷

> When he had painted the naval battle between the Persians and the Egyptians, wishing to make it understood that the battle had taken place on the waters of the Nile, which resemble those of the sea, he expressed through an *argumentum* what he was not able to express simply through his art: on the banks he depicted a donkey drinking along with a crocodile lying in wait for it.

Nealces wished to communicate that the waters on which the battle took place were those of the Nile. But given that the course of the Nile is

---

33. Plin. *Nat. hist.* 35.69.
34. See Corso's note in Conte 1988, 5, 365ff.
35. This is the translation proposed by Mugellesi in Conte 1988, 367 ("risorsa pittorica").
36. Thus Ferri 1946, 155, comparing the word *argumentum* used by Pliny in this context with the Greek *paradeigma*.
37. Plin. *Nat. hist.* 35.142.

very wide, resembling a sea more than a river, it was difficult to allow the viewer of the painting to understand that the expanse of water on which the battle took place belonged to a river and not to the sea. The painter therefore utilizes an *argumentum*—a complex of signs from which it would be possible to infer what his pictorial art was incapable of communicating on its own. On the *litus* of what appeared to be a sea, Nealces painted an ass ambushed by a crocodile. Since the crocodile was an animal typical of the Nile (and definitely not a marine creature), this element rendered the waters immediately identifiable: the viewer would understand that it was a river and not the sea that was depicted there. The same may be said for the fact that an ass was represented in the act of drinking the water in front of it: obviously it is fresh water, rather than sea water, if the ass is drinking it. As for the painter's specific choice of a donkey, it is likely that we have here an illusion to the fact that the king of Persia who was defeated in that battle, Artaxerxes III Ochos, had the surname Onos ("donkey").[38] At this point Nealces' *argumentum* quite resembles what we would call a rebus: a "donkey" (The Great King) ambushed by a "crocodile" (the Nile) functions as a kind of *scholion*—"the king Artaxerxes III Ochos, called Onos, defeated by the Egyptians on the waters of the Nile"—transposed into the figural arts.

Another example. The Spartans Saura and Batracus built the temples that stood inside the Porticus Octaviae. Some maintained that they, being quite wealthy men, had financed the construction themselves in the hope of setting up an inscription that contained their names. This wish was denied. However, it seems that Saura and Batracus obtained their desire in any case: *sunt certe etiamnum in columnarum spiris inscalptae nominum eorum argumento lacerta atque rana* ("There can be seen even now a frog and a lizard carved into the torus of the columns as an *argumentum* of their names").[39] In Greek, *saura* means "lizard" and *batrachos* means "frog," and affixing designs of these two animals to their work, Saura and Batracus had practically "signed" it—thus remedying in some way the absence of the inscription they so desired. Naturally, there is a difference. The inscription would have listed their names explicitly, whereas the carvings of a frog and a lizard could at best allow their names to be "inferred." But for this reason, Pliny says that the two images functioned as an *argumentum*.[40]

We could go on giving examples.[41] However, it seems worth suggesting

---

38. Cf. Ael. *Var. hist.* 4.8; Ferri 1946, 202ff.

39. Plin. *Nat. hist.* 36.42ff.

40. We know other cases of artists who used to "sign" their works with an image instead of their name. See, e.g., the case of the mosaicist Lucius Ceius Pavo who would sign his *nomen* and *praenomen*, but in place of his *cognomen*, would place the image of a peacock (cf. Conte 1988, 603).

41. Plin. *Nat. hist.* 29.54, the interlacing of serpents and their productive union *in causa videtur esse, quare exterae gentes caduceum in pacis argumentis circumdata effigie anguium fecerint* (they put the

that the term *argumentum* in the particular meaning we have identified here—"iconographic symbol"—could be useful in defining an aspect of figural communication for which we lack precise terminology. To see what I mean, let us take at random one of an infinite number of possible examples: Dosso Dossi's *Allegory of Fortune*.[42] In this painting, we see a nude woman framed by a fluttering veil, sitting atop a transparent ball (a kind of bubble of air) and holding a cornucopia. One of her feet is bare and on the other she wears a kind of shoe. In order to describe the functions of these iconographic elements we would probably have to use expressions like "symbol," "sign," "allegorical traits" or any number of other possibilities. In ancient terminology, however, all of these symbolic elements would have been defined as *argumenta*, since from them it is possible to infer the specific qualities of Fortune: her fragility (the air bubble upon which she sits), her erratic and uneven step (her feet, one shod, one bare) and so forth. Imitating Pliny's Latin, we could say that *translucida bulla aere inflata argumentum est Fortunae levitatis*, while *pedes quorum unus calciatus alter nudatus argumenta sunt inconstantiae eius*. And given, then, that these *argumenta*, taken all together, allow us to infer the identity of the female figure of the painting, we could conclude that Dosso Dossi *Fortunam ingenioso quodam argumento pinxit: fecit enim eam translucida bulla sedentem*. . . . In this light, iconographic treatises like Cesare Ripa's *Iconologia* are immense repositories of *argumenta*.

The "Many Meanings" of *Argumentum*

As Quintilian remarks, *argumentum* is a word that has "many meanings":

> argumentum . . . plura significat. nam et fabulae ad actum scaenarum compositae argumenta dicuntur, et <cum> orationum Ciceronis uelut thema [ipse] exponit Pedianus inquit: 'argumentum tale est' (fr. 31 Ofen-

---

image of the serpents around the caduceus as an *argumentum* of peace); 35.101, regarding Protogenes who was supposed to have painted votive boats until he was fifty, *argumentum esse, quod cum Athenis celeberrimo loco Minervae delubri propylon pingeret* . . . *adiecerit parvolas naves longas in iis, quae pictores parergia appellant, ut appareret a quibus initiis ad arcem ostentationis opera sua pervenissent* (the *argumentum* of the presumed occupation of the ship painter were the small transport ships that he added as details when he painted the propylon of the temple of Minerva in Athens). In this case, too, *argumentum* designates a symbol from which one "infers" something: not an iconographic meaning, this time, but a (presumed) message encoded by the painter. Macr. *Sat.* 1.17.68, concerning a statue of Apollo at Hieropolis that combines all the attributes of the son, *hastae atque loricae argumento imago adiungitur Martis* ("the image of Mars is joined with an *argumentum* of a spear and cuirass"). Apul. *Met.* 11.3.4ff., above Isis' brow stands a *plana rotunditas* . . . *argumentum lunae* ("flat disc . . . an *argumentum* of the moon"). And so on.

42. Conserved in the Paul Getty Museum in Malibu, California.

loch) ... *quo apparet omnem ad scribendum destinatam materiam ita appellari. nec mirum, cum id inter opifices quoque sit uulgatum, unde Vergili 'argumentum ingens,' uulgoque paulo numerosius opus dicitur argumentosum.*[43]

Argumentum has many meanings. In fact, the stories composed to be represented on stage are called *argumenta,* and when Pedianus gives the theme of Cicero's orations he says, "the *argumentum* is as follows." ... From this, it ensues that any subject destined to be developed in written form is called by this name. And no wonder, given that this word is very popular among artists, whence the Vergilian "immense *argumentum,*" and that it is commonly said that a scattered work is an *opus argumentosum.*

Quintilian truly appreciates the problem. In fact, in Latin, *argumentum* is largely used in the sense of the "theme" or "subject" of a work—its "argument," as we still say today[44]—and frankly in this instance the inferential character of the word seems entirely absent. The *materia ad scribendum destinata* (whether it is the subject of a comedy or of an oration, or forms the subject of a work of art, such as the story of Io carved on Turnus' shield in Vergil), seems, at least at first glance, to have nothing to do with the flash of light that comes out of the darkness and causes what otherwise would have remained unknown to "stand out." But let us take another look.[45]

The Subject of Figural Narration

There is no dearth of examples of *argumentum* referring to the subject of a work of art. Quintilian claims that this use was "very popular among art-

---

43. Quint. *Inst. orat.* 5.10.8–10.
44. Cf. *TLL* II, 548, 37ff.
45. As for the term *argumentosus* used by Quintilian (*Inst. orat.* 5.10.8) in the syntagma *opus argumentosum* to indicate a work that is disorganized, we may think here that what is being underscored is the excessive domination of the "subject" over its formal realization. *Argumentosus* is in fact a formation in *-osus* like *famosus, ponderosus, damnosus, morbosus, vitiosus,* etc., that underlines the strong predomination of a trait in characterizing something (Leumann 1977², 347, "reich an, versehen mit"; Ernout 1949; Guerrini 1984, 61ff.; Knox 1985, 90ff.). In different cases, the addition of the suffix *-osus* provokes formations with a marked negative sense: in Italian, they can be translated with the adjective *troppo* ("too") as "too heavy" (*ponderosus*), "too talked-about" (*famosus*), "with too many vices" (*vitiosus*), etc. *Argumentosus* would then mean "that has too many themes," that is, without elegance because the theme dominates too much the form that it has received. The vision of a work of art presupposed by such terminology distinguishes cleanly between content and form: one expects that the artists proceeds by giving form to a pre-existing "canvas," rendering it *argumentosus* by means of his formal care. In the case of *opera argumentosa* this process of "giving form" has not been completed.

ists." However, when the "subject" of a work of art is designated by the word *argumentum,* it always corresponds to a story—a narration of the kind that may be represented on a doorway, a shield, a bowl, a sail and so forth.[46] Cicero recounts of Verres that *ex ebore diligentissime perfecta argumenta erant in valvis: ea detrahenda curavit omnia* ("on the doors stood some *argumenta* sculpted in ivory with great precision, all of which he had removed").[47] Meanwhile, in the passage to which Quintilian alludes above, Vergil describes the *imagines* that adorn Turnus' shield like this:

> levem clipeum sublatis cornibus Io
> auro insignebat, iam setis obsita, iam bos
> (argumentum ingens) et custos virginis Argus
> caelataque amnem fundens pater Inachus urna.

In gold Io graced the smooth shield—her horns raised, covered in bristly hairs, already transformed into a cow (an impressive *argumentum*)—along with Argos, the girl's guard and her father Inachus pouring forth his waters from an engraved urn.[48]

There is also Ovid's narration of the contest between Athena and Arachne, with his description of the haughty girl's work: *et vetus in tela deducitur argumentum* ("an old *argumentum* is woven on the cloth").[49] The story represented is that of Europa seduced by the bull, along with other mythologi-

---

46. Cf. *TLL* II, 550, 1ff. where, however, the two meanings of *argumentum*—as "iconographic symbol," that discussed in paragraph 4, and as "subject," or better, an artistically represented "narrative"—are confused.

47. Cic. *Verr.* 6.124.

48. Verg. *Aen.* 7.789ff. One notes, in fact, that in this regard Serv. in *Aen.* 7.791 makes a curious attempt to attribute an inferential value also to the *argumentum* named by Vergil in the case of Turnus' shield: *'argumentum ingens' aut fabula, ut Cicero argumenta in valvis aut re vera argumentum, quod se Graecum probare cupiebat. hoc enim Amata superius dixit 'Inachus Acrisiusque patres mediaeque Mycenae'* ("*'argumentum ingens'* means either the subject, as when Cicero says, 'on the doorway stood some *argumenta*' or *argumentum* in its proper sense, because doing so he wished to show that he was Greek. Amata, in fact, had said this same thing before, 'Inachus and Acrisius and the center of Mycenae are his ancestors.'") We need to consider that Servius refers to the moment in which Amata declares that, if Lavinia strictly needs to find a foreign husband, Turnus also fits the bill. Consequently, the commentator suggests that Vergil had Turnus carry those images on his shield to 'show' his Greek origin. Vergil certainly did not mean this by his *argumentum*. Nevertheless, from a more general point of view, we cannot say Servius was wrong, either: in fact, Turnus does have this story on his shield, and not another, in order to declare his own origin. Servius is forcing the meaning of the text, taking advantage of the fact that in the story those images function objectively as an iconographic *argumentum* from which it is possible to "infer" the hero's origins, in order to attribute the meaning of "inferential sign" to the word *argumentum* used by Vergil in the text; however, here it means something else.

49. Ov. *Met.* 6.69.

cal tales of the same type. And again when he describes the bowl given to Aeneas: *fabricaverat Alcon / Myleus et longo caelaverat argumentum* ("Alcon of Mylos had made it and upon it he had engraved a long *argumentum*").[50] Many more examples could be given. But it is worth examining this final passage of Ovid in greater detail.[51]

The scene represented by Alcon on the bowl is the war of the Seven Against Thebes. Ovid, that master of artistic description, ingeniously alerts his audience to what *argumentum* is engraved on the bowl when he writes that *urbs erat et septem posses ostendere portas: / hae pro nomine erant et, quae foret illa, docebant* ("there was represented a city—you could point out each of its seven gates, which stood in place of its name, and explained what city it was")[52] and later that *ante urbem exsequiae tumulique ignesque rogique / effusaeque comas et apertae pectora matres / significant luctum* ("before the city funerals, graves, flames, pyres, mothers with their hair let loose and their breasts bared indicate mourning").[53] In some sense, Ovid pushes the limits of *ekphrasis* here: not limiting himself to merely describing a work of art, he also entertains himself in revealing how it functions. The reader is not given a description of the scene mediated—that is, already interpreted—by the poet, but is allowed to behold the bare figural elements. At the same time, the poet explains to him how to proceed in their interpretation. The peculiarity of Ovid's method really stands out when compared with how Vergil goes about his description of Turnus' shield. Vergil announces the "subject" of the work immediately, giving the names of the characters, and so on: there is Io, already transformed into a cow; there is Argus who watches over her, and Inachus who pours forth his waters from an urn. Ovid proceeds in reverse. He does not say "there was the city of Thebes with its seven gates; there were the Theban mothers in grief, with their hair let loose and their breasts bared." Instead, he begins with what the reader/viewer actually sees, and only then invites him to guess the "subject" of the work. He describes a city with seven gates, saying that these gates stood for the city's "name"; he represents funeral pyres, women with their hair let loose and their breasts bared, and only later declares that this "signifies" mourning.

---

50. Ov. *Met.* 13.683ff.

51. Prop. *Carm.* 3.9.13ff. (artists excel in art for various reasons, Lysippus for statues that appear to be alive, Calamis for having perfected the horse, etc.: *argumenta magis sunt Menotis addita formae* (the *argumenta* are, in a particular fashion, present in the casts of Mentor)—Mentor was considered the most illustrious of engravers; see also Suet. *Tib.* 44.2, *Parrhasi quoque tabulam . . . legatam sibi sub condicione, ut si argumento offenderetur decies pro ea sestertium acciperet* ("a painting of Parrhasius . . . left to him on condition that if he was offended by the *argumentum*, he could receive a million sesterces instead"), etc. Ov. *Met.* 6.69.

52. Ov. *Met.* 13.685ff.

53. Ov. *Met.* 13.687ff.

Ovid is very true to life, since our enjoyment of figural narration works exactly in this way. In order to guess the subject of a work of art, the viewer makes inferences from the individual figural elements that he sees before him. If he does not have an interpreter to mediate this process for him—a poet to describe the work ecphrastically, *didaskalia,* a Touring Guide—the viewer must infer on his own that the city with seven gates is Thebes, that women with their hair let loose and their breasts bared must mean "mourning." Only then does the subject of the scene become clear: the war of the Seven Against Thebes, which caused so much grief for those involved.

Argumentum therefore maintains its inferential character when it is used to indicate the subject of a work of the figural arts. In fact, what a viewer "really" has in front of him is simply a complex of incompletely codified signs: it is up to him to infer from them the "subject" represented there. For this reason, a story narrated by means of a figural code may rightfully be called an *argumentum.* The figural signs are "names," elements that signify something—and the audience must use them as an *argumentum* to identify what it is they communicate.

The Subject of a Literary Text

What about the *argumentum* of a comedy or an oration? When Mercury, in the prologue of *Amphitruo,* declares *nunc animum advortite / dum huius argumentum eloquar comoediae* ("now pay attention, so I can tell you the *argumentum* of this comedy"),[54] the spectators know that what follows will be a narration: a summary of the comedy, its content. The same holds true for the summaries of Cicero's orations that Quintus Asconius Pedianus supplies as a preface to his commentaries. There does not seem to be anything to infer here. Naturally, we might conclude that the use of *argumentum* to indicate the subject of a literary work is simply transferred from the figural arts. Quintilian tells us that the term *argumentum* was popular among *opifices:* We might not be surprised, then, if *argumentum*—used "properly" by artists to indicate the subjects of their own works—was then used "improperly" to define any type of theme or subject, even in the total absence of the inferential process. This explanation is not very convincing, however: we have seen that *argumentum* tends to maintain its relation to the world of signs and inference, even when this seems to be absent. But—to make a small play on words—we can actually use this observation as an *argumentum*

---

54. Plaut. *Am.* 95ff. The use of *argumentum* in the sense of "subject of the comedy" is very common: cf. *TLL* II, 548, 37ff.

of the fact that *argumentum,* even when it designates the subject of a literary text, maintains its connection to the semiotic sphere. At any rate, this "inference" can be confirmed by a simple consideration.

The *argumentum* of a literary work is not the work itself; it is a brief description of its contents. The play *Amphitruo* is one thing (a comedy by the playwright Plautus, recited on stage). The summary of its plot given in the prologue by Mercury is something else entirely. Suetonius even employs the verb *explicare* to describe the relationship between the plot (the "sketch" or "outline" of a play) and its realization on stage: *parabatur et in noctem spectaculum, quo argumenta inferorum per Aegyptios et Aethiopas explicarentur* ("a night time showing was also being prepared, in which the *argumenta* of the infernal beings were to be 'performed' by Egyptian and Ethiopian actors").[55] Likewise for the summaries of Cicero's speeches: Asconius Pedianus does not pretend that his summaries are a substitute for the orations themselves: they are simply "sketches." Only shameless students and unscrupulous professors would consider reading a summary of the *Aeneid* an acceptable substitute for reading the actual poem. A summary of the *Aeneid* is a tool—something that helps us get an idea of Vergil's work, referring us back to the original. But it is something different from the work itself.

The inferential principle holding for the elements of a work of art realized by an *opifex* now appears to hold in the case of the *argumentum* of a literary work, as well—albeit in different form. From the summary of *Amphitruo* provided by Mercury in the play's prologue, the spectator can only infer what the drama true and proper will be. Here again is that "flash of light" shining forth from the darkness: the subject of the comedy "stands out" through the *argumentum.* But the *argumentum* recited by Mercury is not the comedy itself; it is a complex of signs that permit the audience to know, in brief, the plot of the comedy about to see performed. So too for the speeches of Cicero summarized by Asconius Pedianus in the prefaces to his commentaries. Each *argumentum* is a sign that stands for and refers to the original work, allowing us to recall it. In some sense, it is a real pity that for us the "argument" of a work means simply its "topic" or "subject." In normal linguistic perception, the semiotic value of "the summary" has in fact been lost: No one today would consider the CliffsNotes version of the *Aeneid* an *argumentum* from which it is possible to "infer" the epic poem written by Vergil.[56]

---

55. Suet. *Cal.* 57.10.

56. As the "summary" of a theatrical work or of any literary text, *argumentum* also bears the sense that we give to words such as "action," "plot." On the relationships between the send of *argumentum* as *Inhaltsangabe* of a work (the normal sense in Plautus and Terence) and as a "theme" to develop, cf. Primmer 1964, 61ff., esp. 64–65. On Cic. *Inv.* 1.27 and the problematic rhetoric connected to *argumentum* as "subject" of a work, above all in regard to the novel, see Barwick 1928,

The Apologue and Unlimited Semiosis

In one area of ancient literary production, the term *argumentum* seems to have enjoyed particularly good fortune: the Aesopic fable, the apologue. Already at the conclusion of Ennius' celebrated "fable of the lark" we read: *hoc erit tibi argumentum semper in promptum situm, / ne quid expectes amicos quod tute agere possies* ("you will have this *argumentum* always at hand, so you don't expect your friends to do what you can do yourself").[57] In Ennius' opinion, this fable would be a good *argumentum* for sustaining a certain theory of behavior: namely, not expecting your friends to do what you can do yourself. Phaedrus frequently uses this word in a similar sense—for finding a "moral" in a fable, for showing the reader how he can apply what he has read to his own life. For example, take the story of the brigands who kill the mule that proudly carried their sacks of money, while sparing one that humbly carried sacks of barley: *hoc argumento tuta est hominum tenuitas / magnae periclo sunt opes obnoxiae* ("on the basis of this *argumentum*, men's poverty is secure, while great wealth is subject to danger").[58] Or that of the viper that bites a file: *mordaciorem qui improbo dente adpetit / hoc argumento se describi sentiat* ("He who rashly bites that which is more biting than him should recognize that he himself is described here").[59] Or that of the thief who lights a lantern at the altar of Jupiter only to sack the temple by its light: *quot res contineat hoc argumentum utiles, / non explicabit alius quam qui repperit: / significant primo . . . secundum ostendit . . . novissime interdicit . . .* ("none can explain better than he who wrote this *argumentum* how many useful things are contained within it: in the first place, it means . . . in the second place, he shows . . . , and finally he warns . . . ").[60] Or that of the billy-goats who complain to Jupiter because he gave beards not only to them, but also to young she-goats: *hoc argumentum monet ut sustineas tibi / habitu esse similes, qui sint virtute impares* ("this *argumentum* warns us to accept that those who are unequal to us in worth are similar to us in aspect").[61] Or—finally—that of the bald man who hits himself over the head trying to swat a fly: *hoc argumento ei modo decet veniam dari, / qui casu peccat* ("on the basis of this *argumentum*, one should pardon he who does wrong involuntarily").[62]

261ff.
    57. Enn. *Sat.* 57ff. Vahlen[2] (= Aul. Gell. *NA.* 2.29.1ff.) Cf. Menna 1983, 105ff. (on these lines in particular: 125, n. 31).
    58. Phaed. *Fab.* 2.7.13ff.
    59. Phaed. *Fab.* 4.8.1ff.
    60. Phaed. *Fab.* 4.11.14ff.
    61. Phaed. *Fab.* 4.17.7ff.
    62. Phaed. *Fab.* 5.3.11ff.

In each case, *argumentum* refers directly to the fable—to its narrative. Thus, it is not a summary to which *argumentum* refers, but the text itself (even if the text of a fable is necessarily synthetic and brief). Of course, the Aesopic fable is a very special kind of text, since its chief purpose is not to entertain but to teach. It is a kind of apologue, a text that exists only to be immediately interpreted and turned into a concrete application on the moral plane. As Ennius says, a fable is an *argumentum* to keep on hand in order to avoid making a certain mistake. Phaedrus, as we have seen, goes on listing the various "morals" that may be gleaned from the fable/*argumentum* he has just recounted.[63] This Roman use of *argumentum* to designate the paradigmatic and didactic power of the apologue is quite interesting. It is as if the conventional *ho muthos dēloi* of the Aesopic tradition has undergone a reversal of perspective, transformed into an explicit process of inference. It is not so much the fable that "reveals" certain truths (*ho muthos dēloi*), but rather the audience that must infer them (*argumentum*).[64]

In the case of Aesopic fable, then, the inferential meaning of *argumentum* remains apparent: the text is not so much valuable in itself as in the fact that something else may be inferred from it (a moral, a precept that can be immediately applied elsewhere). As an *argumentum,* a fable of the Aesopic tradition contains an explicit invitation to enlist its text in the process of unlimited semiosis.

---

63. Phaed. *Fab.* 4.10.14ff..

64. Moreover, it has been rightly noted that Phaedrus tends to attribute an explicitly "judicial" character to the structure of the Aesopic fable: Manetti 1987, 227ff. Cf. also Gibbs 1999.

BIBLIOGRAPHY

Abbott, G. 1903. *Macedonian Folklore.* Cambridge: Cambridge University Press.
Accame, S. 1949. *I re di Roma nella leggenda e nella storia.* Naples: Libreria Scientifica Editore.
Adler, A., ed. 1931. *Suidae Lexicon.* Leipzig: Teubner.
Afanasjev, A. 1953. *Antiche fiabe russe.* Turin: Einaudi.
Ahl, F. 1991. *Sophocles' Oedipus: Evidence and Self-Convinction.* Ithaca: Cornell University Press.
Albert-Llorca, M. 1991. *L'ordre des choses: Les recits d' origine des animaux et de plantes en Europe.* Paris: Editions du C.T.H.S.
Aldrovandi, U. 1610. *Ornithologia lib. XVII.* Frankfurt.
Alessio, G. 1969. "Etimologie latine." In *Studi linguistici in onore di Vittore Pisani,* 19–21. Brescia: Paideia.
Alföldi, A. 1965. *Early Romans and the Latins.* Ann Arbor: University of Michigan Press.
———. 1966. *Les cognomina des magistrats de la republique Romaine.* Mélanges Piganiol 2. Paris: R. Chevalier.
Alinei, M. 1983. "Altri zoonimi parentelari." *Quaderni di Semantica* 4: 241–55.
———. 1986. "Belette." In *Atlas Linguarum Europae,* 145–222. Assen-Maastricht: Van Gorcum.
Altheim, F. 1938. *A History of Roman Religion.* London: Methuen.
Anderson, W. S. 1963. "Multiple Changes in the *Metamorphoses.*" *Transactions of the American Philological Association* 94: 1–27.
———. 1994 (1969). *The Art of the Aeneid.* Bristol Classical Paperbacks.
André, J. 1961. *L'alimentation et la cuisine à Rome.* Paris: Klincksieck.
———. 1962. "Notes Philologiques." *Revue de Philologie* 36: 23–35.
———. 1964. "Arbor felix, arbor infelix." In M. Renard and R. Schilling, eds., *Hommages à J. Bayet,* 35–46. Brussels: Latomus.
———. 1991. *Le vocabulaire latin de l'anatomie.* Paris: Belles Lettres.

Arthaber, A. 1989 (1927). *Dizionario comparato dei proverbi e modi proverbiali*. Milan: Hoepli.
Asbjørnsen, P., and J. Moe. 1962. *Fiabe norvegesi*. Turin: Einaudi.
Assmann, J. 1997. *La memoria culturale: Scrittura, ricordo e identità politica nelle grandi civiltà antiche*. Turin: Einaudi. Orig. publ. as *Das kulturelle Gedächtnis: Schrift, Erinnerung und politische Identität in frühen Hochkulturen*, Munich: Beck, 1992.
Audollent, A. 1967 (1904). *Defixionum tabellae*. Paris: Fontenmoig. Rpt., Frankfurt.
Austin, J. 1987. *Come fare cose con le parole*. Genoa: Marietti. Orig. publ. as *How to Do Things with Words*, London: Oxford University Press, 1962.
Avalle, D. 1989. "La 'Folie Tristan.'" In *Le maschere di Guglielmino*, 92–111. Naples: Ricciardi.
Baehrens, A., ed. 1882. *Poetae latini minores*. Leipzig: Teubner.
Bambeck, M. 1973. "Kulturgeschichtliche Marginalien zu einer Wieselbezeichnung in Nordspanien und Südwestfrankreich." In K. Körner and K. Ruhl, eds., *Studia Iberica: Festschrift für Hans Flasche*, 63–74. Munich: Francke.
Bandler, R., and J. Grinder. 1981. *La struttura della magia*. Rome: Astrolabio. Orig. publ. as *The Structure of Magic*, Palo Alto: Science and Behavior Books, 1975.
Barabino, G., A. Nazzaro, and A. Scivoletto. 1994. *Interpretationes Vergilianae Minores*. Genoa: Dipartimento di Archeologia e Filologia Classica.
Barchiesi, A. 1978. "Il lamento di Giuturna." *Materiali e discussioni per l'analisi dei testi classici* 1: 99–121.
Barchiesi, M. 1975. "Gli esametri di Baudelaire e la preistoria del Cygne." In *Studi Triestini di Antichità in onore di Luigia Achillea Stella*, 481–500. Trieste: Facoltà di Lettere e Filosofia.
Barghop, D. 1996. *Forum der Angst*. Munich: Campus Verlag.
Barnes, H. 1957. "The Case of Sosia versus Sosia." *The Classical Journal* 53: 19–24.
Barwick, K. 1928. "Die Gliederung der Narratio in der rhetorischen Theorie und ihre Bedeutung für die Geschichte des antiken Romans." *Hermes* 63: 261–87.
Basile, G. 1925. *Il Pentamerone ossia la fiaba delle fiabe*. Bari: Laterza.
Battaglia, S. 1956. "Lupus in fabula." *Filologia romanza* 3: 292–95.
Baudelaire, C. 1976. *Oeuvres complètes*. Ed. by C. Pichois. 2 vols. Paris: Gallimard.
Bayet, J. 1971. *Croyances et rites dans la Rome antique*. Paris: Payot.
Beck, H. 1895. *Geoponica sive Cassiani Bassi scholastici de re rustica eclogue*. Leipzig: Teubner.
——— and U. Walter, eds. 2005. *Die frühen Römischen Historiker*. Darmstadt: Wissenschaftliche Buchgesellschaft.
Beckmann, F. 1928. *Zauberei und Recht in Roms Frühzeit*. Osnabrück: V. Nolte.
Bedier, J. 1893. *Les fabliaux*. Paris: Bouillon.
Benfey, T. 1859. *Pantschatantra*. Leipzig: Brockhaus.
Benveniste, E. 1948. *Noms d'agent et noms d'action en Indo-Européen*. Paris: Maisonneuve.
———. 1962. *Hittite et Indo-Europeen*. Paris: Maisonneuve.
———. 1966. "Le système sublogique des prepositions en latin." In *Problèmes de linguistique générale*, 132–39. Paris: Gallimard.
———. 1971. "Struttura delle relazioni di persona nel verbo." In *Problemi di linguistica generale*, 269–81. Milan: Il Saggiatore. Orig. publ. as *Problèmes de linguistique générale*, Paris: Gallimard, 1966.
———. 1974. *Il vocabolario delle istituzioni indoeuropee*. Turin: Einaudi. Orig. publ. as *Le vocabulaire des institutions indo-européennes*, Paris: Seuil, 1969.

Bernardelli, G. 1976. "*Le cygne:* Baudelaire tra Virgilio e Chateaubriand." *Aevum* 50: 625–33.

Bernstein, F. 1998. *Ludi Publici: Untersuchungen zur Entstehung und Entwicklung der öffentlichen Spiele im republikanischen Rom.* Historia Einzelschriften 119. Stuttgart: Franz Steiner.

Bertini, F., ed. 1980. "Vitale di Blois, Geta." In *Commedie latine del XII e XIII secolo,* 139–242. Genoa: Dipartimento di Archeologia e Filologia Classica.

———. 1981. "Anfitrione e il suo doppio: Da Plauto a Gulherme Figueiredo." In G. Ferroni, ed., *La semiotica del doppio teatrale,* 307–51. Naples: Liguori.

———. 1997. *Plauto e dintorni.* Bari: Laterza.

Bettini, M. 1972. "Corydon Corydon." *Studi classici e orientali* 21: 261–76.

———. 1983. "L'arcobaleno, l'incesto e l'enigma: A proposito dell'*Oedipus* di Seneca." *Dioniso* 54: 137–53.

———. 1985. "Lettura divinatoria di un incesto (Sen. *Oed.* 366 ss.)." *Materiali e discussioni per l'analisi dei testi classici* 12: 149–59.

———. 1988a. "La correptio iambica." In *Metrica classica e linguistica, 89–205.* Urbino: Atti del Convegno. Rpt., Urbino: Quattro Venti 1991.

———, ed. 1988b. *Lo straniero, ovvero l'identità culturale a confronto.* Bari: Laterza.

———. 1991a. *Anthropology and Roman Culture:* Baltimore: Johns Hopkins University Press.

———. 1991b. *Verso un'antropologia dell'intreccio: Le strutture semplici della trama nelle commedie di Plauto.* Urbino: Quattro Venti.

———, ed. 1991c. *La maschera, il doppio e il ritratto: Strategie dell'identità.* Bari: Laterza.

———. 1994. *I classici nell'età dell'indiscrezione.* Turin: Einaudi.

———. 1998. *Nascere: Storie di donne, donnole, madri ed eroi.* Turin: Einaudi.

———. 1999a. *The Portrait of the Lover.* Trans. by Laura Gibbs. Berkeley: University of California Press.

———. 1999b. "Le contraddizioni della nudità." In G. Fossi, ed., *Il Nudo: Eros, natura, artificio,* 8–21. Florence: Giunti.

———. 2000. "Alle soglie dell'autorità." Introduction to B. Lincoln, *Autorità: Costruzione e corrosione,* vii–xxxiv, Turin: Einaudi.

———, and A. Borghini. 1980. "Il bambino e l'eletto." *Materiali e discussioni per l'analisi dei testi classici* 3: 121–53.

Bianchi Bandinelli, R. 1976. *Roma: L'arte romana nel centro del potere.* Milan: Rizzoli.

Bianco, G., ed. 1984. "Mos." In *Enciclopedia Virgiliana.* Rome: Istituto dell'Enciclopedia Italiana.

Biraschi, A. M. 1982. "Enea a Butroto: Genesi, sviluppo e significato di una tradizione troiana in Epiro." *Annali della Facoltà di Lettere e Filosofia, Studi Classici, Università di Perugia,* n.s., 19 (5): 278–91.

Bischoff, H. 1932. "Der Warner bei Herodot." Ph.D dissertation, University of Marburg.

Blaise, A. 1954. *Dictionnaire Latin–Français des Auteurs Chrétiens.* Turnhout: Brepols.

Bloch, E. 1960. "Die Form der Detektivgeschichte und die Philosophie." *Die neue Rundschau* 71: 665–83.

Bloch, R. 1963. *Les prodiges dans l'antiquité classique.* Paris: Puf. Trans. into Italian as *Prodigi e divinazione nel mondo antico: Greci, etruschi e romani,* Rome: Newton Compton, 1976.

———. 1965. *Tite-Live et les premiers siècles de Rome.* Paris: Belles Lettres.

Bloom, H. 1996. *Il canone occidentale.* Milan: Bompiani. Orig. publ. as *The Western Canon,* New York: Harcourt Brace & Company, 1994.

Blümner, H. 1911. *Die Romische Privataltertumer.* Munich: Beck.
Bochart, S. 1721. *Hierozoicon, sive de animalibus Sacrae Scripturae.* Leiden.
Boehm, F. 1905. "De symbolis Pythagoreis." Ph.D. dissertation, University of Berlin.
Boisseau, F. G. 1821. "Nostalgia." In *Encyclopédie Methodique: Medicine.* Paris: Agasse.
Bolisani, E., ed. 1937. *I Logistorici varroniani.* Padua: Tipografia del Messaggero.
Bolzoni, L. 1995. *La stanza della memoria: Modelli letterari e iconografici nell'eta della stampa.* Turin: Einaudi.
Bömer, F., ed. 1980. *P. Ovidius Naso: Metamorphosen. Kommentar. Buch. X–XI.* Heidelberg: Carl Winter.
Bonfante, G. 1987. "L'etimo del latino forma." *La Parola del Passato* 42: 37–38.
Borghi Cedrini, L. 1989. *La cosmologia del villano.* Alessandria: Edizioni dell'Orso.
Bosshardt, E. 1942. *Die Nomina auf -eus.* Zurich: Aschmann & Scheller.
Bottéro, J. 1982. "Sintomi, segni, scritture nell'antica Mesopotamia." In J.-P. Vernant, ed., *Divinazione e razionalità,* Turin: Einaudi.
———. 1998. *La plus vieille religion en Mésopotamie.* Paris: Gallimard.
Bouché-Leclercq, A. 1882. *Histoire de la divination dans l'antiquité.* Paris: E. Leroux.
Bouhot, J. P., and G. Madec. 1987. "*Soliloquiorum libri duo* (W. Hörmann)." *Revue des études augustiniennes* 33: 332–33.
Bowra, C. 1973. *La lirica greca da Alcmane a Simonide.* 2nd ed. Florence: La Nuova Italia. Orig. publ. as *Greek Lyric Poetry,* Oxford: Clarendon Press, 1962.
Bremmer, J. 1983. "Scapegoat Rituals in Ancient Greece." *Harvard Studies in Classical Philology* 87: 299–320.
Briggs, W. W., Jr. 1980. *Narrative and Simile from the Georgics in the Aeneid.* Leiden: Brill.
Bright, D. F. 1981. "Aeneas' Other Nekuia." *Vergilius* 27: 40–47.
Brillante, C. 1988. "Metamorfosi di un'immagine." In G. Guidorizzi, ed., *Il sogno in Grecia,* 19–23. Bari: Laterza.
Brix, J. 1884. *Ausgewählte Komodien des T. Maccius Plautus, IV, Miles gloriosus.* Leipzig: Teubner.
Brown, N. 1990. *Hermes the Thief.* Great Barrington: Lindisfarne Press.
Brusatin, M. 2000. *L'arte dell'oblio.* Turin: Einaudi.
Bulgakov, M. 1991. *Notes on the Cuff & Other Stories.* Trans. by Alison Rice. Ann Arbor: Ardis.
Burck, E. 1934. *Die Erzählungskunst des T. Livius.* Berlin: Weidmann. Rpt., Berlin/Zurich 1964.
Burkert, W. 1962. *Weisheit und Wissenschaft.* Nürnberg: Hans Carl.
———. 1987. *Mito e rituale in Grecia.* Bari: Laterza. Orig. publ. as *Structure and History in Greek Mythology and Ritual,* Berkeley: University of California Press, 1979.
Butler, H. E., and E. A. Barber, eds. 1969. *The Elegies of Propertius.* Hildesheim: Olms.
Butler, S. 1897. *The Authoress of the Odyssey.* London: Macmillan.
———. 1975 (1872). *Erewhon.* London: Penguin.
Calboli, G. 1969. *Cornifici: Rhetorica ad C. Herennium.* Bologna: Pàtron.
Cantarella, E. 1995. *Secondo natura.* Milan: Rizzoli. Rpt., Rome: Editori Riuniti, 1988.
Cassola, F., ed. 1975. *Inni omerici.* Milan: Mondadori.
Cawley, A., ed. 1958. *Geoffrey Chaucer: Canterbury Tales.* London: Everyman's Library.
Cetti, F. 1774. *I quadrupedi in Sardegna.* Sassari: Piattoli.
Chadwick, H. M., and N. K. Chadwick. 1986 (1932–40). *The Growth of Literature.* 3 vols. Cambridge: Cambridge University Press.

Chamisso, A. von. 1989. *La meravigliosa storia di Peter Schlemihl.* Trans. by G. Jaager-Grassi. Pordenone: Studio Tesi.
Chantraine, P. 1968. *Dictionnaire étymologique de la langue grecque.* Paris: Klincksieck.
Chastaing, M. 1980. "La casa del delitto." In R. Cremante and L. Rambelli, eds., *La trama del delitto: Teoria e analisi del racconto poliziesco,* 209–25. Parma: Pratiche.
Chiarini, G. 1972. "Variazioni sopra un verso plautino." *Studi classici e orientali* 21: 277–98.
Ciani, M. 1983. "I silenzi dei corpi: Difetto e assenza di comunicazione in Ippocrate." In *Le ragioni del silenzio,* 159–72. Padua: Bloom.
Cipriani, G. 1992. "Il vocabolario latino dei baci." *Aufidus* 17: 69–102.
Cipriano, P. 1978. *Fas e nefas.* Rome: Universita degli Studi di Roma, Istituto di Glottologia.
Cocchiara, G. 1963. *Il mondo alla rovescia.* Turin: Boringhieri.
Cohen, G. 1979. "Latin *voltus/vultus* = Face, Expression (On Face)." *Latomus* 38: 337–44.
Cohn, L. 1894. "Antipatros von Akanthos." In *Realencyclopädie* I-2, col. 2517.
Collart, J. 1954. *Varron grammarien latin.* Paris: Belles Lettres.
Comparetti, D. 1943 (1872). *Virgilio nel Medio Evo.* Florence: La Nuova Italia.
Conington, J., and H. Nettleship, eds. 1894. *The Works of Virgil.* London: Wittaker & Co. Rpt., Hildesheim: Olms, 1979.
Conte, G. B., ed. 1988. *Plinio: Storia naturale.* Turin: Einaudi.
Cook, A. B. 1905. "The European Sky-God." *Folklore* 16: 260–332.
Corbett, P. E. 1969 (1933). *The Roman Law of Marriage.* Oxford: Clarendon Press.
Corominas, J. 1954. *Diccionario crítico etimológico de la lengua castellana.* Bern: Francke.
Corsano, A. 1974. "Vico, Plauto e Cartesio." *Bollettino del Centro di Studi vichiani* 4: 140–42.
Courtney, E., ed. 1993. *The Fragmentary Latin Poets.* Oxford: Clarendon Press.
Cova, P. 1992. "Per una lettura narratologica del terzo libra dell'*Eneide.*" In P. Cova, et al., *Letteratura latina dell'Italia settentrionale,* 87–139. Milan: Vita e Pensiero.
———. 1994. *Il libro terzo dell'Eneide.* Milan: Vita e Pensiero.
Crawford, J. W., ed. 1994. *M. Tullius Cicero: The Fragmentary Speeches.* Atlanta: Scholars Press.
Croce, C. 1943. *Bertoldo, Bertoldino e Cacasenno.* Ed. by A. Baldini. Rome: Colombo.
Croisille, J. M., ed. 1985. *Pline l'ancien: Histoire naturelle.* Paris: Belles Lettres.
Crusius, O. 1887. "Über die Sprichwortersammlung des Maximus Planudes." *Rheinisches Museum* 42: 386–425.
Cutt, T., and J. Nyenhuis. 1970. *Plautus: Amphitruo.* Detroit: Wayne State University Press.
Dalyell, J. G. 1845. *The Darker Superstitions of Scotland.* Glasgow: Richard Griffin & Co.
Daremberg, C., and E. Saglio, eds. 1877–1919. *Dictionnaire des antiquités grecques et romaines.* 5 vols. Paris: Hachette.
Davidson, H., ed. 1980. *Saxo Grammaticus: History of the Danes.* Cambridge: Brewer.
De Chateaubriand, F. R. 1966. *Genie du Christianisme.* Paris: Flammarion.
Degani, E., ed. 1983. *Hipponax: Testimonia et fragmenta.* Leipzig: Teubner.
Degrassi, A., ed. 1963. *Inscriptiones Latinae Liberae Rei Publicae.* Florence: La Nuova Italia.
De Gubernatis, A. 1872. *Zoological Mythology.* London: Trübner & Co.
De la Cerda, L., ed. 1612. *P. Virgili Maronis priores sex libri Aeneidos argumentis, explicationibus notis illustrati.* London: H. Cardon.
Delcourt, M. 1938. *Stérilité mystérieuse et naissances maléfiques dans l'antiquité classique.* Paris: Droz.

Delrius, M. 1633. *Disquisitionum Magicarum Libri Sex*. Cologne.
De Martino, E. 1975. *Morte e pianto rituale: Dal lament funebre antico al pianto di Maria*. Turin: Boringhieri. Orig. publ. as *Morte e pianto rituale nel mondo antico*, 1958.
Deonna, W., and M. Renard, 1994. *A tavola con i Romani*. Parma: Pratiche. Orig. publ. as *Croyances et superstitions de table dans la Rome antique*, Brussels: Collection Latomus, 1961.
De Sanctis, G. 1956. *Storia dei Romani: 1. La conquista del primato in Italia*. 2nd ed. Florence: La Nuova Italia.
De Santillana, G., and H. von Dechend. 1983. *Il mulino di Amleto: Saggio sui mito e sulla struttura del tempo*. Milan: Adelphi. Orig. publ. as *Hamlet's Mill: An Essay on Myth and the Frame of Time*, Boston: Gambit, 1969.
Detienne, M. 1962. *Homere, Hesiode et Pythagore*. Brussels: Berchem.
Detlefsen, D., ed. 1866–82. *C. Plinii Secundi Naturalis Historia*. Berlin: Weidmann.
Devereux, G. 1976. *Dreams in Greek Tragedy*. Oxford: Blackwell.
De Zulueta, F. 1963. *Institutes of Gaius*. Oxford: Clarendon Press.
Di Cesare, M. 1974. *The Altar and the City*. New York: Columbia University Press.
Diels, H., and W. Kranz, eds. 1969 (1935). *Die fragmente der Vorsokratiker*. Berlin: Weidmann.
Dihle, A. 1959. "Ptolemaios Chennos." In *Realencyclopädie* XXIII-2, col. 1862.
Dindorf, G., ed. 1855. *Scholia Graeca in Homeri Odysseam*. Oxford.
Dolezel, L. 1985. "Le triangle du double: Un champ thématique." *Poétique* 64: 463–72.
Dollerup, C. 1975. *Denmark, Hamlet, and Shakespeare: A Study of Englishmen's Knowledge of Denmark Towards the End of the Sixteenth Century with Special Reference to Hamlet*. Salzburg: Institut für Englische Sprache und Literatur.
Doniger, W. 1984. *Dreams, Illusions, and Other Realities*. Chicago: University of Chicago Press.
Dornseiff, F. 1922. *Das Alphabet in Mystik und Magie*. Leipzig: Teubner.
Dostoyevsky, F. 1985. *The Double: Two Versions*. Trans. by E. Harden. Ann Arbor: Ardis.
Dumézil, G. 1954. "Ordre, phantasie, changement dans les pensees archaiques de l'Inde à Rome." *Revue des études latines* 32: 139–62.
Dupont, F. 1986a. *L'Acteur roi ou le theatre dans la rome antique*. Paris: Belles Lettres.
———. 1986b. "L'autre-corps de l'empereur-dieu." In C. Malamoud and J.-P. Vernant, eds., *Corps de dieux*, 231–52. Paris: Gallimard.
———. 1989. *La vie quotidienne du citoyen romain sous la republique*. Paris: Hachette.
———. 2000. *L'orateur sans visage: Essai sur l'acteur romain e son masque*. Paris: Puf.
Eco, U. 1990. *I limiti dell'interpretazione*. Milan: Bompiani.
Eitrem, S. 1914. *Opferritus und Voropfer der Griechen und Römer*. Kristiania: Dybwad.
Elworthy, F. 1895. *The Evil Eye*. London: Murray.
Endicott, N., ed. 1967. *The Prose of Sir Thomas Browne*. New York: Anchor Books.
Erbse, H., ed. 1950. "*Pausaniae Atticistae fragmenta*." In *Untersuchungen zu den attizistischen Lexica*, 152–221. Berlin: Akademie-Verlag.
Ernout, A. 1949. *Les adjectifs en -osus et en -ulentus*. Paris: Klincksieck.
———, and A. Meillet. 1965. *Dictionnaire étymologique de la langue latine*. Paris: Klincksieck.
Fauth, W. 1976. "Der Traum des Tarquinius." *Latomus* 35: 469–503.
Feeney, D. 1984. "The Reconciliations of Juno." *Classical Quarterly* 34: 179–94.
Feldherr, A. 1997. "Livy's Revolution: Civic Identity and the Creation of the *Res Publica*." In T. Habinek and A. Schiesaro, eds., *The Roman Cultural Revolution*, 136–57. Cambridge: Cambridge University Press.

Feldman, L. 1958. "Ascanius and Astyanax: A Comparative Study of Virgil and Homer." *The Classical Journal* 53: 361–66.
Fenik, B. 1960. "The Influence of Euripides on Vergil's *Aeneid.*" Ph.D. dissertation, Princeton University.
Ferri, S. 1946. *Plinio il vecchio: Storia delle arti antiche.* Rome: Palombi.
Firdousi, A. 1876. *Le livre des rois.* Trans. by M. J. Mohl. 7 vols. Paris: Imprimerie Nationale.
Flechia, G. 1876. "Postille etimologiche." *Archivio Glottologico Italiano* 2: 49–52.
Flobert, P. 1973. "Mos." *Latomus* 32: 567–69.
Flower, H. 1996. *Ancestor Masks and Aristocratic Power in Roman Culture.* Oxford: Clarendon Press.
Fontana, F. 2000. "Su alcuni modelli latini di *Historia Regum Britanniae*, 137–138: Ovidio, Plauto e Virgilio." *Studi Medievali* 41 (2): 809–26.
Forbes Irving, P. 1990. *Metamorphosis in Greek Myth.* Oxford: Clarendon Press.
Forehand, W. 1971. "Irony in Plautus' *Amphitruo.*" *American Journal of Philology* 92: 633–51.
Fowler, W. W. 1898. *A Year with the Birds.* London: Macmillan.
———. 1917. "Duplicated Altars and Offerings in Verg. *Ecl.* V. 65; *Aen.* III.305; and *Aen.* V. 77ff." *The Classical Review* 31: 163–67.
———. 1919. *The Death of Turnus.* Oxford: Blackwell.
Fraenkel, E. 1962. *Aeschylus: Agamemnon.* Oxford: Clarendon Press.
———. 1993. *Orazio.* Rome: Salerno Editrice. Orig. publ. as *Horace,* Oxford: Clarendon Press, 1957.
Franco, C. 2000. "Kýneos nóos: Il cane e il femminile nell'immaginario greco." Ph.D. dissertation, Università di Siena.
Frazer, J. G. 1898. *Pausanias's Description of Greece.* London: Macmillan. Rpt., New York: Biblo and Tannen, 1965.
———. 1911. *The Golden Bough, Part II: Taboo and the Perils of the Soul.* London: Macmillan.
———. 1913. *The Golden Bough, Part VI: The Scapegoat.* London: Macmillan. Rpt., London: Basingstoke, 1980.
———. 1918. *Folklore in the Old Testament.* London: Macmillan.
———, ed. 1921. *Apollodorus Atheniensis: The Library.* Cambridge: Harvard University Press. Rpt., London: Heinemann, 1976–79. Trans. into Italian as *Apollodoro: Biblioteca,* Milan: Adelphi, 1995.
———. 1931. "Some Popular Superstitions of the Ancients." In *Garnered Sheaves,* 128–50. London: Macmillan.
Frentz, W. 1967. *Mythologisches in Vergils Georgica.* Meisenheim am Glan: Hain.
Freud, S. 1966. *L'interpretazione dei sogni.* In C. Musatti, ed., *Opere* III, xxxiv–616. Turin: Boringhieri. Orig. publ. as *Die Trumdeutung,* in S. Freud, *Gesammelte Werke,* Frankfurt: Fischer, 1940–50.
———. 1970. *Psicopatologia della vita quotidiana.* In C. Musatti, ed., *Opere* IV, 51–297. Turin: Boringhieri. Orig. publ. as *Zur Psychopathologie des Alltagsleben,* in S. Freud, *Gesammelte Werke,* Frankfurt: Fischer, 1940–50.
———. 1972a. *Il motto di spirito e la sua relazione con l'inconscio.* In C. Musatti, ed., *Opere* V, 1–211. Turin: Boringhieri. Orig. publ. as *Der Witz und Seine Beziehung zum Unbewussten,* in S. Freud, *Gesammelte Werke,* Frankfurt: Fischer, 1940–50.
———. 1972b. *Analisi della fobia di un bambino di cinque anni.* In C. Musatti, ed., *Opere* V, 475–589. Turin: Boringhieri. Orig. publ. as *Analyse der Phobie eines fünfjährigen Knaben,* in S. Freud, *Gesammelte Werke,* Frankfurt: Fischer, 1940–50.

———. 1977a. *Il perturbante.* In C. Musatti, ed., *Opere* IX, 77–118. Turin: Boringhieri. Orig. publ. as *Das Unheimliche,* in S. Freud, *Gesammelte Werke,* Frankfurt: Fischer, 1940–50.

———. 1977b. *Sogno e telepatia.* In C. Musatti, ed., *Opere* IX, 379–407. Turin: Boringhieri. Orig. publ. as *Traum und Telepathie,* in S. Freud, *Gesammelte Werke,* Frankfurt: Fischer, 1940–50.

Frontisi, F. 1985. "Le Dionysos masque des *Bacchantes* d'Euripide." *L'homme* 93: 31–58.

———. 1988. "Prosopon, valeurs grecques du masque et du visage." Ph.D. dissertation, École des Hautes Études en Sciences Sociales, Paris.

———. 1991a. *Le dieu-masque.* Paris: La Decouverte.

———. 1991b. "Senza maschera né specchio: L'uomo greco e i suoi doppi." In M. Bettini, ed., *La maschera, il doppio e il ritratto,* 131–58. Bari: Laterza.

Fugier, H. 1963. *Recherches sur l'expression du sacre dans la langue latine.* Paris: Belles Lettres.

Funari, E., ed. 1986. *Il doppio fra patologia e necessità.* Milan: Cortina.

Fusillo, M., 1998. *L'altro e lo stesso.* Florence: La Nuova Italia.

Gabba, E. 1969. "Il *Brutus* di Accio." *Dioniso* 43: 377–83.

Gagé, J. 1955. *Apollon Romain: Essai sur le culte d'Apollon et le developpement du "ritus Graecus" à Rome des origines à Auguste.* Paris: De Boccard.

Galinsky, G. K. 1969. *Aeneas, Sicily, and Rome.* Princeton: Princeton University Press.

———. 1976. *La chute des Tarquins et les debuts de la republique Romaine.* Paris: Payot.

Gentili, B. 1989. *Poesia e pubblico nella Grecia antica.* 2nd ed. Bari: Laterza.

Georg, H., ed. 1905–6. *Tiberi Claudi Donati Interpretationes Vergilianae.* Leipzig: Teubner.

Gernet, L. 1968. "Le temps dans les formes archaiques du droit." In *Droit et institutions en Grece antique,* 263–314. Paris: Flammarion.

Giannini, S., and G. Marotta. 1989. *Fra grammatica e pragmatica.* Pisa: Giardini.

Gibbs, L. 1999. "Lost in a Town of Pigs: The Story of Aesop's *Fables*." Ph.D. dissertation, University of California, Berkeley.

Gilson, E. 1943. *Introduction à l'etude de Saint-Augustin.* Paris: J. Vrin.

Gjerstad, E. 1962. *Legends and Facts of Early Roman History.* Lund: Gleerup.

Goetz, G., ed. 1888–1923. *Corpus Glossariorum Latinorum.* Leipzig: Teubner. Rpt., Amsterdam: Hakkert, 1965.

Gogol', N. 1989. *Le veglie alla fattoria di Dikanka.* Turin: Einaudi.

Gollancz, I. 1926. *The Sources of Hamlet.* London: Humphrey Milford.

Gomme, G. L. 1908. *Folklore as an Historical Science.* London: Methuen. Rpt., Detroit: Singing Tree Press, 1968.

Grassmann-Fischer, B. 1966. *Die Prodigien in Vergil Aeneis.* Munich: Fink.

Graur, A. 1929. *Les consonnes géminées en Latin.* Paris: Champion.

Greene, T. 1986. "History and Anachronism." In G. S. Morson, ed., *Literature and History,* 205–20. Stanford: Stanford University Press.

Greimas, A. 1974. *Del senso.* Milan: Bompiani. Orig. publ. as *Du sens,* Paris: Seuil, 1970.

Griffiths, J. 1970. *Plutarchi de Iside et Osiride.* Cardiff: University of Wales Press.

Grimm, R. E. 1967. "Aeneas and Andromache in *Aeneid* III." *American Journal of Philology* 88: 151–62.

Griscom, A., ed. 1929. *Historia Regum Britanniae of Geoffrey of Monmouth.* London: Longmans.

Groh, V. 1928. "La cacciata dei re romani." *Athenaeum* 6: 289–324.

Grondona, M. 1980. *La religione e la superstizione nella Cena Trimalchionis.* Brussels: Latomus.

Guastella, G. 1997. *Comunicare, ricordare: Fra gli antichi e noi.* Milan: Technologos.
———, ed. 1999. *Gaius Suetonius Tranquillus: L'imperatore Claudio. Vite dei Cesari 5.* Venice: Marsilio.
Guérios, M. 1956. *Tabus lingüísticos.* Rio de Janeiro: Organização Siniões.
Guerrini, R. 1984. "*Lentiginosi oris,* Val. Max., I, 7, ext. 6. Gli aggettivi in *-osus* nei *Fatti e Detti memorabili.*" *Athaeneum* 82 (1): 61–74.
Gugel, H. 1970. "Caesars Tod." *Gymnasium* 77: 5–22.
Guidorizzi, G. 1988. *Il sogno in Grecia.* Bari: Laterza.
———. 1991. "Lo specchio e il doppio: Un sistema di intersezioni." In M. Bettini, ed., *La maschera, il doppio e il ritratto: Strategie dell'identità,* 31–46. Bari: Laterza.
Gwynn, L. 1914. "Cináed úa hAatacáin's Poem on Brugh na Bóinne." *Ériu* 7: 210–38.
Halbwachs, M. 1952. *Les cadres sociaux de la memoire.* Paris: Puf. Trans. into Italian as *I quadri sociali della memoria,* Naples: Ipermedium, 1997.
Halliday, W. R. 1928. *The Greek Questions of Plutarch.* Oxford: Clarendon Press.
———. 1967 (1913). *Greek Divination: A Study of its Methods and Principles.* Chicago: Argonaut.
Hanakdan, B. 1967. *Fables of the Jewish Aesop: From the Fox Fables of Hanakdan.* Trans. by M. Hadas. New York: Columbia University Press.
Hansen, W. F. 1983. *Saxo Grammaticus and the Life of Hamlet.* Lincoln: University of Nebraska Press.
Hardy, T. 1953. *Vita e morte del sindaco di Casterbridge.* Milan: Rizzoli. Orig. publ. as *The Mayor of Casterbridge: The Life and Death of a Man of Character,* London: Smith, Elder & Co., 1886.
Hartland, E. S. 1894. *Legend of Perseus.* London: D. Nutt.
Havthal, F., ed. 1899. *Acronis et Porphyrionis commentarii in Q. Horatium Flaccum.* Berlin: Springer. Rpt., Amsterdam: Schippers, 1966.
Hayman, H. 1873. *The Odyssey of Homer.* London: D. Nutt.
Heine, H. 1993. "Still ist die Nacht." In K. Heine, ed., *Sämtliche Gedichte in zeitlicher Folge,* 167. Frankfurt am Main: Insel Verlag.
Heinze, R. 1982 (1915). *Vergils Epische Technik.* Stuttgart: Teubner.
Henderson, P. 1967. *Samuel Butler: The Incarnate Bachelor.* New York: Barnes and Noble.
Henry, R., ed. 1960. *Photius, Bibliotheque.* Paris: Belles Lettres.
Hermann, T. 1948. "La tragedie nationale chez les Romains." *Classica et medievalia* 9: 141–54.
Herskovits, M. 1948. *Man and His Works.* New York: Knopf.
Heyne, C., ed. 1833. *P. Virgili Maronis Opera.* Leipzig. Rpt., Hildesheim: Olms, 1968.
Hofer, J. 1688. *Dissertatio medica de nostalgia oder Heimwehe.* Basil.
Hoffmann, E. 1984. *Die Abenteuer der Sylvesternacht.* Frankfurt am Main: Insel Verlag.
Hofmann, J. B.1936. *Lateinische Umgangssprache.* 2nd ed. Heidelberg: Carl Winter.
Hörmann, W., ed. 1986. *Augustini soliloquiorum libri duo. De immortalitate animae. De quantitate animae.* Corpus Scriptorum Ecclesiasticorum Latinorum 89. Wien: Österreichischen Akademie der Wissenschaften.
Hornsby, R. A. 1970. *Patterns of Action in the Aeneid: An Interpretation of Vergil's Epic Similes.* Iowa City: University of Iowa Press.
Hough, J. N. 1974. "Bird Imagery in Roman Poetry." *The Classical Journal* 70: 1–13.
Hübner, W. 1970. *Dirae im Römischen Epos.* Hildesheim: Olms.
Hutchinson, R. W. 1966. "The Little Lady." *Folklore* 77: 222–27.
Iodice Martino, M. 1986. "L'aggettivo *argutus* nella tradizione letteraria latina." *Atene e Roma* 31: 34–43.

Jacobi, H. 1952. *Amphytrion in Frankreich und Deutschland.* Zurich: Suris Verlag.
Jacoby, F. 1957. *Die Fragmente der griechischen Historiker.* Leiden: Brill.
Jaeger, M. 1997. *Livy's Written Rome.* Ann Arbor: University of Michigan Press.
Jaager-Grassi, G. and L. Mazzucchetti. 1989. *Adelbert von Chamisso. La meravigliosa storia di Peter Schlemihl.* Pordenone: Studio Tesi.
Jakobson, R. 1966. "Linguistica e poetica." In *Saggi di linguistica generale,* 181–218. Milan: Feltrinelli. . Orig. publ. as *Essais de linguistique générale,* Paris: Minuit, 1963.
Jauss, H. R. 1979. "Poetik und Problematik der Identität und Rolle in Geschichte des Amphitryon." In O. Marquard and K. Stierle, eds., *Identität,* 213–53. Munich: Fink.
Jeanneret, M. 1918. *La langue des tablettes d'execration latines.* Paris: Attinger.
Jervis, G. 1984. *Presenza e identità.* Milan: Garzanti.
Jones, E. 1986. *Amleto e Edipo.* Milan: Mondadori. Orig. publ. as *Hamlet and Oedipus,* London: Gollancz, 1949.
Jouanny, R., ed. 1962. *Oeuvres complètes de Molière.* 2 vols. Paris: Garnier.
Kajanto, I. 1965. *The Latin Cognomina.* Helsinki: Helsingfors.
Kant, I. 1970. "Antropologia dal punta di vista pragmatico." In P. Chiodi, ed., *Scritti morali,* 541–747. Turin: Utet.
Kantoriwicz, E. 1957. *The King's Two Bodies: A Study in Mediaeval Political Theology.* Princeton: Princeton University Press. Kassel, R., and C. Austin, eds. 1989. *Poetae Comici Graeci.* Berlin: De Gruyter.
Keil, H., ed. 1868. *Grammatici Latini.* Leipzig. Rpt., Hildesheim: Olms, 1961.
Keppler, C. F. 1972. *The Literature of the Second Self.* Tucson: University of Arizona Press.
Kiessling, A., and R. Heinze. 1914. *Quintus Horatius Flaccus: Briefe.* Berlin: Weidmann.
Klibansky, R., E. Panofsky, and F. Saxl. 1983. *Saturno e la melanconia: Studi di storia della filosofia naturale, religione e arte.* Turin: Einaudi. Orig. publ. as *Saturn and Melancholy: Studies in the History of Natural Philosophy, Religion and Art,* London: Nelson, 1964.
Knaack, G. 1907. "Eresios." In *Realencyclopädie* VI-I, col. 420.
Knauer, G. N. 1964. *Die Aeneis und Homer.* Göttingen: Vandenhoeck & Ruprecht.
Knight, R. 1950. *Racine et la Grece.* Paris: Boivin.
Knox, B. 1957. *Oedipus at Thebes.* New Haven: Yale University Press.
Knox, P. 1985. "Adjectives in *-osus* and Latin Poetic Diction." *Glotta* 64: 90–101.
Koch, L., and M. Cipolla. 1993. *Sassone Grammatico: Le gesta dei re e degli eroi danesi.* Turin: Einaudi.
Körte, A., and A. Thierfelder, eds. 1959. *Menandri quae supersunt.* Leipzig: Teubner.
Krahe, H. 1939. "Die Vorgeschichte des Griechentums nach dem Zeugnis der Sprache." *Die Antike* 15: 175–90.
Labate, M. 1991. "Città morte, città future: Un tema nella poesia augustea." *Maia,* n. s., 4 (3): 167–84.
Lahusen, G. 1984. *Schriftquellen zum romischen Bildnis.* Bremen: Heye.
Lamacchia, R. 1976. "Aspetti di civiltà diverse in alcune espressioni idiomatiche tradizionali." Miscellanea di studi in onore di Marino Barchiesi. *Rivista di cultura classica e medioevale* 18 (3): 957–86.
Lang, C., ed. 1881. *Cornuti Theologiae Graecae Compendium.* Leipzig: Teubner.
Langen, P., ed. 1964. *C. Valeri Flacci Settimi Balbi Argonauticon libri octo.* Hildesheim: Olms.
Lanza, D. 1997. *Lo stolto.* Turin: Einaudi.
Last, D., and R. Ogilvie. 1958. "Claudius and Livy." *Latomus* 17: 476–87.
Latte, K., ed. 1953. *Hesychii Alexandrini Lexicon.* Copenhagen: Munksgaard.

Lawson, J. C. 1910. *Modern Greek Folklore and Ancient Greek Religion: A Study in Survivals.* Cambridge: Cambridge University Press. Rpt., New York: University Books, 1965.
Lazzeroni, R. 1994. "Rileggendo Benveniste: Le relazioni di persona nel verbo." *Rivista di linguistica* 6: 267–74.
Leach, E. 1964. "Anthropological Aspects of Language: Animal Categories and Verbal Abuse." In E. H. Lenneberg, ed., *New Directions in the Study of Language*, 23–63. Cambridge: MIT Press.
Leaf, W. 1900–1902. *The Iliad.* London: Macmillan. Rpt., Amsterdam: Akkert, 1971.
Le Boulluec, A., ed. 1981. *Clement d'Alexandrie: Les Stromates.* Paris: Editions du Cerf.
Le Bras, G. 1959. "Capacité personnelle et structures sociales dans le tres ancien droit de Rome." In *Droits de l'antiquité et sociologie juridique: Mélanges Henri Lévy-Bruhl*, 417–29. Paris: Sirey.
Le Brun, C. 1992. *Le figure delle passioni.* Milan: Cortina. Orig. publ. as *Conference de Monsieur Le Brun, premier peintre du roy de France . . . sur l'expression générale et particuliere*, Paris, 1698.
Lecrivain, C. 1877. "*Libertus, libertinus.*" In C. Daremberg and E. Saglio, *Dictionnaire des antiquités grecques et romaines*, 1212. Paris: Hachette.
Le Fanu, W. R. 1893. *Seventy Years of Irish Life.* London: Arnold.
Leibniz, G. W. 2003. *Discourse on Metaphysics.* Trans. by G. Montgomery. Whitefish, MT: Kessinger.
Lenchantin De Gubernatis, M. 1912. "La leggenda romana e le praetextae." *Rivista di filologia e istruzione classica* 4: 444–62.
Lesky, A. 1929. "Sphinx." In *Realencyclopädie* III A-2, coll. 1703–49.
Leumann, M. 1976. *Lateinische Laut- und Formenlehre.* Munich: Beck.
Leutsch, E., ed. 1851. *Corpus Paroemiographorum Graecorum.* Göttingen. Rpt., Hildesheim: Olms, 1965.
Lévi-Strauss, C. 1964. *Il pensiero selvaggio.* Milan: Il Saggiatore. Orig. publ. as *La pensée sauvage*, Paris: Plon, 1962.
———. 1966. "La struttura e la forma." In V. Propp, *Morfologia della fiaba*, Turin: Einaudi.
———. 1978. *Antropologia strutturale due.* Milan: Il Saggiatore. Orig. publ. as *Anthropologie structurale deux*, Paris: Plon, 1972.
———. 1983a. "Mythe et Oubli." In *Le regard éloigné*, 253–61. Paris: Plon. Trans. into Italian as "Mito e oblio," in *Lo sguardo da lontano*, Turin: Einaudi, 1984.
———. 1983b. "Race et culture." In *Le regard éloigné*, 21–48. Paris: Plon. Trans. into Italian as "Razza e cultura," in *Lo sguardo da lontano*, Turin: Einaudi, 1984.
———. 1985. *La potière jalouse.* Paris: Plon. Trans. into Italian as *La vasaia gelosa: Il pensiero mitico nelle due Americhe*, Turin: Einaudi, 1987.
Liddell, H. G., and R. Scott. 1940. *A Greek-English Lexicon.* Revised by H. S. Jones. Oxford: Clarendon Press.
Liebrecht, K., ed. 1856. *Gervasio da Tilbury: Otia imperialia.* Hannover: C. Rümpler.
Lincoln, B. 2000. *Autorità: Costruzione e corrosione.* Turin: Einaudi. Orig. publ. as *Authority: Construction and Corrosion*, Chicago: University of Chicago Press, 1994.
Lindberger, O. 1956. *The Transformations of Amphitryon.* Stockholm: Almqvist & Wiksell.
Lindsay, W. 1894. "The Shortening of Long Syllables in Plautus." *Journal of Philology* 22 (43): 1–8.
———, ed. 1903. *Nonii Marcelli De compendiosa Doctrina libri XX.* Leipzig: Teubner. Rpt., Hildesheim: Olms, 1964.

———, ed. 1913. *Sexti Pompei Festi De verborum significatione quae supersunt cum Pauli epitome.* Leipzig: Teubner. Rpt., Hildesheim: Olms, 1965.
Lloyd, R. R. 1957a. "Aeneid III: A New Approach." *American Journal of Philology* 78: 133–51.
———. 1957b. "Aeneid III and the Aeneas Legend." *American Journal of Philology* 78: 382–400.
Lot, F. 1949. "Le baiser à la terre: Continuation d'un rite antique." In *Pankrateia: Mélanges H. Grégoire,* 435–41. Brussels: Institut de Philologie et d'Histoire Orientales et Slaves.
Luck, G. 1977. *P. Ovidius Naso: Tristia.* Heidelberg: Carl Winter.
Lumpe, A., ed. 1984. *"Argumentum."* In O. Hiltbrunner, ed., *Bibliographie zur lateinischen Wortforschung,* 299. Bern: Francke.
Mac Cana, P. 1972. "Mongán mac Fiachna and Immram Brain." *Ériu* 23: 102–42.
Macchia, G., ed. 1984. "Baudelaire, Charles." In *Enciclopedia Virgiliana,* 1: 467–71. Rome: Istituto dell'Enciclopedia Italiana.
Mackail, J. W. 1930. *The Aeneid of Vergil.* Oxford: Clarendon Press.
McKay, A. G. 1973. "Review of R. A. Hornsby, *Patterns of Action in the Aeneid.*" *American Journal of Philology* 94 (3): 315–17.
Mackie, C. 1988. *The Characterization of Aeneas.* Edinburgh: Scottish Academic Press.
Maguinness, W. S. 1964. *Aeneid Book XII.* Letchworth: Bradda Books.
Mainoldi, C. 1984. *L'image du loup et du chien dans la Grece ancienne.* Paris: Ophrys.
Maiullari, F. 1999. *L'interpretazione anamorfica dell'Edipo re.* Rome: Istituti Editoriali e Poligrafici Internazionali.
Malinowski, B. 1953. "The Problem of Meaning in Primitive Language." In C. K. Ogden and I. A. Richards, *The Meaning of Meaning,* 296–336. New York: Harcourt, Brace & Co. Trans. into Italian as *Il significato del significato,* Milan: Il Saggiatore, 1966.
Manetti, G. 1987. *Le teorie del segno nell'antichità classica.* Milan: Bompiani.
Mann, T. 1998. *La montagna incantata.* Milan: Corbaccio. Orig. publ. as *Der Zauberberg,* Frankfurt am Main: Fischer, 1971.
Mantinband, J. H., and C. Passage. 1974. *Amphitryon.* Chapel Hill: University of North Carolina Press.
Marquardt, J. 1886. *Das Privatleben der Romer.* Leipzig: Hirzel.
Martin, P. M. 1975. "Dans le sillage d'Énée." *Athenaeum* 53: 212–44.
Marx, F., ed. 1857. *C. Lucilii Carminum reliquiae.* Leipzig: Teubner. Rpt., Hildesheim: Olms, 1981.
Mastrocinque, A. 1983. "La cacciata di Tarquinio il Superbo." *Athenaeum* 61: 457–80.
———. 1988. *Lucio Giunio Bruto.* Trento: Pubblicazioni di Storia Antica, Università di Trento.
Mathews, R. H. 1972. *Mathews' Chinese-English Dictionary* (revised American edition). Cambridge: Harvard University Press.
Mayhoff, K. 1874. *Novae Lucubrationes Plinianae.* Leipzig: Teubner.
McCartney, E.-S. 1920. "Marginalia from Vergil." *Classical Weekly* 13: 217–21.
Mencacci, F. 1996. *I fratelli amici: La rappresentazione dei gemelli nella cultura romana.* Venice: Marsilio.
———. 2001. "La costruzione dei viri illustres: Genealogia metaforica e maiores collettivi." In M. Coudry and T. Spaeth, eds., *L'invention des grands hommes de la Rome antique,* 421–37. Paris: De Boccard.
Menna, F. 1983. "La ricerca dell'adiuvante." *Materiali e discussioni per l'analisi dei testi classici* 10 (2): 105–32.

Meyer, K. 1895. *The Voyage of Bran, Son of Febal.* London: D. Nutt.
Miceli, S. 1984. *Il demiurgo trasgressivo: Studio sui trickster.* Palermo: Sellerio.
Michel, F., ed., 1862. *Gesta Regum Britanniae.* London: Cambrian Archaeological Association.
Michels, A. K. 1951. "The Drama of the Tarquins." *Latomus* 10: 13–24.
Migne, J.-P., ed. 1844–64. *Patrologia Latina.* Paris.
Moggi, M. 1988. "Straniero due volte: I barbari e il mondo greco." In M. Bettini, ed., *Lo straniero, ovvero l'identità culturale a confronto,* 51–76. Bari: Laterza.
———, and M. Osanna, eds. 2000. *Pausania: Guida della Grecia, Libro VII, L'Acaia.* Milan: Mondadori.
Molière [Poquelin, J.-B.]. 1962. *Amphitryon.* Paris: Garnier.
Momigliano, A. 1975. "The Origin of the Roman Republic." In *Quinto contributo alla storia degli studi classici,* 293–321. Rome: Edizioni di Storia e di Letteratura.
Mommsen, T. 1864. *Romische Forschungen.* Berlin: Weidmann.
———, ed. 1883. *Corpus Inscriptionum Latinarum* X. Berlin.
———. 1969 (1887–88). *Römisches Staatsrecht.* 3 vols. Graz: Akademische Druck- u. Verlagsanstalt.
Montaigne, M. E. de. 1952. *The Essays.* Trans. by C. Cotton. Ed. by W. C. Hazlitt. Chicago: Encyclopaedia Britannica.
Moretti, G. 1982. "Lessico giuridico e modello giudiziario nella favola fedriana." *Maia,* n.s., 34: 227–40.
Morris, D. 1983. *I gesti.* Milan: Mondadori. Orig. publ. as *Gestures,* London: Cape, 1979.
Morris, R. 1985. "Uther and Igerne: A Study in Uncourtly Love." In R. Barber, ed., *Arthurian Literature,* 70–92. Woodbridge: D. S. Brewer.
Müller, C. 1975. *Sextus Pompeius Festus. De verborum significatione quae supersunt cum Pauli epitome.* Hildesheim: Olms.
Müller, K. 1851–70. *Fragmenta Historicorum Graecorum.* Paris: Didot
Münzer, F. 1909. "Q. Fabius Maximus (Cunctator)." In *Realencyclopädie* VI-2, coll. 1814–30.
———. 1931. "L. Iunius Brutus." In *Realencyclopädie* V (Suppl.), coll. 369–85.
———. 1953. "A. Postumius Albinus." In *Realencyclopädie* XXII-I, coll. 902–8.
Murray, G. 1907. *The Rise of the Greek Epic.* Oxford: Clarendon Press.
Musti, D. 1988. "Una città simile a Troia: Città troiane da Siri a Lavinio." In *Strabone e la Magna Grecia,* 95–122. Padua: Programma.
Negri, A. M. 1984. *Gli psiconimi in Virgilio.* Bologna: Pàtron.
Nelson, L. 1961. "Baudelaire and Virgil: A Reading of *Le Cygne.*" *Comparative Literature* 13: 332–45.
Niebuhr, B.-G. 1873. *Romische Geschichte.* Ed. by M. Isler. Berlin: Reimer.
Niedermann, M. 1918. *Essais d'etymologie et de critique verbale latines.* Paris: Attinger.
Norman, D. 1995. *Le cose che ci fanno intelligenti.* Milan: Feltrinelli.
Nutt, A. 1897. *The Celtic Doctrine of Rebirth.* London: D. Nutt.
Ó Broin, T. 1961. "Classical Source of the 'Conception of Mongan.'" *Zeitschrift für celtische Philologie* 28: 262–71.
Oder, E., ed. 1903. *Hermerus, Claudius, Mulomedicina Chironis.* Leipzig: Teubner.
Oesterley, H., ed. 1872. *Gesta Romanorum.* Berlin: Weidmann.
Ogilvie, R. M. 1965. *A Commentary on Livy, Books 1–5.* Oxford: Clarendon Press.
Ogle, M. B. 1911. "The House-Door in Greek and Roman Religion and Folklore." *American Journal of Philology* 32: 252–71.

Olck, F., ed. 1897. "Biene." In *Realencyclopädie* III-I, coll. 431–57.
———. 1909. "Feige." In *Realencyclopädie* VI-2, coll. 2100–151.
Olrik, J., and H. Raeder, eds. 1931. *Saxonis Gesta Danorum.* Copenhagen: Levin & Munksgaard.
Oniga, R. 1985. "Il canticum di Sosia: Forme stilistiche e modelli culturali." *Materiali e discussioni per l'analisi dei testi classici* 14: 113–208.
———. 1991. *Tito Maccio Plauto: Anfitrione.* Venice: Marsilio.
———. 1993. "Intorno al latino *cultura:* Osservazioni fra linguistica e antropologia." *Incontri linguistici* 16: 123–45.
Ooteghem, J. van. 1937. "Énée à Buthrotum." *Les études classiques* 6: 8–13.
Orbeli, I. 1956. *Fables of Medieval Armenia* [*Basni srednevekovoj Armenii*]. Moscow.
Orlando, F. 1993. *Gli oggetti desueti nelle immagini della letteratura.* Turin: Einaudi.
Otis, B. 1964. *Virgil: A Study in Civilized Poetry.* Oxford: Clarendon Press.
Otto, A. 1890. *Die Sprichworter und Sprichwortlichen Redensarten der Romer.* Leipzig: Teubner.
Pagani, G. 1846. *Opere di L. Giunio Moderato Columella.* Venice: Antonelli.
Page, D. 1973. *Folktales in Homer's Odyssey.* Cambridge: Harvard University Press.
Page, T., ed. 1926–29. *P. Vergilius Maro Aeneid.* London: Macmillan.
Pais, E. 1926. *Storia di Roma.* Rome: Optima.
Parke, H. W., and D. Wormell. 1956. *The Delphic Oracle.* Oxford: Basil Blackwell.
Parker, R. 1983. *Miasma, Pollution and Purification in Early Greek Religion.* Oxford: Clarendon Press.
Passage, E. 1954. *Dostoevsky the Adapter.* Chapel Hill: University of North Carolina Press.
Pauly, A., and G. Wissowa, eds. 1893–. *Realencyclopädie der classischen Altertumswissenschaft.* Stuttgart: Druckenmüller.
Pease, A. S., ed. 1881. *M. Tulli Ciceronis De natura deorum.* Cambridge: Harvard University Press. Rpt., New York: Arno Press, 1979.
———, ed. 1920–23. *M. Tulli Ciceronis De divinatione libri duo.* Urbana: University of Illinois Studies in Language and Literature. Rpt., Darmstadt: Wissenschaftliche Buchgesellschaft, 1977.
Peppe, L. 1984. *Posizione giuridica e ruolo sociale della donna romana in eta repubblicana.* Milan: Giuffrè.
Perlman, P. 1983. "Plato *Laws* 833c–834b and the Bears of Brauron." *Greek, Roman and Byzantine Studies* 24: 113–28.
Permiakov, G. L. 1979. *From Proverb to Folk-Tale.* Moscow: Central Department of Oriental Literature.
Perret, J. 1942. *Les origines de la légende Troyenne de Rome.* Paris: Belles Lettres.
———. 1961. *Les dérivés latins en -men et -mentum.* Paris: Klincksieck.
Perry, B. E. 1952. *Aesopica.* Urbana: University of Illinois Press.
Peter, H., ed. 1870. *Veterum Historicorum Romanorum fragmenta.* Leipzig: Teubner.
Petrocelli, C. 1999. "'Mystery story' fra antichità classica e narrativa moderna." In L. Canfora, *Studi sulla tradizione classica per Mariella Cagnetta,* 391–412. Bari: Laterza.
Pettine, E., ed. 1992. *Plutarco: La loquacità.* Naples: D'Auria.
Peuckert, W. E. 1987. "Wolf." In H. Bächtold-Stäubli and E. Hoffmann-Krayer, eds., 716–94. *Handworterbuch des deutschen Aberglaubens.* Berlin: De Gruyter.
Pierio Valeriano, G. 1556. *Hieroglyphica.* Basel.
Piganiol, A. 1917. *Essai sur les origines de Rome.* Paris: De Boccard.

Pistelli, E., ed. 1888. *Iamblichi protrepticus ad fidem codicis Florentini.* Leipzig: Teubner. Rpt., 1967.
Pitrè, G. 1875. *Fiabe, novelle e racconti popolari siciliani.* Palermo: Pedone-Lauriel.
———. 1889. *Usi e costumi, credenze e pregiudizi.* Palermo: Pedone-Lauriel.
Plummer, C., ed. 1910. *Vitae Sanctorum Hiberniae.* Oxford: Clarendon Press.
Poe, E. A. 1970. "The Murders in Rue Morgue." In *The Fall of the House of Usher and Other Writings,* London: Penguin.
———. 1992. "William Wilson." In *The Complete Stories,* ed. by John Seelye, 400–18. New York: Knopf.
Pogorel'skij, A. 1990. *Il Sosia ovvero le mie serate nella Piccola Russia.* Ed. by R. Mauro. Pordenone: Studio Tesi.
Pollard, J. 1975. *Birds in Greek Life and Myth.* Plymouth: Thomas and Hudson.
Portalupi, F., ed. 1974. *M. Cornelio Frontone: Opere.* Turin: Utet.
Powell, F. Y., ed. 1894. *Saxo Grammaticus: The First Nine Books of the Danish History.* Trans. by O. Elton. London: D. Nutt.
Prete, A., ed. 1992. *Nostalgia: Storia di un sentimento.* Milan: Cortina.
Primmer, A. 1964. "Zum Prolog des *Heautontimorumenos.*" *Wiener Studien* 77: 61–75.
Propp, V. J. 1966. *Morfologia della fiaba.* Turin: Einaudi. Orig. publ. as *Morfologiya skazki,* Leningrad: Academia, 1928.
———. 1972. *Le radici storiche dei racconti di fate.* Turin: Boringhieri. Orig. publ. as *Istoricheskie korni volshebnoi skazki,* Leningrad: Leningrad University Press, 1946.
———. 1975. *Edipo alla luce del folclore.* Turin: Einaudi.
Pucci, G. 1991. "La statua, la maschera e il segno." In M. Bettini, ed., *La maschera, il doppio e il ritratto,* 107–28. Bari: Laterza.
———. 1992. "Le forme della comunicazione." In S. Settis, ed., *Civiltà dei Romani: Il rito e la vita privata,* 233–314. Milan: Electa.
———. 1997. "Imago imperii, imperium imaginis." In *Annali della Facoltà di Lettere e Filosofia dell'Università di Siena* 17: 177–88.
Purcell, N. 1999. "Does Caesar Mime?" *Studies of the History of Art* 156: 181–93.
Putnam, M. 1967. *The Poetry of the Aeneid.* Cambridge: Harvard University Press.
———. 1980. "The Third Book of the *Aeneid:* From Homer to Rome." *Ramus* 9: 1–21.
Quint, D. 1982. "Painful Memories: *Aeneid* 3 and the Problem of the Past." *The Classical Journal* 78 (1): 30–38.
Raccanelli, R. 1987. "Prima di Plauto: il racconto di Anfitrione e le sue varianti." Ph.D. dissertation, Università "Ca' Foscari" di Venezia.
Racine, J. 1950. *Oeuvres complètes.* Ed. by R. Picard. 2 vols. Paris: Gallimard.
Radin, P., C. Jung, and K. Kerény. 1965. *Il briccone divino.* Milan: Bompiani. Orig. publ. as *Der gottliche Schelm,* Zurich: Rhein-Verlag, 1954.
Raina, G., ed. 1993. *Pseudo-Aristotele: Fisiognomica.* Milan: Rizzoli.
Rank, O. 1914. *Der Doppelgänger.* Wien: Turia & Kant. Trans. into Italian as *Il doppio: Il significato del sosia nella letteratura e nel folklore,* Milan: Sugarco, 1978.
———. 1987. *Il mito della nascita dell'eroe.* Milan: Sugarco. Orig. publ. as *Der Mythus von Gerburt des Helden,* Wien: Turia & Kant, 1906.
Rech, H. 1936. "Mos maiorum: Wesen und Wirkung der Tradition in Rom." Ph.D. dissertation, University of Marburg.
Rees, A., and B. Rees. 1961. *Celtic Heritage.* London: Thames and Hudson.
Remotti, F. 1990. *Noi primitivi.* Turin: Bollati Boringhieri.
———. 1996. *Contro l'identità.* Bari: Laterza.

Ribbeck, O. 1875. *Die Romische Tragodie*. Leipzig: Teubner.
———, ed. 1897. *Scaenicae romanorum poesis fragmenta: I. Tragicorum romanorum fragmenta*. 3rd ed. Leipzig: Teubner.
———, ed. 1898. *Scaenicae romanorum poesis fragmenta: II. Comicorum romanorum fragmenta*. Leipzig: Teubner.
Ricci, G. 1998. *Il principe e la morte*. Bologna: Il Mulino.
Ricottilli, L. 1984. *La scelta del silenzio*. Bologna: Pàtron.
———. 2000. *Gesto e parola nell'Eneide*. Bologna: Pàtron.
Riess, E. 1893. "Aberglaube." In *Realencyclopädie* I-I, coll. 29–93.
———. 1939. "Omen." In *Realencyclopädie* XVIII-I, coll. 350–78.
Rigault, N. 1805. *Artemidori Oneirocritica*. Leipzig: Siegfred Lebrecht Crusius.
Ripa, C. 1766. *Iconologia*. Perugia.
Riposati, B., ed. 1939. *M. Terenti Varronis: De vita populi Romani*. Milan: Vita e Pensiero.
Risch, E. 1947. "Namensdeutungen und Worterklärungen bei den ältesten griechischen Dichtern." In *Eumusia: Festgabe für Ernst Howald zum sechzigsten Geburtstag am 20. April 1947*, 72–91. Zurich: Erlenbach..
Rogers, R. 1970. *A Psychoanalitic Study of the Double in Literature*. Detroit: Wayne State University Press.
Rohde, E. 1888. "Ein griechisches Märchen." *Rheinisches Museum*, n.s., 43: 303–5.
———. 1970. *Psiche*. Bari: Laterza. Orig. publ. as *Psyche: Seelencult und Unsterblichkeitsglaube der Griechen*, Freiburg im Brisgau, 1890–94.
Rohlfs, G. 1928. *Sprache und Kultur*. Berlin: Bruschweig.
Roiron, F. 1908. *Études sur l'imagination auditive de Virgile*. Paris: Leroux.
Rolland, E. 1877. *Faune populaire de la France*. Paris: Maisonneuve.
Roloff, H. 1967. "Maiores bei Cicero." In H. Oppermann, ed., *Romische Wertbegriffe*, 274–322. Darmstadt: Wissenschaftliche Buchgesellschaft.
Romaldo, A. 1994. "I demoni e la lanterna: Plauto, *Most*. 487." *Annali della Facolta di Lettere e Filosofia dell'Universita di Siena* 15: 31–39.
Rosati, G. 1985. *Ovidio: I cosmetici delle donne*. Venice: Marsilio.
Roscher, W. 1894–97. *Ausfürliches Lexicon der griechischen und romischen Mythologie*. Leipzig: Teubner. Rpt., Hildesheim: Olms, 1978.
Rose, V., ed. 1963. *Hygini Fabulae*. Leiden: Sijthoff.
Rosinus, J. 1585. *Romanarum antiquitatum libri decem ex variis scriptoribus*. Lyon: Sibylle de La Porte.
Rossi, E. 1994. *Les détours obscures: Le annotazioni di Racine alle tragedie greche*. Biblioteca dei Quaderni del Seicento Francese 8. Fasano: Schena.
Royds, T. F. 1914. *The Beasts, Birds and Bees of Virgil*. Oxford: Blackwell.
Rzach, A., ed. 1913. *Hesiodi Carmina*. Leipzig: Teubner.
Samter, E. 1894. "Der Pileus der Romischen Priester und Freigelassenen." *Philologus* 53: 535–43.
Scarpi, P. 1983. "L'eloquenza del silenzio." In M. Ciani, ed., *Le ragioni del silenzio*, 31–50. Padua: Bloom.
Schachermeyr, F. 1932. "L. Tarquinius (Superbus)." In *Realencyclopädie* IV A-2, coll. 2380–89.
Scheid, J. 1989. "Religione e società." In A. Schiavone, ed., *Storia di Roma, 4, Caratteri e morfologie*, 631–60. Turin: Einaudi.
Schilling, R., ed. 1977. *Pline l'Ancien: Histoire naturelle VII*. Paris: Belles Lettres.
Schöne, R. 1872. "Zu Hygin. fab. 95." *Hermes* 6: 125–26.

Schwartz, E. 1887. *Scholia in Euripidem*. Berlin: Reimer.
Schwarzbaum, H. 1979. *The* Mishle Shu'alim *(Fox Fables) of Rabbi Berechiah Ha-Nakdan: A Study in Comparative Folklore and Fable Lore*. Kiron: Institute for Jewish and Arab Folklore Research.
Sébillot, P. 1984. *Le folklore de la France, vol. 5: La faune*. Paris: Imago.
Segre, C. 1990. "Quattro tipi di follia medioevale." In *Fuori del mondo: I modelli nella follia e nelle immagini dell'aldilà*, 89–102. Turin: Einaudi.
Sheer, E., ed. 1908. *Lycophronis Alexandra*. Berlin: Weidmann.
Šklovskij, V. 1968. "La struttura della novella e del romanzo." In T. Todorov, ed., *I formalisti russi*, 205–30. Turin: Einaudi.
Skutsch, O. 1985. *The Annals of Q. Ennius*. Oxford: Oxford University Press.
Snell, B., and H. Mähler, eds. 1975. *Pindari carmina cum fragmentis*. Leipzig: Teubner.
Soltau, W. 1909. *Die Anfänge der Romische Geschichtschreibung*. Leipzig.
Soverini, L., 1992. "Parole, voce, gesti del commerciante nella Grecia classica." *Annali della Scuola Normale Superiore di Pisa* 3 (22): 811–33.
———. 1994. "Psithyros: Hermes, Afrodite e il sussurro nella Grecia antica." In *Ἱστορίη: Studi offerti dagli allievi a Giuseppe Nenci*, 433–60. Galatina: Congedo.
Squillante Saccone, M. 1985. *Le Interpretationes Vergilianae di Tiberio Donato*. Naples: Società Editrice Napoletana.
Stallbaum, J. 1825–30. *Eustathii Commentarii ad Homeri Odysseam*. Leipzig: Weigel. Rpt., Hildesheim: Olms, 1960.
Stärk, E. 1982. "Die Geschichte des Amphitryonstoffes vor Plautus." *Rheinisches Museum* 125: 275–303.
Starry West, G. 1983. "Andromache and Dido." *American Journal of Philology* 104: 257–67.
Steinwenter, A. 1933. "Mores." In *Realencyclopädie* XVI-I, coll. 290–98.
Stephanius, S. 1664. *Saxonis Grammatici Historiae Danicae libri XVI*. Sora.
Stramaglia, A. 1998. *Res inauditae, incredulae: Storie di fantasmi nel mondo greco-latino*. Bari: Levante.
Strodach, K. 1933. *Latin Diminutives in -ello/a- and -illo/a-: A Study in Diminutive Formation*. Philadelphia: Linguistic Society of America.
Suerbaum, W. 1967. "Aeneas zwischen Troja und Rom." *Poética* 1: 176–204.
Svennung, J. 1935. *Untersuchungen zu Palladius*. Uppsala: Almquist & Wiksells.
Syme, R. 1974. *La rivoluzione romana*. Turin: Einaudi. Orig. publ. as *The Roman Revolution*, Oxford: Clarendon Press, 1939.
Taguieff, P.-A. 1999. *Il razzismo*. Milan: Cortina. Orig. publ. as *Le racisme*, Paris: Flammarion, 1997.
Tatlock, J. 1950. *The Legendary History of Britain*. Berkeley: University of California Press.
Temporini, H., and W. Haase. 1986. *Aufstieg und Niedergang der romischen Welt*. Berlin: De Gruyter.
Thesaurus Linguae Latinae. 1900–. Leipzig: Teubner,
Thiel, H. van. 1971. "Sprichwörter in Fabeln." *Antike und Abendland* 17: 105–18.
Thilo, G., ed. 1887. *Servii grammatici qui feruntur in Vergilii Bucolica et Georgica commentarii*. Leipzig: Teubner. Rpt., Hildesheim: Olms, 1961.
Thomas, J. 1981. *Structure de l'imaginaire dans l'Eineide*. Paris: Belles Lettres.
Thompson, L. A. 1989. *Romans and Blacks*. Norman: University of Oklahoma Press.
Thompson, S. 1966. *Motif-Index of Folk-Literature*. 2nd ed. Bloomington: Indiana University Press.

———. 1967. *La fiaba nella tradizione popolare.* Milan: Il Saggiatore.
Thraemer, E. 1901. "Dardanos." In *Realencyclopädie,* IV-2, col. 2179.
Todorov, T. 1989. *Nous et les autres.* Paris: Seuil.Trans. into Italian as *Noi e gli altri: La riflessione francese sulla diversità umana,* Turin: Einaudi, 1990.
Tomaševskij, B. 1968. "La costruzione dell'intreccio." In T. Todorov, ed., *I formalisti russi,* 305–50. Turin: Einaudi.
Tosi, R. 1991. *Dizionario delle sentenze greche e latine.* Milan: Rizzoli.
Toynbee, J. 1971. *Death and Burial in the Roman World.* London: Thames & Hudson.
Traina, A. 1989. "Le traduzioni." In G. Cavallo, P. Fedeli, and A. Giardina, eds., *Lo spazio letterario di Roma antica,* 93–123. Rome: Salerno.
Treggiari, S. 1991. *Roman Marriage.* Oxford: Clarendon Press.
Tullio Altan, C. 1983. *Antropologia: Storia e problemi.* Milan: Feltrinelli.
Tümpel, K. 1894. "Mnemon." In W. Roscher, ed., *Ausfürliches Lexicon der griechischen und romischen Mythologie,* II-2, coll. 3075–76. Leipzig: Teubner. Rpt., Hildesheim: Olms, 1978.
Tupet, A. M. 1986. "Rites magiques dans l'antiquite romaine." In H. Temporini and W. Haase, eds., *Aufstieg und Niedergang der romischen Welt II,* 2591–675. Berlin: De Gruyter.
Tylor, E. 1871. *Primitive Culture.* London: Murray.
Tymms, R. 1949. *Doubles in Literary Psychology.* Cambridge: Bowes & Bowes.
Ugolini, L. 1932. *Albania antica.* Milan: Treves-Treccani-Tumminelli.
———. 1937. *Butrinto: Il mito di Enea, gli scavi.* Rome: Istituto Grafico Tiberino.
Usener, H. 1948 (1895). *Gotternamen.* Frankfurt am Main: Schulte-Bulmke.
Ussing, J. 1875. *T. Macci Plauti Comoediae.* Copenhagen: Librariae Gyldendalianae.
Väänänen, V. 1937. *Le latin vulgaire des inscriptions pompéiennes.* Helsinki: Annales Academiae Fennicae.
Vahlen, J., ed. 1903. *Ennianae Poesis reliquiae.* 2nd ed. Berlin: Weidmann.
Valenti Pagnini, R. 1981. "Lupus in fabula: Trasformazioni narrative di un mito." *Bollettino di studi latini* 11 (1/2): 3–22.
Vander, P., ed. 1961 (1703). *Desideri Erasmi Roterodami Opera Omnia.* Hildesheim: Olms.
Van der Valk, M., ed. 1971. *Eustathii archiepiscopi Thessalonicensis Commentarii ad Homeri Iliadem pertinentes.* Leiden: Brill.
Varner, E. 2004. *Mutilation and Transformation: Damnatio Memoriae and Roman Imperial Portraiture.* Leiden: Brill.
Vasaly, A. 1993. *Representations: Images of the World in Ciceronian Oratory.* Berkeley: University of California Press.
Vermuele, E. 1979. *Aspects of Death in Early Greek Art and Poetry.* Berkeley: University of California Press.
Vernant, J.-P. 1965a. "Aspects mythiques de la memoire." In *Mythe et pensée chez les Grecs,* 49–78. Paris: Maspero.
———. 1965b. "Figuration de l'invisible et catégorie psychologique du double: Le colossòs." In *Mythe et pensée chez les Grecs,* 251–64 Paris: Maspero.
———. 1965c. "Hestia-Hermès: sur l'expression religieuse de l'espace et du mouvement chez les Grecs." In *Mythe et pensée chez les Grecs,* 97–143. Paris: Maspero
———. 1975. "Image et apparence dans la theorie platonicienne de la 'Mimesis.'" *Journal de Psychologie* 2: 133–60.
———. 1976. "Ambiguità e rovesciamento: Sulla struttura enigmatica dell'*Edipo re.*" In J.-P. Vernant and P. Vidal-Naquet, *Mito e tragedia nell'antica Grecia,* 88–120. Turin: Einaudi.

———. 1982. *Divinazione e razionalità*. Turin: Einaudi. Orig. publ. as *Divination et rationalité*, Paris: Seuil, 1974.
———. 1988. "L'individu dans la cité." In *L'individu, la mort, l'amour*, 211–32. Paris: Gallimard.
———. 1990. *Figures, idoles, masques*. Paris: Juillard.
———. 1991. "Psyche: Simulacro del corpo o immagine del divino?" In M. Bettini, ed., *La maschera, il doppio e il ritratto: Strategie dell'identità*, 3–11. Bari: Laterza.
———. 1995. *Passé et présent: Contributions à une psychologie historique*, vol. 2. Rome: Edizioni di Storia e di Letteratura.
———, and F. Frontisi. 1983. "Figures du masque en Grece ancienne." *Journal de Psychologie* 80: 53–69.
———, and P. Vidal-Naquet. 1976. *Mito e tragedia nell'antica Grecia*. Turin: Einaudi.
Vico, G. B. 1968 (1914). *De antiquissima Italorum sapientia: I. Le orazioni inaugurali*. In G. Gentile and F. Nicolini, eds., *De Italorum sapientia e le polemiche*, 203–76. Bari: Laterza.
Vigotsky, L. 1987. *I processi cognitivi*. Turin: Boringhieri.
Walde, A., and J. B. Hofmann. 1954. *Lateinisches Etymologisches Wörterbuch*. Heidelberg: Winter.
Walter, A. 1964. *Proverbia sententiaeque Latinitatis medii aevi*. Göttingen: Vandenhoeck & Ruprecht.
Wardrop, M. 1894. *Georgian Folk-Tales*. London: D. Nutt.
Wentzel, G. 1896. "Asklepiades von Myrlea." In *Realencyclopädie* II-2, coll. 1628–31.
Wessner, P., ed. 1905. *Aeli Donati quod fertur commentum Terentii*. Leipzig: Teubner.
———, ed. 1931. *Scholia in Iuvenalem vetustiora*. Leipzig: Teubner. Rpt., Stuttgart: Teubner, 1967.
West, R. 1933. *Romische Porträtsplastik*. Munich: Eher.
Wilkin, S., ed. 1852. *The Works of Sir Thomas Browne*. London: Bohn.
Williams, R. D. 1962. *P. Vergili Maronis Aeneidos Liber Tertius*. Oxford: Clarendon Press.
———. 1972. *The Aeneid of Vergil*. London: Macmillan.
Wiseman, T. P. 2003. "The Legend of Lucius Brutus," In M. Citroni, ed., *Memoria e identità. La cultura romana costruisce la sua immagine*, 21–38. Florence: Università degli Studi di Firenze, Dipartimento di scienze dell'antichità "Giorgio Pasquali."
Wissowa, G. 1912. *Religion und Kultus der Romer*. Munich: Beck.
Witton, W. 1960. "Two Passages in the Third Book of the *Aeneid*." *Greece and Rome* 7: 171–72.
Wolters, X. 1935. *Notes on Antique Folklore on the basis of Pliny's Natural History L. XXVIII. 22–29*. Amsterdam: H. J. Paris.
Wood, R. 1973 (1769). *An Essay on the Original Genius of Homer*. Washington, D.C.: McGrath Publishing Company.
Wright, H. 1910. *The Recovery of Lost Roman Tragedy*. New Haven: Yale University Press.
Zadoks, A., and J. Jitta. 1932. *Ancestral Portraiture in Rome and the Art of the Last Century of the Republic*. Amsterdam: Noord-Hollandsche Uitgevers Maatschappij.
Zaganianis, N. 1973. "Le mythe de Teree dans la littérature grecque et latine." *Platon* 25: 208–23.
Zambon, F., ed. 1975. *Il Fisiologo*. Milan: Adelphi.
Zeppini Bolelli, A., 1989. *Proverbi toscani*. Florence: Salani.
Ziegler, K. 1936. "Timolaos ek Makedonías." In *Realencyclopädie* VI, AI, coll. 1275–76.
Ziolkowsky, T. 1977. *Disenchanted Images*. Princeton: Princeton University Press.

INDEX

Achilles, 33–34
actors: undergarments of, 104; and imitation, 198–99, 230–31
Admetus, 12, 213, 221
Aeneas, 34, 110, 137, 148, 200–211, 215–16, 218, 220–24, 231, 250
alimentary code, 48
Amelethus, 45, 62–63, 68–69, 71–76
Amleth. *See* Amelethus
Amphitruo: reception of, 176
Amphitryon, 103, 171–72, 176–78, 182, 186–87, 191–92, 240, 251–52
Andromache, 137, 200–208, 211, 213–20, 222–23
animals: as *argumenta*, 245–47; crocodile, 245–46; dog, 57–58; donkey (*onos*), 246; "face" of, 135–36, 139n36; he-goat (*hircus*), 55–56; ibis, 7–9; ram (*aries*), 43, 51–56, 76; serpent, 57, 60, 246–47; sheep (*ovis*), 52–53; speaking, 57; as symbols of language, 7–10; as symbols of stupidity, 50–58, 77; weasel, 7–10, 37; wether (*vervex*), 55. *See also* dogs; wolf
Apollo, 9, 33–34, 38, 64–65, 109, 247
apologue, 253–54

aposiopesis, 20, 24
appearance, physical: and identity, 155–57; imitation of, 148, 152–53, 175–77, 198–99, 230–32; and sight, 132–34; vocabulary of, 158–68, 191. *See also* resemblance
arguere: etymology of, 242–44
argumentosus, 248n45
argumentum: of fables, 253–54; in iconography, 244–47; *ingens,* 248–49; of a play, 251–52; of a work of art, 248–52
argūtus: meaning of, 231–32; etymology of, 243–44
Arruns, 57–61, 75–77
Ascanius, 148, 193–94, 208, 215–18, 231
aspectus, 133–34, 152, 167
Assmann, 113, 116–19
Astyanax, 215–17
auctoritas: and *mos,* 101–3, 128–30
Augustine, 79, 213–14

barbarians, 88–89, 95, 121
behavior: and *mos,* 94–101, 104–6, 113, 117, 125–29

275

Benveniste, Émile, 5, 22–23, 101, 162, 225, 243
birth: through the mouth, 7–8; or ears, 37
Brutus: as animal, 50–58; and false identification, 46–50; portrait of, 49–50; and riddling, 58–70; and stumbling, 75–83; and stupidity, 42–46
brutus: meaning of, 43, 50–52, 57, 64
Buthrotum, 210–211

Caesar, 72, 78, 82–83, 101, 121, 129, 226, 234
Calvisius Sabinus, 28–30
caricature. *See* imitation
Chateaubriand, René de, 222–23
Cinder Boy, 61, 68, 76
Circe, 190–93
Claudius, 44, 57, 76, 139
cognitio. See identity
communication: and Hermes, 6–14, 39; interruption of, 21–26; between living and dead, 26–27; localization of, 3–4; and memory, 29–39; metaphors of, 7–9; and silence, 14–21
commutare. See transformation
consensus: and *mos,* 97–102, 103–13, 123–26
consuetudo, 98–103, 107–8, 118, 128, 135
conversation, 12–28
cornus (cornel), 64–67
cosmetics, 152–54
Creusa, 208, 216
cultural models, 48, 95–96, 109, 131–34, 138–39, 142, 194
cultural relativism, 87–96. *See also* ethnocentrism
cultures, "hot"/"cold," 113
Cupid, 126, 136–37, 150–51, 193
customs. *See mos, mores*

Darius, 91–93
death: and doubles, 185–86, 196–99, 225–37; and memory, 26–30, 193; and silence, 11–13
deception, 148–51

desiderium, 219–21, 233
devil: in proverbs, 15–19
Dido, 148, 193, 205, 218
divination, 4–6. *See also klēdōn*
dogs: and Hermes, 14; sacrifice of, 67n162. *See also* animals
Doppelgänger. *See* doubles
Dostoyevsky, Fyodor, 177n21, 179n28, 184–86
doubles: ancient and modern, 194–96; "aristocratic," 196–99, 226–33; of city, 207–13; and comedy, 172–73; and *honos,* 235–37; and identity, 174–80; and memory, 222–24; and telepathy, 173–74; and transformation, 184–92
dreams: Tarquin's, 43, 51–52, 56–57; of falling, 81–82; and Morpheus, 136; and transformation, 194–95

ears, 4, 6–9; ringing in, 16–17, 25; and memory, 36–39
effigies, 154; as "artificial image," 164–65, 221; and funerary practice, 225–29
emotions, 139–40, 146–49
Encolpius, 238–40
ethnocentrism, 87–88, 94, 119–21. *See also* cultural relativism
Eumolpus, 238–39
exempla: and memory, 115–19
eyes: and *argutus,* 231, 243; as locus of soul, 143–47

(Quintus) Fabius (Maximus Cunctator), 52–53
fables, 61, 70, 74, 80, 83; *argumentum* of, 253–54
face: as expression of interiority (*vultus*), 139–60; Greek concept of, 132–33; and identity, 136–39, 150–54, 167–68, 236; as locus of speech (*os*), 134–38, 144; as manufactured image, 159–62; as natural features (*facies*), 141–43, 148, 151–54. *See also* appearance, physical
facies. See face

Index

falling. *See* stumbling
figs: bitter (*grossuli*), 46–50; in proverb, 18, 21–26
folktales, 41–42, 45–46, 48–49, 54, 59, 61–64, 67–74, 83–84, 192n70
frons (forehead), 145–46
forgetfulness. *See* memory
forma, 160, 165–67, 175–76, 187
Freud, Sigmund, 24, 41, 52, 81–82, 148, 173
frutex, 54–55, 65
funerary practice, 116, 158, 197–98, 225–30, 232–37
funus imaginarium, 227n9

gait: in identity, 136–37, 150, 168, 217, 230–31
gaze: wolf's, 19–21
Giton, 238–40
gressus. See gait
guilt: and stumbling, 79

hair, 35, 138, 183, 238–39, 250–51
Hamlet, 40–43, 50–51, 62, 71. *See also* Amelethus
Hector, 33–34, 137, 201–9, 213–18, 223
Helenus, 200–216, 220–23
Hermes, 4–14, 47, 55, 166, 173–76, 181–83, 191, 197, 240–41, 251–52
honos, 235–37

identification, false, 48–49
identity, 25–26, 167–68, 223–24; features of, 132, 136–39, 177–84; loss of, 186–94; of minority group, 123; as recognition, 139, 154–59
images: and identity, 186–92; "living," 172n3; and memory, 212–30; and proverbs, 17–23
imagines, 157–59, 196–99, 225–26, 232–37. *See also* masks
imitation, 116, 136–37, 148–50, 197–99, 227–37
immutare. See transformation
incessus. See gait

infelix, arbor, 65–67, 82
intelligence, hidden, 68, 77. *See also* stupidity
intolerance. *See* ethnocentrism

Juno, 109, 137, 209, 224
Jupiter, 109–10, 186, 191–92, 209, 224, 253

Khusràw, 41, 48, 62
klēdōn, 4–6, 9, 10

Lentulus, 111–12, 198
levirate: Andromache's, 201–3
Lichas, 238–40
lupus in fabula, proverb, 15–26

magic, 9n31, 187–90, 192–96
maiores: and *imagines*, 158, 197–98, 225–28, 233–37; and *mos*, 103–19
marriage, 94, 120; of Helenus and Andromache, 201–3; of Trojans and Latins, 109–10
masks, 116, 131, 138–39, 146–47, 158, 197n86. *See also* images
memory, 26–39, 192–93; and *mos*, 114–19
Mercury. *See* Hermes
metamorphosis. *See* transformation
mimētai, 198–99, 229–37. *See also* imitation
mirror: and identity, 179–80
mnēmones, 31–36. *See also* memory
Montaigne, Michel de, 88–91, 94–95, 107, 130
mos (*mores*): flexibility of, 106–19; "majority," 102–4, 119–22; "minority," 123–28; normative function of, 97, 104–5, 114; and orality, 113–17; and *vultus*, 141
mutare. See transformation

name: and identity, 174–75

nomenclatores, 31, 36–37
nostalgia: and images, 218–22

Odysseus, 16, 26, 30–34, 41, 174, 190–93, 217
omens, 4–6, 9, 57, 60, 77–82

Palaestrio, 156–57, 187–90
Parrhasius, 244–45, 250
Patroclus, 33–34, 186
person, verbal: Benveniste's theory of, 22–23
Pharae, 4–5, 9–10
Philocomasium, 156–57, 188
plague: and incest, 59–60
pronouns, personal, 22–23, 180–84. *See also* person, verbal
Propp, Vladimir, 59, 68, 70, 74–75
prosōpon, 131–32, 138–40, 142, 151
Protesilaus, 34, 78
proverbs, 12–13, 15–26, 29n91, 40, 53–54, 146

Racine, Jean-Baptiste, 203, 216
remembrance. *See* memory
resemblance, 138, 165, 176–77, 198–99, 213–18, 229–33
riddles, 42, 46, 58–59, 62–65, 68–69, 73–75

sabucus (elder), 65–66
satyrs, 227–28, 236
Sceledrus, 156–57, 182, 188–89, 193
Servilius, 127–29
sight, 19, 151; and the face, 132–34, 143–44
signs, 78–80, 163; and inference, 239–42, 249
silence, 7; folk-beliefs about, 12–26; and memory, 26–30
slaves: and identity, 180–84; and *ius imaginum*, 196–99; as "memory aids," 28–36
Sosia, 25, 58, 103, 119, 123, 166–67, 171–87, 189–97, 199, 240–41
symbolic condensation: Freud's theory of, 56
soul: 38–39, 140–42, 146–47, 151–52, 160
species, 40, 66, 133–34, 167
statues, 4, 9, 49n54, 67, 70, 74n196, 158, 163, 221, 235
sticks, gold in the, 64, 68–74, 76
stumbling, 78–82
stupidity, 42–56, 58, 60–70, 69–70, 72, 75–77, 143
substitutes. *See* doubles

Tarquin(ius Superbus), 41–44, 51–52, 56–60, 65, 76
(Titus Manlius) Torquatus, 53, 57–58
transformation, 185–96
translation: and Hermes, 10–11
Trickster, 48–49
Trojans, 109–11, 150, 200–224 *passim*
Troy, 172n3
Turnus, 206, 248–50

Vernant, Jean-Pierre, 4–5, 27, 31, 36, 131–32, 186, 199, 233
versipellis, 191–92, 195–96
Vespasian, 198, 228–29
voice: of animals, 57–58, 60; and Hermes, 4–11; and identity, 137–39, 148; folk-beliefs about, 19–22
vultus. *See* face

"William Wilson" (Poe), 176–79, 183–84, 195
wolf: folk-beliefs about, 15–23
writing, 3, 8–9, 31–32, 36; and cultural memory, 113–15, 118–19

www.ingramcontent.com/pod-product-compliance
Lightning Source LLC
Chambersburg PA
CBHW030108010526
44116CB00005B/153